300 Best
Rice Cooker
Recipes

300 Best Rice Cooker Recipes

ALSO INCLUDING
Legumes and Whole Grains

Katie Chin

Robert
ROSE

For complete cataloguing information, see page 384

Disclaimer
The recipes in this book have been carefully tested by our kitchen and our tasters. To the best of our knowledge, they are safe and nutritious for ordinary use and users. For those people with food or other allergies, or who have special food requirements or health issues, please read the suggested contents of each recipe carefully and determine whether or not they may create a problem for you. All recipes are used at the risk of the consumer. Consumers should always consult their rice cooker manufacturer's manual for recommended procedures and cooking times.

We cannot be responsible for any hazards, loss or damage that may occur as a result of any recipe use.

For those with special needs, allergies, requirements or health problems, in the event of any doubt, please contact your medical adviser prior to the use of any recipe.

Design and Production: Kevin Cockburn/PageWave Graphics Inc.
Editor: Sue Sumeraj
Recipe editor: Jennifer MacKenzie
Proofreader: Kelly Jones
Indexer: Gillian Watts
Photographer: Colin Erricson
Associate Photographer: Matt Johannsson
Food Stylist: Kathryn Robertson
Prop Stylist: Charlene Erricson

Cover image: Lemony Risotto with Shrimp (page 238)

We acknowledge the financial support of the Government of Canada through the Book Publishing Industry Development Program (BPIDP) for our publishing activities.

Published by Robert Rose Inc.
120 Eglinton Avenue East, Suite 800, Toronto, Ontario, Canada M4P 1E2
Tel: (416) 322-6552 Fax: (416) 322-6936
www.robertrose.ca

Printed and bound in Canada

1 2 3 4 5 6 7 8 9 TCP 19 18 17 16 15 14 13 12 11

FSC
www.fsc.org
MIX
Paper from
responsible sources
FSC® C011825

Contents

Acknowledgments

First and foremost, this book would never have happened if not for the inspiration and example set by my mother, Leeann Chin, who throughout her life inspired my passion for cooking, respect for food and all the joy that comes from feeding and teaching others.

I'd like to thank my amazing posse of recipe testers: Jean Chin, Adam Drucker, Steven Durbahn, Jennifer Garcia, Stacy Mears, Neil Newman, Susie Romano, Ryan Ting and Laura Walston. I was incredibly blessed with this enthusiastic crew, who worked tirelessly under a tight deadline to test more than 300 recipes, never complained (even while managing three rice cookers at once), gave wonderful suggestions to enhance and simplify, tasted everything and even kept me pumped up when I was sick with the flu and couldn't keep my grains straight (yes, recipe testing is a glamorous business).

Thank you also to Maria Bejarano, Bill Chin, Katie Chin, Danielle Chitwood, Emily Dodi, Scott Fields, Sharon Lawson, Michele Morken, Galina Prosyak and Judy Rusignuolo at the USA Rice Federation and Terry Stanley for their support and input. And thanks to Katie Workman for her friendship and inspiration.

Special thanks to Bob Dees of Robert Rose Inc. for his belief in me and for making this book possible. I also want to thank my editors, Sue Sumeraj and Jennifer MacKenzie, for their support, guidance, patience, skill, kindness, sense of humor, encouragement . . . I could go on and on. Many thanks as well to Marian Jarkovich and Martine Quibell of Robert Rose for their marketing and promotion prowess; to Kevin Cockburn of PageWave Graphics for his design skill and meticulousness; to photographer Colin Erricson, associate photographer Matt Johannsson, food stylist Kathryn Robertson and prop stylist Charlene Erricson for the beautiful photographs; and to Kelly Jones for her careful proofread.

Thanks also to my agent, Sally Ekus of The Lisa Ekus Group, for all her support and general awesomeness.

Much appreciation to Roland Products, Melissa's Produce and Cuisinart for donating their wonderful products for testing.

Finally, I'd like to thank my friends and family for their love, support and encouragement, especially my husband, Matthew Jonas, who never whined, even when I sent him on a wild goose chase to find rose water and Himalayan red rice.

Introduction

As the youngest child growing up in an Asian-American household in the '70s in the Midwestern United States, it was always my job to wash the rice before placing it in the nifty rice cooker that held its rightful place on our countertop. In our household, rice was a very important part of every meal: you could not leave the table until everyone had finished every single grain in their bowl. And it had to be perfectly cooked. Over the years, I became very fond of that rice cooker. It served me well, and I considered it part of our family.

I am not alone. Since the 1940s, rice cookers have been a staple appliance for millions of households all over the world — and it's no wonder. A rice cooker ensures perfect rice every time, without the hassle of watching over it or fearing the rice will burn, and in an almost magical way, it turns itself off automatically when the rice is done. Rice cookers are portable, take up very little counter space and are extremely easy to clean. They are great for any kitchen and a boon to college students and others who may not have access to a full suite of appliances. My sister, a gourmet who prides herself on her "cook's kitchen" at home, takes her rice cooker along on weekend getaways to her rustic cabin on one of the thousands of lakes in Minnesota.

So, great, it's a handy gizmo that makes great rice. "I don't make rice that often, so I don't use it all the time" or "I got one of those as a wedding present, but I'm not sure what to do with it." I've heard my friends respond this way over the years when I've mentioned the rice cooker to them, and I never knew where to go from there. Now I do, and you can too.

Through my years as a busy chef and caterer, I was always looking for ways to create delicious meals for my family that would save me time and cleanup, and there it was, sitting on my counter the whole time. Rice is just the beginning! What I've discovered is that the rice cooker is about so much more than rice; it is an incredibly useful kitchen tool that also makes wonderfully healthy grains and legumes. It's sort of like a fast slow cooker that allows you to make tasty one-dish meals for every occasion, from risottos (without the constant stirring!) and stews to pilafs, polenta and creamy oatmeal.

As a working mother of twins, I have found the rice cooker to be a lifesaver — I can put a home-cooked meal on the table without a lot of effort or supervision. A friend of mine recently commented, "I am frankly not organized enough to buy everything and put it in my slow cooker in the morning before I go to work, so the rice cooker has been a huge plus for our family."

As I tried out recipes for this book at countless dinner parties in my home, the main reaction I got was this: "You made *that* in a rice cooker? Incredible!" For busy home cooks and seasoned chefs everywhere, this book will open your eyes to a whole new way of cooking that will save you time and help you integrate more whole grains into your diet.

"What if I don't have one of those fancy machines?" Although amazing technological advancements have been made in the rice cooker realm, the majority of the recipes in this book will work in everything from simple on/off machines (which can cost as little as $15) to the higher-end models (which run upwards of $200) and everything in between (more on this in "Types of Automatic Rice Cookers," page 8).

Inspired by flavors from around the corner and around the world, I have worked hard to create recipes that offer a little something for everyone. For your next dinner party, try serving Italian Sausage and Mushroom Risotto (page 241), and to spice up a weekday meal for the family, try an Arroz con Pollo (page 191) that everyone will love.

With an eye toward a healthier diet, I've also included everyday recipes for a broad range of grains and legumes, including barley, quinoa, polenta, oatmeal, lentils and black beans. Dishes such as Black Bean Quinoa Chili (page 163) and Lentils and Barley with Caramelized Onions (page 308) will surprise and delight your family and friends.

In every chapter, there are plenty of step-by-step instructions and directions for using the rice cooker cycles, as well as useful hints and tips.

I hope you will enjoy making these recipes as much as I did creating them, and that your rice cooker will earn its rightful place as the superhero on your countertop.

Getting to Know Your Rice Cooker

The rice cooker was first invented in the 1940s to meet the demands of Japanese households that consume rice on a daily basis. It was a simple machine that mimicked the rice cooking process on a stovetop, with a curved bowl that mirrored the *okame* — the traditional Japanese metal pot used to cook rice.

Today's basic models are quite similar. The rice cooker is an electrical appliance that consists of a main body, an inner cooking bowl, an electric heating plate and a thermal sensing device (a small, spring-loaded thermometer that gauges the temperature of the contents of the bowl). Rice cookers guide rice through four cooking stages: sitting in water, boiling, absorbing water (steaming) and resting.

Once rice and water are added to the cooking bowl, the bowl's weight depresses the thermal sensing device and the heating plate quickly brings the water to a boil. Water boils at 212°F (100°C). Once it reaches a steady boil, it won't get any hotter. As long as there is water in the pan, the temperature is stable. Once the rice absorbs all the water in the pan, the temperature starts to rise. The rice cooker senses this change and switches from the Cook cycle to the Keep Warm cycle (or to

Off if the machine has no Keep Warm cycle). The rice has finished cooking and enters its resting phase.

This is the basic cooking process in on/off machines. For fuzzy logic models, it's slightly different. Fuzzy logic machines have a computer chip (think rice cooker with a brain), which gives them the ability to react. They constantly monitor the amount of heat during the cooking process and make small adjustments in temperature and cooking time according to what the thermal sensing device senses.

Types of Automatic Rice Cookers

There are three types of automatic rice cookers: on/off models, fuzzy logic models and induction heating models.

On/Off Models

On/off models are the most basic and least expensive machines. Popular brands include Aroma, Salton, National, Sanyo, Panasonic, Cuisinart, Oster, Jarden, Zojirushi, Black & Decker, Krups and Breville. They come in two types: "cook and shut off" and "keep warm."

The on/off "cook and shut off" machine is the most basic and least expensive. It has no indicator light to tell you when the rice is done, but you will hear a click when the water has boiled off and the rice has finished cooking. The rice stays warm for about 2 hours after the cooker turns itself off. Basic "cook and shut off" machines run between $15 and $30.

Most on/off "keep warm" rice cookers are exactly like on/off "cook and shut off" machines, except that they automatically switch to a Keep Warm cycle after the rice has finished cooking. They also typically have a built-in steaming period after the rice has finished cooking so the rice is ready to eat once the machine switches to the Keep Warm cycle. This type of cooker will keep the rice warm for up to 4 hours without forming a thick crust on the bottom; however, some machines will form a light crust shortly after switching to the Keep Warm cycle. You must unplug the machine to turn it off.

Some "keep warm" machines now offer digital controls with a multitude of cycles, such as a Brown Rice cycle, which has a longer soaking period to compensate for the extra bran layer. Some brands, such as Aroma, even offer a patent-pending "sauté then simmer" technology. If you own an on/off "keep warm" model that has these advanced capabilities, you can easily adapt the recipes in this book for use with your machine.

Many "keep warm" machines come with a steamer tray or basket. This accessory provides a convenient way to steam an array of dishes. You can even steam rice at the same time that you are steaming meat or vegetables, making it possible to create complete meals in your machine. Some models also come with a condensation collector that channels excess moisture away from the rice to maintain the ideal moisture level. It's a good idea to regularly detach the collector to clean it.

On/off "cook and shut off" machines come in a pot style, similar to the original Japanese design. On/off "keep warm" machines come either in the pot style or a cool-touch design in which the cooking bowl and steam tray are housed within the cool-touch unit, which remains cool to the touch even during the cooking cycle. This feature makes the machine safer, as well as making it a portable serving vessel. Many on/off models come with nonstick coating, which I highly recommend.

Within the on/off category is a special Persian-style rice cooker. These machines (such as Pars) are capable of producing popular Iranian rice dishes with a rice crust (*tah dig*).

Fuzzy Logic (Sensor Logic) Models

A fuzzy logic rice cooker (also called a sensor logic rice cooker or a micro-computerized rice cooker) has a microcomputer that allows the machine to regulate time and temperature according to the type of rice being cooked (brown rice, for example, cooks at a lower temperature than white rice). Fuzzy logic rice cookers allow the rice cooker to think for itself, constantly monitoring and adjusting the heat during the cooking process. Simply put, these machines have an internal monitoring computer that is programmed to "pay attention" to how the rice is cooking, making fine adjustments in temperature and cooking times along the way.

Fuzzy logic rice cookers come with programmable settings in the form of a menu that enables you to select the type of grain or cooking method you desire: brown rice, sushi rice, sticky rice, porridge, etc. Once you select a grain type, the computer optimizes the cooking temperature to enhance that grain's flavor and texture. These machines also have a function that lets you pick your preferred texture (hard versus soft). Some models even offer settings for cake, slow cooking, oatmeal and soup.

Fuzzy logic machines have a built-in soaking period that soaks the rice (ensuring greater penetration of liquid into each grain, for better results) for approximately

20 minutes. To bypass this step, there is a Quick Cook cycle. The Quick Cook cycle is also great for sautéing ingredients for risottos, pilafs and other recipes.

Some fuzzy logic models come with a steamer tray or basket, along with a steamer menu. Most of these models also have a timer that lets you program a specific time for the dish to finish — great for waking up to piping hot oatmeal!

Fuzzy logic machines and those with Sensor Logic technology are popular in Asian households because they make amazing rice. They are also wonderful for porridge and other recipes that require gentler heat, such as risottos and polenta. They are pricy, however, with models starting at around $100. Some popular brands include Cuisinart, Zojirushi, Panasonic, Sanyo, Tiger and Aroma.

Induction Heating Models

Induction heating rice cookers are similar to fuzzy logic models but take precision a step further by obtaining their heat from an alternating electric current in the wall outlet. In on/off and fuzzy logic models, heat is applied from the electrical plate directly under the rice cooker bowl. Induction rice cookers have electric coils that generate a magnetic field when the device is turned on. This means the rice cooker bowl instantly becomes hot and the pot itself becomes the source of heat within the machine.

Who knew cooking rice could be this scientific? What it all boils down to is this: induction heating rice cookers improve the cooking process because their temperature-sensing methods are more accurate, allowing for fine-tuned adjustments. They also produce more evenly cooked food because heat encompasses the rice cooker bowl, rather than simply radiating up from below. In the event of a human measuring error, an induction heating rice cooker can make minute adjustments to both the time and the temperature of the selected program. They really do make perfect rice.

All this precision comes with a price. Induction heating rice cookers start at around $250 and go up to $500 plus for top of the line. Popular brands include Zojirushi and Sanyo.

What's the Best Rice Cooker for Me?

If you're looking to cook simple, plain pots of rice and maybe do some steaming, I'd suggest a small or medium no-frills on/off machine. If you want to experiment with some of the non-traditional techniques in this book, such as pilafs and risottos, and you plan to entertain, I'd go with a higher-end medium or large on/off "keep warm" model with digital controls. If you plan to take advantage of the full array of capabilities, such as sticky rice and porridge, that fuzzy logic and induction heating models have to offer, splurge and go for the best in class.

Features, Cycle Settings and Options

The list below includes just some of the features, cycle settings and options available on rice cookers. The terminology varies with each manufacturer and model type, so always consult the manual for your machine.

On/Off Switch

On/off rice cookers have a switch that clicks down into the Cook position. Click up for the Keep Warm cycle or to shut off the machine. As soon as you plug in an on/off machine, it will begin heating up depending on the position of the switch (Cook or Keep Warm mode). The Cook position is the same as the Regular cycle on fuzzy logic machines.

Steamer Tray or Basket

Many on/off machines and some fuzzy logic machines come with a steamer tray or basket that enables you to steam dumplings, appetizers, vegetables, fish and meats. You can even steam rice at the same time that you're steaming items on the tray. Some of the steamer baskets have two or three tiers — very convenient for making larger quantities. When steaming in an on/off machine, you will need to set a timer. Most fuzzy logic machines that offer steaming have a built-in timer so you can program steaming time.

Keep Warm Cycle

The Keep Warm cycle is available on certain on/off models and on fuzzy logic and induction heating machines. When the rice is finished cooking, the machine automatically switches to the Keep Warm cycle, where it rests at a constant low temperature for up to 4 hours, or even more (check your manual for your machine's capability). Fuzzy logic machines will often give you a digital read-out of how long the machine has been on the Keep Warm cycle. Some machines come with a two-phase cycle in which the machine stays warm for 3 hours, then switches to a second lower-temperature mode for an additional 8 hours. Certain models allow you to turn the Keep Warm cycle off without unplugging the machine. The Keep Warm cycle is also an excellent way to reheat some dishes.

I've included a rest period on the Keep Warm cycle at the end of many of the recipes in this book. This small amount of extra time results in a superior rice, grain or legume dish. It's best to serve recipes containing meat, fish or vegetables immediately, to prevent spoilage. Also be aware that brown rice can sour if left for more than 1 hour on the Keep Warm cycle. I recommend transferring soups and certain stews to a serving dish right away; otherwise, the grains will continue absorbing liquid and will become mushy.

Timer

Some fuzzy logic machines come with a built-in timer that enables you to program

an end time. This is great when you want to come home to steaming hot rice after a long day's work, or wake up to piping hot oatmeal. Do not use the timer function when a recipe calls for perishable ingredients.

Menu

Fuzzy logic and sensor logic machines, as well as some digital on/off models, include a control panel, a menu of sorts, that allows you to choose from various cycles. Below is a short guide to some basic cycles. Remember that every machine has its own personality, so it's best to refer to your manufacturer's manual.

- **Regular:** Fuzzy logic machines are automatically set for a white rice cycle usually called the Regular cycle (or Normal on some machines). Use this cycle for long-, medium- and short-grain white rice. Some machines give you a choice between Softer (for a softer consistency) and Harder (best for rice salads) on this cycle. The Regular cycle is also best for a variety of other grains, including barley, millet, amaranth and couscous. On fuzzy logic machines, the Regular cycle has a built-in soaking period of about 20 minutes. This allows the liquid to penetrate the grains, resulting in superior rice.
- **Brown Rice:** Use this cycle for all brown rice, red rice and non-glutinous black rice varieties. It's also ideal for wild rice. The Brown Rice cycle is generally twice as long as the Regular cycle, because brown rice takes longer to cook than white rice. It also has a built-in soaking period of 1 hour. Because brown rice retains its bran layers (unlike white rice, in which the bran layer has been polished off), this soaking step is very important, as it allows water to penetrate through the tough bran layers, helping to release nutrients and improving the texture.
- **Quick Cook:** When you're short on time, you can select this cycle to bypass the soaking period in the Regular and Brown

Rice cycles, though you will sacrifice the superior texture that soaking provides. The Quick Cook cycle can also be used to sauté ingredients before cooking on the Regular or Porridge cycle.

- **Porridge:** This cycle is wonderful for congees, grits, polenta and creamy oatmeal. It's also terrific for risotto (though some fuzzy logic models have a dedicated Risotto cycle). It has a constant medium-low temperature that is ideal for these types of recipes.
- **Reheat:** This cycle is great for leftovers and refrigerated rice, or to bring rice that has been on the Keep Warm cycle to a hotter temperature. Just add some water or broth to add moisture. The machine will beep when it reaches the proper temperature, about 5 to 10 minutes after you press the Reheat button.
- **Steam:** For this cycle, you'll use the steaming tray or basket that came with the machine. This cycle enables you to steam everything from dumplings to full meals. You can steam rice in the bottom and a fish fillet with some vegetables on top, for example.
- **Sweet/Sticky:** Use this cycle (labeled either Sweet or Sticky) for all glutinous rice, such as Thai black rice, and for sushi rice if your machine doesn't have a Sushi cycle. The machine calibrates the soaking time to achieve the most desirable sticky texture.
- **Sushi:** This cycle produces a sticky texture that is ideal for making sushi rice. The machine calibrates the soaking time to achieve the most desirable sticky texture.

Some fuzzy logic rice cookers come with advanced cycles, such as Risotto, Soup, Cake and Slow Cook. You can easily adapt the recipes in this book to take advantage of these capabilities if you own a state-of-the-art fuzzy logic machine.

Rice Cooker Tips

- Read your manufacturer's use and care manual and orient yourself with safety precautions before using your rice cooker. Bear in mind that brands do differ.
- Each machine has its own unique personality, which you will get to know by experimenting with these recipes. When in doubt, refer to the manufacturer's manual.
- Never immerse your machine in water. I recommend washing the rice cooker bowl by hand.
- Use a long-handled wooden spoon or nonstick spatula when sautéing or stirring ingredients in the rice cooker bowl.
- Spray the rice cooker bowl with nonstick cooking spray to prevent sticking, if desired.
- When cooking rice, never lift the lid, as the steam will evaporate and interrupt the cooking process.
- Unplug the machine from the outlet when it's not in use and before cleaning. Let it cool before putting on or taking off parts.
- When using perishable ingredients, do not use the timer to instruct the machine to cook later in the day or overnight.
- For a superior result, use filtered water to cook rice, grains and beans.
- Position the unit away from the wall and out from under cabinets so the steam can be released freely.
- Serve all recipes that call for fish, meat or vegetables immediately to prevent spoilage and refrigerate any leftovers promptly.

How to Use This Book

All of the recipes in this book can be made using an electronic rice cooker. The majority can be made in either a standard on/off machine or a fuzzy logic machine. For some recipes, however, fuzzy logic is either preferred or required.

Please note that some rice cooker models are labeled to reflect the measured volume of *cooked* white rice the machine will yield — for example, "10-cup rice cooker (cooked rice)" — while others are labeled to reflect the amount of measured *raw* white rice the rice cooker bowl will accommodate — for example, "10-cup rice cooker" — but actually hold about double the volume of cooked rice. The recipes in this book instruct you to use either a medium or a large machine. When the recipe calls for a medium rice cooker, it should be able to hold 14 to 16 cups (3.5 to 4 L) of cooked white rice; when it calls for a large machine, it should be able to hold 19 to 22 cups (4.75 to 5.5 L) of cooked white rice. Recipes that call for a medium machine can generally also be made in a larger machine.

If you're not sure of the size of your rice cooker, fill the bowl with water using a 1-cup (250 mL) measuring cup and count the number of cups it takes to fill the bowl to the top inside ridge. The total volume of the water will equal the volume of cooked rice the bowl holds.

Because each rice cooker has its own personality, some recipes may require some fiddling on your part to perfect them. In time, you will learn to appreciate your machine's unique attributes.

Using the Various Cycles

All recipes include instructions on which cycle(s) to use. Here are some tips that will help you get the most out of each cycle.

The Regular Cycle

If you're using a standard on/off rice cooker without digital controls, the Regular cycle is simply the main cooking cycle. Push down on the on/off switch, and the machine will begin heating up. When the cycle completes, the machine will either turn off or switch to the Keep Warm cycle. (You can manually reset the machine for the Keep Warm cycle by flipping the switch up or by unplugging the machine, plugging it back in and then flipping the switch up.)

When you are sautéing on the Regular cycle using an on/off machine, keep in mind that some machines will switch to the Keep Warm cycle unless the lid is kept down. Lift the lid when necessary to stir ingredients, then close it again. Other machines may switch to the Keep Warm cycle even with the lid down. In that case, you may need to manually hold the switch down so it stays in the cooking mode while you are sautéing. Once you add liquid, unplug the machine and reset for the Regular cycle by plugging the machine back in, then flipping the switch down.

The Regular cycle also refers to the white rice cycle on fuzzy logic machines. If you are going to sauté on the Regular cycle in a fuzzy logic machine, remember that it will take 20 minutes to heat up, due to the built-in soaking period.

The Brown Rice Cycle

The Brown Rice cycle is available on fuzzy logic machines. Some recipes call for resetting to or cooking on the Brown Rice cycle. The soaking period for the Brown Rice cycle is 1 hour, so bear this in mind, as you'll need to add an hour to the total cooking time when using this cycle (as noted in specific recipes). This may not be the fastest cooking method, but it's worth the wait for superior results.

The Quick Cook Cycle

The Quick Cook cycle, available on fuzzy logic machines, bypasses the soaking period and heats up immediately. In the recipes in this book, I use the Quick Cook cycle primarily to sauté ingredients, then reset the machine for the Regular, Brown Rice or Porridge cycle. Some recipes, especially pilafs, can be cooked completely on the Quick Cook cycle, but please follow the specific directions for each recipe.

Some fuzzy logic models won't allow you to sauté on the Quick Cook cycle (they keep switching to the Keep Warm cycle), and others may not let you reset to another cycle once you've sautéed and added liquid. In either case, heat the machine on the Regular, Brown Rice or Porridge cycle, do your sautéing, then let the machine complete the cycle once you've added the liquid. Refer to the manufacturer's guide that came with your machine for more information.

The Porridge Cycle

The Porridge cycle on fuzzy logic machines cooks at a constant low boil instead of the rolling medium boil of the Regular cycle on standard on/off machines. This low boil makes the Porridge cycle an excellent choice for risottos, congees, oatmeal, grits and polenta. Some cooks run the Porridge cycle a second time for super-creamy grits and polenta, but I have not found this to be necessary.

The Steam Cycle, Sweet/Sticky Cycle and Sushi Cycle

These specialized cycles are available only on certain fuzzy logic models. If your machine doesn't have these cycles, you can use the Regular cycle for the same functions, though the results may not be quite as good. The Sweet/Sticky cycle and the Sushi cycle are interchangeable.

The Keep Warm Cycle

Most rice cookers switch to the Keep Warm cycle once they have completed the cooking cycle. The Keep Warm cycle can also be manually activated via the Keep Warm button or function on fuzzy logic machines and the Keep Warm switch on on/off "keep warm" machines. If a recipe asks you to reset to the Keep Warm cycle, you may have to unplug the machine to reset it. When cooking side dishes, and rice pilaf in particular, I've noticed that in some on/off "keep warm" machines the rice can begin to harden on the bottom during the Keep Warm cycle. Try spraying the bottom of the bowl with nonstick cooking spray. You may also need to unplug the machine when it switches to the Keep Warm cycle and let it rest for a few minutes.

The Long, Medium and Short of It: A Guide to Rice

The Origins of Rice

There's a good reason people throw rice at weddings — the tiny grain is a symbol of prosperity and fertility. It's also the most important staple food for much of the world's population, and research suggests it's been sating appetites for more than 5,000 years.

From its first cultivation in the Yangtze River Valley, the water- and sun-loving crop spread from Asia to India to Pakistan until it ended up in the United States, where it found fertile ground in the Carolinas and Georgia. Later, it spread across the South. Those early American fields took root by accident, literally, when a sea captain gave the South Carolina locals a bag of rice he'd brought from Madagascar as payment for fixing his wrecked ship. After that chance meeting some 400 years ago, rice production became a major part of the U.S. agricultural scene and continues to be today.

In the Philippines, there's an expression that says, "One grain of rice equals one bead of sweat." In other words, it's a labor-intensive crop, and in some countries it still requires hundreds of man-hours for each acre that's cultivated. It's grown on nearly every continent, with prolific producers like Korea, Vietnam, Thailand, Japan, Bangladesh and Indonesia leading the way.

Because it's nutritious and tasty, rice is in constant demand, with consumption around the world increasing dramatically every year for the past several decades. It's naturally fat-, sodium- and cholesterol-free, and American long-grain white rice contains a measly 103 calories per $\frac{1}{2}$-cup (125 mL) serving.

The four major categories of rice — indica, japonica, aromatic and glutinous — are distinguished by their shape and texture, varying from long-grain and fluffy, like basmati, to short-grain and sticky, used to make mochi. Rice is brown or white depending on how it's processed. Brown rice, which is chewier, nuttier and richer in nutrients, still has the bran surrounding the kernel. White rice, more tender and delicate, no longer has the bran and germ.

In addition to being served on their own, the different types of rice are used to make baby food, flour, milk, noodles, snacks, breakfast cereals, beer and wine.

And as for tossing it onto the lucky bride and groom after the "I do's," many churches have banned the tradition. Why? Is it potentially lethal for birds to eat the rice that falls to the ground? Not true, say avian experts, who report that birds have long used rice fields as their own personal feeders, with no ill effects. No one knows the origin of that myth, but there's a more practical reason to stop throwing rice: wedding guests might slip and fall on it. That's why it's usually flower petals and not rice raining down on the happy couple.

Long-Grain Rices

Long-grain rice is usually described as rice that is about four to five times as long as it is wide. Most of the long-grain types grown today are descendants of *Oryza sativa indica*, which produced the famous Indian basmati rice. Though likely first cultivated in and around India, long-grain rice is grown in tropical regions throughout Asia and the southern United States.

Basmati Rices
Varieties and forms:
White basmati, brown basmati, kalijira

Basmati is a variety of long-grain rice grown in India and Pakistan, known for its fragrance and delicate, nuanced flavor. Its name means "the fragrant one" in Sanskrit, but it can also mean "the soft rice," and the word coincidently means "my smile" in Arabic. India is the largest cultivator and exporter of this rice, followed by Pakistan; it is primarily grown in the lush fields of the Punjab region. White basmati rice is the most common. Brown basmati rice still has its hull intact. Kalijira rice, a miniature version, is an ancient strain grown in Bangladesh and is so expensive that it's typically reserved for holidays in India.

Basmati rice has a light, dry texture and is lightly perfumed. The grains are fluffy and stay separate when cooked. These are ideal rices for Middle Eastern pilafs and biryani dishes. Keep in mind that basmati is more filling than many other varieties of white rice, so you may have to cook a little bit less per person.

Since basmati rice is imported, it's necessary to rinse it before use.

Southern Long-Grain Rices
Varieties and forms:
American long-grain white, American long-grain brown, parboiled (Converted), instant

The most common rice in the world, Southern long-grain rice is also known as Carolina long-grain rice or Carolina gold. Long and slender, it is the most widely grown rice in the United States. American long-grain brown rice is unhulled, meaning it's a whole grain with its bran and outer layer of fiber intact. Parboiled (Converted) rice has been parboiled and dried before refining, a process that causes the grains to absorb many of the nutrients from the husk. When cooked, the grains are more nutritious, firmer and less clingy than white rice grains. You may use parboiled (Converted) rice in place of long-grain rice, but bear in mind that it requires more water and, therefore, takes longer to cook. Instant rice has been precooked and dehydrated. I don't recommend using instant rice for the recipes in this book.

American long-grain white rice cooks up tender, dry, fluffy and separate. It has a somewhat bland, sweet grain flavor. Long-grain brown rice has a chewier, nuttier flavor. Instant rice is blander than regular rice and cooks up quite mushy.

Brown rice is a whole grain, so it contains all the vitamins and minerals rice has to offer. Because of its high oil content, it is best to keep brown rice refrigerated or frozen, rather than on the shelf, where it can go rancid. Brown rice takes at least twice as long to cook as white rice.

Jasmine Rices

Varieties and forms:
Thai jasmine, brown jasmine

Jasmine rice, also known as Thai fragrant rice after its country of origin, is the most popular rice in Thailand and Southeast Asia. It is the second most popular aromatic rice in the United States. Its high quality, combined with the crop's low yield, makes it more expensive than other rice varieties. Brown jasmine rice is jasmine rice with its hull intact.

Jasmine is an aromatic rice with a distinctive jasmine aroma. Sweet, nutty and mild, it tastes a bit like popcorn when cooked. Round and starchy, jasmine rice cooks up soft, moist and sticky.

Jasmine rice should be cooked within 6 months of purchase or it will lose not only its freshness, but also its delicate jasmine flavor.

American Aromatics

Varieties and forms:
American jasmine, Jasmati, Texmati, Kasmati, Calmati, wild pecan, Louisiana pecan

American aromatics are domestic versions of basmati and jasmine rices. American jasmine and Jasmati are jasmine rices adapted to grow in the southern United States. Texmati and Kasmati rices are American-grown basmati rices. Calmati, grown in California, is a cross between basmati and Carolina long-grain rice. Louisiana pecan and wild pecan rice are basmati hybrids grown in the bayou area of Louisiana. They get their names from the process of being dried on pecan husks.

American aromatics have the flavor and texture of basmati and/or jasmine rice. Louisiana pecan rice and wild pecan rice have a rich, nutty flavor derived from their unique drying process.

Long-Grain Sticky Rices

Varieties and forms:
Thai, sticky jasmine, glutinous (aka "sticky" or "sweet") white, Thai sticky (black or purple)

Long-grain sticky rice is known as *kow neow* in Thailand. Popular throughout Thailand and Southeast Asia, it is traditionally formed into balls and eaten with your hands like bread. Thai and sticky jasmine rices are most popular in Northern Thailand. Glutinous white rice is an ancient strain of rice found in Laos, Vietnam, Cambodia, Indonesia, Bangladesh, China and Japan. Legend has it that the Chinese used glutinous rice as mortar in the making of the Great Wall. Thai black and purple sticky rices are used primarily in sweetened desserts.

It is interesting to note that glutinous rice does not, in fact, contain gluten. It is sticky because it has no amylose (a type of starch that is waxy and sets up a stiff gel in rice grains, making them stiffer and more separate) and has high amounts of amylopectin (a pectin-type starch that produces a sticky and/or creamy result).

Sticky yet firm, long-grain sticky rices are aromatic and have a sweet flavor. They are traditionally soaked overnight and steamed instead of boiled. They become translucent when cooked.

Red Rices

Varieties and forms:
California red, wehani, Himalayan red, red cargo, riz rouge (camargue)

Red rices are technically brown rices with a pink, red or mahogany hull. Some are bred to be red; others are red by lucky happenstance. California red is an offshoot of traditional red rices found in Asia. Wehani is an Indian basmati and red rice hybrid. With a russet hue, Himalayan red has been grown in Asia for centuries. Red cargo rice gets its name from the fact that it is usually exported in bulk, rather than in prepackaged bags. Considered a gourmet delicacy, riz rouge ("red rice" in French) was first planted in the 1940s by Chinese and Madagascarean troops in the marshy lands on the Mediterranean coast of France.

Generally more expensive than standard brown rices, red rices have a similar taste to brown varieties. Plump and nutty in flavor, they have a chewy texture and are less sticky than brown rices.

Because their hulls are intact, red rices contain all the nutrients, vitamins and minerals rice has to offer. Red rices take longer to cook than white rices, but slightly less time than brown.

Short- and Medium-Grain Rices

Short- and medium-grain rices are also known as japonica rices. Requiring a special temperate climate found in only a few places in the world, japonica rices are grown in Japan, Korea, Australia, the United States and parts of Europe.

Smooth, plump and moist, with a subtle flavor, japonica rices are extremely versatile. They are ideal for sushi, stuffings and mixed rice dishes, and they hold together well for chopsticks. They also make the perfect accompaniment to strongly flavored dishes, from Asian delicacies to paella, the quintessential dish of Spain, made with the japonica variety Valencia. Across Europe and in Italy, Arborio rice, another japonica variety, is used to make risotto.

Japanese-Style Japonica Rices

Most common varieties and forms:
Calrose, Nishiki, Akita Homachi, Koshihikari

Japonica rices grown in Japan are not readily available for export, but several American-grown varieties are widely available. California-grown Calrose, a medium-grain japonica rice, is the most commonly available Japanese-style rice in North America. Medium-grain varieties are oblong, with a length that is two to three times the width. Also known as "pearl rice," short-grain varieties are somewhat round and are harder to find than medium-grain rices. In Japan, the terms "short-grain" and "medium-grain" are used interchangeably and can also mean sushi rice.

In Japan and other parts of Southeast Asia, japonica rices are eaten three times a day and may also be used to make sushi. With their clean, mild taste, japonica rices are considered by many to be the best in the world. Price is a good gauge of quality, and in some Asian markets the price of japonica rices can change before your eyes as it fluctuates with market prices. Popular brands include Pacific International, Tamaki Gold, Kokuhu Rose, Konriko and Tamanishiki. Japanese-style japonica rices need to be soaked for 30 to 60 minutes before use.

Risotto Rices

Varieties and forms:
Arborio, Carnaroli

Risotto rices are rounded, short-grain rices traditionally grown in the Po valley of Northern Italy. They are now also grown in

California and Texas. The most popular are Arborio, named after the Italian town where it is grown, and Carnaroli. Carnaroli has a larger grain than Arborio, but both are used in risotto, paella and puddings. Risotto rices come in different grades, from super-fino (considered by many to be the best) to fino, semi-fino and commune.

As a result of their high starch content, risotto rices are firm, creamy and chewy when cooked. Risotto's signature "bite" is the result of a lucky "defect." During maturation, the starch in the grain's core "deforms," resulting in its firm, toothy center when cooked. It's not recommended to steam Arborio rice in the traditional manner because of its high starch content. For salads and other non-risotto recipes, Arborio or Carnaroli rice should be boiled briefly and drained.

Risotto rice should not be rinsed before cooking, as its high starch content gives it its rich, creamy texture. Risotto is best served "al dente," which literally means "to the teeth," so that it has its characteristic firm, chewy center.

Paella Rices

Varieties and forms:
Valencia, bomba

A staple in Spain, paella rices are medium-grain japonica rices that produce a creamy texture, much like risotto. One variety of paella rice is Valencia, named for the most popular rice-growing region of Spain. Another variety is bomba, which is grown in Calasparra, Spain. Considered by many to be the superior variety, bomba was once on the verge of extinction because it is extremely labor-intensive to grow.

Slightly sticky when cooked, paella rice stays separate, unlike risotto. Its neutral taste allows it to absorb other flavors beautifully. Bomba rice absorbs 30% more liquid than other rices. Bomba also expands widthwise, unlike other rices, which expand lengthwise.

Paella rices should not be overcooked. The center of the grain should have a delicate, chewy bite when cooked.

American Black, Brown, Red and Mahogany Rices

Varieties and forms:
Black japonica rice, medium-grain brown rice, short-grain brown rice

These American-grown specialty aromatic rices are as revered for their beauty as they are for their flavor. American black, brown, red and mahogany rices are considered brown rices because they are unhulled. Black japonica rice is a short-grain rice that originated in California. It is a hybrid of Asian black short-grain rice and medium-grain mahogany rice. Medium-grain brown rice is fiber-rich, moist and chewy. The ubiquitous short-grain brown rice has plump, fat kernels.

Black japonica rice has a musty, mushroom-like flavor that goes well with meats and wild game. Medium-grain brown rice cooks up beautifully and has a heartier texture than short-grain brown rice. With its high starch content, short-grain brown rice has a nutty flavor and is moist and slightly sticky when cooked.

I recommend storing black japonica rice in the refrigerator for extended shelf life. Because of its high oil content, short-grain brown rice can go rancid in the cupboard, so it is best stored in the refrigerator or freezer.

Short-Grain Sticky (Glutinous) Rices

Varieties and forms:
Chinese, Japanese, Korean

Short-grain sticky rice (also called glutinous rice, though it doesn't contain gluten) is widely eaten throughout Asia. The Chinese variation, *nuomi*, is a popular ingredient in dishes served at festivals and New Year's celebrations. Japanese sticky rice, *mochigome*, is often used to make mochi, a traditional rice cake. In Korea, *chapssal* is used for a variety of dishes.

Plump and opaque, short-grain sticky rices are used primarily in desserts and sweet dishes. Especially sticky when cooked, it has a slightly sweet taste.

Rinse short-grain sticky rice before cooking. Soaking it overnight prior to cooking will maximize its expansion when cooked.

Bhutanese Red Rice

A medium-grain rice, Bhutanese red rice is grown exclusively in the tiny kingdom of Bhutan, located high in the eastern Himalayan Mountains. A red japonica rice, it is a staple of rural Bhutanese cuisine. Currently, it is the only agricultural product exported from Bhutan to the United States.

Bhutanese red rice is semi-milled, which means some of its reddish bran remains on the grain. When cooked, it becomes pale pink, and its texture is soft and slightly sticky. It has a strong nutty flavor.

Because it is semi-milled, Bhutanese red rice cooks faster than brown rice, but not as quickly as white rice.

Forbidden Black Rice

Forbidden black rice gets its name because it was originally grown only for the Chinese emperor. Grown in Zhejiang in northern China, it is prized for its color as well as its soft texture and nutty taste. Although relatively new to the United States, it is getting easier and easier to find in American specialty shops.

Forbidden black rice turns a beautiful deep indigo when cooked. Unlike other short-grain black rices, forbidden black rice is not a sticky rice. Rather, it is considered a "rice bowl rice." It is becoming a popular — and strikingly beautiful and tasty — alternative to white rice. It is traditionally used to make congee, the savory Chinese breakfast porridge.

Wild Rice

Technically, wild rice is not a rice at all, but a marsh grass. Found in ponds, lakes and marshes, it is native to the Great Lakes region of North America. It was a staple food of North America's first inhabitants. It is also called Indian rice, Canadian rice, manomin, water oats, blackbird oats and marsh oats.

Wild rice has a distinctly nutty taste and chewy texture. Most often enjoyed with its hull intact, wild rice is a popular ingredient in stuffings and as a substitute for potatoes, white rice or brown rice. When cooked, wild rice cracks open to reveal a white interior. Because of its high oil content, it is best kept refrigerated or frozen.

Buying and Storing Rice

You can find many varieties of rice at a well-stocked grocery store. For the more exotic types, such as Bhutanese red or Thai black, try an Asian market, a health-food store or an online resource such as Lundberg Family Farms or Lotus Foods. Always purchase rice from a trusted source and inspect it for insects or discoloration. As a general rule of thumb, white rice should be pearly, red and black rices should be shiny and brown rices should be evenly tan.

It's best to store rice in a tightly sealed container in a cool pantry. When properly sealed and stored, polished white rice will keep well for 25 to 30 years. Because brown, black and red rices contain healthful oils in their germ layer, these rices can go rancid, so use them within 1 month of purchase, refrigerate them for up to 3 months or freeze them for up to 5 months.

Measuring Rice

For ease of use and familiarity, I have written the recipes using standard imperial and metric measurements. But don't throw away the small cup that came with your machine; it is the standard measurement in Asia for rice cookers and measures 6 ounces ($3/4$ cup or 175 mL) of rice. To measure the right amount of liquid, simply add the amount of water or other liquid that's indicated on the side of the rice cooker bowl (e.g., if you fill the small cup with rice twice, fill the bowl with water up to the 2-cup line). Feel free to use this method when you're making basic pots of rice, particularly when using Asian rices. Otherwise, follow the recipe directions, using standard measurements. Do not mound the rice when measuring. I recommend leveling it off with your finger or a rubber spatula.

As in many Asian households, I was taught to measure the liquid by using my finger, otherwise known as the Mount Fuji technique. With the tip of your index finger just touching the surface of the rice, add water until it reaches the first knuckle. You may feel most secure using a measuring cup or being guided by the lines on the side of the bowl, but know that millions of Asian families swear by this technique. This method should only be used when preparing long-grain white rices, medium-grain Asian rices or short-grain Asian rices.

To Rinse or Not to Rinse

I recommend rinsing all types of rice, with the exception of Arborio and Carnaroli. Rinsing eliminates excess starch, which can make rice mushy. Rinsed rice turns out light and fluffy, and you will never go back. (You don't want to rinse Arborio or Carnaroli rice, because you want it to retain its abundant amylopectin, which it releases to create the creamy texture risottos are known for.)

Many domestic rices are fortified with vitamins and minerals. You may have noticed that the package recommends *not* rinsing the rice so you don't wash away the nutrients. But in my opinion, the improved outcome provided by rinsing far outweighs the minimal nutrients provided by fortified rices. Far better to get your nutrients by maintaining a well-balanced diet.

While rinsing is truly a personal preference for domestic rices, it's a necessity for imported rices, as some mills outside of North America still use polishing additives such as talc, which should be removed. In addition, because they are often stored in bulk, imported rices could contain dirt, bugs and twigs. There is one exception to this rule: a rice labeled "*musenmai*" or "rinse-free" has entered the North American market from Japan. Look for it at Asian markets.

To rinse rice, place it in a bowl and fill the bowl with cool water, stirring the rice with one hand. Drain and repeat until the water in the bowl stays clear.

Soaking Rice

Fuzzy logic rice cookers have built-in soaking times (20 minutes for white rice and 1 hour for brown, red and black rices). If you're using an on/off machine, you may wish to soak brown, red and black rices for 30 to 60 minutes before steaming, for improved nutrients and texture.

Some varieties of rice require an extended soaking period, including short-grain rices (at least 30 minutes) and sticky or sweet rices (4 to 6 hours, or overnight). Refer to specific recipes for soaking instructions.

Coating the Bowl

Some cooks swear by spraying a thin layer of nonstick cooking spray on the bottom of the rice cooker bowl before making rice. It can help separate the grains and prevent them from sticking, but this is a matter of personal preference.

Cooking a Pot of Plain Rice

1. If desired, spray the bottom of the rice cooker bowl with nonstick cooking spray. Place rinsed rice in the bowl and cover with water as specified in the Rice Cooking Chart (page 21). (Alternatively, use chicken or vegetable broth for added flavor.) Add salt to taste, if desired, and swirl to combine.
2. For on/off machines, set for the Regular cycle. For fuzzy logic machines, set for the Quick Cook cycle (if you want to bypass the soaking cycle), the Regular cycle (for long-, medium- or short-grain white rices), the Brown Rice cycle (for long-,

medium- or short-grain brown, black, red and wild rices), the Sweet/Sticky cycle (for sticky rices) or the Sushi cycle (for Japanese short-grain rice). See the Rice Cooking Chart for cycle recommendations. Do not open the lid while rice is cooking!

3. Wait for the cycle to end. The inherent advantage of cooking rice in a rice cooker is that it automatically stops cooking when the grains have absorbed all the water. I have included a list of approximate cooking times in the Rice Cooking Chart to give you a general idea of how long you will need to wait.

4. After the cooking cycle has ended, the rice needs to continue steaming for 10 minutes. In fuzzy logic machines and most on/off "keep warm" machines, the steaming period is built in, so when the timer sounds, your rice is ready to eat. For on/off "cook and shut off" machines, you will need to set a timer for 10 minutes after the machine clicks off.

5. Fluff the rice with a wooden spoon (dipped in water) or plastic paddle. If desired, fold in butter.

Rice Cooking Chart

The following chart is based on using 1 cup (250 mL) rice, which generally yields about 3 cups (750 mL) cooked. For this amount, use a small or medium machine. If you want to double the recipe, you'll need a medium, medium-large or large machine. The amounts of liquid and cooking times in this chart are meant as general guidelines, as each machine is slightly different; you should also refer to the cooking times listed in your rice cooker manual. Personal preference can also affect cooking times (for example, if you like your rice moister, you might add more liquid).

Type of Rice	Amount of Liquid	Cooking Time*	Fuzzy Logic Cycle
American jasmine	1½ cups (375 mL)	25 to 35 minutes	Regular cycle
Bhutanese red	1½ cups (375 mL)	25 to 30 minutes	Brown Rice cycle
Black japonica	2 cups (500 mL)	60 to 70 minutes	Brown Rice cycle
Bomba	2 cups (500 mL)	25 to 35 minutes	Regular cycle
Brown basmati	2 cups (500 mL)	45 to 60 minutes	Brown Rice cycle
Brown jasmine	2 cups (500 mL)	45 to 60 minutes	Regular cycle
Brown kalijira	2 cups (500 mL)	45 to 60 minutes	Brown Rice cycle
California red	2 cups (500 mL)	45 to 60 minutes	Brown Rice cycle
Calmati	2 cups (500 mL)	25 to 35 minutes	Regular cycle
Forbidden black	1¾ cups (425 mL)	40 to 50 minutes	Brown Rice cycle
Himalayan red	2 cups (500 mL)	45 to 60 minutes	Brown Rice cycle
Japanese-style medium-grain (japonica)	1⅓ cups (325 mL)	25 to 35 minutes	Regular cycle
Japanese-style short-grain (japonica)	1 cup + 2 tbsp (280 mL)	25 to 35 minutes	Sushi cycle

* Add 20 minutes to the cooking time if using the Regular cycle on a fuzzy logic machine. Add 1 hour to the cooking time if using the Brown Rice cycle on a fuzzy logic machine. (The additional cooking time reflects the built-in soaking periods in fuzzy logic models.)

Type of Rice	Amount of Liquid	Cooking Time*	Fuzzy Logic Cycle
Jasmati	2 cups (500 mL)	25 to 35 minutes	Regular cycle
Kasmati	2 cups (500 mL)	25 to 35 minutes	Regular cycle
Long-grain brown	2 cups (500 mL)	45 to 60 minutes	Brown Rice cycle
Long-grain sticky	2 cups (500 mL)	45 to 60 minutes	Sweet/Sticky cycle
Long-grain white	1½ cups (375 mL)	25 to 30 minutes	Regular cycle
Louisiana pecan	2 cups (500 mL)	30 to 40 minutes	Brown Rice cycle
Medium-grain brown	2 cups (500 mL)	45 to 60 minutes	Brown Rice cycle
Parboiled (Converted)	2¼ cups (550 mL)	30 to 40 minutes	Regular cycle
Red cargo	2 cups (500 mL)	45 to 60 minutes	Brown Rice cycle
Riz rouge (camargue)	3½ cups (875 mL)	35 to 45 minutes	Brown Rice cycle
Short-grain sticky	1 cup (250 mL)	25 to 35 minutes	Sweet/Sticky cycle
Texmati	2 cups (500 mL)	25 to 35 minutes	Regular cycle
Thai jasmine	1½ cups (375 mL)	25 to 35 minutes	Regular cycle
Valencia	1¾ cups (425 mL)	25 to 35 minutes	Regular cycle
Wehani	2 cups (500 mL)	60 to 70 minutes	Brown Rice cycle
White basmati	1½ cups (375 mL)	25 to 35 minutes	Regular cycle
White kalijira	1½ cups (375 mL)	25 to 35 minutes	Regular cycle
Wild	3 cups (750 mL)	60 to 70 minutes	Regular cycle
Wild pecan	2 cups (500 mL)	30 to 40 minutes	Brown Rice cycle

* Add 20 minutes to the cooking time if using the Regular cycle on a fuzzy logic machine. Add 1 hour to the cooking time if using the Brown Rice cycle on a fuzzy logic machine. (The additional cooking time reflects the built-in soaking periods in fuzzy logic models.)

All About Grains

What Are Whole Grains?

It's easy to understand why grains have been called "the staff of life," since they've been sustaining people as vital food sources for centuries.

Whole grains, specifically, are the seeds of grasses, cultivated for eating. Also called cereals, they come in many shapes and sizes, from large kernels of popcorn to small quinoa seeds. Other examples include barley, buckwheat, bulgur, millet, oatmeal and wild rice, and whole-grain versions of rice, bread, cereal, flour and pasta are now common in groceries, farmers' markets and ethnic markets.

Whole grains are an excellent source of important nutrients, such as potassium, magnesium and selenium. They're far healthier than their refined counterparts, because they contain the bran and germ — the whole grain.

There are three parts to a whole grain: the bran, which is the fiber-rich outer layer; the middle layer, called the endosperm, which is filled with proteins and carbohydrates; and the germ, the small nutrient-rich core, which contains vitamin E, B vitamins, antioxidants and healthy fats. Refined grains, such as those found in white bread, contain only the endosperm.

Picking Your Grain: The Whole-Grain Lexicon

Amaranth

Amaranth is the seed of a bushy plant related to beets, quinoa and spinach. Each plant produces a deep red, flowery head containing as many as 60,000 seeds. An ancient grain, amaranth was a staple in the diet of pre-Colombian Aztecs, who believed it gave them supernatural powers. Buying in to this belief, the invading Spanish conquistadors burned amaranth crops in hopes that it would help destroy this powerful people.

With its nutty flavor and crunchy texture, this "lost grain" is enjoying a resurgence. Amaranth can be ground into flour or cooked whole as a hot cereal or side dish. It can also be popped in a skillet, like popcorn.

Barley

Varieties and forms:
Pearl, hulled (whole), pot, Scotch

Barley has a rich and varied history, from its distinction as the food of gladiators to its prominence during Biblical and Medieval times. It was the first domesticated grain in the Near East. Today, it is a versatile cereal grain that is enjoyed as a nutritious part of meals as well as an ingredient in malt beverages.

The most popular form is pearl barley, also known as peeled or polished barley. Pearl barley is husked and the bran is removed, then it is steamed and polished. It has a rich, nutlike flavor and a chewy, creamy texture when cooked.

Hulled barley, also called whole barley or barley groats, has only the outer husk removed. It takes a bit longer to cook than

pearl barley and is chewier. Pot barley is more refined than hull but retains some of the bran. Scotch barley is husked and coarsely ground.

Bulgur

Bulgur is widely eaten throughout the Middle East and India, as well as in Turkey and other Mediterranean countries. Often confused with cracked wheat, which is raw, bulgur is ground wheat kernels that are parboiled then hulled, dried and ground. "Bulgur" is a Turkish word that stems from the Arabic word *burghul*.

With its mild, nutty flavor and dry, fluffy texture, bulgur is a common accompaniment to stews. It also works well in salads and pilafs. Bulgur is available in fine, medium, coarse and very coarse grinds.

Buckwheat

Varieties and forms:
Buckwheat groats, kasha

First cultivated in 6000 BC in Southeast Asia, buckwheat was then spread throughout the world. Today, buckwheat is most popular in Eastern Europe and Russia. Buckwheat groats are not actually a grain, but the raw, hulled seeds of a plant related to rhubarb and sorrel. Kasha, in turn, is hulled and toasted buckwheat groats. Served at breakfast, lunch and dinner, kasha is so intrinsic to Slavic culture that a popular Russian proverb states, "borscht and kasha are all we need to live on."

Nutty and chewy in texture, kasha is most often cooked in a skillet, sometimes with an egg. It can also be boiled into breakfast porridge. Buckwheat groats are often ground into flour to be used in baking and making noodles.

Corn

Varieties and forms:
Grits, polenta, cornmeal, hominy, hominy grits

An icon of the American culinary tradition, corn (or maize) is Native American in origin. A staple around the dinner table and on the barbecue, corn is often eaten right off the cob. Grits, polenta and cornmeal all come from dried kernels of corn that have been ground into one of three textures: coarse, medium or fine. When the corn is ground, the coarser particles become grits, while finer granules are used for polenta. The most finely ground corn becomes cornmeal, and even cornmeal has varying textures, from coarsely ground to finely ground (also called corn flour).

Stone-ground grits are the coarsest grind and are preferable to instant grits. For the most nutritious and flavorful grits, look for a coarse texture and dark flecks of germ and bran. Grits are typically cooked with boiling water into a porridge-like consistency for breakfast or with savory ingredients as a side dish. Dried polenta can be prepared like grits, but is more often molded into a firm block, then cut into slices and baked or fried. Coarsely ground and medium ground cornmeal is used to make everything from cornmeal mush to cornbread and waffles. Finely ground cornmeal, or corn flour, is used in baking and as a coating for foods that will be fried.

Hominy refers to hulled corn kernels that have been stripped of their bran and germ. Whole hominy is sold fresh, frozen or dried and is a popular breakfast cereal, especially in the southern United States. It is the staple ingredient in the popular Mexican stew pozole. When hominy is partially ground, the result is hominy grits.

Couscous

The traditional grain of Morocco, couscous is actually coarse semolina dough rolled into tiny balls and dried. Its origins date back to the 9th century in North Africa. Today, it is a staple throughout West Africa, France, Spain, the Canary Islands, Portugal, Turkey, Greece and parts of the Middle East. Aside from traditional couscous, there is pearl (or Israeli) couscous, which is extruded through a round mold and toasted, and is actually a wheat-based pasta. There is also whole wheat couscous.

A staple in Moroccan cuisine, couscous is eaten with stews, on its own or in dishes such as tabbouleh. It is something of a misnomer to say "cooking" couscous, as couscous really only needs to be rehydrated. Pearl couscous has a nuttier, chewier texture than traditional couscous and is somewhat easier to prepare, because there isn't much danger of clumping. Whole wheat couscous takes slightly longer to cook.

Cracked Wheat

A truly ancient grain, wheat was first cultivated 12,000 years ago in southwestern Asia. Often confused with bulgur, cracked wheat is raw wheat berries that have been cracked, whereas bulgur has been steamed, hulled, dried and ground. Cracked wheat includes the wheat bran and germ, and is available in fine, medium and coarse grinds.

Cracked wheat has the same nutty flavor as bulgur, but with a heartier texture. It also takes longer to cook because it has not been steamed or toasted.

Farro

A type of wheat, farro is thought to have been first cultivated near Damascus in 7,700 BC. Wild farro can be traced back as far as 17,000 BC. Legend has it that farro sustained the ancient Roman legions. Because of its low yield, farro was gradually pushed aside by other crops, but it remains popular in Albania, Morocco, Spain, Turkey and Switzerland, and especially in the Tuscany region of Italy.

Often confused with spelt, farro has a nutty, wheaty taste and a chewy texture when cooked. It is often eaten as a whole grain in soups. Ground farro is used to make pasta and bread, as it was in ancient Egypt.

Kamut

Kamut is a modern proprietary breed of an ancient grain known as khorasan wheat. First cultivated in the Middle East, khorasan is said to have been found in the tombs of the pharaohs, hence its nickname "King Tut's Wheat." It is also called "prophet's wheat" because it is believed to have been on Noah's ark.

Kamut kernels are two to three times larger than wheat kernels. Kamut has a rich, buttery taste and a chewy texture. It is often ground into flour to be used in bread, breakfast cereals, pastas and crackers. Kamut extract is used to make beverages, such as beer. The grain can also be cooked and eaten whole.

Millet

Believed to be one of the first grains cultivated by man, millet is tiny and beadlike and varies in color from white to gray to yellow to red. A staple in African and South Asian cultures, millet is actually a seed. Until recently, millet was used primarily in the Western world as livestock and bird feed, but it is growing in popularity, especially among people on a wheat-free diet.

Whole-grain millet is the most popular form, but puffed millet is also available. Often served as a side dish with beans and vegetables, millet makes a fine substitute for risotto. Many people choose to toast millet in a skillet before cooking it. Millet is very digestible, making it a favored option for people on a wheat-free diet.

Oats

Varieties and forms:
Oat groats, old-fashioned (large-flake) rolled oats, quick-cooking rolled oats, steel-cut oats

Perhaps due to their hardy nature, or perhaps thanks to their beloved taste, oats have been a favorite breakfast meal for hundreds of years. Oats are available in a variety of forms. Oat groats have been cleaned, toasted and hulled. Old-fashioned (large-flake) rolled oats have also been steamed and flattened. Quick-cooking rolled oats are cut into pieces before they are steamed and rolled. Steel-cut oats have been cut into pieces but not rolled.

Oats in any form are most often cooked as a hot breakfast cereal. Raw rolled oats are often added to granola or muesli. All varieties have a sweet, nutty flavor and a chewy texture. Oat groats and steel-cut oats take longer to cook than the rolled variety. I do not recommend making quick-cooking rolled oats in the rice cooker.

Quinoa

Originally from the Andes, quinoa was first harvested more than 3,000 years ago. Known as the "gold of the Incas," quinoa was considered sacred by the Incan people. They referred to it as *chisaya mama*, or "mother of all grains." Traditionally, the Incan emperor would sow the first seeds of the season, using tools made of gold. Today, quinoa is gaining popularity in modern kitchens throughout the world.

Quinoa is not actually a grain at all, but the seed of a plant related to spinach, beets and Swiss chard. Disk-shaped and nutty and grassy in flavor, it has a crunchy yet soft texture. There are three main varieties of quinoa: white, red and black.

Rye Berries

Rye berries are whole kernels of rye. Rye looks a bit like wheat, but its kernels are longer and thinner. A relative newcomer among grains, rye was not cultivated until about 400 BC. First domesticated in Germany, rye is thought to have originated from a weed that grew among wheat and barley. Today, it is most popular in Scandinavia and Eastern Europe.

Rye berries have a very hearty, distinctive flavor. The flour is most commonly found in traditional rye and pumpernickel bread. Rye berries can also be cooked as a hot cereal or a side dish. It is best to rinse rye berries before cooking them.

Spelt

A cousin to wheat, spelt is an ancient grain native to Iran and southeastern Europe. It is one of the world's most popular grains, and its cultivation dates back 7,000 years. Use of spelt is mentioned in the Bible, and legend has it that spelt was one of the first grains to be made into bread. A staple in many ancient civilizations, such as Greece and Rome, it was offered up to the gods in pagan harvest and fertility ceremonies.

With a sweet, nutty flavor, spelt is most often ground into flour and used in bread, pasta and crackers. It can also be brewed and fermented as a beverage.

Teff

The smallest grain in the world, teff measures only about $\frac{1}{32}$ inch (<1 mm) in diameter. It takes roughly 150 grains of teff to weigh as much as one grain of wheat. "Grain" is a misnomer, for teff is actually the seed of a tufted grass native to northeastern Africa and southwestern Arabia. It is believed to have been first cultivated in Ethiopia around 4,000 BC. Today, it is widely used in Ethiopia, India and Australia. Cultivation of teff has recently begun in South Dakota and Idaho.

Teff has a rich, nutty flavor. In Ethiopia, where it is a staple, teff is most often ground into flour, fermented for 3 days, then made into injera, or Ethiopian flatbread. Teff is also boiled into a porridge and brewed into drinks.

Although teff is tiny, it is dense with nutrients because each grain is mostly bran and germ — the most nutritious part of any seed. It contains no gluten, so it is suitable for wheat-free diets.

Wheat Berries

Second only to corn as the most popular crop on Earth, wheat is a staple in many diets around the world, especially in the United States. Wheat berries are whole wheat kernels with their germ and bran intact. There are several varieties, named after the seasons in which they are cultivated, including hard red winter wheat and hard white winter wheat. Because the germ and bran are intact, wheat berries are the most nutritious form of wheat.

Wheat berries are often added to salads, baked into bread or made into porridge. They have a nutty flavor and a chewy texture similar to that of pasta. It was once believed that wheat berries had to be soaked overnight before cooking, but simply boiling them is enough to achieve a soft, chewy texture.

Buying and Storing Grains

Most of the grains featured in this book are available at health-food stores. Some can be found at well-stocked grocery stores or via online resources such as Bob's Red Mill.

Because whole grains are rich in natural oils, they will go rancid over a period of 1 to 12 months, depending on the grain and the temperature at which it is stored. The bran layer acts as protective coating to the germ, so intact grains aren't as vulnerable as cracked grains. It's important to purchase grains from a store that has high turnover. If you purchase prepackaged grains, check the expiration date. If you're shopping bulk, sniff the grains and make sure they smell sweet or have no aroma at all. If they smell musty or oily, they are rancid or starting to go rancid.

When you get home, make sure to store your whole grains in tightly sealed containers in the refrigerator or freezer.

To Soak or Not to Soak

For most whole grains, I recommend using the fuzzy logic Brown Rice cycle, which has a built-in soaking cycle of 1 hour. Bear this in mind, as you'll need to add an extra hour to cooking times. If you're using a standard on/off machine, you may want to soak grains for 30 to 60 minutes for improved texture and a slight reduction in cooking time.

Rinsing and Draining Grains

I believe many grains should be rinsed, especially if they're bought in bulk, but it's not necessary for all types. Please see specific recipes for directions. If you purchase a batch that seems to be dusty or contain twigs or other matter, always rinse it.

To rinse grains, pour them into a fine-mesh wire sieve. Place the sieve in a bowl and run water over the grains until they're submerged. Swish the water around a few times and drain. Repeat until the water is clear.

Toasting Grains

Some grains, such as millet, benefit from being toasted in a dry skillet over medium heat for 5 minutes before cooking. While it's not necessary, it does add a nice touch.

Cooking Grains

1. Place the grains in the rice cooker bowl and cover with water as specified in the Grains Cooking Chart (below). (Alternatively, use chicken or vegetable broth for added flavor.) Swirl to combine.
2. For on/off machines, set for the Regular cycle. For fuzzy logic machines, set for the Regular cycle (for millet, amaranth and couscous) or the Brown Rice cycle (for all other grains). Do not open the lid while the grains are cooking!
3. Wait for the cycle to end. The inherent advantage of cooking grains in a rice cooker is that it automatically stops cooking when the grains have absorbed all of the water. I have included a list of approximate cooking times in the Grains Cooking Chart to give you a general idea of how long the wait will be.
4. After the cooking cycle has ended, the grains need to continue steaming for 10 minutes. In fuzzy logic machines and most on/off "keep warm" machines, the steaming period is built in, so when the timer sounds, your grains are ready to eat. For on/off "cook and shut off" machines, you will need to set a timer for 10 minutes after the machine clicks off. You may keep your grains on the Warm Cycle for up to 1 hour.
5. Fluff the grains with a wooden spoon (dipped in water) or plastic paddle before eating them or using them in a recipe. If you're not going to use them right away, let them cool completely before refrigerating in an airtight container.

Grains Cooking Chart

The following chart is based on using 1 cup (250 mL) dried grains, which generally yields 2½ to 4 cups (625 mL to 1 L) cooked. For this amount, use a medium machine. If you double the recipe, switch to a medium-large to large machine. The amounts of liquid and cooking times in this chart are meant as general guidelines, as each machine is slightly different. Personal preference can also affect cooking times (for example, if you like your grains moister, you might add more liquid). Some types of grains, such as wheat berries and rye berries, are unpredictable, so don't be surprised if they take up to an extra hour beyond the recommended cooking time.

Type of Grain	Amount of Liquid	Cooking Time*	Fuzzy Logic Cycle
Amaranth	2½ cups (625 mL)	20 to 30 minutes	Regular cycle
Bulgur	2 cups (500 mL)	25 to 35 minutes	Brown Rice cycle
Cornmeal (stone-ground)	3 cups (750 mL)	60 to 90 minutes	Brown Rice cycle
Couscous	1½ cups (375 mL)	13 to 15 minutes	Regular cycle
Cracked wheat	2 cups (500 mL)	45 to 50 minutes	Brown Rice cycle
Farro	2½ cups (625 mL)	35 to 40 minutes	Brown Rice cycle
Hominy, whole	5 cups (1.25 L)	3 to 4 hours	Brown Rice cycle

* Add 20 minutes to the cooking time if using the Regular cycle on a fuzzy logic machine. Add 1 hour to the cooking time if using the Brown Rice cycle on a fuzzy logic machine. (The additional cooking time reflects the built-in soaking periods in fuzzy logic models.)

Type of Grain	Amount of Liquid	Cooking Time*	Fuzzy Logic Cycle
Hulled barley	3 cups (750 mL)	50 to 60 minutes	Brown Rice cycle
Israeli couscous	2 cups (500 mL)	20 to 25 minutes	Regular cycle
Kamut	2½ cups (625 mL)	45 to 60 minutes	Brown Rice cycle
Kasha/buckwheat groats	2 cups (500 mL)	25 to 35 minutes	Brown Rice cycle
Millet	2½ cups (625 mL)	30 to 35 minutes	Regular cycle
Old-fashioned (large-flake) rolled oats	2¾ cups (675 mL)	25 to 35 minutes	Regular cycle
Pearl barley	3 cups (750 mL)	40 to 50 minutes	Regular cycle
Polenta (coarse-grain)	4 cups (1 L)	60 to 90 minutes	Brown Rice cycle
Quinoa	2 cups (500 mL)	20 to 35 minutes	Brown Rice cycle
Rye berries	2 cups (500 mL)	60 to 80 minutes	Brown Rice cycle
Spelt	3 cups (750 mL)	1½ to 2 hours	Brown Rice cycle
Steel-cut oats	3 cups (750 mL)	35 to 45 minutes	Brown Rice cycle
Teff	4 cups (1 L)	30 to 40 minutes	Brown Rice cycle
Wheat berries	2½ cups (625 mL)	60 to 80 minutes	Brown Rice cycle

* Add 20 minutes to the cooking time if using the Regular cycle on a fuzzy logic machine. Add 1 hour to the cooking time if using the Brown Rice cycle on a fuzzy logic machine. (The additional cooking time reflects the built-in soaking periods in fuzzy logic models.)

All About Legumes

Beans, Beans, They're Good for Your Heart . . .

Over the years, beans have gotten a bad rap — they can be rough on the digestive system and have been identified most closely with a cheap way to stretch a meal. Not at all glamorous. But beans have a newfound respect in both cooks' and foodies' vocabularies these days as earthy, flavor-filled staples that can stand alone or add a healthy punch to varied, even exotic dishes.

The complex carbohydrates we call legumes, including beans, lentils, peas and peanuts, are part of the Leguminosae family. They grow in a pod, and we usually chuck the shell and eat the seeds inside. Most beans are dried for longevity and sold either in bulk or in packages, and they need to be soaked before cooking. The varieties are vast, from black beans, used in Mexican, South American and Cuban dishes, to mild and creamy cannellini beans, popular in Italian cooking.

Protein-rich and satisfying, legumes of all types can be used in soups and stews, as hearty side dishes or salads and as meat substitutes for main courses. They add texture, color and interest to recipes. They're easy to prepare, and they're versatile and economical. They can be refried, baked, pressure-cooked, slow-cooked or served with a nice Chianti. And as you're about to find out, your rice cooker is a convenient way to prepare them.

The ancient mathematician Pythagoras, an early vegetarian, thought legumes were "the seat of the soul" because of their life-sustaining qualities. And indeed, beans are naturally low in sodium and fat and are cholesterol-free. They fall under the "good carbs" category, creating energy for the brain and muscles. Legumes are high in fiber, helping to regulate blood glucose levels, which is especially important for diabetics.

And about that downside, here's a tip: if beans bother your stomach, try some of the softer varieties, such as black-eyed peas, lima beans, chickpeas and great Northern beans, which tend to produce less gas. It's best to soak beans for several hours and discard the soaking water before adding any other ingredients, to reduce their natural sugar and make them less likely to cause flatulence. Vinegar is also useful to help eliminate those extra sugars: add 2 to 4 tablespoons (30 to 60 mL) to the soaking water.

Know Your Beans: A Legume Glossary

Adzuki Beans

Popular throughout Asia, and especially in Japan, adzuki beans are small, red and oval. They are about ¼ inch (5 mm) in diameter and have a distinctive white ridge along one side. They are thought to have originated in China, and were introduced into Japan around AD 1000. Today, adzuki beans are one of Japan's largest crops. They are also cultivated in China and Thailand.

Adzuki beans have a strong sweet and nutty flavor. In Japan, adzuki beans are often cooked into a sweet red bean paste and used in desserts. Adzuki beans can also be cooked whole and served with rice, or cooked until soft and served with coconut milk.

Black Beans

The ubiquitous black bean is a staple in many cultures, especially in Latin America. Black beans, also called turtle beans and *frijoles negros*, originated in Peru. They were first introduced to Europe in the 15th century by Spanish and Portuguese explorers, who brought them home from the New World. These same explorers then introduced black beans to Africa and Asia.

Whether dried, canned or fresh, black beans have a rich flavor and velvety texture when cooked. Cooked whole or in a paste, they taste similar to mushrooms. They hold up well after cooking and stand up to the strongest and hottest spices.

Black-Eyed Peas

Black-eyed peas (also called cowpeas) get their name from the large black spot on the surface. First domesticated in West Africa, the black-eyed pea was introduced to the United States in the 17th century. It remains a main ingredient in Southern soul food. A hardy crop, the black-eyed pea is now cultivated around the world, including in Florida, the Carolinas and Virginia.

In some cultures, it is believed to be good luck to eat black-eyed peas on New Year's Day. With their creamy texture and distinctive taste, they are also a popular everyday meal. In the South, black-eyed peas are typically cooked with a pork product for flavoring and served with collards, turnip or mustard greens and a hunk of cornbread.

Chickpeas

One of the earliest cultivated crops, chickpeas are thought to have originated in the Middle East more than 7,000 years ago. Today, they are a staple in many cultures, from the Middle East and Europe to India and western Asia. There are several varieties, such as the cream-colored, round kabuli type (also called garbanzo beans) used primarily in Western cultures, and the smaller, darker desi type used throughout the rest of the world.

There are countless ways to prepare the creamy, soft, lightly flavored chickpea. Whether cooked into stews and curries, ground into flour, roasted as snacks, brewed in drinks or served cold in salads, there are almost as many ways to enjoy chickpeas as there are cultures in the world.

Cranberry Beans

Originating in Colombia and now grown in New Jersey, Massachusetts, Oregon, Washington, Wisconsin, British Columbia and Quebec, cranberry beans (called borlotti in Italy and shell beans in New Zealand), get their name from the deep red patterns against a cream-colored background.

Cranberry beans have a creamy texture and a slightly chestnut-like flavor. When purchasing them in the pod, look for bright pods that yield their beans easily. Popular for their gorgeous color, cranberry beans are often cooked whole as a side dish or tossed into pasta or soups.

Dried Peas

Dried peas have been consumed since prehistoric times and are mentioned in the Bible. They were prized in ancient Egypt, Greece and Rome. Today, the greatest producers of dried peas are Russia, France, China and Denmark. Although they look like lentils, they are, indeed, field peas that have been dried. During the drying process, they are sometimes split along a seam, in which case they are called split peas.

Dried peas are a great substitute for fresh peas in the off-season, or when a recipe calls for a starchier, hardier legume. While most people associate dried peas with a deep green color, they are also available in yellow. Yellow dried peas offer a more delicate flavor and are the type generally preferred in northern European countries.

Fava Beans

Native to North Africa and southwest Asia, fava beans are one of the oldest cultivated plants on earth. They were popular in ancient Greece and Rome, and remain a staple in Mediterranean, Asian and African cuisines. A member of the pea family, fava beans are also known as broad beans, pigeon beans, horse beans and Windsor beans.

Most often used fresh, fava beans have a distinct flavor and a creamy texture. A popular addition to pasta and soups in Italy, fava beans also appear in many forms in the cuisines of Portugal, Greece, Estonia, southwest Asia and North Africa.

Flageolets

Originating in the north of France, flageolets are tiny, kidney-shaped beans that range in color from creamy white to light green. They remain popular in France and are cultivated there, as well as in California. Varieties of the flageolet include the heirloom Chevrier, Elsa, Flambeau and Flamingo.

Considered by many to be the caviar of beans, flageolets are creamy and delicate in flavor. They are very popular in France, especially when served with lamb, ham or bacon.

Kidney Beans

Kidney beans are, indeed, shaped like kidneys and typically have a rich red color, but they can also be white (cannellini beans). Along with black, navy and pinto beans, they are often called "common beans" because they are derived from a common bean originating in Peru. They were introduced in Europe in the 15th century by Spanish explorers. Today, they are common in the Americas, Europe, Africa and Asia. For more information on white kidney beans, see page 32.

Enjoyed in soups, stews, chili, salads and on their own, kidney beans have a smooth texture and a distinct flavor that stands up well to spices and herbs.

Lentils

Originating in Central Asia, lentils have been around since prehistoric times and were one of the first cultivated foods. Round, oval or heart-shaped lentils come in many different colors. The lentils most commonly used in North America are green and brown, but they also come in yellow, black, red and orange. They are sold whole or split in half. Petite French green lentils, also known as puy, are grown in France.

Lentils are enjoyed throughout the world in many different ways. Cooked into soups and curries, eaten with barley or wheat, or ground into flour, lentils are as versatile as they are ubiquitous. Petite French lentils hold their shape when cooked and make a delicious side dish or a bed for entrées.

Lima Beans

Lima beans originated in either Peru or Guatemala. One thing is certain: they have been around for almost 7,000 years. Spanish explorers brought them to Europe, Africa and Asia. They were introduced to the United States relatively late, in the 19th century. Because they grow well in tropical regions, lima beans have become a very important crop throughout Africa and Asia.

Sometimes called butter beans because of their rich, buttery taste, lima beans are probably best known in the United States as an ingredient in succotash. But their delicate flavor and creamy texture are perfectly suited to many dishes, including soups and stews, and make them a wonderful accompaniment to strongly flavored meats, such as lamb.

Confusingly enough, large lima beans are also sometimes called butter beans, but they have an earthier flavor than the smaller variety. Christmas lima beans, used in many Italian dishes, have an intriguing chestnut flavor. Baby lima beans are a petite version of the large lima bean and have a mild flavor and smooth texture. Baby limas are wonderful for succotash.

Mung Beans

Native to Bangladesh, India and Pakistan, the mung bean is very popular in those countries, as well as in China, Burma, Thailand, Japan, Korea and throughout Southeast Asia. Introduced in the United States in the 19th century, it was primarily used as livestock feed, but it is gaining popularity on the dinner table. Small, oval mung beans are green when their hulls are intact and yellow when hulled.

Mung beans are extremely versatile, eaten whole with spicy meat in the Philippines, sprouted in many Asian cuisines and ground into flour for crêpes in India. In China, mung beans are boiled to make the dessert *tang shui*, or sugar water.

Peanuts

Contrary to their name, peanuts are not actually nuts. The peanut is, in fact, a legume. Related to the pea, lentil, chickpea and other beans, the peanut grows in a curious way. As the flower of the peanut plant grows, it gets so heavy that it bends toward the ground and burrows into the soil, where the peanut matures.

Raw or roasted, shelled or unshelled, peanuts are as American as apple pie and baseball, although they are also a common ingredient in candies and Asian dishes. Americans perhaps know the peanut best in its butter form.

Pigeon Peas

Cultivation of the pigeon pea (also called gandules) stretches back at least 3,000 years. It most likely originated in Asia, then was brought to East Africa and the New World. It thrives in tropical and semitropical regions of India and eastern and central Africa. While the legume nourishes people and livestock alike, the pigeon pea plant nourishes the soil in which it grows.

The pigeon pea is extremely versatile. It can be cooked whole or sprouted. In India, dried pigeon peas are used in popular dal dishes. Ethiopian cooking uses not only the pea, but also the pod, shoots and leaves.

Pink Beans

Small, oval and pinkish-brown, pink beans are popular in the western United States and throughout the Caribbean. They are also known as chili beans or by their Spanish name, *habichuela rosadas*. They are grown primarily in California.

Pink beans have a smooth, meaty texture and a sweet, delicate taste. They are available canned or dried, and are used in soups and chili or on their own, alongside rice. When they are unavailable, kidney, pinto or red beans can be used in place of pink beans.

Pinto Beans

Pinto means "painted" in Spanish, and these beans get their name because of their reddish-brown splashes of color. Like all "common beans," including kidney, black and navy beans, pinto beans are descended from an ancient bean originating in Peru. From there, they were introduced into South and Central America, Europe, Africa, Asia and, finally, the United States.

When cooked, their splotches of color fade and pinto beans turn pink all over. Their creamy texture and semisweet taste make them a favorite ingredient in Latin American dishes. They are served whole alongside rice and in stews and soups, and can also be served in a refried paste.

Soybeans

Originating in China more than 13,000 years ago, soybeans are extremely versatile and adaptable. They were introduced in Japan in the 8th century and later made their way into Thailand, Malaysia, Korea and Vietnam. Today, soybeans and soy products are used all over the world.

Soybeans are enjoyed in countless ways. They are eaten fresh, young and green as edamame. They are also dried as soy nuts, fermented as tofu and tempeh, ground into flour, turned into milk and used as an ingredient in many foods, both fresh and packaged. Soy has a slightly nutty flavor, but is valued for its ability to take on the flavor of other ingredients.

White Beans

Varieties and forms:
cannellini (white kidney), gigante, great Northern, navy (white pea)

There are many varieties of white beans. Though typically grouped together and called simply "common beans," these beans go by many names. Cannellini beans, also called white kidney beans, are large, smooth and plump, and are popular in central and southern Italy, especially Tuscany. Native to Central America, the gigante bean is large and flat; it is popular in Mediterranean cooking, especially in Spain and Greece, as well as in African cuisine. Similar in shape to the lima bean but smaller, great Northern beans are grown primarily in the Midwestern United States and are related to the kidney and pinto bean. The navy bean (also called the white pea bean) got its popular name because it was a staple food of the United States Navy in the early 20th century.

All white beans yield a soft and creamy texture. Their flavors range from subtle and nutty to delicate and distinct. They are great in soups, stews and salads or ground for pastes and dips.

Buying and Storing Legumes

You can find most types of beans at well-stocked grocery stores, but you may have to venture to an ethnic market for yellow or red lentils or adzuki beans. You can also try a natural-foods store or an online resource.

When buying beans, avoid packages that contain a lot of broken beans or beans that have broken skins or are discolored. Try to buy beans from stores with a high turnover rate.

It's best to store beans in a tightly sealed container in a cool, dry place. Freezing can dehydrate beans, so avoid doing so.

Sorting and Rinsing Legumes

It's important to sort and pick over legumes to eliminate rocks and other debris. To sort legumes, spread them out evenly on a baking sheet and use your fingers to gently brush them down the pan. Pick out grit and any small rocks (which may have been included in the package because they are roughly the same size and shape as the legumes; the rocks may be any color, but dark gray is typical). After sorting the legumes, rinse them in a colander.

Soaking Legumes

Before you cook dried legumes, you will need to soak them (with the exception of lentils and split peas), as they need to rehydrate to be soft enough for cooking.

- **Overnight Soak:** To 1 pound (500 g) dried legumes (about 2 cups/500 mL) add 6 to 8 cups (1.5 to 2 L) cold water in a large pot. Let stand overnight or for at least 6 to 8 hours. Drain water and rinse beans.
- **Quick Soak:** To 1 pound (500 g) dried legumes (about 2 cups/500 mL) add 6 to 8 cups (1.5 to 2 L) hot water in a large pot. Bring to a rapid boil over high heat; boil for 2 minutes. Remove from heat and let stand for 1 hour. Drain water and rinse beans.

Seasoning Legumes

Legumes can be tough if salt is added during the cooking process; therefore, I recommend waiting to season legumes with salt until after they are cooked (as indicated in the recipes).

Cooking Legumes

1. Place the legumes in the rice cooker bowl and cover with water as specified in the Legumes Cooking Chart (below). (Alternatively, use chicken or vegetable broth for added flavor.) Do not add salt or acid at this time, as they can toughen legumes and increase the cooking time. Swirl to combine.

2. Set for the Regular cycle for both on/off machines and fuzzy logic machines. Because legumes do not absorb liquid in the same way grains do, you will need to set a timer. Refer to the cooking times in the Legumes Cooking Chart. The cooking time starts the moment you close the lid. Check periodically to make sure the legumes are still submerged in water, and replenish with boiling water, if necessary.

3. When the timer sounds, check the legumes for doneness. They should be tender if you're planning to eat them right away; if you'll be adding them to a dish that requires further cooking, such as chili, you may want to stop the rice cooker while the legumes are still slightly al dente. Don't worry if you need as much as an hour longer than the cooking time specified.

4. When the legumes have reached the desired doneness, turn off the rice cooker. Wearing oven mitts, remove the bowl carefully. Drain the legumes, then season them with salt or other seasonings. If you're going to be enjoying them later or using them in another recipe, let them cool completely before refrigerating in an airtight container.

Legumes Cooking Chart

The following chart is based on using 1 cup (250 mL) dried legumes, which generally yields 3 to 4 cups (750 mL to 1 L) cooked. For this amount, use a medium machine. If you double the recipe, switch to a medium-large to large machine. The amounts of liquid and cooking times in this chart are meant as general guidelines, as each machine is slightly different. Many other variables, such as how soft or hard the water is and how old the beans are, can also dramatically affect cooking times. Don't be surprised if some legumes take up to an extra hour beyond the suggested cooking time.

Type of Legume	Amount of Liquid	Cooking Time*
Adzuki beans	3 cups (750 mL)	45 to 60 minutes
Black beans	3 to 4 cups (750 mL to 1 L)	$1\frac{1}{4}$ to $1\frac{1}{2}$ hours

* Add 20 minutes to the cooking time if using a fuzzy logic machine. (This additional time reflects the built-in soaking period in fuzzy logic models.)

Type of Legume	Amount of Liquid	Cooking Time*
Black-eyed peas	3 to 4 cups (750 mL to 1 L)	1 to 1¼ hours
Chickpeas (garbanzo beans)	4 cups (1 L)	2 to 2¼ hours
Cranberry beans	3 to 4 cups (750 mL to 1 L)	1½ to 1¾ hours
Dried peas, green and yellow	2 cups (500 mL)	45 to 60 minutes
Fava beans	3 cups (750 mL)	1½ to 2 hours
Flageolets	3 to 4 cups (750 mL to 1 L)	1¼ to 1½ hours
Kidney beans	3 to 4 cups (750 mL to 1 L)	1 to 1¼ hours
Lentils, brown	2 to 3 cups (500 to 750 mL)	40 to 50 minutes
Lentils, green, yellow, black, red and orange	2 to 3 cups (500 to 750 mL)	30 to 40 minutes
Lentils, petit French (puy)	3 cups (750 mL)	30 to 40 minutes
Lima beans, baby	2 to 3 cups (500 to 750 mL)	1 to 1½ hours
Lima beans, butter beans	3 to 4 cups (750 mL to 1 L)	1¼ to 1½ hours
Lima beans, Christmas	3 to 4 cups (750 mL to 1 L)	2 to 2¼ hours
Lima beans, large	2 to 3 cups (500 to 750 mL)	1½ to 1¾ hours
Mung beans	3 to 4 cups (750 mL to 1 L)	1 to 1½ hours
Pigeon peas	3 to 4 cups (750 mL to 1 L)	1½ to 1¾ hours
Pink beans	3 cups (750 mL)	1 to 1½ hours
Pinto beans	3 to 4 cups (750 mL to 1 L)	1½ to 2 hours
Soybeans	4 cups (1 L)	3 to 4 hours
White beans, cannellini (white kidney)	3 to 4 cups (750 mL to 1 L)	1¼ to 1½ hours
White beans, gigante	4 cups (1 L)	1¼ to 1½ hours
White beans, great Northern	4 cups (1 L)	1½ to 2 hours
White beans, navy (white pea)	4 cups (1 L)	1¼ to 1½ hours

*Add 20 minutes to the cooking time if using a fuzzy logic machine. (This additional time reflects the built-in soaking period in fuzzy logic models.)

Breakfasts

Creamy Breakfast Oatmeal

Makes 3 to 4 servings

This traditional oatmeal is combined with lots of yummy extras for even more flavor, making it the perfect comfort food breakfast. Serve hot with sliced bananas, more milk and a drizzle of maple syrup, if desired.

Steel-Cut Oats

Steel-cut oats are whole-grain groats (the inner portion of the oat kernel) that have been cut into only two or three pieces by steel, rather than being rolled. They are golden in color and resemble small pieces of rice. Because there's less processing, they're more nutritious than rolled oats.

• Medium rice cooker; fuzzy logic only

1½ cups	steel-cut oats	375 mL
1 tsp	ground cinnamon	5 mL
¼ tsp	salt	1 mL
3½ cups	whole milk	875 mL
1 tsp	vanilla extract	5 mL
2 tbsp	pure maple syrup	30 mL
½ cup	raisins or chopped dates	125 mL

1. In the rice cooker bowl, combine oats, cinnamon, salt, milk, vanilla and maple syrup. Set the rice cooker for the Porridge cycle.
2. When the machine switches to the Keep Warm cycle, let stand for 10 minutes. Serve immediately or hold on the Keep Warm cycle for up to 1 hour. Serve sprinkled with raisins.

Variation

Creamy Butterscotch Breakfast Oatmeal: Stir in ½ cup (125 mL) butterscotch chips when the machine switches to the Keep Warm cycle.

Chai-Spiced Oatmeal

Makes 3 to 4 servings

The bold flavors of chai — such as cardamom, part of the ginger family — are combined with traditional oats to give a spicy twist to old-fashioned oatmeal. Serve hot, sprinkled with brown sugar, and with more milk, if desired.

● **Medium rice cooker; fuzzy logic only**

1 cup	old-fashioned (large-flake) rolled oats	250 mL
1 cup	cooked white or brown rice (see page 20)	250 mL
1/2 tsp	ground cinnamon	2 mL
1/4 tsp	salt	1 mL
1/4 tsp	ground cardamom	1 mL
1/8 tsp	ground nutmeg	0.5 mL
2 1/2 cups	whole milk or soy milk	625 mL
1/4 cup	coconut milk	60 mL
3 tbsp	liquid honey	45 mL
1/2 tsp	vanilla extract	2 mL

1. In the rice cooker bowl, combine oats, rice, cinnamon, salt, cardamom, nutmeg, milk, coconut milk, honey and vanilla. Set the rice cooker for the Porridge cycle.
2. When the machine switches to the Keep Warm cycle, let stand for 10 minutes. Serve immediately or hold on the Keep Warm cycle for up to 1 hour.

Becca's Chocolate Banana Oatmeal

Makes 3 to 4 servings

This luscious oatmeal is my daughter's favorite and is sure to be a hit among kids of all ages. Serve hot, with more milk, and garnish with more chocolate chips, if you like. Chocolate is a great helper when it comes to encouraging children to eat more grains!

Tip

If you're out of chocolate chips, you can use 1/4 cup (60 mL) sweetened hot cocoa powder instead.

● **Medium rice cooker; fuzzy logic only**

1 1/4 cups	steel-cut oats	300 mL
3 cups	whole milk, soy milk or almond milk	750 mL
1	ripe banana, mashed	1
1/2 cup	packed brown sugar	125 mL
1/4 cup	semisweet chocolate chips	60 mL

1. In the rice cooker bowl, combine oats and milk. Set the rice cooker for the Porridge cycle.
2. When the machine switches to the Keep Warm cycle, fold in banana, brown sugar and chocolate chips. Let stand for 10 minutes. Serve immediately or hold on the Keep Warm cycle for up to 1 hour.

Variation

Chocolate Peanut Banana Oatmeal: Add 1/4 cup (60 mL) smooth peanut butter with the chocolate chips.

Old-Fashioned Porridge

Makes 3 to 4 servings

Serve hot with milk, maple syrup or honey and the fruit of your choice.

Tip
Load your fuzzy logic machine with oats, salt and water before you go to bed. Set the timer and wake up to a delicious breakfast.

• Medium rice cooker; fuzzy logic or on/off

1¼ cups	steel-cut oats	300 mL
¼ tsp	salt	1 mL
3 cups	water	750 mL

1. In the rice cooker bowl, combine oats, salt and water. Set the rice cooker for the Porridge cycle.
2. When the machine switches to the Keep Warm cycle, let stand for 10 minutes. Serve immediately or hold on the Keep Warm cycle for up to 1 hour.

For On/Off Machines
Set the rice cooker for the Regular cycle and set a timer for 30 minutes. When the timer sounds, switch to the Keep Warm cycle and let stand for 10 minutes.

Rolled Grain Porridge with Cranberries and Walnuts

Makes 4 to 6 servings

Rolled grains (flakes) cook to a thick and creamy porridge that is enhanced by the chewy sweetness of the cranberries and the crunchy saltiness of the walnuts. Serve hot, sprinkled with brown sugar or drizzled with maple syrup, and with more milk if desired.

Tip
You can find mixtures of different rolled grains at natural food stores and online.

• Medium rice cooker; fuzzy logic only

2 cups	mixed rolled grains (flakes)	500 mL
¼ tsp	salt	1 mL
2 cups	whole milk	500 mL
1½ cups	water	375 mL
½ cup	dried cranberries	125 mL
½ cup	walnut halves, toasted (see tip, page 53) and coarsely chopped	125 mL
1 tbsp	butter	15 mL

1. In the rice cooker bowl, combine rolled grains, salt, milk and water. Set the rice cooker for the Porridge cycle.
2. When the machine switches to the Keep Warm cycle, stir in cranberries, walnuts and butter. Let stand for 10 minutes. Serve immediately or hold on the Keep Warm cycle for up to 1 hour.

Millet and Amaranth Breakfast Porridge

Makes 3 to 4 servings

The superpowers of amaranth and millet combine in this terrific porridge — it's a must-try! Serve hot, sprinkled with brown sugar, and with more milk, if desired.

Tips

To bring out a pleasantly nutty aroma, toast the millet and amaranth in a dry skillet over medium heat for 5 minutes before cooking. It's not necessary, but it's a nice touch if you have the time.

For information about rice cooker sizes, see page 13.

• Medium rice cooker; fuzzy logic only

¾ cup	millet	175 mL
¼ cup	amaranth	60 mL
¼ tsp	salt	1 mL
1½ cups	water	375 mL
1½ cups	whole milk or soy milk	375 mL
2 tbsp	chopped dates	30 mL
2 tbsp	chopped apricots	30 mL
1 tsp	ground cinnamon	5 mL
⅛ tsp	ground allspice	0.5 mL
2 tbsp	liquid honey	30 mL
1 tsp	vanilla extract	5 mL

1. In the rice cooker bowl, combine millet, amaranth, salt, water and milk. Set the rice cooker for the Porridge cycle.
2. When the machine switches to the Keep Warm cycle, stir in dates, apricots, cinnamon, allspice, honey and vanilla. Let stand for 10 minutes. Serve immediately or hold on the Keep Warm cycle for up to 1 hour.

Variation

For a vegan porridge, substitute agave nectar for the honey and use soy milk. Serve sprinkled with turbinado sugar rather than brown sugar.

Cherry Almond Amaranth Porridge

Makes 3 to 4 servings

This breakfast concoction is tasty, healthy and satisfying. With the sweet touch of cherries and the golden goodness of honey, it just feels indulgent! Serve hot, with brown sugar and more milk.

Tip

To bring out a pleasantly nutty aroma, toast the amaranth in a dry skillet over medium heat for 5 minutes before cooking.

- **Medium rice cooker; fuzzy logic or on/off**

1 cup	amaranth	250 mL
3 cups	water	750 mL
1/4 cup	dried cherries, coarsely chopped	60 mL
1/4 cup	toasted slivered almonds (see tip, page 45)	60 mL
2 tbsp	liquid honey	30 mL
1 tsp	vanilla extract	5 mL
1/4 cup	whole milk or soy milk	60 mL

1. In the rice cooker bowl, combine amaranth and water. Set the rice cooker for the Regular cycle and set a timer for 30 minutes.
2. When the timer sounds, stir in cherries, almonds, honey and vanilla. Set a timer for 5 minutes.
3. When the timer sounds, switch to the Keep Warm cycle and let stand for 5 minutes. Serve immediately or hold on the Keep Warm cycle for up to 1 hour. Stir in milk.

Variation

For a vegan porridge, substitute agave nectar for the honey and use soy milk. Serve sprinkled with turbinado sugar rather than brown sugar.

Honey Apple Brown Rice Porridge

Makes 3 to 4 servings

The B vitamins in brown rice will help jumpstart your metabolism and boost your immune system. Apples are a crunchy, filling addition to this healthy breakfast dish. Serve hot, with more milk, if desired.

- **Medium rice cooker; fuzzy logic only**

1 cup	brown jasmine rice, rinsed and drained	250 mL
1 1/2 cups	whole milk or almond milk	375 mL
1 1/2 cups	water	375 mL
1	apple, chopped	1
1 tsp	ground cinnamon	5 mL
2 tbsp	liquid honey	30 mL

1. In the rice cooker bowl, combine rice, milk and water. Set the rice cooker for the Porridge cycle.
2. When the machine switches to the Keep Warm cycle, gently stir in apple, cinnamon and honey. Let stand for 10 minutes. Serve immediately or hold on the Keep Warm cycle for up to 1 hour.

Teff Porridge with Honey and Dates

Makes 3 to 4 servings

Teff grains are a healthy, gluten-free alternative to wheat grains. With high levels of calcium, fiber, thiamin and many other nutrients, teff porridge is a wonderful way to jumpstart your morning.

Tip

Experiment with a variety of dried fruits, such as figs, currants or pitted French prunes, to replace the dates in this dish.

● **Medium rice cooker; fuzzy logic or on/off**

1 cup	teff	250 mL
3 cups	water	750 mL
1/3 cup	chopped dates	75 mL
1 tsp	ground cinnamon	5 mL
2 tbsp	liquid honey	30 mL
1 tbsp	butter	15 mL

1. In the rice cooker bowl, combine teff and water. Set the rice cooker for the Porridge cycle.
2. When the machine switches to the Keep Warm cycle, stir in dates, cinnamon, honey and butter. Let stand for 10 minutes, then serve immediately.

For On/Off Machines

Set the rice cooker for the Regular cycle and set a timer for 30 minutes. When the timer sounds, switch to the Keep Warm cycle and continue with step 2.

Forbidden Black Rice Porridge (Jook)

Makes 4 servings

In ancient China, black rice was forbidden to anyone but the emperor. These days, everyone is entitled to enjoy it, so share this easy dish with your friends and family!

Tips

If you use vegetable broth, this recipe is completely vegan.

This porridge may be held on the Keep Warm cycle for up to 1 hour, but is best when served immediately.

● **Medium rice cooker; fuzzy logic only**

2	1-inch (2.5 cm) slices gingerroot	2
3/4 cup	forbidden black rice, rinsed and drained	175 mL
4½ cups	chicken or vegetable broth	1.125 L
1 tbsp	soy sauce	15 mL
	Freshly ground white pepper	
	Chopped green onions (white and green parts)	

1. In the rice cooker bowl, combine ginger, rice, broth and soy sauce. Set the rice cooker for the Porridge cycle.
2. When the machine switches to the Keep Warm cycle, let stand for 10 minutes. Season to taste with pepper. Serve garnished with green onions.

Goo Ma's Cantonese Chicken Porridge (*Jook*)

Makes 4 servings

This traditional Chinese rice dish, which I learned from my *Goo Ma* (Chinese for "aunt"), is my family's idea of the perfect comfort food at any time of day. The natural juices from the chicken infuse the porridge with delicious flavors.

Tips

If you have leftover cooked chicken on hand, omit the chicken thighs and add chopped cooked chicken when the machine switches to the Keep Warm cycle. This also works with any other leftover cooked meat.

This porridge may be held on the Keep Warm cycle for up to 1 hour, but is best when served immediately.

• Medium rice cooker; fuzzy logic only

2	1-inch (2.5 cm) slices gingerroot	2
4 oz	boneless skinless chicken thigh, cut into bite-size pieces	125 g
¾ cup	long-grain white rice, rinsed and drained	175 mL
5 cups	chicken broth	1.25 L
2 tbsp	soy sauce, divided	30 mL
¼ tsp	toasted Asian sesame oil	1 mL
	Freshly ground white pepper	
	Chopped green onions (white and green parts)	

1. In the rice cooker bowl, combine ginger, chicken, rice, broth, 1 tbsp (15 mL) of the soy sauce and sesame oil. Set the rice cooker for the Porridge cycle.
2. When the machine switches to the Keep Warm cycle, let stand for 10 minutes. Stir in the remaining soy sauce and season to taste with pepper. Serve garnished with green onions.

Variation

Ground Pork Jook: Omit the chicken. At the beginning of the Porridge cycle, set a timer for 30 minutes. Meanwhile, in a bowl, combine 12 oz (375 g) ground pork, 2 tsp (10 mL) cornstarch and 2 tsp (10 mL) soy sauce, mixing well. Form into ½-inch (1 cm) meatballs. When the timer sounds, add the meatballs to the rice cooker and let the cycle complete. Continue with step 2.

Berry Breakfast Risotto

Makes 4 to 6 servings

Arborio rice, an Italian short-grain rice, cooks into a warm, creamy risotto. Berries and mint add a refreshing flavor that will brighten up any morning meal.

Tip

For even better flavor, macerate the strawberries and raspberries. Toss them with 1 tsp (5 mL) granulated sugar and let stand for 1 hour.

● Medium rice cooker; fuzzy logic only

1 cup	Arborio rice	250 mL
1/2 cup	granulated sugar	125 mL
2 cups	water	500 mL
1 cup	half-and-half (10%) cream	250 mL
2 tsp	vanilla extract	10 mL
1 cup	raspberries	250 mL
1 cup	sliced strawberries	250 mL
	Fresh mint leaves	

1. In the rice cooker bowl, combine rice, sugar, water, cream and vanilla. Set the rice cooker for the Porridge cycle. Stir thoroughly two or three times while the risotto is cooking.
2. When the machine switches to the Keep Warm cycle, fold in raspberries and strawberries. Serve immediately, garnished with mint.

Farro Breakfast Risotto

Makes 4 to 6 servings

Farro cooks to a creamy risotto, and the thick coconut milk and soft, pulpy mango contribute to a flawless combination of textures and flavors. Serve hot, with more milk, if desired.

Tip

Add more water or apple juice, if necessary, to thin out the risotto before serving.

● Medium rice cooker; fuzzy logic only

1 1/2 cups	farro, rinsed and drained	375 mL
1 1/2 cups	water	375 mL
1 cup	coconut milk	250 mL
1/2 cup	whole milk	125 mL
1/4 cup	unsweetened apple juice	60 mL
1 cup	diced mango	250 mL

1. In the rice cooker bowl, combine farro, water, coconut milk, milk and apple juice. Set the rice cooker for the Porridge cycle.
2. When the machine switches to the Keep Warm cycle, gently stir in mango. Let stand for 10 minutes. Serve immediately or hold on the Keep Warm cycle for up to 1 hour.

Variation

Substitute 1/2 cup (125 mL) sliced dried cherries or apricots for the mango.

Lu's Breakfast Grits

Makes 3 to 4 servings

This fabulous one-pot, Southern-style breakfast was inspired by my friend Lu. The time-honored combination of bacon, eggs and grits is sure to appeal to the whole family.

Tips

For a leaner approach, use turkey bacon and 8 egg whites.

For information about rice cooker sizes, see page 13.

• Medium rice cooker; fuzzy logic or on/off

2	slices bacon, chopped	2
3 tbsp	butter, divided	45 mL
4	large eggs, lightly beaten	4
1 cup	coarse stone-ground grits	250 mL
½ tsp	salt	2 mL
3 cups	water	750 mL
¼ tsp	freshly ground black pepper	1 mL

1. Set the rice cooker for the Quick Cook or Regular cycle. When the bottom of the bowl gets hot, sauté bacon for about 4 minutes or until lightly browned. Remove from bowl and set aside.
2. Carefully wipe bacon fat from bowl with a paper towel. Add 1 tbsp (15 mL) butter to the bowl. Add eggs and scramble for 3 to 4 minutes or until set.
3. Return bacon to the bowl and stir in grits, salt and water. Set the rice cooker for the Porridge or Regular cycle. Stir thoroughly two or three times while the grits are cooking.
4. When the machine switches to the Keep Warm cycle, stir in pepper and the remaining butter. Let stand for 10 minutes, then stir thoroughly and serve immediately.

Grits with Currants and Almonds

Makes 4 servings

The currants infuse these grits with sweetness, and the potassium and iron in this breakfast will boost your immune system and keep you in good health. Serve hot, with more milk, if desired.

Tip

To toast almonds, spread them in a single layer on a baking sheet. Bake in a 325°F (160°C) oven for 5 to 10 minutes or until light brown and fragrant. Stir frequently to ensure even toasting.

• Medium rice cooker; fuzzy logic only

1 cup	coarse stone-ground grits	250 mL
1/4 tsp	salt	1 mL
3 cups	whole milk	750 mL
3 tbsp	liquid honey	45 mL
1/4 cup	currants	60 mL
1/4 cup	toasted sliced almonds (see tip, at left)	60 mL

1. In the rice cooker bowl, combine grits, salt, milk and honey. Set the rice cooker for the Porridge cycle. Stir thoroughly two or three times while the grits are cooking.
2. When the machine switches to the Keep Warm cycle, stir in currants and almonds. Let stand for 10 minutes. Serve immediately or hold on the Keep Warm cycle for up to 1 hour. Stir thoroughly before serving.

Variation

Polenta with Currants and Almonds: Substitute 1 cup (250 mL) coarse-grain yellow polenta for the grits and increase the milk to 4 cups (1 L).

Cowboy Breakfast Tamales

Makes
15 tamales

This Mexican egg, cheese and sausage dish is a great recipe to make on a leisurely weekend, when the whole family can get in on the action.

Tips

Discard any corn husks that are torn or have small holes.

If your rice cooker comes with tiered steamer baskets, arrange an equal number of tamales in each tier.

For information about rice cooker sizes, see page 13.

- **Blender or immersion blender**
- **Large rice cooker with a steamer basket; fuzzy logic or on/off**

Red Chili Sauce

2 oz	dried California chile peppers	60 g
2 oz	dried New Mexico chile peppers	60 g
3 cups	water	750 mL
2	cloves garlic	2
1 tsp	salt	5 mL

Tamales

20	dried corn husks	20
1½ cups	masa harina	375 mL
¾ tsp	baking powder	3 mL
¾ tsp	salt	3 mL
1 tsp	ground cumin	5 mL
⅓ cup	canola oil	75 mL
3 tbsp	butter, softened	45 mL
¾ cup + 3 tbsp	warm chicken broth	220 mL
1	large potato, diced	1
4 oz	fresh chorizo sausage, casings removed	125 g
3	large eggs, lightly beaten	3
	Salt and freshly ground black pepper	
½ cup	shredded Monterey Jack cheese	125 mL
4 cups	water	1 L

1. *Sauce:* In a saucepan, combine California chiles, New Mexico chiles and water. Heat over medium heat until steaming (do not let boil). Remove from heat and let soak for 1 hour.

2. Using a slotted spoon, transfer chiles to blender (or transfer to a tall cup and use an immersion blender). Add garlic, salt and 1½ cups (375 mL) soaking liquid; purée until smooth. Set aside. Discard excess soaking liquid.

3. *Tamales:* Place corn husks in a large bowl and cover with warm water. Let stand for at least 30 minutes or until husks are softened.

4. Meanwhile, in a large bowl, whisk together masa harina, baking powder, salt and cumin.

5. In a small bowl, using an electric mixer, beat oil and butter for about 5 minutes or until very light and creamy. Gradually knead 3 tbsp (45 mL) of the oil mixture into the masa mixture, followed by 3 tbsp (45 mL) of the broth. Continue alternately kneading in oil mixture and broth until a smooth paste forms, 10 to 15 minutes. Set aside.

6. Place potato in a small saucepan and cover with cold water. Bring to a boil over high heat. Boil for 8 to 10 minutes or until tender. Drain.

7. In a nonstick skillet, cook chorizo over medium heat, breaking it up with a spoon, for 4 to 5 minutes or until browned. Drain off excess fat, leaving a small amount in the pan. Stir in potato. Cook, stirring, for about 1 minute. Add eggs and cook, scrambling, until set. Remove from heat and season to taste with salt and pepper. Let cool to room temperature.

8. Add cheese and ½ cup (125 mL) of the chili sauce to the scrambled egg mixture, tossing to coat.

9. Remove a corn husk from the water and pat dry with a clean towel. Place 2 tbsp (30 mL) tamale dough in center of husk. Spread dough to within ½ inch (1 cm) of the wide end and halfway toward the pointed end. Place 1 heaping tablespoon (15 mL) scrambled egg mixture in center of dough. Fold sides of husk in, overlapping them in the center. Fold the pointed end toward the filling. Repeat with another 14 husks and the remaining dough and egg mixture.

10. Pour water into the rice cooker bowl. Set the rice cooker for the Regular or Steam cycle.

11. Arrange tamales seam side down in the steamer basket, stacking them side by side, touching each other. Cover with the remaining husks and tuck the husks around the tamales to form a blanket. When the water in the rice cooker comes to a boil, place the steamer basket in the rice cooker and close the cover. Set a timer for 1 hour.

12. When the timer sounds, transfer the tamales to a serving platter and let cool for 15 minutes. Unwrap tamales from corn husks and discard husks. Serve with the remaining chili sauce.

Variation

Substitute 1 cup (250 mL) diced peeled chayote (about 2 medium) for the potato.

Vanilla and Brown Sugar Breakfast Polenta

Makes 4 to 6 servings

Honey, vanilla and brown sugar add sweetness and flavor to this nutritious, creamy polenta, for a delicious breakfast. Serve hot, with more milk and dusted with more cinnamon, if desired.

Tips

For an even creamier breakfast polenta, run the Porridge cycle a second time.

This polenta may be held on the Keep Warm cycle for up to 1 hour.

• Medium rice cooker; fuzzy logic only

1 cup	coarse-grain yellow polenta	250 mL
1/3 cup	packed brown sugar	75 mL
1/4 tsp	salt	1 mL
1/4 tsp	ground cinnamon	1 mL
1/2	vanilla bean, split lengthwise	1/2
2 cups	water	500 mL
2 cups	whole milk	500 mL

1. In the rice cooker bowl, combine polenta, brown sugar, salt, cinnamon, vanilla bean, water and milk. Set the rice cooker for the Porridge cycle. Stir thoroughly two or three times while the polenta is cooking.
2. When the machine switches to the Keep Warm cycle, stir thoroughly, then let stand for 10 minutes. Discard vanilla bean.

Appetizers, Snacks and Sushi

Dolmades with Lamb and Mint

Makes
36 dolmades

The hint of fresh mint mixed with toasted pine nuts will make you think you're dining al fresco at a beachside restaurant somewhere in the Greek islands. Dipped in the tangy tzatziki, these dolmades are the perfect appetizer to go with wine or ouzo.

Tips

Grape leaves are available at many well-stocked grocery stores and at Middle Eastern markets.

For sweeter dolmades, add ½ cup (125 mL) golden raisins to the lamb mixture.

* **Large rice cooker; fuzzy logic or on/off**

1½ lbs	lean ground lamb or beef	750 g
2 cups	finely chopped onions	500 mL
⅔ cup	long-grain white rice, rinsed and drained	150 mL
⅔ cup	toasted pine nuts (see tip, page 52)	150 mL
¼ cup	finely chopped fresh mint	60 mL
1 tbsp	salt	15 mL
½ tsp	freshly ground black pepper	2 mL
1	jar (8 oz/227 mL) grape leaves, drained and rinsed	1
	Tzatziki (see recipe, opposite)	
	Fresh dill sprigs	

1. In a large bowl, combine lamb, onions, rice, pine nuts, mint, salt and pepper until well combined.

2. Gently open up a grape leaf and place rib side down on a work surface. Place a rounded tablespoon (15 mL) of lamb mixture in the center of the leaf. Fold the bottom of the leaf over the meat, fold in the sides and roll into a tight cylinder. Repeat with the remaining filling (you will have extra grape leaves).

3. Place 2 grape leaves in the bottom of the rice cooker bowl (reserve any remaining leaves for another use). Arrange rolled dolmades carefully in stacks in the rice cooker bowl, seam side down. Place a plate on top to keep the dolmades in place and from unrolling. Pour in enough water to cover dolmades.

4. Set the rice cooker for the Regular or Steam cycle and set a timer for 50 minutes. Check occasionally while cooking and add enough water to keep the dolmades covered.

5. When the timer sounds, check to make sure dolmades are no longer pink inside. If necessary, continue cooking, checking for doneness every 5 minutes. Turn the machine off (or unplug it) and let cool for 8 to 10 minutes. Serve warm, with tzatziki on the side. Garnish each serving with a dill sprig.

Variation

Substitute an equal amount of ground chicken or turkey for the lamb.

Tzatziki

Makes about 2 cups (500 mL)

Cool and creamy, this tangy cucumber dip flavored with garlic is the perfect complement to dolmades and other Greek specialties.

2	cloves garlic, minced	2
½ tsp	crushed anise seeds	2 mL
½ tsp	salt	2 mL
¼ tsp	freshly ground white pepper	1 mL
1 cup	Greek-style plain yogurt	250 mL
2 tbsp	freshly squeezed lemon juice	30 mL
1 cup	diced English cucumber (¼-inch/0.5 cm dice)	250 mL
2 tbsp	finely chopped fresh dill	30 mL
1	fresh dill sprig	1

1. In a medium bowl, combine garlic, anise seeds, salt, pepper, yogurt and lemon juice. Stir in cucumber and dill until well combined. Cover and refrigerate for at least 2 hours, until chilled, or for up to 2 days.
2. Serve garnished with a sprig of fresh dill.

Dolmades with Currants and Herbs

Makes 20 to 24 dolmades

The tang of grape leaves mixed with fresh currants and herbs makes this dish a refreshing appetizer for everything from small gatherings to large events — and it's healthy too! It's been a great way to use long-grain rice for centuries.

Tips

To toast pine nuts, place them in a dry skillet over medium heat and cook, stirring, for about 5 minutes or until browned and fragrant. Immediately transfer to a bowl and let cool.

For information about rice cooker sizes, see page 13.

• Large rice cooker; fuzzy logic or on/off

1 cup	finely chopped red onion	250 mL
¾ cup	long-grain white rice, rinsed and drained	175 mL
⅔ cup	toasted pine nuts (see tip, at left)	150 mL
¼ cup	currants	60 mL
¼ cup	finely chopped fresh parsley	60 mL
¼ cup	finely chopped fresh mint	60 mL
2 tbsp	finely chopped fresh dill	30 mL
1 tsp	salt	5 mL
¼ tsp	freshly ground black pepper	1 mL
1	jar (8 oz/227 mL) grape leaves, drained and rinsed	1
	Tzatziki (see recipe, page 51)	

1. In a large bowl, combine onion, rice, pine nuts, currants, parsley, mint, dill, salt and pepper until well combined.

2. Gently open up a grape leaf and place rib side down on a work surface. Place a rounded tablespoon (15 mL) of rice mixture in the center of the leaf. Fold the bottom of the leaf over the meat, fold in the sides and roll into a tight cylinder. Repeat with the remaining filling (you will have extra grape leaves).

3. Place 2 grape leaves in the bottom of the rice cooker bowl (reserve remaining grape leaves for another use). Arrange rolled dolmades carefully in stacks in the rice cooker bowl, seam side down. Place a plate on top to keep the dolmades in place and from unrolling. Pour in enough water to cover dolmades.

4. Set the rice cooker for the Regular or Steam cycle and set a timer for 50 minutes. Check occasionally while cooking and add enough water to keep the dolmades covered.

5. When the timer sounds, check to make sure rice is tender inside dolmades. If necessary, continue cooking, checking for doneness every 5 minutes. Turn the machine off (or unplug it) and let cool for 8 to 10 minutes. Serve warm or at room temperature, with tzatziki on the side.

Black-Eyed Pea and Walnut Lettuce Wraps

Makes 16 wraps

Walnuts, feta cheese and dried cranberries always work well together, as they do here with black-eyed peas and a dash of sherry vinegar. This is the perfect appetizer to serve as your guests arrive.

Tips

To toast walnut halves, spread nuts in a single layer on a baking sheet. Bake in a 350°F (180°C) oven, stirring often, for 5 to 10 minutes or until light brown and fragrant. Immediately transfer to a bowl and let cool before chopping.

The filling for these wraps can be made up to 1 day ahead. Store in an airtight container in the refrigerator. Bring to room temperature and wrap in lettuce as guests arrive.

2 tbsp	extra virgin olive oil	30 mL
2	cloves garlic, minced	2
1 cup	finely chopped onion	250 mL
1½ cups	cooked black-eyed peas (see page 33), cooled	375 mL
1 cup	dried cranberries	250 mL
¾ cup	walnut halves, toasted (see tip, at left) and coarsely chopped	175 mL
¾ cup	crumbled feta cheese	175 mL
¼ cup	finely chopped fresh parsley	60 mL
¾ cup	sherry vinegar	175 mL
	Salt and freshly ground black pepper	
16	butter lettuce leaves	16

1. In a medium nonstick skillet, heat oil over medium heat. Sauté garlic and onion for about 3 minutes or until onion is softened and translucent.
2. In a medium bowl, combine onion mixture, peas, cranberries, walnuts, feta, parsley and vinegar. Season to taste with salt and pepper.
3. Spoon about ¼ cup (60 mL) of the pea mixture into each lettuce leaf. Fold leaves in half and eat them taco-style.

Variation

Substitute blue cheese for the feta cheese.

Korean Beef Lettuce Wraps

Makes 10 to 12 wraps

This delectable starter dish calls for kiwi juice to be used as a marinade for the beef, making the meat so juicy and tender that it almost melts in your mouth.

Tips

To make kiwi purée, place peeled kiwifruit in a blender or food processor and purée until smooth.

Kiwi purée acts as a tenderizer in Korean beef dishes. You can also use pineapple juice or pear juice for the same effect. Many Koreans use cola to tenderize their meat, and this is also a fine substitute.

To toast sesame seeds, spread seeds in a single layer on a baking sheet. Bake in a 325°F (160°C) oven, stirring often, for 10 to 15 minutes or until light brown and fragrant. Immediately transfer to a bowl and let cool.

1½ lbs	boneless beef rib-eye or top sirloin, cut into ⅛-inch (3 mm) strips	750 g
1 tbsp	kiwi purée (see tip, at left)	15 mL
3	cloves garlic, minced	3
1 tbsp	packed dark brown sugar	15 mL
1½ tsp	minced gingerroot	7 mL
2 tbsp	soy sauce	30 mL
1½ tsp	toasted sesame oil	7 mL
1 tbsp	vegetable oil	15 mL
3 cups	cooked short-grain white rice (see page 20), cooled	750 mL
10 to 12	Boston or Bibb lettuce leaves	10 to 12
2 tsp	toasted sesame seeds (see tip, at left)	10 mL
	Thai chili sauce (such as Sriracha)	

1. In a large bowl, toss beef with kiwi purée; let stand for 15 minutes.
2. In a small bowl, whisk together garlic, brown sugar, ginger, soy sauce and sesame oil. Add to beef mixture and toss to coat.
3. In a large nonstick skillet, heat vegetable oil over medium-high heat. Sauté beef mixture until beef is browned on all sides. Remove from heat.
4. Spoon a small scoop of rice into each lettuce leaf and top with 1 tbsp (15 mL) beef mixture. Sprinkle with sesame seeds. Serve with chili sauce.

Crispy Kasha Croquettes with Coconut Cilantro Sauce

Makes 16 croquettes

If kasha is Jewish soul food, then this recipe takes soul to new heights. Enhanced with a coconut cilantro sauce, these crispy croquettes make for a truly heavenly starter that will be a unique surprise for your guests.

Tips

For the best flavor, toast whole cumin seeds in a skillet over medium-high heat, stirring constantly, for about 3 minutes or until fragrant. Immediately transfer to a spice grinder and let cool, then grind to a fine powder.

Sriracha is a Thai chili sauce available at well-stocked supermarkets and Asian markets. You may substitute your favorite hot sauce.

- **Blender or food processor**

Coconut Cilantro Sauce

1	clove garlic	1
1	1-inch (2.5 cm) piece gingerroot	1
1 cup	finely chopped fresh cilantro	250 mL
¼ tsp	salt	1 mL
¼ cup	coconut milk	60 mL
2 tbsp	freshly squeezed lime juice	30 mL
1 tsp	Thai chili sauce (such as Sriracha)	5 mL

Croquettes

2¼ cups	cooked kasha (see page 27), cooled	550 mL
½ cup	whole wheat flour	125 mL
3	finely chopped green onions	3
2	cloves garlic, minced	2
1 tbsp	dried parsley	15 mL
1 tsp	ground cumin (see tip, at left)	5 mL
1 tsp	salt	5 mL
¼ tsp	freshly ground black pepper	1 mL
	Vegetable oil	

1. *Sauce:* In blender, combine garlic, ginger, cilantro, salt, coconut milk, lime juice and chili sauce; purée until smooth. Transfer to a bowl and set aside.

2. *Croquettes:* In a large bowl, combine kasha and flour, squeezing with your fingers until the dough holds its shape. Work in green onions, garlic, parsley, cumin, salt and pepper. Form dough into sixteen 2-inch (5 cm) patties.

3. In a large skillet, heat ½ inch (1 cm) oil over medium heat. Working in batches as necessary, fry patties, turning once, for 2 to 3 minutes per side or until browned on both sides, adding oil and adjusting heat as needed between batches. Transfer to a baking sheet lined with paper towels and let drain. Serve warm with dipping sauce.

Variation

Add ½ cup (125 mL) puréed tofu to the kasha mixture for added protein.

Pork Tamales with Red Chili Sauce

Makes
15 tamales

Pork tamales have been a tradition for centuries, but making them in a rice cooker? You have to try it to believe it. The combination of California and New Mexico dried chiles in the sauce gives the pork mixture a kick you won't forget.

Tips

Check the corn husks before soaking them and discard any that are torn or have small holes.

If your rice cooker comes with tiered steamer baskets, arrange an equal number of tamales in each tier.

For information about rice cooker sizes, see page 13.

- **Blender or immersion blender**
- **Large rice cooker with a steamer basket; fuzzy logic or on/off**

Red Chili Sauce

2 oz	dried California chile peppers	60 g
2 oz	dried New Mexico chile peppers	60 g
3 cups	water	750 mL
2	cloves garlic	2
1 tsp	salt	5 mL

Tamales

20	dried corn husks	20
1½ cups	masa harina	375 mL
¾ tsp	baking powder	3 mL
¾ tsp	salt	3 mL
1 tsp	ground cumin	5 mL
⅓ cup	canola oil	75 mL
3 tbsp	butter, softened	45 mL
¾ cup + 3 tbsp	warm chicken broth	220 mL
1½ cups	shredded cooked pork (see tip, opposite)	375 mL
4 cups	water	1 L

1. *Sauce:* In a saucepan, combine California chiles, New Mexico chiles and water. Heat over medium heat until steaming (do not let boil). Remove from heat and let soak for 1 hour.
2. Using a slotted spoon, transfer chiles to blender (or transfer to a tall cup and use an immersion blender). Add garlic, salt and 1½ cups (375 mL) soaking liquid; purée until smooth. Set aside, reserving the remaining soaking liquid.
3. *Tamales:* Place corn husks in a large bowl and cover with warm water. Let stand for at least 30 minutes or until husks are softened.
4. Meanwhile, in a large bowl, whisk together masa harina, baking powder, salt and cumin. Set aside.
5. In a small bowl, using an electric mixer, beat oil and butter for about 5 minutes or until very light and creamy. Gradually knead 3 tbsp (45 mL) of the oil mixture into the masa harina mixture, followed by 3 tbsp (45 mL) of the broth. Continue alternately kneading in oil mixture and broth until a smooth paste forms, 10 to 15 minutes. Set aside.

Tip

To cook the pork the traditional way, place 1 lb (500 g) boneless pork shoulder blade (butt) roast in a large saucepan and cover with water. Bring to a boil over medium-high heat. Reduce heat and simmer for 45 minutes or until fork-tender. Let cool, then shred.

6. Place pork in a large bowl. Pour 2 cups (500 mL) of the red chili sauce through a fine-mesh sieve set over the pork. Add the remaining soaking liquid to the sieve, $\frac{1}{2}$ cup (125 mL) at a time, pressing sauce down with the back of a spoon. Discard solids left in sieve. Toss pork with sauce.

7. Remove a corn husk from the water and pat dry with a clean towel. Place 2 tbsp (30 mL) tamale dough in center of husk. Spread dough to within $\frac{1}{2}$ inch (1 cm) of the wide end and halfway toward the pointed end. Place 1 heaping tablespoon (15 mL) pork mixture in center of dough. Fold sides of husk in, overlapping them in the center. Fold the pointed end toward the filling. Repeat with another 14 husks and the remaining dough and pork mixture.

8. Pour water into the rice cooker bowl. Set the rice cooker for the Regular or Steam cycle.

9. Arrange tamales seam side down in the steamer basket, stacking them side by side, touching each other. Cover with the remaining husks and tuck the husks around the tamales to form a blanket. When the water in the rice cooker comes to a boil, place the steamer basket in the rice cooker and close the cover. Set a timer for 1 hour.

10. When the timer sounds, transfer the tamales to a serving platter and let cool for 15 minutes. Unwrap tamales from corn husks and discard husks. Serve with the remaining red chili sauce.

Maria's Chicken Tamales with Tomatillo Cilantro Sauce

Makes
15 tamales

As a Southern California resident, I have tasted tamales cooked in many homes and restaurants, but my friend Maria's authentic Mexican recipe tops my list. The cilantro mixed with the onion and garlic freshens the tamale dough like nothing else.

Tips

Check the corn husks before soaking them and discard any that are torn or have small holes.

To cook the chicken the traditional way, place 1 lb (500 g) chicken breasts in a large saucepan and cover with water. Bring to a boil over medium-high heat. Reduce heat and simmer for 45 minutes or until no longer pink inside. Let cool, then shred.

If desired, serve each tamale sprinkled with 2 tbsp (30 mL) shredded Monterey Jack cheese.

- **Blender or immersion blender**
- **Large rice cooker with a steamer basket; fuzzy logic or on/off**

Tomatillo Cilantro Sauce

6	tomatillos, quartered	6
1	serrano chile pepper	1
3 cups	water	750 mL
2	cloves garlic	2
1	bunch fresh cilantro, large stems removed (about ¾ cup/175 mL packed)	1
2 tbsp	finely chopped onion	30 mL
1 tbsp	freshly squeezed lime juice	15 mL
	Salt and freshly ground black pepper	

Tamales

20	dried corn husks	20
1½ cups	masa harina	375 mL
¾ tsp	baking powder	3 mL
¾ tsp	salt	3 mL
1 tsp	ground cumin	5 mL
⅓ cup	canola oil	75 mL
3 tbsp	butter, softened	45 mL
¾ cup + 3 tbsp	warm chicken broth	220 mL
1½ cups	shredded cooked chicken (see tip, at left)	375 mL
4 cups	water	1 L

1. *Sauce:* In a medium saucepan, bring tomatillo, serrano pepper and water to a boil over medium-high heat. Reduce heat and simmer for 25 minutes. Remove from heat and let cool.
2. Transfer tomatillo mixture to blender (or transfer to a tall cup and use an immersion blender). Add garlic, cilantro, onion and lime juice; purée until smooth. Transfer to a bowl and season to taste with salt and pepper.
3. *Tamales:* Place corn husks in a large bowl and cover with warm water. Let stand for at least 30 minutes or until husks are softened.

Tamales

Tamale literally means "wrapped food." Traditional tamales are packets of corn dough with a savory or sweet filling, typically wrapped in corn husks, which are discarded before eating. Tamales date back to pre-Columbian times, though the actual inventor is unknown. Being both portable and nutritious, they were often carried by Aztec, Mayan and Incan warriors.

4. Meanwhile, in a large bowl, whisk together masa harina, baking powder, salt and cumin. Set aside.

5. In a small bowl, using an electric mixer, beat oil and butter for about 5 minutes or until very light and creamy. Gradually knead 3 tbsp (45 mL) of the oil mixture into the masa harina mixture, followed by 3 tbsp (45 mL) of the broth. Continue alternately kneading in oil mixture and broth until a smooth paste forms, 10 to 15 minutes. Set aside.

6. In another large bowl, combine chicken and 2 cups (500 mL) of the sauce.

7. Remove a corn husk from the water and pat dry with a clean towel. Place 2 tbsp (30 mL) tamale dough in center of husk. Spread dough to within $1/2$ inch (1 cm) of the wide end and halfway toward the pointed end. Place 1 heaping tablespoon (15 mL) chicken mixture in center of dough. Fold sides of husk in, overlapping them in the center. Fold the pointed end toward the filling. Repeat with another 14 husks and the remaining dough and chicken mixture.

8. Pour water into the rice cooker bowl. Set the rice cooker for the Regular or Steam cycle.

9. Arrange tamales seam side down in the steamer basket, stacking them side by side, touching each other. Cover with the remaining husks and tuck the husks around the tamales to form a blanket. When the water in the rice cooker comes to a boil, place the steamer basket in the rice cooker and close the cover. Set a timer for 1 hour.

10. When the timer sounds, transfer the tamales to a serving platter and let cool for 15 minutes. Unwrap tamales from corn husks and discard husks. Serve tamales with the remaining sauce.

Red Lentil and Red Rice Patties with Aïoli

Makes 28 patties

This vegetarian delight is great all year round. The garlic and onion are true complements to the lentils and tofu, and Bhutanese red rice gives the patties a rich texture. They may very well remind you of falafel — you'll even want to put them in pita and dribble them with tahini sauce for a delicious lunch.

Tips

Look for Bhutanese red rice at gourmet stores and online. If you can't find it, substitute red cargo rice or regular red rice.

Increase the amount of hot pepper flakes if you like more heat.

Aïoli

2	cloves garlic, minced	2
½ cup	mayonnaise	125 mL
2 tsp	Dijon mustard	10 mL
1 tsp	freshly squeezed lemon juice	5 mL
1 tsp	extra virgin olive oil	5 mL
	Salt and freshly ground black pepper	

Patties

3 tbsp	extra virgin olive oil	45 mL
2	cloves garlic, minced	2
½ cup	finely chopped onion	125 mL
10 oz	firm tofu, puréed	300 g
3 cups	cooked Bhutanese red rice (see page 20), cooled	750 mL
1½ cups	cooked red lentils (see page 33), cooled	375 mL
½ cup	panko bread crumbs	125 mL
1 tsp	ground cumin	5 mL
½ tsp	hot pepper flakes	2 mL
¼ cup	cornstarch	60 mL
	Vegetable oil	

1. *Aïoli:* In a small bowl, whisk together garlic, mayonnaise, mustard, lemon juice and oil. Season to taste with salt and pepper. Set aside.

2. *Patties:* In a medium nonstick skillet, heat olive oil over medium heat. Sauté garlic and onion for about 3 minutes or until onion is softened and translucent.

3. In a medium bowl, combine onion mixture, tofu, rice, lentils, panko, cumin and hot pepper flakes. Sprinkle cornstarch on a sheet of waxed paper or parchment paper. Form mixture into twenty-eight 1½-inch (4 cm) patties. Dust both sides of each patty with cornstarch.

4. In a large nonstick skillet, heat 1 tbsp (15 mL) vegetable oil over medium-high heat. Working in batches, fry patties, turning once, for about 5 minutes per side or until golden brown on both sides, adding oil and adjusting heat as needed between batches. Transfer to a baking sheet lined with paper towels and let drain. Serve hot with aïoli.

Chickpea Sliders

Makes 10 to 12 sliders

Chickpeas (also known as garbanzo beans) are a versatile legume with a surprising flavor. Here, they're made into sliders and drizzled with lemon juice and tahini. This appetizer will delight and mystify your guests until you fill them in on the secret ingredient.

Tip

The cooked patties can be stored in an airtight container in the freezer for up to 3 months. Reheat from frozen on a baking sheet in a 350°F (180°C) oven for 15 to 20 minutes or until heated through.

Tahini

Tahini is sesame seed paste, and is used in a variety of Middle Eastern dishes. You can make your own tahini by roasting 1 cup (250 mL) sesame seeds on a baking sheet in a 350°F (180°C) oven for 15 minutes or until golden brown. Let cool, then purée in a food processor, drizzling in 1/4 cup (60 mL) extra virgin olive oil through the feed tube until well blended.

- **Preheat oven to 350°F (180°C)**
- **Food processor**
- **Baking sheet, greased**

3	cloves garlic, minced	3
1	large egg, lightly beaten	1
3 cups	cooked chickpeas (see page 33), cooled	750 mL
1 cup	finely chopped onion	250 mL
2 tsp	dried oregano	10 mL
2 tsp	dried parsley	10 mL
1 1/2 tsp	ground cumin	7 mL
1 1/2 tsp	salt	7 mL
1 1/2 tsp	all-purpose flour	7 mL
	Slider rolls or small soft dinner rolls	
	Freshly squeezed lemon juice	
	Tahini	

1. In food processor, combine garlic, egg, chickpeas, onion, oregano, parsley, cumin, salt and flour; pulse until mixture forms a smooth dough. Transfer to a bowl and refrigerate for 20 minutes.
2. Using about 1/4 cup (60 mL) dough per patty, form dough into 2-inch (5 cm) patties. Place patties on prepared baking sheet.
3. Bake in preheated oven for 10 minutes. Turn patties over and bake for 10 minutes or until browned, crispy and hot in the center.
4. Place patties on rolls and drizzle with lemon juice and tahini. Serve hot.

Variation

Serve each patty in a mini pita, with chopped tomatoes, onions and green bell peppers and prepared harissa.

Fontina Risotto Balls (*Arancini*)

Makes 24 balls

These delicious risotto balls, made with Parmesan and semisoft fontina cheese, would make any Sicilian cook proud. I like to make the risotto the night before, shape it into balls the next day, then either cook the balls or freeze them for a later date.

Tips

If you want to prepare these risotto balls and serve them the same day, simply let the risotto cool completely in step 3, then continue with step 4 without refrigerating. The risotto balls won't be quite as good as those made with refrigerated risotto, but they'll still be amazing!

For information about rice cooker sizes, see page 13.

- **Medium or large rice cooker; fuzzy logic or on/off**

Risotto Balls

1 tbsp	extra virgin olive oil	15 mL
5 tsp	butter, divided	25 mL
1	onion, finely chopped	1
1 cup	Arborio rice	250 mL
¼ cup	white wine	60 mL
3 cups	chicken broth	750 mL
½ cup	freshly grated Parmesan cheese	125 mL
1 tsp	salt	5 mL
1½ cups	panko bread crumbs, divided	375 mL
½ cup	packed shredded fontina cheese	125 mL
¾ cup	finely chopped fresh parsley	175 mL
3 tbsp	finely chopped fresh chives	45 mL
1	large egg yolk	1
24	¼-inch (0.5 cm) cubes fontina cheese (about 4 oz/125 g)	24
2	large eggs	2
	Vegetable oil	

Tomato Sauce

1 tbsp	extra virgin olive oil	15 mL
1	clove garlic, minced	1
¼ cup	finely chopped Spanish onion	60 mL
2 tsp	finely chopped fresh basil	10 mL
½ tsp	hot pepper flakes	2 mL
1	can (14 oz/398 mL) whole tomatoes, with juice	1
Pinch	granulated sugar	Pinch
	Salt	

1. *Risotto Balls:* Set the rice cooker for the Quick Cook or Regular cycle. When the bottom of the bowl gets hot, add olive oil and 1 tbsp (15 mL) butter and let butter melt. Sauté onion for about 3 minutes or until softened and translucent.

2. Add rice, stirring to coat. Cook, stirring, for about 4 minutes or until rice is mostly translucent and only a dot of white remains. Stir in wine and cook for 3 to 4 minutes or until wine is evaporated. Stir in broth. Close the lid and reset for the Porridge or Regular cycle. Set a timer for 25 minutes. Stir two or three times while the rice is cooking.

Tips

The cooked risotto balls can be stored in an airtight container in the freezer for up to 3 months. Reheat from frozen on a baking sheet in a 350°F (180°C) oven for 15 to 20 minutes or until heated through.

The sauce can also be made ahead. Let it cool completely, then transfer to an airtight container and refrigerate for up to 3 days. Reheat in a saucepan over medium heat before serving.

3. When the timer sounds, check to see if rice is al dente and most of the liquid is absorbed. If necessary, continue cooking, checking for doneness every 5 minutes. When the proper consistency is achieved, fold in the remaining butter. Fold in Parmesan and salt. Spread risotto in a large pan and let cool completely. Cover and refrigerate overnight.

4. *Sauce:* In a small saucepan, heat oil over medium-high heat. Sauté garlic and onion for about 3 minutes or until onion is softened and translucent. Add basil and hot pepper flakes; sauté for 1 minute. Stir in tomatoes with juice, breaking up tomatoes with the back of the spoon. Reduce heat and simmer for about 15 minutes or until sauce starts to thicken. Stir in sugar and salt to taste. Cover and remove from heat.

5. Remove risotto from the refrigerator and stir in $\frac{1}{2}$ cup (125 mL) of the panko, shredded fontina, parsley, chives and egg yolk. Form 1 rounded tablespoon (15 mL) risotto mixture into a $1\frac{1}{2}$-inch (4 cm) ball, then slightly flatten it in your hand. Place a cube of fontina in the middle of the flattened ball and reform into a tight round ball. Repeat with the remaining risotto mixture and fontina cubes.

6. In a shallow bowl, beat eggs until blended. Place the remaining panko in another shallow bowl. Dip risotto balls in egg, then in panko, coating evenly and shaking off excess. Discard any excess egg and panko.

7. In a large, deep skillet, heat $1\frac{1}{2}$ inches (4 cm) of vegetable oil over medium-high heat until a few crumbs of panko turn golden brown in 5 seconds. Working in batches, fry risotto balls for 1 to 2 minutes or until crisp and brown all over, adding oil and adjusting heat as needed between batches. Transfer to a baking sheet lined with paper towels and let drain. Serve warm with tomato sauce.

Variation

Wild Mushroom Risotto Balls: Sauté $\frac{1}{2}$ cup (125 mL) chopped mixed wild mushrooms with the onion in the rice cooker.

Galina's Meatballs

**Makes
36 meatballs**

When I was growing up, meatballs were often served as appetizers at parties, but they didn't taste like this! This recipe for authentic Russian meatballs was given to me by my friend Rita's mother, who grew up in Kiev. They are enchanting when dipped in a red sauce accented with brown sugar and Tabasco.

Tips

If you like heat, increase the amount of hot pepper sauce.

If serving these meatballs at a party, keep them warm in a chafing dish and set a small container of toothpicks alongside.

Meatballs

4 tbsp	extra virgin olive oil, divided	60 mL
1 cup	finely chopped onion	250 mL
1 lb	lean ground beef (preferably round)	500 g
1 lb	lean ground turkey (preferably dark meat)	500 g
½ cup	cooked long-grain white rice (see page 20), cooled	125 mL
1 tsp	salt	5 mL
¼ tsp	freshly ground black pepper	1 mL
1 tbsp	butter	15 mL

Sauce

2	cans (each 8 oz/227 mL) tomato sauce	2
1 tsp	packed brown sugar	5 mL
¼ cup	water	60 mL
3 tbsp	ketchup	45 mL
½ tsp	hot pepper sauce	2 mL

1. *Meatballs:* In a medium nonstick skillet, heat 1 tbsp (15 mL) oil over medium-high heat. Sauté onion for about 3 minutes or until softened and translucent. Remove from heat and let cool completely.

2. In a large bowl, combine cooled onion, beef, turkey, rice, salt and pepper. Using wet hands, form mixture into thirty-six 1-inch (2.5 cm) meatballs.

3. In a large nonstick skillet, melt butter and 1 tbsp (15 mL) oil over medium-high heat. Working in batches, fry meatballs for 1 to 2 minutes or until browned all over, adding oil and adjusting heat as needed between batches. Transfer meatballs to a plate.

4. *Sauce:* In another large skillet, combine tomato sauce, brown sugar, water, ketchup and hot pepper sauce. Bring to a boil over medium-high heat. Add meatballs, reduce heat and simmer, gently stirring occasionally, for 30 to 40 minutes or until meatballs are no longer pink inside.

Variation

Substitute ground veal for the beef and ground chicken for the turkey.

Mini Bacon and Asparagus Quiche

Makes 24 quiches

What would the French say about a quiche shell made with rice from a rice cooker? "*C'est magnifique!*" would be my guess, once they've tasted the result. The combination of bacon, asparagus and Swiss cheese is a trusted favorite that gets new life here.

Tips

Don't press the crust mixture more than halfway up the sides of the muffin cups; otherwise, the rice may become too hard.

Since it's easy to spill the egg mixture, I like to transfer it to a pitcher or a measuring cup with a spout and pour it into the rice shells after I've placed the muffin pan on the oven rack.

For a lighter version of this recipe, omit the bacon and use whole milk in place of the cream.

- **Preheat oven to 400°F (200°C)**
- **24-cup mini muffin pan, greased**

Crust

1	large egg white	1
1 cup	cooked long-grain brown rice (see page 20), cooled	250 mL
2 tbsp	butter, softened	30 mL

Filling

3 cups	water	750 mL
3	spears asparagus, tough ends removed, blanched (see tip, page 82) and finely chopped	3
2	slices bacon, cooked crisp and chopped	2
1/4 cup	finely chopped onion	60 mL
3/4 cup	shredded Swiss cheese	175 mL
3	large eggs	3
1/2 cup	half-and-half (10%) cream	125 mL
3/4 tsp	salt	3 mL
1/4 tsp	freshly ground black pepper	1 mL
1/4 cup	freshly grated Parmesan cheese	60 mL

1. *Crust:* In a medium bowl, combine egg white, rice and butter until well blended. Press into bottom and halfway up sides of prepared muffin cups. Bake in preheated oven for 8 to 9 minutes or until set. Let cool slightly in pan. Reduce oven temperature to 350°F (180°C).
2. *Filling:* In another medium bowl, combine asparagus, bacon, onion and Swiss cheese. Spoon into rice shells, dividing equally.
3. In a small bowl, whisk together eggs, cream, salt and pepper until well blended. Pour over asparagus mixture, dividing equally. Sprinkle with Parmesan.
4. Bake for 25 to 30 minutes or until a tester inserted in the center of a quiche comes out clean. Let cool in pan on a wire rack for about 15 minutes, then carefully remove quiches from pan. Serve warm.

Variation

Mini Sausage and Spinach Quiche: Substitute 1/2 cup (125 mL) crumbled cooked sausage for the bacon and a 10-oz (300 g) package of frozen spinach, thawed and sautéed, for the asparagus.

Wild Rice Pancakes with Smoked Salmon and Crème Fraîche

Makes 48 small pancakes

I served this elegant appetizer at a New Year's Day open house, and the crowd simply went wild. I suggest doubling the recipe, as these pancakes are a big hit at parties.

Tips

The pancakes can be made ahead and refrigerated in an airtight container overnight. Warm on a baking sheet in a 300°F (150°C) oven for 10 minutes before serving.

Canola oil is heart-healthy, but you may also use vegetable oil or corn oil for frying.

● **Preheat oven to 200°F (100°C)**

1 cup	all-purpose flour	250 mL
2 tbsp	baking powder	30 mL
1 tsp	salt	5 mL
3	large eggs, lightly beaten	3
1¼ cups	whole milk (approx.)	300 mL
¼ cup	melted butter	60 mL
2 tbsp	finely chopped shallots	30 mL
1½ cups	cooked wild rice (see page 20), cooled	375 mL
	Vegetable oil	
6 oz	thinly sliced smoked salmon, cut into 48 small pieces	175 g
½ cup	crème fraîche	125 mL
2 oz	red caviar (optional)	60 g
2 tbsp	finely chopped fresh chives	30 mL

1. In a large bowl, combine flour, baking powder and salt. Stir in eggs, milk, butter and shallots until batter is smooth. (The batter should be a bit thinner than pancake batter; stir in more milk, if necessary.) Stir in wild rice.

2. In a large nonstick skillet, heat 1 tbsp (15 mL) oil over medium heat. Spoon in about 1 tbsp (15 mL) batter per pancake and cook for about 1 minute or until bubbles appear uniformly on top and bottoms are browned. Turn pancakes over and cook for about 1 minute or until bottoms are browned. Transfer to a baking sheet and place in warm oven. Repeat with the remaining batter, adding oil and adjusting heat as needed between batches.

3. Place pancakes on a serving platter. Top each with smoked salmon, a small dollop of crème fraîche, caviar and a sprinkle of chives.

Thai Crab Cakes

Makes 12 to 14 crab cakes

For years, I thought crab cakes from Maryland were the absolute best. But then we honeymooned in Thailand, and I was inspired to make these — exquisite! You'll appreciate the way the fresh cilantro and chili sauce complement the succulent flavor of the crab.

Tip

If you prefer denser crab cakes, add 1 tbsp (15 mL) cornstarch to the crabmeat mixture and refrigerate breaded patties for 30 minutes before frying.

Panko

Panko bread crumbs, a product from Japan, coat food in a delicate yet sturdy sheath. They are available at well-stocked supermarkets and Asian markets. You can substitute regular dry bread crumbs if you can't find panko.

Dipping Sauce

½ cup	mayonnaise	125 mL
1 tsp	sambal oelek or other hot Asian chili sauce	5 mL
1 tsp	freshly squeezed lime juice	5 mL

Crab Cakes

2 tbsp	extra virgin olive oil	30 mL
1	clove garlic, minced	1
½ cup	finely chopped red onion	125 mL
5 oz	cooked lump crabmeat, picked over to remove shell fragments	150 g
2 tbsp	finely chopped fresh cilantro	30 mL
½ tsp	salt	2 mL
1 tbsp	fish sauce (nam pla)	15 mL
½ tsp	sambal oelek or other hot Asian chili sauce	2 mL
1½ cups	cooked brown jasmine rice (see page 20), cooled	375 mL
1	large egg, lightly beaten	1
½ cup	panko bread crumbs	125 mL
	Vegetable oil	
	Additional finely chopped fresh cilantro	

1. *Sauce:* In a small bowl, combine mayonnaise, sambal oelek and lime juice. Set aside.
2. *Crab Cakes:* In a medium nonstick skillet, heat olive oil over medium heat. Sauté garlic and red onion for about 3 minutes or until onion is softened and translucent. Remove from heat and let cool.
3. In a large bowl, using a fork, combine cooled onion mixture, crabmeat, cilantro, salt, fish sauce and sambal oelek. Stir in cooked rice. Stir in egg until well blended. Form mixture into twelve to fourteen 1½-inch (4 cm) patties.
4. Sprinkle panko on a sheet of waxed paper or parchment paper. Dredge each patty in bread crumbs, coating evenly and shaking off excess. Discard any excess panko.
5. In a large nonstick skillet, heat 1 tbsp (15 mL) vegetable oil over medium-high heat. Working in batches, fry patties, turning once, for about 5 minutes per side or until golden brown on both sides and hot in the center, adding oil and adjusting heat as needed between batches. Transfer to a baking sheet lined with paper towels and let drain.
6. Arrange crab cakes on a serving platter and sprinkle evenly with cilantro. Serve immediately, with dipping sauce on the side.

Thai Shrimp Cakes with Mango Coconut Sauce

Makes 32 shrimp cakes

The mango coconut sauce adds an exotic flair to a party, or even a weeknight dinner. It's like bringing the tropics right to your table. I love the kick of the Thai chili sauce combined with the sweetness of the coconut milk.

Tips

To purée mango, first dice it, then purée in a blender or food processor until smooth. You'll need about 1/4 mango for 1/4 cup (60 mL) puréed mango.

A 14-oz (400 mL) can of coconut milk will provide just the amount you need for this recipe.

Fish sauce is a condiment made from fermented fish, used in Southeast Asian cooking. It imparts an umami flavor to food thanks to its glutamate content. Fish sauce is available at well-stocked supermarkets and Asian markets.

Mango Coconut Sauce

2 tbsp	butter	30 mL
2	cloves garlic, minced	2
1 tbsp	finely chopped green onions (white and green parts)	15 mL
1 tbsp	finely chopped fresh cilantro	15 mL
1 tbsp	minced gingerroot	15 mL
1 tbsp	minced lemongrass (tender inner layers only)	15 mL
1/4 cup	puréed mango (see tip, at left)	60 mL
2 tbsp	liquid honey	30 mL
1/2 tsp	salt	2 mL
1 cup	coconut milk	250 mL
2 tsp	Thai chili sauce (such as Sriracha)	10 mL

Shrimp Cakes

1 lb	medium cooked shrimp, peeled and deveined, cut into 1/2-inch (1 cm) pieces	500 g
1 1/2 cups	cooked jasmine rice (see page 20), cooled	375 mL
1 cup	all-purpose flour	250 mL
1/4 cup	finely chopped green onions (white and green parts)	60 mL
1/4 cup	finely chopped fresh cilantro	60 mL
2 tsp	baking powder	10 mL
1 tsp	salt	5 mL
1 tbsp	fish sauce (nam pla)	15 mL
3	large eggs, lightly beaten	3
2/3 cup	coconut milk	150 mL
1/4 cup	melted butter	60 mL
	Vegetable oil	

1. *Sauce:* In a medium saucepan, melt butter over medium heat. Sauté garlic, green onions, cilantro, ginger and lemongrass for about 4 minutes or until fragrant. Add mango, honey and salt; sauté for 2 to 3 minutes or until warmed through. Stir in coconut milk and Thai chili sauce; simmer, stirring occasionally, for 5 minutes. Remove from heat, cover and set aside.
2. *Shrimp Cakes:* In a large bowl, combine shrimp, rice, flour, green onions, cilantro, baking powder, salt and fish sauce until well mixed. Gently stir in eggs, coconut milk and butter.

Tip

For a clean, bright flavor in Asian shrimp dishes, soak the shrimp in a mixture of warm water and 1 tsp (5 mL) salt for 5 minutes, then rinse and pat dry before chopping.

Mango

Mango is primarily a summer fruit and can be eaten both green and ripe. Low in calories, mangos are packed with dietary fiber, vitamins, antioxidants and minerals. Recent studies suggest that they are also powerful cancer fighters. When choosing a mango, it should yield nicely to a light press with a fingertip. Under-ripe mangos will ripen in a day or two if put in a paper bag in a warm place.

3. In a large nonstick skillet, heat 2 tbsp (30 mL) oil over medium-high heat. For each shrimp cake, drop 1 tbsp (15 mL) shrimp mixture into skillet, flattening it slightly so that the cake is about 2 inches (5 cm) in diameter. Cook cakes, turning once, for about 5 minutes per side or until golden brown on both sides. Repeat with the remaining shrimp mixture, adding oil and adjusting heat as needed between batches. Serve warm, drizzled with sauce.

Variation

Thai Scallop Cakes with Mango Coconut Sauce: Coarsely chop 1 lb (500 g) cooked scallops in a blender or food processor and use in place of the shrimp.

Quinoa and Eggplant "Caviar"

Makes 6 to 8 servings

Although an ideal appetizer, this recipe also makes a great lunch or dinner for two to three people, thanks to the protein-rich quinoa. The black quinoa looks just like caviar!

Tip

Black quinoa imparts a beautiful ebony, caviar-like quality to this dish, but you can use regular or red quinoa in its place.

- Preheat broiler
- Shallow roasting pan
- Food processor

3	eggplants (each about 2 lbs/1 kg)	3
2 tbsp	extra virgin olive oil	30 mL
2	cloves garlic, minced	2
1 cup	finely chopped onion	250 mL
2	plum (Roma) tomatoes, seeded and finely chopped	2
1½ cups	cooked black quinoa (see page 27), cooled	375 mL
3 tbsp	finely chopped fresh cilantro	45 mL
3 tbsp	finely chopped fresh parsley	45 mL
2 tbsp	freshly squeezed lemon juice	30 mL
	Salt and freshly ground black pepper	
	Pita chips	

1. Place eggplants in roasting pan. Broil for about 40 minutes, turning every 5 minutes, until skin is blackened all over and is falling off. Let cool until cool enough to handle, then peel away the blackened skin.
2. In a medium nonstick skillet, heat oil over medium heat. Sauté garlic and onion for about 3 minutes or until onion is softened and translucent. Remove from heat and set aside.
3. Place eggplant flesh in food processor and pulse until puréed. Transfer to a large bowl and add onion mixture, tomatoes, quinoa, cilantro, parsley and lemon juice. Season to taste with salt and pepper.
4. Spoon onto pita chips and serve warm or at room temperature.

Lentil Walnut Pâté

Makes 6 to 8 servings

When I make this pâté for my family, there are never any leftovers. And because walnuts are packed with protein, I know they're getting good nutrition. The blend of fresh lemon juice and olive oil gives the lentils and walnuts a rich Mediterranean flavor.

Walnuts

You can maintain the fresh taste of walnuts by storing them in the refrigerator or freezer. Walnuts go rancid when exposed to warm temperatures for long periods of time. Fresh walnuts smell mildly nutty and taste sweet. If your walnuts smell like paint thinner, throw them away. Store walnuts in an airtight container in the refrigerator or in an airtight plastic bag in the freezer for up to 3 months.

• **Food processor**

2	cloves garlic	2
3 cups	cooked red lentils (see page 33), cooled	750 mL
1/2 cup	toasted walnut halves (see tip, page 53)	125 mL
2 tsp	ground cumin	10 mL
1/4 cup	extra virgin olive oil	60 mL
2 tbsp	freshly squeezed lemon juice	30 mL
	Salt and freshly ground black pepper	
	Whole-grain crackers or toast points	
	Chopped fresh parsley	

1. In food processor, combine garlic, lentils, walnuts and cumin; purée until smooth. With the motor running, through the feed tube, drizzle in oil and lemon juice; process until blended. Transfer to a bowl and season to taste with salt and pepper.
2. Spread on crackers and garnish with parsley.

Variation

Substitute green or yellow lentils for the red lentils, or try a combination of all three.

Moroccan Bean Dip (*Bessara*)

Makes 10 to 12 servings

This dip, made with dried fava beans and seasonings, is a great appetizer to serve with pita wedges and vegetable crudités. Accompanied by mint tea or wine of any variety, it's perfect for all types of parties. It also makes an excellent accompaniment, along with couscous and salad, to a lamb or chicken main course.

Fava Beans

Fava beans are also known as broad beans, horse beans, English beans, faba beans and Windsor beans. While their season is fleeting, it's a wonderful treat to cook with fresh fava beans, and worth the effort. When shopping for fava beans, select small pods; those that bulge with beans are past their prime. Two pounds (500 g) of unshelled beans yields about 1 cup (250 mL) shelled.

- **Medium rice cooker; fuzzy logic or on/off**
- **Food processor**

1½ cups	dried fava beans	375 mL
6 cups	water	1.5 L
2	cloves garlic	2
1½ tsp	salt	7 mL
1 tsp	ground cumin	5 mL
½ tsp	sweet paprika	2 mL
½ tsp	cayenne pepper	2 mL
¼ cup	freshly squeezed lemon juice	60 mL
⅓ cup	extra virgin olive oil	75 mL
	Additional sweet paprika	
	Finely chopped fresh parsley	

1. Sort, rinse and soak fava beans (see pages 32–33). Drain and peel off skins.
2. Place soaked fava beans and water in the rice cooker bowl. Set the rice cooker for the Regular cycle and set a timer for 1½ hours.
3. When the timer sounds, check to see if fava beans are tender. If necessary, continue cooking, checking for doneness every 5 minutes. Drain, reserving 3 tbsp (45 mL) cooking liquid.
4. In food processor, combine fava beans, reserved cooking liquid, garlic, salt, cumin, paprika, cayenne and lemon juice; purée until smooth. With the motor running, through the feed tube, drizzle in oil; process until blended.
5. Transfer bean mixture to a large saucepan and heat over medium heat, stirring, until warmed through.
6. Transfer to a shallow serving bowl. Dust with paprika and garnish with parsley.

Perfect Sushi Rice

Makes about 5 cups (1.25 L)

There is a delicate art to making the perfect sushi rice, but this recipe will help you turn out a sweet, sticky rice that will make rolling a breeze.

Mirin

Mirin is a clear, gold Japanese cooking wine that adds a mild sweetness, aroma and luster to many Japanese dishes. It can be found at well-stocked grocery stores and Asian markets. If you can't find it, substitute an equal amount of sake and a pinch of granulated sugar.

- **Medium or large rice cooker; fuzzy logic or on/off**
- **Large, non-metallic, flat-bottomed bowl**
- **Handheld fan**

2 cups	Japanese-style short- or medium-grain japonica rice (such as Calrose)	500 mL
2 cups	water	500 mL
3 tbsp	granulated sugar	45 mL
2 tsp	salt	10 mL
¼ cup	seasoned rice vinegar	60 mL
2 tbsp	mirin	30 mL

1. Place rice in a colander and rinse under cool running water until water runs clear. Let drain for 1 hour.
2. Place rice and water in the rice cooker bowl, swirling to combine. Set the rice cooker for the Regular or Sushi cycle.
3. Meanwhile, in a small saucepan, combine sugar, salt, vinegar and mirin. Heat over medium-low heat until sugar and salt are dissolved (do not let boil). Remove from heat and set aside.
4. When the cycle is completed, transfer rice to the flat-bottomed bowl, spreading it out evenly with a plastic paddle or wooden spoon. Make some space in the center of the rice and slowly add the vinegar mixture. Lift and mix the rice with the paddle, using a slicing motion. Use the handheld fan to cool the rice. Mix, fan and mix again, repeating until all of the grains are coated with vinegar mixture. Cover rice with a damp cloth until ready to use, for up to 1 hour. Do not refrigerate.

Assorted Sushi (*Nigirizushi*)

Makes 40 pieces

Nigirizushi, meaning "hand-formed sushi," consists of a mound of rice with fish draped over top. This most basic form of sushi is traditionally served in pairs.

Tips

When using salmon, it's best to cover the fish with salt and refrigerate it in an airtight container for 1 hour. This adds flavor and firms up the fish slightly, making it easier to cut. Rinse off salt and pat dry.

Yellowtail (hamachi) is a member of the jack family and has a flavor similar to tuna. It is available wild or farmed. Farmed yellowtail has a whiter color because of its higher fat content.

You can buy a nigiri sushi rice mold at Japanese markets.

4 oz	skinless sushi-grade tuna	125 mL
4 oz	skinless sushi-grade salmon (see tip, at left)	125 mL
4 oz	skinless sushi-grade yellowtail (hamachi)	125 mL
	Wasabi paste	
3 cups	Perfect Sushi Rice (page 73), cooled	750 mL
	Soy sauce	
	Pickled ginger slices (*gari*)	

1. Using a very sharp knife, cut tuna, salmon and yellowtail into uniform 2- by 1-inch (5 by 2.5 cm) slices about $\frac{1}{4}$ inch (0.5 cm) thick. Rub a pinch of wasabi paste down the center of each slice.
2. Dampen your hands with water. Scoop up enough sushi rice to fill the center of your palm. Shape rice into a rounded mound and place on a serving plate. Lay a slice of fish on top of mound, wasabi side down. Repeat with the remaining rice and fish.
3. Serve immediately with soy sauce, ginger and more wasabi.

Shrimp and Asparagus Rolls (*Maki*)

Makes 6 servings

In these creative rolls, the freshness of the steamed shrimp and the crunch of the asparagus make for a blissful fusion of flavors and textures.

Tips

Roasted nori (seaweed sheets) can be found at well-stocked grocery stores and Asian markets. Make sure to store it in a sealable food storage bag in the refrigerator, as it can get damp and lose its flavor. Use it within 1 month.

"Julienne" is a culinary term for a preparation in which food is cut into long, thin strips similar to matchsticks.

- **Steamer basket**
- **Sushi mat, covered with plastic wrap**

6	jumbo shrimp, peeled and deveined	6
6	sheets roasted nori (see tip, at left)	6
	Bowl of cold water	
4½ cups	Perfect Sushi Rice (page 73), cooled	1.125 L
12	julienned carrot sticks (about 2 inches/5 cm long)	12
12	spears asparagus, blanched (see tip, page 82) and halved lengthwise	12
	Soy sauce	
	Pickled ginger slices (*gari*)	
	Wasabi paste	

1. Bring a medium saucepan of water to a boil over high heat. Place shrimp in steamer basket and set over boiling water. Cover and steam for 5 to 7 minutes or until pink and opaque. Using a slotted spoon, transfer shrimp to a cutting board. Let cool, then cut in half lengthwise.

2. Lay 1 sheet of nori, shiny side down, on prepared sushi mat, with the long end toward you. Wet your hands with cold water. Working from left to right, spread ¾ cup (175 mL) sushi rice evenly over nori, leaving a 1-inch (2.5 cm) strip at the top. Arrange 2 shrimp halves, 2 carrot strips and 2 asparagus spears in a thin horizontal line across the middle of the rice.

3. Wet your hands again and roll the sushi mat firmly away from you, using the mat and plastic wrap to guide the nori roll and peeling the mat and plastic back as you go, rolling to the top edge. Rub a small amount of cold water on the edge of the nori and wrap the nori around to complete the sushi roll. Press the mat and plastic around nori to seal the roll. Let rest, seam side down, for 5 minutes.

4. Peel off sushi mat. Dip a sharp knife in water and slice sushi roll into 8 pieces.

5. Repeat steps 2 to 4 with the remaining ingredients. Serve immediately with soy sauce, ginger and wasabi.

Tuna Rolls (*Maki*)

Makes 4 to 6 servings

The tuna roll is a favorite in any sushi bar. For those who love spicy tuna, try tossing the tuna in Sriracha sauce for that extra kick.

Tip

Tuna contains omega-3 fatty acids, which have been proven to lower blood pressure and assist with cardiovascular health. It is also packed with protein and low in calories — a delicious *and* nutritious treat.

- **Sushi mat, covered with plastic wrap**

4	sheets roasted nori (see tip, page 75), cut in half crosswise	4
	Bowl of cold water	
3 cups	Perfect Sushi Rice (page 73), cooled	750 mL
4 tsp	wasabi paste	20 mL
8 oz	skinless sushi-grade yellowfin or ahi tuna, cut into ¾-inch (2 cm) strips	250 g
	Soy sauce	
	Pickled ginger slices (*gari*)	
	Additional wasabi paste	

1. Lay 1 sheet of nori, shiny side down, on prepared sushi mat, with the long end toward you. Wet your hands with cold water. Working from left to right, spread ¾ cup (175 mL) sushi rice evenly over nori, leaving a 1-inch (2.5 cm) strip at the top. Brush ½ tsp (5 mL) wasabi paste in a thin horizontal line across the rice, about 1 inch (2.5 cm) from the side nearest you. Arrange one-quarter of the tuna in a horizontal line on top of the wasabi, cutting tuna as necessary to fit.

2. Wet your hands again and roll the sushi mat firmly away from you, using the mat and plastic wrap to guide the nori roll and peeling the mat and plastic back as you go, rolling to the top edge. Rub a small amount of cold water on the edge of the nori and wrap the nori around to complete the sushi roll. Press the mat and plastic around nori to seal the roll. Let rest, seam side down, for 5 minutes.

3. Peel off sushi mat. Dip a sharp knife in water and slice sushi roll into 6 pieces.

4. Repeat steps 1 to 3 with the remaining ingredients. Serve immediately with soy sauce, ginger and wasabi.

Variations

Salmon Rolls: Replace the tuna with 8 oz (250 g) sushi-grade salmon, cut into ¾-inch (2 cm) strips.

Cucumber Rolls: Replace the tuna with 2 Japanese cucumbers, cut into long sticks.

California Rolls

Makes 4 to 6 servings

California rolls are a variation on the basic crab roll, but rolled inside out and with avocado added to the filling. Because the rice is on the outside of the seaweed, these rolls have a pleasing texture that is popular with many sushi eaters.

Tips

Imitation crab has become prevalent at sushi restaurants everywhere. While this is an adequate choice for everyday, I love to splurge on fresh crab, especially when entertaining.

As you cut the avocado, sprinkle it with a little lemon juice to prevent it from browning.

• Sushi mat, covered with plastic wrap

¾ cup	cooked crabmeat or imitation crab	175 mL
2 tbsp	mayonnaise	30 mL
½ tsp	salt	2 mL
4	sheets roasted nori (see tip, page 75)	4
	Bowl of cold water	
4 cups	Perfect Sushi Rice (page 73), cooled	1 L
4 tbsp	toasted sesame seeds (see tip, page 54)	60 mL
1	avocado, peeled and cut into strips (see tip, at left)	1
	Soy sauce	
	Pickled ginger slices (*gari*)	
	Wasabi paste	

1. In a small bowl, combine crab, mayonnaise and salt. Set aside.
2. Lay 1 sheet of nori, shiny side down, on prepared sushi mat, with the long end toward you. Wet your hands with cold water. Working from left to right, spread 1 cup (250 mL) sushi rice evenly over nori, leaving a 1-inch (2.5 cm) strip at the top. Sprinkle 1 tbsp (15 mL) sesame seeds evenly over rice.
3. Turn the nori over so that the seaweed is on top. Arrange one-quarter of the crab mixture and avocado strips in a thin horizontal line across the middle of the seaweed.
4. Wet your hands again and roll the sushi mat firmly away from you, using the mat and plastic wrap to guide the nori roll and peeling the mat and plastic back as you go, rolling to the top edge. Rub a small amount of cold water on the edge of the nori and wrap the nori around to complete the sushi roll. Press the mat and plastic around rice to seal the roll. Let rest, seam side down, for 5 minutes.
5. Peel off sushi mat. Dip a sharp knife in water and slice sushi roll into 8 pieces.
6. Repeat steps 2 to 5 with the remaining ingredients. Serve immediately with soy sauce, ginger and wasabi.

Variation

Tempura Rolls: After cutting each roll into 8 pieces, tuck a piece of shrimp tempura on top of the crab and avocado in each piece, letting it stick out the top.

Sushi Bowl (*Chirashizushi*)

Makes 4 to 6 servings

Chirashizushi **translates as "scattered sushi." If you're craving sushi but don't have the time to roll, this is an easy and very satisfying dish.**

Tips

You can buy powdered dashi mix at Asian markets, but I suggest making it from scratch (see page 185), as it's simple and the taste will be superior. If you can't find either the powdered mix or the bonito shavings you need to make dashi, you can substitute fish stock.

When buying sashimi, make sure to ask if it's sashimi-grade fish. Avoid any fish that is discolored or has a strong "fishy" smell. Return home as soon as possible after purchasing sashimi and store it in the refrigerator. I always strive to use sashimi the same day I purchase it.

Be creative and experiment with different types of sashimi-grade fish. Or add ½ cup (125 mL) sliced cooked meat.

8 oz	skinless sashimi-grade tuna	250 g
3 tbsp	soy sauce, divided	45 mL
8	dried shiitake mushrooms	8
2 cups	warm water	500 mL
1 tbsp	granulated sugar, divided	15 mL
¼ cup	dashi (see tip, at left)	60 mL
1 tsp	mirin	5 mL
2	large eggs	2
2 tbsp	vegetable oil, divided	30 mL
5 cups	Perfect Sushi Rice (page 73), cooled	1.25 L
4 to 6	cooked peeled jumbo shrimp, butterflied	4 to 6
1	cucumber, peeled and julienned (see tip, page 75)	1
2 tbsp	sesame seeds	30 mL
2 tbsp	pickled ginger slices (*gari*), shredded	30 mL
	Soy sauce	
	Wasabi paste	

1. Cut tuna into slices ¼ to ½ inch (0.5 to 1 cm) thick and 1 to 1½ inches (2.5 to 4 cm) long. Place in a small glass bowl and add 2 tbsp (30 mL) of the soy sauce. Cover and refrigerate for 10 minutes.
2. Place shiitake mushrooms in a bowl and cover with warm water. Let stand for 15 to 20 minutes or until mushrooms are rehydrated. Drain, reserving ⅔ cup (150 mL) of the soaking liquid. Squeeze out excess water from mushrooms, remove stems and slice mushrooms into thin strips.
3. In a small saucepan, combine mushrooms, reserved soaking liquid, 2 tsp (10 mL) of the sugar, dashi, the remaining soy sauce and mirin. Bring to a boil over medium-high heat. Reduce heat and simmer for about 10 minutes or until almost all of the liquid has evaporated. Transfer to a bowl and set aside.
4. In a small bowl, beat eggs and the remaining sugar. In a medium nonstick skillet, heat 1 tbsp (15 mL) oil over medium heat. Pour in ¼ cup (60 mL) of the egg mixture and cook, without stirring, until bottom is set. Turn omelet over and cook until set. Transfer omelet to a plate. Repeat with the remaining oil and egg mixture. Cut omelets into thin strips.
5. Divide sushi rice among 4 to 6 serving bowls. Spread mushroom mixture on top of rice. Place omelet strips, shrimp and cucumber on top of mushrooms. Top with sashimi. Sprinkle with sesame seeds and place pickled ginger on the side of the bowl. Serve immediately with soy sauce and wasabi.

Stuffed Japanese Rice Balls (*Onigiri*)

Makes 8 servings

These portable rice balls are a common staple of Japanese cuisine and are often packed in Japanese lunch boxes, or *bento*. Take liberties with the ingredients, as you can put almost anything in them. And get the kids involved in this one!

Tips

Bonito shavings (dry fish flakes) are made from a type of tuna and are the base for many Japanese sauces and stocks. They have a strong, salty flavor and can be found at Asian markets.

Onigiri is a great treat for school lunches. Get creative and use cut-up nori to make smiley faces or even cat faces, complete with nori whiskers!

¼ cup	bonito shavings (dried fish flakes)	60 mL
1 tbsp	soy sauce	15 mL
½ tsp	salt	2 mL
1½ cups	cold water	375 mL
4 cups	Perfect Sushi Rice (page 73), cooled	1 L
2	sheets roasted nori (see tip, page 75), cut into ½-inch (1 cm) strips	2
2 tbsp	toasted sesame seeds (see tip, page 54)	30 mL

1. In a bowl, combine bonito shavings and soy sauce until bonito shavings are moistened.

2. In another bowl, dissolve salt in cold water. Dampen your hands and divide sushi rice into 8 portions. Working with one portion at a time, divide rice into 2 half-balls. Make a dimple in the center of one half and fill with a heaping teaspoon (5 mL) of bonito shavings. Cover with the other half and press lightly to enclose the filling. Gently form into a pyramid. Repeat with the remaining rice and bonito shavings.

3. Wrap each rice pyramid with a strip of nori, using a bit of salted water to seal the ends. Sprinkle with sesame seeds. Serve immediately or wrap in plastic wrap and store in the refrigerator for up to 2 days.

Variations

Instead of the bonito, try filling the rice balls with one of these other classic Japanese fillings: pickled plum (*umeboshi*), flaked cooked salted salmon (*shake* or *shiozake*), cooked salty cod roe (*tarako*) or chopped pickles (*tsukemono*).

Experiment with non-traditional fillings, such as cooked ground beef, chicken or turkey seasoned with curry, or canned tuna mixed with mayonnaise.

Rice-Stuffed Tofu Pouches (*Inarizushi*)

Makes 6 servings

These stuffed pouches are super-portable, making for a yummy and unique lunch-on-the-go. If you're eating them at home, serve them with soy sauce, pickled ginger and wasabi.

Tips

You can buy powdered dashi mix at Asian markets, but I suggest making it from scratch (see page 185), as it's simple and the taste will be superior.

Deep-fried tofu cakes (*abubrage*) can be found at Asian markets. Look for them in cans or fresh in the refrigerated section. For convenience, buy extra to keep on hand in your pantry (canned) or freezer (fresh).

For information about rice cooker sizes, see page 13.

• **Large rice cooker with a steamer basket; fuzzy logic or on/off**

2½ cups	Perfect Sushi Rice (page 73), cooled	625 mL
3 tbsp	toasted sesame seeds (see tip, page 54)	45 mL
3 cups	water	750 mL
6	shiitake mushrooms, stemmed and finely chopped	6
1	carrot, diced	1
½ tsp	toasted sesame oil	2 mL
3 tbsp	granulated sugar	45 mL
½ tsp	salt	2 mL
1 cup	dashi (see tip, at left) or chicken broth	250 mL
¼ cup	soy sauce	60 mL
3 tbsp	seasoned rice vinegar	45 mL
6	deep-fried tofu cakes (*abubrage*), each about 2 inches (5 cm) square, cut in half	6
	Additional toasted sesame seeds	
	Daikon radish sprouts	

1. In a large bowl, combine sushi rice and sesame seeds. Set aside.
2. Place water in the rice cooker bowl. Set the rice cooker for the Regular or Steam cycle.
3. Place mushrooms and carrot in the steamer basket. When the water in the rice cooker comes to a boil, place the steamer basket in the rice cooker and close the cover. Set a timer for 20 minutes.
4. When the timer sounds, transfer vegetables to a small bowl. Add rice mixture and sesame oil; toss to coat. Set aside.
5. In a medium saucepan, combine sugar, salt, dashi, soy sauce and vinegar. Bring to a boil over high heat. Add tofu cakes, reduce heat to medium-low, cover and simmer for 15 to 20 minutes or until liquid is almost completely absorbed. Transfer tofu cakes to a plate and let cool slightly.
6. Using your hands, open each tofu cake into a pouch and stuff it with rice mixture, dividing mixture equally among pouches. Top with sesame seeds and garnish with daikon radish sprouts.

Salads

Garlic Steak Warm Rice Salad

Makes 4 entrée servings

Does garlic steak even require an introduction? Any beef lover will eat this delicious salad quickly and be asking for more. Be prepared and make extra!

Tips

To blanch asparagus, bring a small saucepan of water to a boil over high heat. Add asparagus and boil for 2 to 4 minutes or until bright green and tender-crisp. Using a slotted spoon, transfer asparagus to a bowl of ice water and let cool completely. Drain well, then chop.

It's important to cut steak across the grain to ensure tenderness.

Arugula

Arugula is a tangy, zesty salad green. In Roman times, it was grown for both its leaves and its seed, which was used to flavor oils. Arugula can be eaten raw in salads or added to stir-fries, soups and pasta sauces.

- **Broiling pan**

Steak

1 lb	boneless beef steak(s) (such as top or strip loin, rib eye or tenderloin), about 1 inch (2.5 cm) thick	500 g
4	cloves garlic, minced	4
¼ cup	red wine vinegar	60 mL
½ cup	extra virgin olive oil	125 mL
	Garlic powder	

Dressing

2 tsp	salt	10 mL
	Freshly ground black pepper	
½ cup	red wine vinegar	125 mL
3 tbsp	freshly squeezed lemon juice	45 mL
2 tsp	liquid honey	10 mL
1 cup	extra virgin olive oil	250 mL

Salad

6	spears asparagus, tough ends removed, blanched (see tip, at left) and chopped	6
2 cups	cooked long-grain white rice (see page 20), kept warm	500 mL
2 cups	arugula	500 mL
½ cup	cherry tomatoes, halved	125 mL
½ cup	chopped yellow bell pepper	125 mL
⅓ cup	finely chopped fresh flat-leaf (Italian) parsley	75 mL

1. *Steak:* Place steak in a deep pan or bowl. Add garlic, vinegar and oil. Generously sprinkle each side of steak with garlic powder. Cover and refrigerate for 2 hours, turning once.

2. Meanwhile, preheat broiler. Remove steak from marinade, discarding marinade, and place on broiling pan. Broil for 4 to 7 minutes per side for medium-rare or to desired doneness. Transfer to a cutting board; let stand for 10 minutes, then cut across the grain into thin slices.

3. *Dressing:* In a small bowl, whisk together salt, pepper to taste, vinegar, lemon juice and honey. Gradually whisk in oil until well blended.

4. *Salad:* In a serving bowl, combine asparagus, rice, arugula, tomatoes, yellow pepper and parsley. Add all but 2 tbsp (30 mL) dressing and toss to combine. Arrange steak on top of salad. Drizzle the remaining dressing over steak.

Arborio Rice Salad with Asparagus

Makes 6 side servings

I love asparagus so much that I could never have enough ways to serve it. This is one of my favorite dishes to bring to potluck picnics, and I am always asked to share the recipe.

Tips

Because of its high starch content, Arborio rice can't be steamed in a rice cooker in the traditional fashion. Instead, it's boiled for 10 minutes.

The tough end of an asparagus stalk naturally breaks off when you bend it, but for a prettier presentation, you can slice it off with a paring knife before chopping the rest of the stalk.

● **Large rice cooker; fuzzy logic or on/off**

Rice

4 cups	water	1 L
¾ cup	Arborio rice	175 mL

Dressing

2	cloves garlic, minced	2
1 tsp	finely chopped fresh thyme	5 mL
½ tsp	salt	2 mL
¼ tsp	freshly ground black pepper	1 mL
3 tbsp	red wine vinegar	45 mL
2 tbsp	freshly squeezed lemon juice	30 mL
1 tsp	Dijon mustard	5 mL
¼ cup	extra virgin olive oil	60 mL

Salad

6	spears asparagus, tough ends removed, blanched (see tip, page 82) and chopped	6
3	green onions (green and white parts), chopped	3
1 cup	cherry tomatoes, halved	250 mL
¼ cup	toasted pine nuts (see tip, page 52)	60 mL
1 tbsp	finely chopped fresh parsley	15 mL
1 tbsp	finely grated lemon zest	15 mL
	Additional toasted pine nuts	

1. *Rice:* Place water in the rice cooker bowl. Set the rice cooker for the Regular cycle. When the water comes to a boil, add rice. Set a timer for 10 minutes.

2. When the timer sounds, check to make sure rice is al dente. If necessary, continue cooking, checking for doneness every 5 minutes. Drain in a fine-mesh sieve and rinse under cool water. Drain well and set aside.

3. *Dressing:* In a small bowl, whisk together garlic, thyme, salt, pepper, vinegar, lemon juice and mustard. Gradually whisk in oil until well blended.

4. *Salad:* In a serving bowl, combine rice, asparagus, green onions, tomatoes, pine nuts, parsley and lemon zest. Add dressing and toss to combine. Cover and refrigerate for at least 30 minutes, until chilled, or for up to 2 hours. Garnish with pine nuts.

Chinese Black Rice Salad with Orange and Avocado

Makes 6 side servings

This delicious salad dresses up any table. The combination of contrasting colors, creamy textures and bright flavors will be the hit of your next lunch gathering.

Tips

To blanch snow peas, bring a small saucepan of water to a boil over high heat. Add trimmed peas and boil for 1 minute or until tender-crisp. Using a slotted spoon, transfer peas to a bowl of ice water and let cool completely. Drain well, then thinly slice.

To toast sliced almonds, spread them in a single layer on a baking sheet. Bake in a 325°F (160°C) oven, stirring often, for 5 to 10 minutes or until light brown and fragrant. Immediately transfer to a bowl and let cool.

Dressing

1 tbsp	granulated sugar	15 mL
2 tsp	grated gingerroot	10 mL
½ tsp	salt	2 mL
½ tsp	freshly ground black pepper	2 mL
3 tbsp	soy sauce	45 mL
3 tbsp	freshly squeezed orange juice	45 mL
1 tbsp	rice vinegar	15 mL
2½ tbsp	extra virgin olive oil	37 mL
2 tsp	toasted sesame oil	10 mL

Salad

2 cups	cooked forbidden black rice (page 20), cooled, rinsed and drained	500 mL
1 cup	finely chopped orange bell pepper	250 mL
¾ cup	cubed avocado	175 mL
¾ cup	thinly sliced blanched snow peas (see tip, at left)	175 mL
½ cup	drained canned mandarin oranges	125 mL
¼ cup	drained canned sliced water chestnuts	60 mL
¼ cup	finely chopped green onions (white and green parts)	60 mL
2 tbsp	finely chopped fresh cilantro	30 mL
¼ cup	toasted sliced almonds (see tip, at left)	60 mL
2 tbsp	toasted sesame seeds (see tip, page 54)	30 mL
	Additional chopped fresh cilantro and toasted sesame seeds	

Gingerroot

Fresh gingerroot is a knobby root with thick, globular offshoots. It has a tangy, sweet and somewhat spicy taste. Before grating fresh ginger, try putting it in the freezer for 1 hour. This will dry it out a bit, making it easier to grate.

1. *Dressing:* In a small bowl, whisk together sugar, ginger, salt, pepper, soy sauce, orange juice and vinegar. Gradually whisk in olive oil and sesame oil until well blended.

2. *Salad:* In a serving bowl, combine rice, orange pepper, avocado, snow peas, oranges, water chestnuts, green onions and cilantro. Add dressing and toss to combine. Cover and refrigerate for at least 30 minutes, until chilled, or for up to 2 hours. Just before serving, add almonds and sesame seeds; toss to combine. Garnish with cilantro and sesame seeds.

Variations

Add 1 cup (250 mL) shredded cooked rotisserie-style chicken when tossing the salad with the dressing.

Substitute any non-glutinous rice, such as brown kalijira or long-grain brown rice, for the forbidden black rice.

Forbidden Black Rice Thai Salad

Makes 4 to 6 side servings

The rice may be forbidden, but this salad is a must-have. The combination of papaya, ginger, chile pepper and fresh mint really gives it some *pow*!

Tips

Rinsing and draining the rice after it's been cooked helps to eliminate starch and loosen it before it is tossed with other ingredients.

If you prefer more heat in the dressing, leave the seeds in the chile pepper. But beware — they pack a fiery punch.

Dressing

½	dried Thai chile pepper, seeded (see tip, at left) and finely chopped	½
2 tbsp	packed brown sugar	30 mL
2 tsp	minced gingerroot	10 mL
3 tbsp	freshly squeezed lime juice	45 mL
2 tbsp	fish sauce (nam pla)	30 mL
¼ cup	extra virgin olive oil	60 mL

Salad

2	green onions (white and green parts), finely chopped	2
1	papaya, diced	1
2 cups	cooked forbidden black rice (see page 20), cooled, rinsed and drained	500 mL
1 cup	chopped red bell pepper	250 mL
¼ cup	finely chopped fresh mint	60 mL
¼ cup	toasted pine nuts (see tip, page 52)	60 mL

1. *Dressing:* In a small bowl, whisk together chile pepper, brown sugar, ginger, lime juice and fish sauce. Gradually whisk in oil until well blended.
2. *Salad:* In a serving bowl, combine green onions, papaya, rice, red pepper, mint and pine nuts. Add dressing and toss to combine.

Variations

Forbidden Black Rice Thai Steak Salad: Use only half the dressing to toss the salad. Arrange thin slices of grilled steak on top of the salad. Drizzle the remaining dressing over the steak.

If you can't find forbidden black rice, substitute Arborio rice.

Asian Japonica Rice Salad with Edamame

Makes 6 side servings

Fresh lime juice, real maple syrup and just enough cayenne pepper give this refreshing salad some real zing.

Tips

Tamari is made with more soybeans than ordinary soy sauce, resulting in a smoother, more balanced, more complex flavor. It is available at well-stocked grocery stores and Asian markets.

To cook the frozen shelled edamame, simply follow the package directions, then drain and let them cool.

Black Sesame Seeds

Black sesame seeds make for a beautiful presentation and, as a bonus, contain calcium and protein. They are used in Chinese medicine to help increase liver and kidney function. Look for them at gourmet specialty shops and Asian markets. You may substitute white sesame seeds, if you prefer.

Dressing

2	cloves garlic, minced	2
1 tbsp	minced gingerroot	15 mL
1/2 tsp	salt	2 mL
1/4 tsp	freshly ground black pepper	1 mL
1/8 tsp	cayenne pepper	0.5 mL
2 tbsp	rice vinegar	30 mL
2 tbsp	freshly squeezed lime juice	30 mL
2 tbsp	water	30 mL
1 1/2 tbsp	tamari	22 mL
2 tsp	pure maple syrup or light (fancy) molasses	10 mL
1/4 cup	extra virgin olive oil	60 mL
1 tsp	toasted sesame oil	5 mL

Salad

1	carrot, diced	1
2 cups	cooked black japonica rice (see page 20), cooled, rinsed and drained	500 mL
1 cup	frozen shelled edamame, cooked (see tip, at left)	250 mL
1 cup	diagonally sliced celery	250 mL
1/2 cup	chopped red bell pepper	125 mL
1/2 cup	diagonally sliced green onions (white and green parts)	125 mL
1 tbsp	toasted black sesame seeds (see tip, page 54)	15 mL
	Additional diagonally sliced green onions and toasted black sesame seeds	

1. *Dressing:* In a small bowl, whisk together garlic, ginger, salt, black pepper, cayenne, vinegar, lime juice, water, tamari and maple syrup. Gradually whisk in olive oil and sesame oil until well blended.

2. *Salad:* In a serving bowl, combine carrot, rice, edamame, celery, red pepper, green onions and sesame seeds. Add dressing and toss to combine. Cover and refrigerate for at least 30 minutes, until chilled, or for up to 2 hours. Garnish with green onions and sesame seeds.

Minted Red Rice Salad
with Shallot Dressing

Makes 8 side servings

I just love red cargo rice because it tastes great, looks pretty and is so good for you. I like to make this tasty salad with fresh mint and parsley from my herb garden, to give it that homegrown feeling.

Shallots

Shallots are a member of the lily family and are closely related to the onion, but have a cluster of small bulbs, similar to garlic. They have a papery, reddish-brown skin and white flesh that is sweeter than even mild onions. Shallots are a culinary darling among chefs because of their firm texture and sweet, aromatic yet pungent flavor and firm texture. They are also low in calories!

Dressing

1 tbsp	finely minced shallots	15 mL
1 tsp	granulated sugar	5 mL
½ tsp	salt	2 mL
¼ tsp	freshly ground black pepper	1 mL
¼ cup	freshly squeezed lemon juice	60 mL
2 tbsp	water	30 mL
2 tbsp	red wine vinegar	30 mL
½ cup	extra virgin olive oil	125 mL

Salad

3 cups	cooked red cargo rice (see page 20), cooled, rinsed and drained	750 mL
1 cup	diced seeded cucumbers	250 mL
¼ cup	finely chopped fresh parsley	60 mL
¼ cup	finely chopped fresh mint	60 mL

1. *Dressing:* In a small bowl, whisk together shallots, sugar, salt, pepper, lemon juice, water and vinegar. Gradually whisk in oil until well blended.
2. *Salad:* In a serving bowl, combine rice, cucumbers, parsley and mint. Add dressing and toss to combine. Cover and refrigerate for at least 30 minutes, until chilled, or for up to 2 hours.

Variations

If you're pressed for time, try using Bhutanese red rice, which requires only 25 to 30 minutes cooking time (red cargo rice takes 45 to 60 minutes).

This salad would be delicious with some leftover grilled chicken thrown in.

Wehani Rice Salad with Mango

Makes 6 side servings

My producer, Melanie, introduced me to a version of this salad when we were shooting a TV show outside Honolulu a few years ago. The crisp, fresh flavors bring me (and my guests) back to the islands every time I serve it!

Tip

Rinsing and draining the rice after it's been cooked helps to eliminate starch and loosen it before it is tossed with other ingredients.

Watercress

Packed with phytochemicals and antioxidants, watercress packs a lot of nutrition into its delicate leaves. In fact, some studies indicate that a regular consumption of watercress may reduce your risk of developing certain types of cancer.

Dressing

½ tsp	finely grated orange zest	2 mL
¼ cup	freshly squeezed orange juice	60 mL
3 tbsp	freshly squeezed lemon juice	45 mL
2 tbsp	balsamic vinegar	30 mL
¼ cup	extra virgin olive oil	60 mL
2 tsp	toasted sesame oil	10 mL
	Salt and freshly ground black pepper	

Salad

2 cups	cooked wehani rice (see page 20), cooled, rinsed and drained	500 mL
½ cup	chopped red bell pepper	125 mL
½ cup	chopped green bell pepper	125 mL
2	mangos, diced	2
1 cup	trimmed watercress	250 mL

1. *Dressing:* In a small bowl, whisk together orange zest, orange juice, lemon juice and vinegar. Gradually whisk in olive oil and sesame oil until well blended. Season to taste with salt and pepper.

2. *Salad:* In a serving bowl, combine rice, red pepper and green pepper. Add dressing and toss to combine. Just before serving, add mangos and watercress; toss to combine.

Variation

If you're pressed for time, try using long-grain white rice or Thai jasmine rice, which require only 25 to 35 minutes cooking time (wehani rice takes 60 to 70 minutes).

Basmati Rice Salad with Dried Apricots

Makes 6 side servings

Although I have yet to visit Marrakesh, this is the salad I fantasize making with the bounty of ingredients I could find strolling through the stalls in the marketplace.

Tip

To toast walnut and pecan halves, spread nuts in a single layer on a baking sheet. Bake in a 350°F (180°C) oven, stirring often, for 5 to 10 minutes or until light brown and fragrant. Immediately transfer to a bowl and let cool before chopping.

Dressing

1/2 tsp	salt	2 mL
1/2 tsp	ground ginger	2 mL
1/4 tsp	ground turmeric	1 mL
1/4 tsp	ground cumin	1 mL
1/4 tsp	ground cinnamon	1 mL
1/4 tsp	freshly ground black pepper	1 mL
1/4 cup	freshly squeezed lemon juice	60 mL
2 tbsp	plain yogurt	30 mL
2 1/2 tsp	liquid honey	12 mL
1/4 cup	extra virgin olive oil	60 mL
1 tbsp	walnut oil	15 mL

Salad

2 cups	cooked brown basmati rice (see page 20), cooled, rinsed and drained	500 mL
1 cup	chopped celery	250 mL
1/2 cup	pecan halves, toasted (see tip, at left) and coarsely chopped	125 mL
1/2 cup	walnut halves, toasted and coarsely chopped	125 mL
1/2 cup	chopped dried apricots	125 mL
	Baby spinach leaves	

1. *Dressing:* In a small bowl, whisk together salt, ginger, turmeric, cumin, cinnamon, pepper, lemon juice, yogurt and honey. Gradually whisk in olive oil and walnut oil until well blended.
2. *Salad:* In a large bowl, combine rice, celery, pecans, walnuts and apricots. Add dressing and toss to combine. Serve immediately or cover and refrigerate for at least 30 minutes, until chilled, or for up to 2 hours. Serve on a bed of baby spinach.

Variation

Substitute brown kalijira rice for the basmati rice.

Chickpea Basmati Salad

Makes 6 side servings

I discovered this refreshing salad at the home of a Middle Eastern friend, who had learned it from her mother. It is quick to make and always impresses.

Toasted Sesame Oil

Toasted sesame oil (also called Asian sesame oil) is darker and has a stronger flavor than regular sesame oil. It is used in small quantities for flavoring and not for cooking. It is available at well-stocked grocery stores and Asian markets.

Dressing

1	clove garlic, minced	1
½ tsp	salt	2 mL
¼ tsp	ground cumin	1 mL
¼ tsp	ground cardamom	1 mL
¼ tsp	ground turmeric	1 mL
¼ tsp	freshly ground black pepper	1 mL
3 tbsp	freshly squeezed lemon juice	45 mL
1 tbsp	white wine vinegar	15 mL
¼ cup	extra virgin olive oil	60 mL
1 tbsp	toasted sesame oil	15 mL

Salad

1	can (14 to 19 oz/398 to 540 mL) chickpeas, drained and rinsed	1
2 cups	cooked white basmati rice (see page 20), cooled, rinsed and drained	500 mL
1 cup	chopped red bell pepper	250 mL
1 cup	chopped yellow bell pepper	250 mL
½ cup	chopped celery	125 mL
¼ cup	chopped fresh parsley	60 mL
	Arugula	

1. *Dressing:* In a small bowl, whisk together garlic, salt, cumin, cardamom, turmeric, pepper, lemon juice and vinegar. Gradually whisk in olive oil and sesame oil until well blended.

2. *Salad:* In a large bowl, combine chickpeas, rice, red pepper, yellow pepper, celery and parsley. Add dressing and toss to combine. Cover and refrigerate for at least 30 minutes, until chilled, or for up to 2 hours. Serve on a bed of arugula.

Variation

Substitute brown basmati rice for the white basmati.

Warm Jasmine Rice Salad with Shrimp and Thai Herbs

Makes 8 side servings or 4 entrée servings

This gem is a great complement to any Asian-themed meal and also makes a light and healthy main dish. You may want to make a little extra, as my guests always ask for seconds when I serve it.

Mesclun Salad Greens

Mesclun salad greens are a mix of assorted small, young salad leaves. The traditional mix, which originated in Provence, France, includes chervil, arugula, leafy lettuces and endive in equal proportions. In North America, you may also find a mix by this name containing spinach, frisée, radicchio and other leafy greens.

Dressing

2 tsp	minced gingerroot	10 mL
2 tsp	packed brown sugar	10 mL
2 tbsp	freshly squeezed lime juice	30 mL
2 tbsp	fish sauce (nam pla)	30 mL
½ tsp	sambal oelek or other hot Asian chili sauce	2 mL
¼ cup	vegetable oil	60 mL
1 tsp	toasted sesame oil	5 mL

Salad

12	cooked peeled medium shrimp	12
2 cups	cooked Thai jasmine rice (see page 20), kept warm	500 mL
⅓ cup	chopped seeded cucumber	75 mL
⅓ cup	chopped red bell pepper	75 mL
¼ cup	finely chopped fresh cilantro	60 mL
3 tbsp	dry-roasted peanuts, crushed	45 mL
	Mesclun salad greens	

1. *Dressing:* In a small bowl, whisk together ginger, brown sugar, lime juice, fish sauce and sambal oelek. Gradually whisk in vegetable oil and sesame oil until well blended.
2. *Salad:* In a large bowl, combine shrimp, rice, cucumber, red pepper, cilantro and peanuts. Add dressing and toss to combine. Serve immediately on a bed of salad greens.

Variation

For even more color and nutrients, add 1 cup (250 mL) sliced mango or papaya.

Shrimp Jambalaya Salad with Wild Pecan Rice

Makes 6 entrée servings

Nutty, crunchy, zesty and spicy, this mouthwatering salad makes a terrific entrée. It brings together so many familiar flavors of the Big Easy that you will be whistling Dixie for another helping.

Tip

This salad is perfect when you have leftover grilled shrimp. Skip step 1 and add the grilled shrimp with the other salad ingredients.

Shrimp

2 tbsp	extra virgin olive oil	30 mL
2	cloves garlic, minced	2
¼ cup	finely chopped onion	60 mL
18	medium shrimp, peeled and deveined	18
½	bay leaf	½
1 tsp	dried thyme	5 mL

Dressing

1	clove garlic, minced	1
½ tsp	salt	2 mL
¼ tsp	freshly ground black pepper	1 mL
¼ tsp	dried oregano	1 mL
2 tbsp	red wine vinegar	30 mL
1 tbsp	freshly squeezed lemon juice	15 mL
1 tsp	coarse-grain mustard	5 mL
½ tsp	hot pepper sauce	2 mL
¼ cup	extra virgin olive oil	60 mL

Salad

1	tomato, seeded and chopped	1
2 cups	cooked wild pecan rice (see page 20), cooled, rinsed and drained	500 mL
1 cup	finely chopped green bell pepper	250 mL
½ cup	diagonally sliced celery	125 mL
½ cup	finely chopped fresh parsley	125 mL

1. *Shrimp:* In a large nonstick skillet, heat oil over medium-high heat. Sauté garlic and onion for about 2 minutes or until onion is softened. Add shrimp, bay leaf and thyme; sauté for about 4 minutes or until shrimp are pink and opaque. Transfer to a serving bowl and set aside.
2. *Dressing:* In a small bowl, whisk together garlic, salt, pepper, oregano, vinegar, lemon juice, mustard and hot pepper sauce. Gradually whisk in oil until well blended.
3. *Salad:* Add tomato, rice, green pepper, celery and parsley to the shrimp. Add dressing and toss to combine. Serve warm or cover and refrigerate for at least 30 minutes, until chilled, or for up to 2 hours.

Turkey and Wild Rice Curry Salad

Makes 4 entrée servings

This salad is great for a summertime lunch. The cool fresh fruit and vegetables — and just enough curry — give it an exotic feel.

Tips

Rinsing the rice and draining it after it's been cooked helps to eliminate starch and loosen before tossing with other ingredients.

"Julienne" is a culinary term for a preparation in which food is cut into long, thin strips similar to matchsticks.

To toast almonds, spread them in a single layer on a baking sheet. Bake in a 325°F (160°C) oven for 5 to 10 minutes or until light brown and fragrant. Stir frequently to ensure even toasting.

Dressing

1	clove garlic, minced	1
1 tbsp	granulated sugar	15 mL
1 tsp	mild curry powder	5 mL
½ tsp	salt	2 mL
¼ tsp	freshly ground black pepper	1 mL
¼ cup	white wine vinegar	60 mL
2 tsp	Dijon mustard	10 mL
¼ cup	extra virgin olive oil	60 mL

Salad

2 cups	cooked wild rice (see page 20), cooled, rinsed and drained	500 mL
1½ cups	cubed cooked turkey	375 mL
1 cup	red seedless grapes	250 mL
1 cup	chopped celery	250 mL
½ cup	julienned carrots (see tip, at left)	125 mL
½ cup	toasted sliced almonds (see tip, at left)	125 mL
2 tbsp	finely chopped red onion	30 mL

1. *Dressing:* In a small bowl, whisk together garlic, sugar, curry powder, salt, pepper, vinegar and mustard. Gradually whisk in oil until well blended.
2. *Salad:* In a serving bowl, combine rice, turkey, grapes, celery, carrots, almonds and red onion. Add dressing and toss to combine.

French Barley Salad

Makes 8 side servings or 4 entrée servings

This is a great salad for a warm day, delicious on the side but hearty enough for a main dish. The combination of barley and green beans (I prefer them with a slight crunch) gives it a rich flavor and texture, while the dressing, full of garden-fresh herbs, lends a refreshing zest.

Tip

To blanch green beans, bring a small saucepan of water to a boil over high heat. Add green beans and boil for 1 minute or until tender-crisp. Using a slotted spoon, transfer green beans to a bowl of ice water and let cool completely. Drain well, then slice.

Dressing

2 tbsp	finely chopped fresh thyme	30 mL
2 tbsp	finely chopped fresh parsley	30 mL
1 tbsp	finely minced shallots	15 mL
2 tbsp	sherry vinegar	30 mL
4 tsp	Champagne vinegar (see tips, page 106)	20 mL
4 tsp	Dijon mustard	20 mL
⅔ cup	extra virgin olive oil	150 mL
	Salt and freshly ground black pepper	

Salad

3 cups	cooked hulled barley (see page 27), cooled	750 mL
2 cups	French green beans, blanched (see tip, at left) and sliced lengthwise	500 mL
1 cup	chopped red bell pepper	250 mL
1 cup	diced carrots	250 mL

1. *Dressing:* In a small bowl, whisk together thyme, parsley, shallots, sherry vinegar, Champagne vinegar and mustard. Gradually whisk in oil until well blended. Season to taste with salt and pepper.
2. *Salad:* In a serving bowl, combine barley, green beans, red pepper and carrots. Add dressing and toss to combine. Cover and refrigerate for at least 30 minutes, until chilled, or for up to 2 hours.

Variations

Substitute cooked wheat berries or rye berries for the barley.

Store-bought honey-glazed walnuts would be a fantastic addition to this salad, providing texture, sweetness and protein. Sprinkle them over top just before serving.

Barley Salad with Sweet Corn and Cilantro

Makes 8 side servings or 4 entrée servings

I visited Santa Fe a few years ago and fell in love with the food, the artwork and especially the people. I can't wait to return, but in the meantime I created this recipe to evoke the feeling of the Southwest through bright colors and fresh flavors.

Tip

You may use dried herbs if you don't have fresh on hand. Just halve the quantity.

Dressing

2	shallots, minced	2
¼ cup	finely chopped fresh cilantro	60 mL
¼ cup	finely chopped fresh mint	60 mL
2 tsp	packed brown sugar	10 mL
2 tbsp	white wine vinegar	30 mL
1 tbsp	freshly squeezed lime juice	15 mL
½ cup	extra virgin olive oil	125 mL
	Salt and freshly ground black pepper	

Salad

4	tomatoes, seeded and chopped	4
3 cups	cooked hulled barley (see page 27), cooled	750 mL
1 cup	cooked fresh or thawed frozen corn kernels	250 mL

1. *Dressing:* In a small bowl, whisk together shallots, cilantro, mint, brown sugar, vinegar and lime juice. Gradually whisk in oil until well blended. Season to taste with salt and pepper.
2. *Salad:* In a serving bowl, combine tomatoes, barley and corn. Add dressing and toss to combine. Cover and refrigerate for at least 30 minutes, until chilled, or for up to 2 hours.

Variation

Substitute cooked wheat berries, spelt, Kamut, rye berries or farro for the barley.

Bulgur Chickpea Salad

Makes 4 side servings

This side dish is a favorite at barbecues because its flavors go perfectly with smoky ribs or well-seasoned tri-tip.

Tip

Balsamic vinegar imparts a rich complexity to salad dressings. If you need to substitute, mix 2 tbsp (30 mL) red wine vinegar with 2 tsp (10 mL) granulated sugar, but there's nothing like the real thing.

Dressing

2 tsp	finely chopped fresh mint	10 mL
½ tsp	salt	2 mL
¼ tsp	freshly ground black pepper	1 mL
¼ tsp	ground coriander	1 mL
¼ tsp	ground cumin	1 mL
2 tbsp	freshly squeezed lime juice	30 mL
2 tbsp	balsamic vinegar	30 mL
¼ cup	extra virgin olive oil	60 mL

Salad

1	can (14 to 19 oz/398 to 540 mL) chickpeas, drained	1
2 cups	cooked bulgur (see page 27), cooled	500 mL
½ cup	julienned carrots (see tip, page 94)	125 mL
⅓ cup	dried cranberries	75 mL
¼ cup	toasted slivered almonds (see tip, page 94)	60 mL

1. *Dressing:* In a small bowl, whisk together mint, salt, pepper, coriander, cumin, lime juice and vinegar. Whisk in oil until well blended.
2. *Salad:* In a serving bowl, combine chickpeas, bulgur, carrots and cranberries. Add dressing and toss to combine. Cover and refrigerate for at least 30 minutes, until chilled, or for up to 2 hours. Just before serving, add almonds and toss to combine.

Variation

Barley Chickpea Salad: Substitute cooked barley for the bulgur.

Israeli Couscous Summer Chopped Salad

Makes 4 entrée servings

This is one of my standard recipes for summer night picnics at the Hollywood Bowl. It is easy to make, store and serve, and gets a standing ovation every time. It pairs well with poached salmon.

Tip

Chiffonade means to cut herbs or leafy green vegetables into very thin ribbons, which makes for a lovely presentation. To chiffonade, stack the leaves a few at a time, fold them over to secure them, then slice them from one side parallel to the central stem and stopping just short of the stem. Flip the leaves over and repeat on the other side. You should be left with just the central stem, which you can then discard.

Dressing

2 tbsp	finely chopped fresh tarragon	30 mL
2 tsp	finely chopped fresh parsley	10 mL
1½ tsp	dried oregano	7 mL
½ tsp	salt	2 mL
¼ tsp	freshly ground black pepper	1 mL
3 tbsp	freshly squeezed lemon juice	45 mL
3 tbsp	red wine vinegar	45 mL
1 tbsp	liquid honey	15 mL
¼ cup	extra virgin olive oil	60 mL

Salad

12	cherry tomatoes, quartered	12
5	spears asparagus, tough ends removed, blanched (see tip, page 82) and chopped	5
1	small to medium zucchini, chopped	1
1	small to medium yellow summer squash (yellow zucchini), chopped	1
2 cups	cooked Israeli couscous (see page 27), cooled, rinsed and drained	500 mL
¾ cup	chopped yellow bell pepper	175 mL
3 tbsp	fresh basil chiffonade (see tip, at left)	45 mL
3 tbsp	chopped fresh flat-leaf (Italian) parsley	45 mL

1. *Dressing:* In a small bowl, whisk together tarragon, parsley, oregano, salt, pepper, lemon juice, vinegar and honey. Gradually whisk in oil until well blended.
2. *Salad:* In a serving bowl, combine tomatoes, asparagus, zucchini, summer squash, couscous, yellow pepper, basil and parsley. Add dressing and toss to combine. Cover and refrigerate for at least 30 minutes, until chilled, or for up to 2 hours.

Farro and Sun-Dried Tomato Salad

Makes 6 to 8 side servings

This elegant and flavorful salad was inspired by a romantic Italian dinner in Beverly Hills at which the chef featured farro as a side for a number of classic dishes.

Tips

Sun-dried tomatoes add a gourmet touch and a burst of flavor to this salad. They are readily available, but if you want to make your own, simply slice plum (Roma) tomatoes in half lengthwise and place in a 200°F (100°C) oven for 6 to 12 hours or until tomatoes are dry but still flexible. Let cool and store in an airtight container indefinitely.

To blanch sugar snap peas, bring a small saucepan of water to a boil over high heat. Add peas and boil for 1 minute or until tender-crisp. Using a slotted spoon, transfer peas to a bowl of ice water and let cool completely. Drain well.

Dressing

2	cloves garlic, minced	2
1/2 cup	finely chopped sun-dried tomatoes (see tip, at left)	125 mL
2 tbsp	finely chopped fresh basil	30 mL
2 tsp	drained capers	10 mL
1/2 tsp	salt	2 mL
1/4 tsp	freshly ground black pepper	1 mL
2 tbsp	balsamic vinegar	30 mL
1/2 cup	extra virgin olive oil	125 mL

Salad

2 1/2 cups	cooked farro (see page 27), cooled	625 mL
1 cup	trimmed sugar snap peas, blanched (see tip, at left)	250 mL
1 cup	chopped red bell pepper	250 mL
1/2 cup	diagonally sliced green onions (white and green parts)	125 mL
1/2 cup	julienned carrots (see tip, page 94)	125 mL

1. *Dressing:* In a small bowl, whisk together garlic, sun-dried tomatoes, basil, capers, salt, pepper and vinegar. Gradually whisk in oil until well blended.

2. *Salad:* In a serving bowl, combine farro, peas, red pepper, green onions and carrots. Add dressing and toss to combine. Serve immediately or cover and refrigerate for at least 30 minutes, until chilled, or for up to 2 hours.

Variation

Substitute cooked barley, wheat berries, spelt, Kamut or rye berries for the farro.

Roasted Vegetable and Farro Salad

Makes 6 to 8 side servings

This is one of my favorites for cool evenings. The robust flavors of the herbs and freshly roasted vegetables make it a great side dish.

Tip

If you have fresh herbs available, swap them out for the dried. Double the quantity when using fresh.

Balsamic Vinegar

Balsamic vinegar is made from grape pressings that have not been permitted to ferment. It has a rich, slightly sweet flavor. True balsamic vinegars, labeled "Aceto Balsamico Tradizionale," are aged in oak for at least 12 years. They can be quite expensive, but are nice to have on hand to be used sparingly in special-occasion recipes. Most balsamic vinegars you'll find on a supermarket shelf have been aged for less time and will not have "Tradizionale" on the label. These are appropriate for everyday use.

- **Preheat oven to 400°F (200°C)**
- **Rimmed baking sheet, lined with foil**

Salad

2	small to medium zucchini, diced	2
2	small to medium yellow summer squash (yellow zucchini), diced	2
2	carrots, diced	2
1	large onion, quartered	1
1 cup	chopped red bell pepper	250 mL
¼ cup	extra virgin olive oil	60 mL
	Salt and freshly ground black pepper	
2½ cups	cooked farro (see page 27), cooled	625 mL
1 cup	halved cherry tomatoes	250 mL

Dressing

½ tsp	dried thyme	2 mL
½ tsp	dried oregano	2 mL
½ tsp	dried parsley	2 mL
½ tsp	salt	2 mL
¼ tsp	freshly ground black pepper	1 mL
2 tbsp	balsamic vinegar	30 mL
1 tbsp	Dijon mustard	15 mL
¼ cup	extra virgin olive oil	60 mL

1. *Salad:* In a large bowl, combine zucchini, summer squash, carrots, onion and red pepper. Add oil and toss to coat. Spread vegetables in a single layer on prepared baking sheet and sprinkle with salt and pepper to taste. Roast in preheated oven for 35 to 40 minutes or until tender and beginning to brown. Transfer to a large heatproof serving bowl and let cool for 15 minutes.

2. *Dressing:* In a small bowl, whisk together thyme, oregano, parsley, salt, pepper, vinegar and mustard. Gradually whisk in oil until well blended.

3. Add farro and cherry tomatoes to the roasted vegetables. Add dressing and toss to combine. Serve immediately.

Millet, Sweet Corn and Avocado Salad

Makes 3 to 4 entrée servings

Millet is a popular grain in Asia and Africa. This is a great make-ahead recipe, as the millet will continue to absorb flavor as it chills.

Tip

To bring out a pleasantly nutty aroma, toast the millet in a dry skillet over medium heat, stirring constantly, for 5 minutes before adding it to the rice cooker. (This is not necessary, but it's a nice touch if you have the time.)

- **Blender or food processor**

Dressing

1	clove garlic, smashed	1
1	bunch fresh cilantro, including stems (about 2 cups/500 mL)	1
½ tsp	salt	2 mL
¼ tsp	freshly ground black pepper	1 mL
⅓ cup	buttermilk	75 mL
¼ cup	sour cream	60 mL
¼ cup	mayonnaise	60 mL
1½ tbsp	freshly squeezed lime juice	22 mL
2 tsp	balsamic vinegar	10 mL

Salad

2	tomatoes, seeded and diced	2
2 cups	cooked fresh or thawed frozen corn kernels	500 mL
1½ cups	cooked millet (see page 27), cooled	375 mL
½ cup	finely chopped red onion	125 mL
¼ cup	chopped seeded poblano peppers	60 mL
2	avocados	2

1. *Dressing:* In blender, combine garlic, cilantro, salt, pepper, buttermilk, sour cream, mayonnaise, lime juice and vinegar; purée until smooth.
2. *Salad:* In a serving bowl, combine tomatoes, corn, millet, red onion and poblano pepper. Add dressing and toss to combine. Cover and refrigerate for at least 30 minutes, until chilled, or for up to 2 hours. Just before serving, cut avocados into cubes, add to salad and toss to combine.

Variation

Millet with Roasted Corn and Avocado: Preheat barbecue grill to medium for indirect heat. Place each of 3 corn cobs on a sheet of heavy-duty foil. Drizzle with 1 tbsp (15 mL) water and spread evenly with melted butter. Wrap very tightly, so the packages will not leak. Place over unlit side and grill for 45 minutes or until tender. Let cool, then cut off kernels. Substitute for the fresh corn.

Quinoa Tabbouleh

**Makes 4 to
5 side servings**

Here's a great dish to
bring to a summer
picnic. These little
lettuce wraps are
healthy, delicious and
light enough to keep
you energetic and active
throughout the day.

Tip

If your tomatoes are
super-juicy, save the
seeds and juices and
push them through
a fine-mesh sieve,
discarding the seeds.
Add the juices to the
lemon juice before
making the dressing.

3	tomatoes, seeded (see tip, at left) and chopped	3
2	cucumbers, seeded and diced	2
1½ cups	cooked quinoa (see page 27), cooled	375 mL
1 cup	chopped green onions (white and green parts)	250 mL
1 cup	chopped fresh parsley	250 mL
¼ cup	finely chopped fresh mint	60 mL
⅓ cup	freshly squeezed lemon juice	75 mL
⅓ cup	extra virgin olive oil	75 mL
1 tsp	salt	5 mL
8 to 10	romaine lettuce leaves	8 to 10

1. In a large bowl, combine tomatoes, cucumbers, quinoa, green onions, parsley and mint.
2. In a small bowl, whisk together lemon juice, oil and salt until well blended. Add to the tomato mixture and stir to combine. Cover and refrigerate for at least 30 minutes, to blend the flavors, or for up to 2 hours.
3. For the best flavor, bring to room temperature before serving. To serve, scoop tabbouleh into lettuce leaves and eat like a taco.

Variation

Millet Tabbouleh: Substitute cooked toasted millet (see tip, page 101) for the quinoa.

Roasted Corn and Quinoa Salad

Makes 6 side servings

This salad is packed with protein and antioxidants, but my kids don't even realize it's healthy. The bright flavors and mix of textures from the quinoa, corn, edamame and red peppers make it a family favorite.

Tip

You can use thawed frozen corn kernels in a pinch. You can also roast the wrapped ears of corn in a 350°F (180°C) oven, directly on the oven rack, for 30 minutes.

Edamame

In Japan, edamame (green soybeans) are a popular snack food, and they have gained popularity in North America not only because they're yummy, but also because they're a complete protein, containing all of the amino acid building blocks. The reported health benefits of adding edamame to your diet include reduction of the risk of heart disease, improvement of bone health and reduction of certain types of cancer.

- **Preheat barbecue grill to medium for indirect heat**
- **Blender or food processor**

Salad

3	ears corn, husked	3
3 tbsp	water	45 mL
	Melted butter	
3 cups	cooked quinoa (see page 27), cooled	750 mL
1 cup	frozen shelled edamame, cooked (see tip, page 87)	250 mL
¾ cup	finely chopped red onion	175 mL
½ cup	finely chopped red bell pepper	125 mL

Dressing

1	clove garlic, smashed	1
1	bunch fresh cilantro, including stems (about 2 cups/500 mL)	1
2 tbsp	packed fresh mint leaves	30 mL
2 tsp	packed golden brown sugar	10 mL
2 tbsp	rice vinegar	30 mL
1 tbsp	freshly squeezed lime juice	15 mL
¼ cup	extra virgin olive oil	60 mL
	Salt and freshly ground pepper	
	Additional finely chopped fresh cilantro and mint	

1. *Salad:* Place each cob on a sheet of heavy-duty foil. Drizzle with 1 tbsp (15 mL) water and spread evenly with butter. Wrap very tightly, so the packages will not leak. Place over unlit side of barbecue and grill for 45 minutes or until tender. Let cool, then cut off kernels and place in a large bowl.
2. Add quinoa, edamame, red onion and red pepper to the corn. Toss to combine.
3. *Dressing:* In blender, combine garlic, cilantro, mint, brown sugar, vinegar and lime juice; purée until smooth. With the motor running, through the feed tube, drizzle in oil; process until incorporated.
4. Add dressing to the quinoa mixture and toss well to combine. Season to taste with salt and pepper. Transfer to a serving platter and sprinkle with cilantro and mint.

Tex-Mex Quinoa Salad

Makes 6 side servings

Just serve margaritas alongside this summer salad and you'll have a party that will get people talking.

Tip
The best tool for grating citrus zest is a rasp grater, such as a Microplane.

• **Blender or food processor**

Dressing

1	clove garlic, smashed	1
½ tsp	finely grated lime zest	2 mL
½ tsp	salt	2 mL
¼ tsp	freshly ground black pepper	1 mL
⅓ cup	sour cream	75 mL
3 tbsp	freshly squeezed lime juice	45 mL
2 tbsp	red wine vinegar	30 mL
1 tbsp	liquid honey	15 mL
⅓ cup	extra virgin olive oil	75 mL

Salad

1	tomato, seeded and chopped	1
1	can (14 to 19 oz/398 to 540 mL) black beans, drained and rinsed	1
2 cups	cooked quinoa (see page 27), cooled	500 mL
1 cup	cooked fresh or thawed frozen corn kernels	250 mL
½ cup	finely chopped fresh cilantro	125 mL
¼ cup	crumbled Cotija or feta cheese	60 mL
¼ cup	shredded Monterey Jack cheese	60 mL
2	avocados	2

1. *Dressing:* In blender, combine garlic, lime zest, salt, pepper, sour cream, lime juice, vinegar and honey; purée until smooth. With the motor running, through the feed tube, drizzle in oil; process until incorporated.

2. *Salad:* In a serving bowl, combine tomato, beans, quinoa, corn, cilantro, Cotija and Monterey Jack. Add dressing and toss to combine. Cover and refrigerate for at least 30 minutes, until chilled, or for up to 2 hours. Just before serving, cut avocados into cubes, add to salad and toss to combine.

Variations

Tex-Mex Millet Salad: Substitute cooked toasted millet (see tip, page 101) for the quinoa.

Add cooked shrimp, chicken or beef to this salad to make it a complete meal.

Mediterranean Red Quinoa Salad

Makes 4 to 6 side servings

I could eat this combination of ingredients with just about any main course, and the red quinoa adds a protein punch. This salad also looks great and has a wonderful texture.

Tip

You can use store-bought marinated artichoke hearts (from a jar or from the deli counter) or make your own. To marinate artichoke hearts, drain a 14-oz (398 mL) can of water-packed artichoke hearts and cut artichokes in half. In an airtight container, whisk together $\frac{1}{3}$ cup (75 mL) extra virgin olive oil, $\frac{1}{4}$ cup (60 mL) white vinegar, 1 tbsp (15 mL) minced onion and $\frac{1}{8}$ tsp (0.5 mL) each salt, freshly ground black pepper, dry mustard and dried basil. Add artichokes and toss to coat. Cover and refrigerate for at least 8 hours or up to 1 week.

Dressing

$\frac{3}{4}$ tsp	dried oregano	3 mL
$\frac{3}{4}$ tsp	dried basil	3 mL
$\frac{1}{2}$ tsp	salt	2 mL
$\frac{1}{2}$ tsp	freshly ground black pepper	2 mL
3 tbsp	freshly squeezed lemon juice	45 mL
2 tbsp	red wine vinegar	30 mL
$\frac{1}{2}$ tsp	Dijon mustard	2 mL
$\frac{1}{4}$ cup	extra virgin olive oil	60 mL

Salad

$1\frac{1}{2}$ cups	cooked red quinoa (see page 27), cooled	375 mL
1 cup	cherry tomatoes, halved and seeded	250 mL
$\frac{1}{2}$ cup	pitted and sliced kalamata olives	125 mL
$\frac{1}{2}$ cup	chopped drained marinated artichoke hearts (see tip, at left)	125 mL
$\frac{1}{3}$ cup	finely chopped fresh parsley	75 mL
$\frac{1}{3}$ cup	finely chopped fresh cilantro	75 mL
$\frac{1}{2}$ cup	crumbled feta cheese	125 mL

1. *Dressing:* In a small bowl, whisk together oregano, basil, salt, pepper, lemon juice, vinegar and mustard. Gradually whisk in oil until well blended.

2. *Salad:* In a serving bowl, combine quinoa, tomatoes, olives, artichokes, parsley and cilantro. Fold in feta. Add dressing and toss to combine. Cover and refrigerate for at least 30 minutes, until chilled, or for up to 2 hours.

Rye Berry Salad with Cranberries and Pistachios

Makes 6 side servings

I usually serve this hearty salad at the end of summer, but it's terrific any time of year. The dried cranberries and pistachios give it a sweet, salty and crunchy taste that will excite your taste buds.

Tips

Champagne vinegar is a light, mild vinegar that creates delicate salad dressings. If you can't find it, you can substitute white wine vinegar.

To make Champagne vinegar at home, pour Champagne or other sparkling wine into wide-mouth jars and leave the jars open; after about 6 weeks, you will have Champagne vinegar. Taste-test it — if it tastes like vinegar, it's done. Cover tightly and store at room temperature for up to 6 months.

Dressing

1 tbsp	minced shallots	15 mL
1 tsp	finely grated orange zest	5 mL
1/2 tsp	salt	2 mL
1/4 tsp	freshly ground black pepper	1 mL
1/4 cup	freshly squeezed orange juice	60 mL
1/4 cup	Champagne vinegar (see tips, at left)	60 mL
1/4 cup	extra virgin olive oil	60 mL

Salad

2 cups	cooked rye berries (see page 27), cooled	500 mL
1/2 cup	finely chopped celery	125 mL
1/4 cup	dried cranberries	60 mL
1/4 cup	pistachios, coarsely chopped	60 mL
1/4 cup	finely chopped red onion	60 mL

1. *Dressing:* In a small bowl, whisk together shallots, orange zest, salt, pepper, orange juice and vinegar. Gradually whisk in oil until well blended.
2. *Salad:* In a serving bowl, combine rye berries, celery, cranberries, pistachios and red onion. Add dressing and toss to combine. Cover and refrigerate for at least 30 minutes, until chilled, or for up to 2 hours.

Variation

For a luxurious dressing, substitute truffle oil for 1 tbsp (15 mL) of the olive oil.

Wheat Berry Waldorf Salad

Makes 8 side servings

My updated version of the classic Waldorf salad brings together all the crunchy goodness of the original with a hearty and healthy approach. Wheat berries add a delicious texture to balance the apples and nuts, and provide dietary fiber to boot.

Tips

If you like a tart dressing, add a bit more lemon juice.

To toast walnut halves, spread nuts in a single layer on a baking sheet. Bake in a 350°F (180°C) oven, stirring often, for 5 to 10 minutes or until light brown and fragrant. Immediately transfer to a bowl and let cool before chopping.

You can prepare the dressing and combine the salad ingredients up to 2 hours ahead, but refrigerate them separately until just before serving.

Dressing

1/2 tsp	salt	2 mL
1/4 tsp	freshly ground black pepper	1 mL
1/2 cup	mayonnaise or plain yogurt	125 mL
1/4 cup	sour cream	60 mL
1 tbsp	freshly squeezed lemon juice	15 mL
1 tsp	liquid honey	5 mL

Salad

2 cups	cooked wheat berries (see page 27), cooled	500 mL
1 cup	walnut halves, toasted (see tip, at left) coarsely chopped	250 mL
1 cup	chopped Granny Smith or other tart apple	250 mL
1 cup	sliced red seedless grapes	250 mL

1. *Dressing:* In a small bowl, whisk together salt, pepper, mayonnaise, sour cream, lemon juice and honey until well blended.

2. *Salad:* In a serving bowl, combine wheat berries, walnuts, apple and grapes. Add dressing and toss to combine. Serve immediately.

Variation

Barley Waldorf Salad: Substitute cooked barley for the wheat berries.

Sesame Ginger Wheat Berry Salad

Makes 8 side servings

Fresh Asian spices and crisp vegetables give this wheat berry salad wonderful texture and flavor.

Tips

When shredding bok choy, cut across the stems and leaves.

To shred cabbage, remove the outer leaves and cut off the stem. Cut cabbage in half and place flat side down on a cutting board. Beginning at the outer edge, make diagonal cuts across the cabbage, as close together as you can — $\frac{1}{4}$ inch (0.5 cm) is a good width. When you're done shredding, cut the strips in half.

Napa Cabbage

Napa cabbage is a variety of Chinese cabbage that originated near Beijing and is widely used in East Asian cuisine. It is lighter in color than other Chinese cabbages, such as bok choy. It has a light, delicate taste and is often used in stir-fries, soups or slaw.

- • **Blender or food processor**

Dressing

1	clove garlic, smashed	1
1 tbsp	chopped green onion (white part only)	15 mL
1 tbsp	minced gingerroot	15 mL
$\frac{1}{2}$ tsp	dry mustard	2 mL
$\frac{1}{2}$ tsp	hot pepper flakes	2 mL
$\frac{1}{4}$ cup	rice vinegar	60 mL
1 tbsp	soy sauce	15 mL
1 tbsp	liquid honey	15 mL
1 tbsp	hoisin sauce	15 mL
1 tsp	creamy peanut butter	5 mL
$\frac{1}{4}$ cup	peanut oil	60 mL
1 tsp	toasted sesame oil	5 mL

Salad

1	carrot, thinly sliced	1
2 cups	shredded napa cabbage	500 mL
$1\frac{1}{2}$ cups	cooked wheat berries (see page 27), cooled	375 mL
$\frac{1}{2}$ cup	shredded bok choy (see tip, at left)	125 mL
$\frac{1}{2}$ cup	thinly sliced blanched snow peas (see tip, page 84)	125 mL
$\frac{1}{4}$ cup	diagonally sliced green onions (white and green parts)	60 mL

1. *Dressing:* In blender, combine garlic, green onion, ginger, dry mustard, hot pepper flakes, vinegar, soy sauce, honey, hoisin sauce and peanut butter; purée until smooth. With the motor running, through the feed tube, drizzle in peanut oil and sesame oil; process until incorporated.
2. *Salad:* In a serving bowl, combine carrot, cabbage, wheat berries, bok choy, peas and green onions. Add dressing and toss to combine.

Fava Bean Wheat Berry Salad

Makes 6 entrée servings

Don't even think about simply serving fava beans with Chianti. This combination of slightly crunchy beans, scrumptious wheat berries, feta cheese and pine nuts makes for a wonderful lunch. You'll be in a Mediterranean state of mind for the rest of the afternoon!

Tips

Green garlic (also called garlic scapes) is young garlic that is harvested before the cloves have begun to mature. The resulting vegetable resembles a scallion and is milder than garlic. Look for green garlic at farmers' markets. You can substitute green onions, if you prefer.

To prepare and blanch fava beans, remove the beans from their pods. Bring a small saucepan of water to a boil over high heat. Add beans and boil for 1 minute or until tender-crisp. Using a slotted spoon, transfer beans to a bowl of ice water and let cool completely. Remove the tough outer skins from the beans by pinching the skin between your thumb and forefinger; discard skins.

Dressing

½ tsp	salt	2 mL
¼ tsp	freshly ground black pepper	1 mL
2 tbsp	red wine vinegar	30 mL
6 tbsp	extra virgin olive oil	90 mL

Salad

1	stalk green garlic (bulb and tender greens), thinly sliced	1
2 cups	cooked wheat berries (see page 27), cooled	500 mL
2 cups	fresh or thawed frozen shelled fava beans, blanched if fresh (see tips, at left)	500 mL
½ cup	crumbled feta cheese	125 mL
¼ cup	toasted pine nuts (see tip, page 52)	60 mL
2 tbsp	finely chopped fresh flat-leaf (Italian) parsley	30 mL
1 tbsp	finely chopped fresh chives	15 mL
	Additional toasted pine nuts	

1. *Dressing:* In a small bowl, whisk together salt, pepper and vinegar. Gradually whisk in oil until well blended.
2. *Salad:* In a serving bowl, combine green garlic, wheat berries, fava beans, feta, pine nuts, parsley and chives. Add dressing and toss to combine. Cover and refrigerate for at least 30 minutes, until chilled, or for up to 2 hours. Garnish with pine nuts.

Variation

Fava Bean Barley Salad: Substitute cooked barley for the wheat berries.

Japanese Adzuki Bean Salad

Makes 4 entrée servings

Bright red adzuki beans make a yummy salad filled with the flavors of the Far East. I love to serve it for brunch to give my table international flair.

Tip

With wasabi powder, a little goes a long way, so if you decide to increase the heat in this dressing, add more sparingly.

Tamari

Tamari is a Japanese soy sauce made from fermented soybeans. It is thicker, darker and richer than regular soy sauce and has a stronger flavor. Japanese soy sauces typically include wheat as a primary ingredient, which tends to give their sauces a slightly sweeter flavor than Chinese soy sauces. However, tamari is almost always produced without wheat, which makes it popular with those eating wheat-free diets. You can use tamari in any recipe that calls for soy sauce, though you may want to use a bit less.

Dressing

2 tsp	wasabi powder	10 mL
2 tsp	granulated sugar	10 mL
2 tbsp	rice vinegar	30 mL
2 tsp	tamari	10 mL
3 tbsp	extra virgin olive oil	45 mL
2 tbsp	toasted sesame oil	30 mL
	Salt and freshly ground black pepper	

Salad

1½ cups	cooked adzuki beans (see page 33), cooled	375 mL
1 cup	diced seeded cucumber	250 mL
¾ cup	chopped blanched snow peas (see tip, page 84)	175 mL
1 tsp	toasted sesame seeds (see tip, page 54)	5 mL
1 tsp	finely chopped fresh chives	5 mL
1½ cups	mesclun salad greens	375 mL
⅔ cup	trimmed watercress	150 mL
	Additional toasted sesame seeds and snipped fresh chives	

1. *Dressing:* In a small bowl, whisk together wasabi powder, sugar, vinegar and tamari. Gradually whisk in olive oil and sesame oil until well blended. Season to taste with salt and pepper.

2. *Salad:* In a bowl, combine beans, cucumber and peas. Add dressing and toss to combine. Cover and refrigerate for at least 30 minutes, until chilled, or for up to 2 hours. Add sesame seeds and chives; toss to combine. Serve on a bed of salad greens and watercress. Garnish with sesame seeds and chives.

Soups

Greek Lemon and Rice Soup (*Avgolemono*)

Makes 6 servings

This delightfully tangy Greek favorite will have you saying *"Opa!"* Try adding chicken for a higher-protein version.

Tips

It's important to switch to the Keep Warm cycle before adding the broth and egg mixture. If it boils, the eggs will overcook, and it will be a Greek tragedy!

The rice will continue to absorb liquid if this soup is kept warm in the rice cooker, so make sure to serve it immediately.

For information about rice cooker sizes, see page 13.

- **Medium rice cooker; fuzzy logic or on/off**

2 tbsp	butter	30 mL
¼ cup	minced green onions (white and green parts)	60 mL
½ cup	long-grain white rice, rinsed and drained	125 mL
4 cups	chicken broth	1 L
6	large egg yolks	6
	Finely grated lemon zest	
¼ cup	freshly squeezed lemon juice	60 mL
	Salt and freshly ground black pepper	
	Finely chopped fresh mint	

1. Set the rice cooker for the Quick Cook or Regular cycle. When the bottom of the bowl gets hot, add butter and let it melt. Sauté green onions for about 2 minutes or until softened.
2. Stir in rice and broth. Close the lid and reset for the Regular cycle. Set a timer for 20 minutes.
3. Meanwhile, in a medium bowl, whisk together egg yolks and lemon juice until well blended.
4. When the timer sounds, check to make sure rice is tender. If necessary, continue cooking, checking for doneness every 5 minutes. Switch to the Keep Warm cycle. Gradually add half the broth from the rice cooker to the egg yolk mixture and whisk until well blended. Pour egg mixture into the rice cooker bowl and stir constantly until thickened. Season to taste with salt and pepper. Serve immediately, garnished with mint and lemon zest.

Variation

Add 1 cup (250 mL) shredded cooked chicken when you switch to the Keep Warm cycle.

Creamy Wehani Coconut Rice Soup

Makes 6 servings

Wehani is an aromatic brown rice that generally keeps a low profile, but it adds wonderful texture to this soup. It should be slightly chewy, with a hint of crunch.

Tips

Although cooking this soup on the Brown Rice cycle takes an hour longer, it's worth it for the superior results.

Studies suggest that Thai chile peppers, also known as bird's eye chiles, can improve sleep, lower blood pressure and cholesterol and reduce inflammation. But they can pack a punch, so adjust accordingly if you like things less spicy.

● **Medium rice cooker; fuzzy logic or on/off**

2 tbsp	vegetable oil	30 mL
2	cloves garlic, minced	2
1	shallot, minced	1
1 cup	finely chopped onion	250 mL
1 tsp	ground turmeric	5 mL
1 tsp	ground cumin	5 mL
1½ tsp	Thai red curry paste	7 mL
1	Thai chile pepper, seeded and minced	1
1 cup	wehani rice, rinsed and drained	250 mL
1 tbsp	packed brown sugar	15 mL
3 cups	chicken or vegetable broth	750 mL
1 tbsp	fish sauce (nam pla)	15 mL
1	can (14 oz/400 mL) coconut milk	1
	Freshly squeezed lime juice	
	Salt and freshly ground black pepper	

1. Set the rice cooker for the Quick Cook or Regular cycle. When the bottom of the bowl gets hot, add oil and swirl to coat. Sauté garlic, shallot and onion for about 3 minutes or until shallot and onion are softened and translucent. Add turmeric, cumin and curry paste; sauté for 1 minute.

2. Stir in chile pepper, rice, brown sugar, broth and fish sauce. Close the lid and reset for the Regular cycle. Set a timer for 45 minutes. (Or reset for the Brown Rice cycle and set a timer for 1¾ hours.)

3. When the timer sounds, stir in coconut milk. Set the timer for 15 minutes.

4. When the timer sounds, check to make sure rice is tender. If necessary, continue cooking, checking for doneness every 5 minutes. Switch to the Keep Warm cycle. Stir in lime juice to taste. Season to taste with salt and pepper. Let stand for 5 minutes, then serve immediately.

Variation

Add 1 cup (250 mL) chopped cooked shrimp when you switch to the Keep Warm cycle.

Wild Mushroom and Barley Soup

Makes 4 servings

A nice, earthy soup is a perennial favorite and this one doesn't disappoint. Best enjoyed next to a roaring fire with someone special.

Tips

Unless your mushrooms are extremely dirty, you can simply wipe them with a damp paper towel to clean them. If you need to wash them, rinse them in a colander and wipe them dry with a paper towel. Never soak fresh mushrooms, as they'll absorb too much water.

Marsala, a sweet wine used in many Italian dishes, comes from Sicily. You may substitute another sweet wine, such as port or sherry.

• Medium rice cooker; fuzzy logic or on/off

3 tbsp	butter	45 mL
2	cloves garlic, minced	2
½ cup	finely chopped onion	125 mL
1½ tsp	finely chopped fresh thyme	7 mL
1	carrot, finely chopped	1
1 cup	finely chopped celery	250 mL
1 cup	mixed wild mushrooms (such as cremini, chanterelle and porcini), chopped	250 mL
¼ cup	Marsala	60 mL
⅓ cup	pearl barley, rinsed and drained	75 mL
4 cups	chicken broth	1 L
2 cups	water	500 mL
	Salt and freshly ground black pepper	

1. Set the rice cooker for the Quick Cook or Regular cycle. When the bottom of the bowl gets hot, add butter and let it melt. Sauté garlic and onion for about 3 minutes or until onion is softened and translucent. Add thyme and sauté for 1 minute. Add carrot, celery and mushrooms; sauté for 4 to 5 minutes or until softened. Stir in Marsala and cook for 3 to 4 minutes or until liquid has evaporated.

2. Stir in barley, broth and water. Close the lid and reset for the Regular cycle. Set a timer for 45 minutes.

3. When the timer sounds, check to make sure barley is tender. If necessary, continue cooking, checking for doneness every 5 minutes. Switch to the Keep Warm cycle. Season to taste with salt and pepper. Let stand for 10 minutes, then serve immediately.

Tomato Soup with Israeli Couscous

Makes 6 servings

I like to think of this as an elegant version of an after-school favorite. It's a great light meal for a brisk afternoon.

Tips

If you don't have any fresh cilantro on hand, you can substitute 1 tbsp (15 mL) ground coriander, adding it with the cumin.

For information about rice cooker sizes, see page 13.

● **Large rice cooker; fuzzy logic or on/off**

2 tbsp	extra virgin olive oil	30 mL
4	cloves garlic, minced	4
1 cup	finely chopped onion	250 mL
2	carrots, chopped	2
1	can (14 oz/398 mL) diced tomatoes, with juice	1
1⅓ cups	Israeli couscous	325 mL
¼ tsp	ground cumin	1 mL
Pinch	cayenne pepper	Pinch
6 cups	chicken or vegetable broth	1.5 L
2 tbsp	finely chopped fresh mint	30 mL
2 tbsp	finely chopped fresh cilantro	30 mL
	Salt and freshly ground black pepper	

1. Set the rice cooker for the Quick Cook or Regular cycle. When the bottom of the bowl gets hot, add oil and swirl to coat. Sauté garlic and onion for about 3 minutes or until onion is softened and translucent. Add carrots and sauté for 3 to 4 minutes or until softened.

2. Stir in tomatoes with juice, couscous, cumin, cayenne and broth. Close the lid and reset for the Regular cycle. Set a timer for 20 minutes.

3. When the timer sounds, check to make sure couscous is tender. If necessary, continue cooking, checking for doneness every 5 minutes. Switch to the Keep Warm cycle. Stir in mint and cilantro. Season to taste with salt and pepper. Serve immediately.

Corn Chowder with Quinoa and Millet

Makes 4 servings

This is a fantastic soup to make in the summer, when fresh corn is plentiful, but it's still a nice treat during other seasons. And it's chock full of hearty grains and veggies. Delightful!

Tips

To clean leeks, fill a sink with warm water. Split leeks lengthwise and submerge in water, swishing them around to remove dirt. Rinse thoroughly under cool water and drain.

To bring out a pleasantly nutty aroma, toast the millet in a dry skillet over medium heat, stirring constantly, for 5 minutes before adding it to the rice cooker. (This is not necessary, but it's a nice touch if you have the time.)

For a lighter soup, use fat-free evaporated milk instead of cream.

Although cooking this soup on the Brown Rice cycle takes an hour longer, it's worth it for the superior results.

- **Medium rice cooker; fuzzy logic or on/off**
- **Blender or food processor**

3 tbsp	butter, divided	45 mL
1 cup	finely chopped sweet onion (such as Vidalia)	250 mL
1½ cups	finely chopped leeks (white and light green parts only)	375 mL
1 cup	finely diced celery	250 mL
½ cup	finely chopped red bell pepper	125 mL
½ cup	quinoa, rinsed and drained	125 mL
¼ cup	millet	60 mL
¼ tsp	dried thyme	1 mL
4 cups	chicken or vegetable broth, divided	1 L
4 cups	cooked fresh or thawed frozen corn kernels, divided	1 L
1 cup	half-and-half (10%) cream	250 mL
	Salt and freshly ground black pepper	
2 tbsp	finely chopped fresh flat-leaf (Italian) parsley	30 mL

1. Set the rice cooker for the Quick Cook or Regular cycle. When the bottom of the bowl gets hot, add 2 tbsp (30 mL) butter and let it melt. Sauté onion for about 3 minutes or until softened and translucent. Add leeks, celery and red pepper; sauté for 3 to 4 minutes or until softened.

2. Stir in quinoa, millet, thyme and 3 cups (750 mL) of the broth. Close the lid and reset for the Regular cycle. Set a timer for 25 minutes. (Or reset for the Brown Rice cycle and set a timer for 85 minutes.)

3. Meanwhile, in blender, combine 3 cups (750 mL) of the corn and the remaining broth; purée until smooth.

4. When the timer sounds, stir in corn purée and the remaining corn. Set the timer for 10 minutes.

5. When the timer sounds, check to make sure quinoa and millet are tender. If necessary, continue cooking, checking for doneness every 5 minutes. Switch to the Keep Warm cycle. Stir in cream and the remaining butter. Season to taste with salt and pepper. Serve immediately, garnished with parsley.

Tuscan Wheat Berry Soup

Makes 6 servings

Wheat berries provide great texture. I love the combination of white beans, rosemary and wheat berries in this rustic dish.

Tips

If you prefer not to use wine, purée the beans with a combination of the liquid from the can and chicken or vegetable broth.

Although cooking this soup on the Brown Rice cycle takes an hour longer, it's worth it for the superior results.

For information about rice cooker sizes, see page 13.

- **Large rice cooker; fuzzy logic or on/off**
- **Blender or food processor**

2	cans (each 14 to 19 oz/398 to 540 mL) cannellini (white kidney) or other white beans, drained and rinsed, divided	2
1 cup	dry white wine	250 mL
2 tbsp	extra virgin olive oil	30 mL
3	cloves garlic, minced	3
1 cup	finely chopped onion	250 mL
2 tsp	finely chopped fresh rosemary	10 mL
1	carrot, chopped	1
1½ cups	chopped celery	375 mL
1	can (14 oz/398 mL) whole tomatoes, drained and chopped	1
1½ cups	wheat berries, rinsed and drained	375 mL
6 cups	chicken or vegetable broth	1.5 L
	Salt and freshly ground black pepper	

1. Place half the beans in blender and add wine; purée until smooth. Set aside.

2. Set the rice cooker for the Quick Cook or Regular cycle. When the bottom of the bowl gets hot, add oil and swirl to coat. Sauté garlic and onion for about 3 minutes or until onion is softened and translucent. Add rosemary and sauté for 1 minute. Add carrot and celery; sauté for 3 to 4 minutes or until softened.

3. Stir in bean purée, tomatoes, wheat berries and broth. Close the lid and reset for the Regular cycle. Set a timer for 1 hour. (Or reset for the Brown Rice cycle and set a timer for 2 hours.)

4. When the timer sounds, check to make sure wheat berries are tender. If necessary, continue cooking, checking for doneness every 5 minutes. Switch to the Keep Warm cycle. Stir in the remaining beans. Season to taste with salt and pepper. Let stand for 10 minutes, then serve immediately.

Variation

Substitute an equal amount of rye berries for wheat berries.

Curried Squash Soup

Makes 6 to 8 servings

When I feel the first chill of autumn, it inspires me to stir up a pot of my friend Robert's favorite squash soup. The spice of the curry combined with the sweetness of the squash and coconut milk tickle your taste buds and warm your soul.

Tip

For a creamier version, after switching to the Keep Warm cycle in step 3, transfer half of the soup to a blender or food processor and purée until smooth. (Or use an immersion blender in the rice cooker bowl and pulse a few times.) Return to the bowl (if necessary) and continue with step 3.

• Large rice cooker; fuzzy logic or on/off

3 tbsp	extra virgin olive oil	45 mL
2	cloves garlic, minced	2
1 cup	finely chopped onion	250 mL
3 tbsp	minced gingerroot	45 mL
1½ tbsp	curry powder	22 mL
1 tsp	ground cumin	5 mL
1	carrot, diced	1
2 cups	diced peeled butternut squash	500 mL
1 cup	finely chopped celery	250 mL
1 cup	dried red lentils, sorted and rinsed	250 mL
6 cups	chicken or vegetable broth	1.5 L
1	can (14 oz/400 mL) coconut milk	1
2 tbsp	finely chopped fresh cilantro	30 mL
1 tbsp	freshly squeezed lime juice	15 mL
	Salt and freshly ground black pepper	

1. Set the rice cooker for the Quick Cook or Regular cycle. When the bottom of the bowl gets hot, add oil and swirl to coat. Sauté garlic, onion and ginger for about 3 minutes or until onion is softened and translucent. Add curry powder and cumin; sauté for 1 minute. Add carrot, squash and celery; sauté for 4 to 5 minutes or until softened.

2. Stir in lentils and broth. Close the lid and reset for the Regular cycle. Set a timer for 40 minutes.

3. When the timer sounds, check to make sure lentils are tender. If necessary, continue cooking, checking for doneness every 5 minutes. Switch to the Keep Warm cycle. Stir in coconut milk, cilantro and lime juice. Season to taste with salt and pepper. Let stand for 10 minutes, then serve immediately.

Spicy Pumpkin and Split Pea Soup

Makes 4 to 6 servings

The colors of this soup scream "autumn" to me, and that's the perfect time of year to enjoy it. The fresh parsley garnish adds beautiful contrast.

Tips

Yellow split peas are used in many Indian dishes and can be found at well-stocked grocery stores and Indian markets.

For information about rice cooker sizes, see page 13.

• Large rice cooker; fuzzy logic or on/off

¼ tsp	crushed saffron threads	1 mL
¼ cup	hot water	60 mL
2 tbsp	extra virgin olive oil	30 mL
2 cups	finely chopped onions	500 mL
1 tsp	curry powder	5 mL
½ tsp	ground cinnamon	2 mL
¼ tsp	ground ginger	1 mL
¼ tsp	hot pepper flakes	1 mL
3 cups	cubed peeled pumpkin (½-inch/1 cm cubes)	750 mL
¾ cup	dried yellow split peas, sorted and rinsed	175 mL
5 cups	chicken broth	1.25 L
	Salt and freshly ground black pepper	
	Finely chopped fresh parsley	

1. In a measuring cup or small bowl, combine saffron threads and hot water; set aside to steep.
2. Set the rice cooker for the Quick Cook or Regular cycle. When the bottom of the bowl gets hot, add oil and swirl to coat. Sauté onion for about 3 minutes or until softened and translucent. Add curry powder, cinnamon, ginger and hot pepper flakes; sauté for 1 minute.
3. Stir in saffron-infused water, pumpkin, split peas and broth. Close the lid and reset for the Regular cycle. Set a timer for 1 hour.
4. When the timer sounds, check to make sure pumpkin and peas are tender. If necessary, continue cooking, checking for doneness every 5 minutes. Switch to the Keep Warm cycle. Season to taste with salt and black pepper. Let stand for 5 minutes, then serve immediately, garnished with parsley.

Variation

Butternut Squash and Split Pea Soup: Substitute cubed butternut squash for the pumpkin.

Thick and Hearty Split Pea Soup

Makes 8 servings

A vegan soup that's thick and hearty? You bet. This soup always gets a warm response on a blustery winter day.

Tips

For a smoky flavor, add 1 tsp (5 mL) liquid smoke with the broth.

For information about rice cooker sizes, see page 13.

- **Large rice cooker; fuzzy logic or on/off**
- **Blender, food processor or immersion blender**

2 tbsp	extra virgin olive oil	30 mL
2	cloves garlic, minced	2
1 cup	finely chopped onion	250 mL
1	carrot, diced	1
1½ cups	chopped celery	375 mL
2	potatoes, cut into ½-inch (1 cm) cubes	2
2 cups	dried green or yellow split peas, sorted and rinsed	500 mL
1	bay leaf	1
1 tsp	dried basil	5 mL
1 tsp	dried thyme	5 mL
½ tsp	celery seeds	2 mL
6 cups	vegetable broth	1.5 L
¼ cup	finely chopped fresh parsley	60 mL
	Salt and freshly ground black pepper	

1. Set the rice cooker for the Quick Cook or Regular cycle. When the bottom of the bowl gets hot, add oil and swirl to coat. Sauté garlic and onion for about 3 minutes or until onion is softened and translucent. Add carrot and celery; sauté for 3 to 4 minutes or until softened.
2. Stir in potatoes, peas, bay leaf, basil, thyme, celery seeds and broth. Close the lid and reset for the Regular cycle. Set a timer for 1½ hours.
3. When the timer sounds, check to make sure peas are tender. If necessary, continue cooking, checking for doneness every 5 minutes. Switch to the Keep Warm cycle.
4. Transfer half of the soup to blender and purée until smooth. (Or use an immersion blender in the rice cooker bowl and pulse a few times.) Return to the bowl (if necessary). Stir in parsley. Let stand for 10 minutes. Season to taste with salt and pepper. Serve hot.

Variation

Add a 4-oz (125 g) smoked ham hock with the broth. When you switch to the Keep Warm cycle, transfer ham hock to a cutting board. Remove the meat from the bone and discard bone, fat and skin. Cut ham into bite-size pieces and return to the rice cooker after puréeing half the soup.

Southwestern Anasazi Bean Soup

Makes 8 servings

Ana-what? Good thing you can focus on eating, rather than pronouncing, this delicious bean soup. I love that you don't have to presoak the beans. Easy peasy.

Tips

Anasazi beans are one of the few beans that don't need to be soaked before cooking.

For a spicier soup, try using a serrano pepper in place of the jalapeño.

● **Large rice cooker; fuzzy logic or on/off**

2	slices bacon, finely diced	2
2	cloves garlic, minced	2
1	jalapeño pepper, seeded and finely chopped	1
1 cup	finely chopped onion	250 mL
1 cup	dried anasazi beans	250 mL
½ tsp	ground cumin	2 mL
¼ tsp	ground coriander	1 mL
7 cups	chicken or vegetable broth	1.75 L
	Salt and freshly ground black pepper	
2 tbsp	finely chopped green onions (white and green parts)	30 mL
2 tbsp	chopped fresh cilantro	30 mL

1. Set the rice cooker for the Quick Cook or Regular cycle. When the bottom of the bowl gets hot, sauté bacon for about 8 minutes or until browned. Drain off all but 1 tbsp (15 mL) of the fat.

2. Stir in garlic, jalapeño, onion, beans, cumin, coriander and broth. Close the lid and reset for the Regular cycle. Set a timer for 1½ hours.

3. When the timer sounds, check to make sure beans are tender. If necessary, continue cooking, checking for doneness every 5 minutes. Switch to the Keep Warm cycle. Season to taste with salt and pepper. Serve immediately, garnished with green onions and cilantro.

Steven's Old-Fashioned Black Bean Soup

Makes 6 to 8 servings

The smoked ham hock and rich molasses elevate this dish from a soup to a symphony of flavors. Inspired by my friend Steven's family recipe, it's a favorite in my house.

Tips

To avoid tearing up when you're chopping onions, try refrigerating the onions for 30 minutes first, and don't cut the root off.

If you prefer, you can substitute packed brown sugar or pure maple syrup for the molasses.

Ham hocks are a cut of pork from the ankle joint of a pig. They contribute a lot of flavor to soups and stews. You can find them at some grocery stores and at Asian and Latin markets.

- **Large rice cooker; fuzzy logic or on/off**
- **Blender, food processor or immersion blender**

2 cups	dried black beans	500 mL
2 tbsp	extra virgin olive oil	30 mL
3	cloves garlic, minced	3
2 cups	finely chopped onions	500 mL
1 tbsp	ground cumin	15 mL
1 tsp	chili powder	5 mL
1	small carrot, finely chopped	1
1½ cups	finely chopped celery	375 mL
2	bay leaves	2
1	smoked ham hock (about 4 oz/125 g)	1
6½ cups	chicken broth	1.625 L
1 cup	finely chopped red bell pepper	250 mL
1 tbsp	dark (cooking) molasses	15 mL
½ cup	finely chopped fresh cilantro	125 mL
3 tbsp	freshly squeezed lime juice	45 mL
	Salt and freshly ground black pepper	
	Sour cream	
	Chopped avocado	
	Lime wedges	

1. Sort, rinse, soak and drain beans (see pages 32–33).
2. Set the rice cooker for the Quick Cook or Regular cycle. When the bottom of the bowl gets hot, add oil and swirl to coat. Sauté garlic and onions for about 3 minutes or until onions are softened and translucent. Add cumin and chili powder; sauté for 1 minute. Add carrot and celery; sauté for 3 to 4 minutes or until softened.
3. Stir in soaked beans, bay leaves, ham hock and broth. Close the lid and reset for the Regular cycle. Set a timer for 1½ hours.

Tips

If you prefer a chunkier soup, purée one-quarter instead of half.

Using salt during the cooking process can toughen beans and make take them longer to cook. Wait until the end to add salt and pepper to taste.

4. When the timer sounds, discard bay leaves and transfer ham hock to a cutting board. Stir red pepper and molasses into the rice cooker. Set the timer for 30 minutes.

5. Meanwhile, remove ham meat from the bone and discard bone, fat and skin. Cut ham into bite-size pieces. Set aside.

6. When the timer sounds, check to make sure beans are tender. If necessary, continue cooking, checking for doneness every 5 minutes. Switch to the Keep Warm cycle.

7. Transfer half of the soup to blender and purée until smooth. (Or use an immersion blender in the rice cooker bowl and pulse a few times.) Return to the bowl (if necessary). Stir in ham, cilantro and lime juice. Season to taste with salt and pepper. Let stand for 10 minutes. Serve immediately, topped with sour cream and garnished with avocado and lime wedges.

Brazilian Black Bean Soup

Makes 6 to 8 servings

Here's a zesty twist on a hearty favorite! I love the delicate yet robust flavor combination. This soup is perfect for a late summer evening.

Tips

Using salt during the cooking process can toughen beans and make them take longer to cook. Wait until the end to add salt and pepper to taste.

Double the amount of cayenne pepper if you like more heat.

Freshly squeezed orange juice is preferable for this recipe, but a good-quality, not-from-concentrate orange juice is an acceptable alternative.

For information about rice cooker sizes, see page 13.

- **Large rice cooker; fuzzy logic or on/off**
- **Blender, food processor or immersion blender**

2 cups	dried black beans	500 mL
2 tbsp	extra virgin olive oil	30 mL
6	cloves garlic, minced	6
½ cup	finely chopped onion	125 mL
2 tbsp	ground cumin	30 mL
½ tsp	cayenne pepper	2 mL
1	carrot, diced	1
1 cup	finely chopped red bell pepper	250 mL
9 cups	chicken broth	2.25 L
2 tbsp	finely grated orange zest	30 mL
1½ cups	orange juice	375 mL
	Salt and freshly ground black pepper	
	Sour cream	
2 tbsp	finely chopped fresh cilantro	30 mL

1. Sort, rinse, soak and drain beans (see pages 32–33).
2. Set the rice cooker for the Quick Cook or Regular cycle. When the bottom of the bowl gets hot, add oil and swirl to coat. Sauté garlic and onion for about 3 minutes or until onion is softened and translucent. Add cumin and cayenne; sauté for 1 minute. Add carrot and red pepper; sauté for 3 to 4 minutes or until softened.
3. Stir in soaked beans, broth and orange juice. Close the lid and reset for the Regular cycle. Set a timer for 1½ hours.
4. When the timer sounds, stir in orange zest. Set the timer for 15 minutes.
5. When the timer sounds, check to make sure beans are tender. If necessary, continue cooking, checking for doneness every 5 minutes. Switch to the Keep Warm cycle.
6. Working in batches, transfer soup to blender and purée until smooth. (Or use an immersion blender in the rice cooker bowl and pulse a few times.) Season to taste with salt and black pepper. Serve immediately, topped with sour cream and garnished with cilantro.

Variation

Vegan Brazilian Black Bean Soup: Substitute vegetable broth for the chicken broth and vegan sour cream for the sour cream.

Chickpea, Porcini and Farro Soup

Makes 4 to 6 servings

Fresh mushrooms and white wine make a great combination! I love to serve this earthy soup on a cold winter night.

Tips

Fresh porcini mushrooms can be hard to find in North America, so cremini mushrooms are a good substitute. Another option is to use $1/2$ oz (14 g) dried porcini mushrooms, which are more readily available. Avoid packages with too much dust or crumbled pieces, as the flavor is not likely to be very strong. To rehydrate dried porcini mushrooms, soak them in hot water for 30 minutes and squeeze out liquid before using. There's no need to sauté them; simply add them with the farro in step 3.

Although cooking this soup on the Brown Rice cycle takes an hour longer, it's worth it for the superior results.

- **Medium rice cooker; fuzzy logic or on/off**
- **Blender or food processor**

1	can (14 to 19 oz/398 to 540 mL) chickpeas, drained and rinsed	1
1 cup	dry white wine	250 mL
2 tbsp	extra virgin olive oil	30 mL
2 tbsp	butter	30 mL
2	cloves garlic, minced	2
1 cup	finely chopped onion	250 mL
1 tbsp	finely chopped fresh thyme	15 mL
1 cup	sliced porcini or cremini mushrooms	250 mL
1	sprig fresh rosemary	1
$1/3$ cup	farro, rinsed and drained	75 mL
4 cups	vegetable broth or water	1 L
	Salt and freshly ground black pepper	

1. In blender, combine chickpeas and wine; purée until smooth. Set aside.
2. Set the rice cooker for the Quick Cook or Regular cycle. When the bottom of the bowl gets hot, add oil and butter and let butter melt. Sauté garlic and onion for about 3 minutes or until onion is softened and translucent. Add thyme and sauté for 1 minute. Add mushrooms and sauté for 4 to 5 minutes or until softened.
3. Stir in chickpea purée, rosemary, farro and broth. Close the lid and reset for the Regular cycle. Set a timer for 45 minutes. (Or reset for the Brown Rice cycle and set a timer for $1\frac{3}{4}$ hours.)
4. When the timer sounds, check to make sure farro is tender. If necessary, continue cooking, checking for doneness every 5 minutes. Switch to the Keep Warm cycle. Season to taste with salt and pepper. Let stand for 5 minutes, then serve immediately.

Farro Minestrone

Makes 6 to 8 servings

In this new take on an Italian classic, farro adds fiber and nutrients, and its texture perfectly complements the heartiness of the soup. *Mangia!*

Tips

The rind from a wedge of Parmesan is traditionally simmered in a pot of minestrone. Whenever you grate Parmesan, save the rind for this soup. If you don't have a rind saved, carefully trim the rind off your wedge of cheese using a sharp knife.

For easy removal of the thyme sprigs, bay leaf and Parmesan rind, tie them up in a square of cheesecloth, making a "bouquet garni."

Although cooking this soup on the Brown Rice cycle takes an hour longer, it's worth it for the superior results.

• **Large rice cooker; fuzzy logic or on/off**

3 tbsp	extra virgin olive oil, divided	45 mL
1 cup	finely chopped onion	250 mL
2 tbsp	minced garlic	30 mL
2	carrots, chopped	2
1	zucchini, chopped	1
1 cup	chopped celery	250 mL
2	sprigs fresh thyme	2
1	bay leaf	1
1	Parmesan cheese rind (see tip, at left)	1
2 cups	diced tomatoes	500 mL
1 cup	farro, rinsed and drained	250 mL
6 cups	chicken or vegetable broth	1.5 L
1	can (14 to 19 oz/398 to 540 mL) cannellini (white kidney) beans, drained and rinsed	1
½ cup	chopped fresh parsley	125 mL
	Freshly grated Parmesan cheese	
	Salt and freshly ground black pepper	

1. Set the rice cooker for the Quick Cook or Regular cycle. When the bottom of the bowl gets hot, add 2 tbsp (30 mL) oil and swirl to coat. Sauté onion and garlic for about 3 minutes or until onion is softened and translucent. Add carrots, zucchini and celery; sauté for 3 to 4 minutes or until softened.

2. Stir in thyme sprigs, bay leaf, Parmesan rind, tomatoes, farro and broth. Close the lid and reset for the Regular cycle. Set a timer for 1 hour. (Or reset for the Brown Rice cycle and set a timer for 2 hours.)

3. When the timer sounds, stir in beans. Set the timer for 15 minutes.

4. When the timer sounds, check to make sure farro is tender. If necessary, continue cooking, checking for doneness every 5 minutes. Switch to the Keep Warm cycle. Discard thyme sprigs, bay leaf and Parmesan rind. Stir in parsley. Season to taste with salt and pepper. Serve immediately, garnished with grated Parmesan and drizzled with the remaining oil.

Variation

Wheat Berry Minestrone: Substitute wheat berries for the farro.

Lentil and Potato Dal

Makes 4 to 6 servings

Ghee (better known as clarified butter in this part of the world) provides the base for this delicious Indian dish.

Tips

If you don't have time to make ghee, it is available in jars where Indian foods are sold or you can substitute butter or olive oil.

For information about rice cooker sizes, see page 13.

• Medium rice cooker; fuzzy logic or on/off

2 tbsp	ghee (see recipe, page 203)	30 mL
4	cloves garlic, minced	4
1 cup	finely chopped onion	250 mL
1 tbsp	minced gingerroot	15 mL
1 tsp	ground cumin	5 mL
1 tsp	ground turmeric	5 mL
½ tsp	ground coriander	2 mL
½ tsp	mustard seeds	2 mL
½ tsp	ground cardamom	2 mL
¼ tsp	cayenne pepper	1 mL
2	potatoes, peeled and cut into ½-inch (1 cm) cubes	2
2	tomatoes, cored, seeded and chopped	2
1 cup	dried small red lentils, sorted and rinsed	250 mL
3 cups	chicken or vegetable broth	750 mL
½ cup	finely chopped fresh parsley	125 mL
2 tbsp	red wine vinegar	30 mL
	Salt and freshly ground black pepper	
	Greek-style plain yogurt	

1. Set the rice cooker for the Quick Cook or Regular cycle. When the bottom of the bowl gets hot, add ghee and swirl to coat. Sauté garlic, onion and ginger for about 3 minutes or until onion is softened and translucent. Add cumin, turmeric, coriander, mustard seeds, cardamom and cayenne; sauté for 1 minute.

2. Stir in potatoes, tomatoes, lentils and broth. Close the lid and reset for the Regular cycle. Set a timer for 40 minutes.

3. When the timer sounds, check to make sure lentils are tender. If necessary, continue cooking, checking for doneness every 5 minutes. Switch to the Keep Warm cycle. Stir in parsley and vinegar. Season to taste with salt and black pepper. Serve immediately, topped with yogurt.

Ginger Salmon and Rice Soup

Makes 6 servings

This soup is equal parts delicate and hearty, and is deceptively easy to make! But it's so good your diners will think you swam upstream to get this on the table.

Tips

I like to use my food processor to mince large quantities of gingerroot. Place the minced ginger in a plastic freezer bag and flatten in out. Freeze for up to 3 months and simply snap off as much as you need as you go.

For information about rice cooker sizes, see page 13.

● **Medium rice cooker; fuzzy logic or on/off**

1½ lb	skinless salmon fillet, cut into 8 pieces	750 g
2 tbsp	soy sauce	30 mL
1 tbsp	toasted sesame oil	15 mL
¾ cup	long-grain white rice, rinsed and drained	175 mL
2 tbsp	finely chopped fresh cilantro stems	30 mL
3	¼-inch (0.5 cm) slices gingerroot	3
½ tsp	salt	2 mL
4 cups	chicken broth	1 L
2 cups	water	500 mL
2	green onions (white and green parts), chopped	2
2 tsp	minced fresh cilantro	10 mL

1. In a large bowl, toss salmon with soy sauce and sesame oil. Set aside.
2. In the rice cooker bowl, combine rice, cilantro stems, ginger, salt, broth and water. Set the rice cooker for the Regular cycle and set a timer for 20 minutes.
3. When the timer sounds, stir in salmon and marinade. Set the timer for 10 minutes.
4. When the timer sounds, check to make sure salmon is opaque and flakes easily with a fork. If necessary, continue cooking, checking for doneness every 3 minutes. Switch to the Keep Warm cycle. Let stand for 5 minutes. Discard ginger slices. Serve immediately, garnished with green onions and cilantro.

Variation

Substitute 1½ lbs (750 g) rainbow trout fillets, which have a flavor and texture similar to salmon.

Japanese Rice Soup (*Zohsui*)

Makes 6 to 8 servings

Dashi is a traditional Japanese soup base, but don't be intimidated: it's just a simple broth. This is sure to become a go-to soup favorite in your house!

Tips

You can buy powdered dashi mix at Asian markets, but I suggest making it from scratch (see page 185), as it's simple and the taste will be superior. If you can't find either the powdered mix or the bonito shavings you need to make dashi, you can substitute fish stock or equal parts water and clam juice.

Look for Japanese chili powder (*ichimi tohgarashi*) at Japanese food stores.

• Large rice cooker; fuzzy logic or on/off

1 cup	Japanese-style short-grain japonica rice (such as Calrose)	250 mL
7 cups	dashi (see tip, at left)	1.75 L
2 cups	packed spinach leaves	500 mL
1 cup	lump crabmeat, picked over to remove shell fragments	250 mL
2	large eggs, beaten	2
	Salt and freshly ground white pepper	
	Japanese chili powder (optional)	
	Soy sauce	
1 tsp	toasted sesame oil	5 mL

1. Place rice in a bowl and add enough cool water to cover by 1 inch (2.5 cm); let soak for 30 minutes. Rinse and drain (see page 20).
2. In the rice cooker bowl, combine soaked rice and dashi. Set the rice cooker for the Regular cycle and set a timer for 30 minutes.
3. When the timer sounds, check to make sure rice is tender. If necessary, continue cooking, checking for doneness every 5 minutes. Switch to the Keep Warm cycle. Stir in spinach and crab. Whisk in eggs. (The eggs should form into soft strings throughout the soup.) Season to taste with salt, pepper, chili powder (if using) and soy sauce. Let stand for 10 minutes, then serve immediately, drizzled with sesame oil.

Variation

Use cooked shrimp in place of or as a complement to the crab.

Shrimp, Corn and Quinoa Soup

Makes 4 servings

Some things just go well together — in this case, shrimp, corn and quinoa. This refreshing soup is light yet filling, so it is perfect as a light lunch.

Tips

For the best flavor, toast whole cumin seeds in a dry skillet over medium-high heat, stirring constantly, for about 3 minutes or until fragrant. Immediately transfer to a spice grinder and let cool, then grind to a fine powder.

Celery seeds impart a celery flavor to stews, soups and other dishes, but use them sparingly — a little goes a long way. You can substitute dill seeds or 1 tbsp (15 mL) minced celery leaves.

Although cooking this soup on the Brown Rice cycle takes an hour longer, it's worth it for the superior results.

- **Medium rice cooker; fuzzy logic or on/off**

2 tbsp	extra virgin olive oil	30 mL
2	cloves garlic, minced	2
1/2 cup	finely chopped onion	125 mL
1	small carrot, finely chopped	1
1	stalk celery, finely chopped	1
1/2 tsp	celery seeds	2 mL
1/4 tsp	cayenne pepper	1 mL
1/4 tsp	ground cumin	1 mL
1/4 tsp	ground turmeric	1 mL
1/2 cup	quinoa, rinsed and drained	125 mL
4 cups	chicken or vegetable broth	1 L
8 oz	medium shrimp, peeled and deveined	250 g
1 cup	cooked fresh or thawed frozen corn kernels	250 mL
3 tbsp	finely chopped fresh cilantro	45 mL
1 tsp	salt	5 mL
2 tbsp	freshly squeezed lemon or lime juice	30 mL

1. Set the rice cooker for the Quick Cook or Regular cycle. When the bottom of the bowl gets hot, add the oil and swirl to coat. Sauté garlic and onion for about 3 minutes or until onion is softened and translucent. Add carrot and celery; sauté for 3 to 4 minutes or until softened. Add celery seeds, cayenne, cumin and turmeric; sauté for 1 minute.

2. Stir in quinoa and broth. Set the rice cooker for the Regular cycle and set a timer for 30 minutes. (Or set the rice cooker for the Brown Rice cycle and set a timer for 1 1/2 hours.)

3. When the timer sounds, check to make sure quinoa is tender. If necessary, continue cooking, checking for doneness every 5 minutes. Switch to the Keep Warm cycle. Stir in shrimp and corn. Let stand for 15 minutes or until shrimp are pink and opaque. Stir in cilantro, salt and lemon juice. Serve immediately.

Variation

Shrimp, Corn and Millet Soup: Substitute cooked toasted millet (see tip, page 116) for the quinoa.

Thai Chicken Soup with Forbidden Black Rice

Makes 4 servings

The complex flavors that develop in this soup belie the relatively quick and simple process. It's a surefire way to impress your guests!

Tips

Thai red curry paste contains aromatic herbs, such as lemongrass, galangal and fresh red chile peppers, harvested at their peak of freshness and carefully blended with fragrant spices. It is available at well-stocked grocery stores and Asian markets.

Although cooking this soup on the Brown Rice cycle takes an hour longer, it's worth it for the superior results.

The rice will continue to absorb liquid if this soup is kept warm in the rice cooker, so make sure to serve it immediately.

• **Medium rice cooker; fuzzy logic or on/off**

4	boneless skinless chicken thighs, cut into bite-size pieces	4
4	green onions, thinly sliced (keep white and green parts separate)	4
1	can (14 oz/398 mL) diced tomatoes, with juice	1
½ cup	forbidden black rice, rinsed and drained	125 mL
¼ cup	finely chopped red bell pepper	60 mL
1	can (14 oz/400 mL) coconut milk	1
3 cups	chicken broth	750 mL
1 tbsp	Thai red curry paste	15 mL
2 tbsp	finely chopped fresh basil	30 mL
2 tbsp	finely chopped fresh cilantro	30 mL
3 tbsp	freshly squeezed lime juice	45 mL
1 tbsp	fish sauce (nam pla)	15 mL

1. In the rice cooker bowl, combine chicken, white part of green onions, tomatoes with juice, rice, red pepper, coconut milk, broth and curry paste. Set the rice cooker for the Regular cycle and set a timer for 30 minutes. (Or set the rice cooker for the Brown Rice cycle and set a timer for 1½ hours.)

2. When the timer sounds, check to make sure juices run clear when chicken is pierced. If necessary, continue cooking, checking for doneness every 5 minutes. Switch to the Keep Warm cycle. Stir in green part of green onions, basil, cilantro, lime juice and fish sauce. Let stand for 15 minutes, then serve immediately.

Wild Rice Soup with Chicken

Makes 6 servings

Go wild with this dish! It's healthy, hearty and (wildly) delicious.

Tips

For convenience, use any type of leftover cooked chicken.

Try using a wild rice blend, such as Lundberg Farms.

If you're not counting calories, you can use 1½ cups (375 mL) heavy or whipping (35%) cream instead of evaporated milk, for an even richer soup.

Although cooking this soup on the Brown Rice cycle takes an hour longer, it's worth it for the superior results.

• **Medium rice cooker; fuzzy logic or on/off**

3 tbsp	butter	45 mL
2	cloves garlic, minced	2
1 cup	finely chopped onion	250 mL
1 tsp	dried oregano	5 mL
¼ tsp	dried basil	1 mL
¼ tsp	freshly ground black pepper	1 mL
2	carrots, diced	2
1 cup	diced celery	250 mL
¾ cup	wild rice, rinsed and drained	175 mL
6 cups	chicken broth	1.5 L
¼ cup	all-purpose flour	60 mL
1	can (12 oz or 370 mL) evaporated milk	1
2 cups	diced rotisserie chicken	500 mL
1 cup	cooked fresh or thawed frozen peas	250 mL
2 tbsp	red wine	30 mL

1. Set the rice cooker for the Quick Cook or Regular cycle. When the bottom of the bowl gets hot, add butter and let it melt. Sauté garlic and onion for about 3 minutes or until onion is softened and translucent. Add oregano, basil and pepper; sauté for 1 minute. Add carrots and celery; sauté for 3 to 4 minutes or until softened.

2. Stir in wild rice and broth. Close the lid and reset for the Regular cycle. Set a timer for 45 minutes. (Or reset for the Brown Rice cycle and set a timer for 1¾ hours.)

3. Meanwhile, in a bowl, whisk together flour and evaporated milk.

4. When the timer sounds, stir in flour mixture. Set the timer for 15 minutes.

5. When the timer sounds, check to make sure wild rice is tender and soup is thickened. If necessary, continue cooking, checking for doneness every 5 minutes. Switch to the Keep Warm cycle. Stir in chicken, peas and wine. Let stand for 10 minutes, then serve immediately.

Chicken and Barley Chowder

Makes 6 servings

Lentils, barley and green split peas pack this rich chicken chowder with nutrients. Serve it piping hot for a satisfying meal.

Tips

To intensify the tomato flavor in this soup, substitute fire-roasted tomatoes.

For the best flavor, buy whole dried sage leaves and crush them with your fingers.

For information about rice cooker sizes, see page 13.

- **Large rice cooker; fuzzy logic or on/off**

4	boneless skinless chicken thighs, cut into bite-size pieces	4
3	carrots, finely chopped	3
2	potatoes, peeled and cut into 1/4-inch (0.5 cm) dice	2
2 cups	finely chopped onions	500 mL
2 cups	finely chopped celery	500 mL
1 1/2 cups	fresh or thawed frozen corn kernels	375 mL
1/4 cup	dried green lentils, sorted and rinsed	60 mL
1/4 cup	dried green split peas, sorted and rinsed	60 mL
1/4 cup	pearl barley, rinsed and drained	60 mL
1 tbsp	dried rubbed sage	15 mL
1 tbsp	dried oregano	15 mL
3 cups	chicken broth	750 mL
3 cups	water	750 mL
1	can (28 oz/796 mL) whole tomatoes, with juice	1
2 cups	finely chopped red bell pepper	500 mL
	Salt and freshly ground black pepper	

1. In the rice cooker bowl, combine chicken, carrots, potatoes, onions, celery, corn, lentils, peas, barley, sage, oregano, broth and water. Stir in tomatoes with juice, breaking the tomatoes up with your fingers as you add them. Set the rice cooker for the Regular cycle and set a timer for 30 minutes.
2. When the timer sounds, stir in red pepper. Set the timer for 15 minutes.
3. When the timer sounds, check to make sure juices run clear when chicken is pierced. If necessary, continue cooking, checking for doneness every 5 minutes. Switch to the Keep Warm cycle. Season to taste with salt and pepper. Let stand for 5 minutes, then serve immediately.

Variation

Turkey and Barley Chowder: Substitute turkey stock for the chicken broth and 2 cups (500 mL) chopped cooked turkey for the chicken thighs, adding the turkey when you switch to the Keep Warm cycle.

Hot and Sour Soup

Makes 4 to 6 servings

This classic Szechuan recipe is both spicy and sour, not to mention easy and delicious. You really *can* have it all!

Tips

You may refrigerate the marinated pork for up to 24 hours before making the soup.

The rice will continue to absorb liquid if this soup is kept warm in the rice cooker, so make sure to serve it immediately.

For information about rice cooker sizes, see page 13.

- **Medium rice cooker; fuzzy logic or on/off**

6	dried black or shiitake mushrooms	6
1/3 cup	Thai jasmine rice, rinsed and drained	75 mL
1 1/2 tsp	salt, divided	7 mL
5 cups	chicken broth	1.25 mL
3 tbsp	white vinegar	45 mL
1 tbsp	soy sauce	15 mL
1/2 cup	canned shredded bamboo shoots, drained and rinsed	125 mL
1 cup	shredded cooked pork tenderloin (about 4 oz/125 g)	250 mL
1/2 tsp	cornstarch	2 mL
1/2 tsp	soy sauce	2 mL
1 cup	medium-firm tofu, cut into 1 1/2- by 1 1/4-inch (4 by 3 cm) pieces	250 mL
1 tsp	Thai chili sauce (such as Sriracha)	5 mL
2 tbsp	cornstarch	30 mL
2 tbsp	cold water	30 mL
2	large eggs, lightly beaten	2
1	green onion, finely chopped	1
	White pepper	

1. Place mushrooms in a bowl and add enough hot water to cover; let stand for about 30 minutes or until softened. Rinse and drain. Remove stems and cut caps into thin slices.
2. In the rice cooker bowl, combine rice, 1 tsp (5 mL) of the salt, broth, vinegar and 1 tbsp (15 mL) soy sauce. Set the rice cooker for the Regular cycle. When the mixture comes to a boil, stir in mushroom slices and bamboo shoots. Set a timer for 20 minutes.
3. Meanwhile, in a medium bowl, combine pork, the remaining salt, 1/2 tsp (2 mL) cornstarch and 1/2 tsp (2 mL) soy sauce. Cover and refrigerate for 10 minutes.
4. When the timer sounds, stir in pork, tofu and chili sauce. Set the timer for 5 minutes.
5. Meanwhile, in a small bowl, combine 2 tbsp (30 mL) cornstarch with cold water.
6. When the timer sounds, check to make sure rice is tender. If necessary, continue cooking, checking for doneness every 5 minutes. Switch to the Keep Warm cycle. Slowly pour in cornstarch mixture, stirring constantly until soup thickens. Using a fork, slowly stir in eggs until shreds form. Stir in green onion. Season to taste with white pepper. Serve immediately.

Pancetta and Spelt Soup

Makes 6 servings

Cooking with pancetta sometimes feels like cheating. Its flavor works overtime to do all the heavy lifting for you, so you can save your energy for more important things — like enjoying a delicious meal with your loved ones.

Tips

For the ultimate convenience, I like to use boxed ready-to-use organic chicken broth for this recipe.

Pancetta is an Italian dry-cured meat similar to bacon (though bacon is smoked, not cured). You can substitute bacon in this soup, but you may want to blanch it first to eliminate its smoky flavor. To do so, cook bacon in boiling water for 4 minutes; drain and pat dry.

Although cooking this soup on the Brown Rice cycle takes an hour longer, it's worth it for the superior results.

• Medium rice cooker; fuzzy logic or on/off

6 oz	pancetta, diced	175 g
1 tbsp	extra virgin olive oil	15 mL
2	cloves garlic, minced	2
1 cup	finely chopped onion	250 mL
2	tomatoes, cored, seeded and diced	2
1	bay leaf	1
1	sprig fresh thyme	1
½ cup	spelt or farro, rinsed and drained	125 mL
6 cups	chicken or vegetable broth	1.5 L
	Finely chopped fresh flat-leaf (Italian) parsley	
	Freshly grated Parmesan cheese	

1. Set the rice cooker for the Quick Cook or Regular cycle. When the bottom of the bowl gets hot, sauté pancetta for 3 to 4 minutes or until browned. Transfer pancetta to a bowl and set aside.

2. Add oil to the rice cooker bowl and swirl to coat. Sauté garlic and onion for about 3 minutes or until onion is softened and translucent.

3. Stir in pancetta, tomatoes, bay leaf, thyme sprig, spelt and broth. Close the lid and reset for the Regular cycle. Set a timer for 45 minutes. (Or reset for the Brown Rice cycle and set a timer for 1¾ hours.)

4. When the timer sounds, check to make sure spelt is tender. If necessary, continue cooking, checking for doneness every 5 minutes. Switch to the Keep Warm cycle. Discard bay leaf and thyme sprig. Let stand for 10 minutes, then serve immediately, garnished with parsley and Parmesan.

Easy Chorizo and Hominy Soup

Makes 4 to 6 servings

Your family will absolutely love this simple spin on Mexican pozole. The chorizo offers a nice kick.

Tip

Increase the amount of chorizo if you like more heat and a meatier soup.

Chorizo

Chorizo is a highly seasoned ground pork sausage. The Mexican version is typically fresh and is seasoned with chile peppers and vinegar. The Spanish version is made with pork, white wine, sweet paprika and garlic and is usually cured and fermented. Many chorizos are deep red in color because they contain pimentón (Spanish smoked paprika).

- **Medium rice cooker; fuzzy logic or on/off**

2 tbsp	extra virgin olive oil	30 mL
2	cloves garlic, minced	2
6 oz	fresh chorizo sausage, finely chopped	175 g
1 tbsp	ground cumin	15 mL
2	carrots, finely chopped	2
1 cup	finely chopped celery	250 mL
1	can (28 oz/796 mL) white hominy, drained and rinsed	1
4 cups	chicken broth	1 L
1/2 cup	finely chopped fresh cilantro	125 mL
	Fresh cilantro leaves	
4 to 6	corn tortillas, warmed	4 to 6

1. Set the rice cooker for the Quick Cook or Regular cycle. When the bottom of the bowl gets hot, add oil and swirl to coat. Sauté garlic for about 1 minute or until fragrant. Add chorizo and cumin; sauté for 2 minutes. Add carrots and celery; sauté for 3 to 4 minutes or until softened.

2. Stir in hominy and broth. Close the lid and reset for the Regular cycle. Set a timer for 30 minutes.

3. When the timer sounds, switch to the Keep Warm cycle. Stir in chopped cilantro. Let stand for 5 minutes, then serve immediately, garnished with cilantro leaves and with warm tortillas on the side.

Portuguese Kale and Rice Soup

Makes 6 to 8 servings

Kale isn't just an ordinary cabbage — it's a superfood. Which means it packs a mighty punch, especially in this robust stew.

Tips

The rice will continue to absorb liquid if this soup is kept warm in the rice cooker, so make sure to serve it immediately.

For a green, kale is unusually high in fiber, which keeps you feeling full for a long time.

For information about rice cooker sizes, see page 13.

● **Large rice cooker; fuzzy logic or on/off**

2 tbsp	extra virgin olive oil	30 mL
1	clove garlic, minced	1
1/2 cup	finely chopped onion	125 mL
2	carrots, diced	2
1/2	large turnip, peeled and diced	1/2
2	cured chorizo sausages, cut diagonally into 1/4-inch (0.5 cm) thick slices	2
2	bay leaves	2
1	can (14 to 19 oz/398 to 540 mL) red kidney beans, drained and rinsed	1
3/4 cup	long-grain white rice, rinsed and drained	175 mL
2 tbsp	dried parsley	30 mL
2 tbsp	dried thyme	30 mL
1 tsp	salt	5 mL
1/4 tsp	freshly ground black pepper	1 mL
4 cups	chicken or vegetable broth	1 L
2 cups	water	500 mL
1/2	bunch kale, stemmed and chopped (about 1/2 cup/125 mL)	1/2

1. Set the rice cooker for the Quick Cook or Regular cycle. When the bottom of the bowl gets hot, add oil and swirl to coat. Sauté garlic and onion for about 3 minutes or until softened and translucent. Add carrots and turnip; sauté for 3 to 4 minutes or until softened.

2. Stir in chorizo, bay leaves, beans, rice, parsley, thyme, salt, pepper, broth and water. Close the lid and reset for the Regular cycle. Set a timer for 40 minutes.

3. When the timer sounds, check to make sure rice is tender. If necessary, continue cooking, checking for doneness every 5 minutes. Switch to the Keep Warm cycle. Stir in kale. Let stand for 15 minutes, then serve immediately.

Sopa de Albóndigas

Makes 6 to 8 servings

This classic Mexican soup is bursting with flavor. The *albóndigas* (meatballs) steal the show!

Tips

I like to double the meatball recipe and keep a batch in my freezer. Freeze meatballs on a baking sheet lined with parchment paper. Once frozen, transfer to a plastic freezer bag and freeze for up to 3 months. Thaw them overnight in the refrigerator before adding them to the soup (or to other recipes).

For information about rice cooker sizes, see page 13.

- **Large rice cooker; fuzzy logic or on/off**

Meatballs

1	large egg, lightly beaten	1
1 lb	ground beef or turkey (dark meat, preferably)	500 g
1/3 cup	long-grain white rice, rinsed and drained	75 mL
1/4 cup	finely chopped fresh mint	60 mL
1/4 cup	finely chopped fresh parsley	60 mL
1 1/2 tsp	salt	7 mL
1/4 tsp	freshly ground black pepper	1 mL

Soup

2 tbsp	extra virgin olive oil	30 mL
2	cloves garlic, minced	2
1 cup	finely chopped onion	250 mL
2	large carrots, diced	2
2	zucchini, diced	2
4 cups	water	1 L
4 cups	chicken broth	1 L
1/2 cup	tomato sauce	125 mL
1 1/2 cups	cooked fresh or thawed frozen peas	375 mL
1/4 tsp	cayenne pepper	1 mL
1 tbsp	finely chopped fresh oregano	15 mL
	Salt and freshly ground black pepper	

1. *Meatballs:* In a large bowl, combine egg, beef, rice, mint, parsley, salt and pepper. Roll into 1-inch (2.5 cm) balls. Set aside.

2. *Soup:* Set the rice cooker for the Quick Cook or Regular cycle. When the bottom of the bowl gets hot, add oil and swirl to coat. Sauté garlic and onion for about 3 minutes or until onion is softened and translucent. Add carrots and zucchini; sauté for 3 to 4 minutes or until softened.

3. Stir in water, broth and tomato sauce. Close the lid and reset for the Regular cycle. When the mixture comes to a boil, drop in meatballs. Set a timer for 20 minutes.

4. When the timer sounds, check to make sure meatballs are no longer pink inside. If necessary, continue cooking, checking for doneness every 5 minutes. Switch to the Keep Warm cycle. Stir in peas, cayenne and oregano. Season to taste with salt and black pepper. Let stand for 10 minutes, then serve immediately.

Stews and Chilis

Lentil and Farro Stew

Makes 6 to 8 servings

With its unique blend of spices and vegetables, this delectable stew will transport you to a quaint Italian bistro. As an added bonus, the farro and lentils pack a healthy punch.

Tips

If you don't have cheesecloth to make a bouquet garni, simply add the fresh herbs with the tomatoes. Just remember to remove the thyme sprigs and bay leaf before serving.

Although cooking this stew on the Brown Rice cycle takes an hour longer, it's worth it for the superior results.

• Large rice cooker; fuzzy logic or on/off

3	fresh thyme sprigs	3
1	bay leaf	1
1 tsp	chopped fresh oregano	5 mL
3	slices bacon, cut into thin strips	3
1 cup	finely chopped onion	250 mL
2	carrots, cut into rounds	2
1 cup	finely chopped red bell pepper	250 mL
1 cup	finely chopped yellow bell pepper	250 mL
1 cup	farro, rinsed and drained	250 mL
1	can (14 oz/398 mL) diced tomatoes, with juice	1
1½ cups	dried green lentils, sorted and rinsed	375 mL
Pinch	cayenne pepper	Pinch
6 cups	chicken or vegetable broth	1.5 L
½ cup	dry white wine	125 mL
	Finely chopped fresh parsley	

1. Tie thyme sprigs, bay leaf and oregano in a square of cheesecloth, making a bouquet garni. Set aside.
2. Set the rice cooker for the Quick Cook or Regular cycle. When the bottom of the bowl gets hot, sauté bacon until crisp. Drain off all but 1 tbsp (15 mL) fat. Add onion and sauté for about 3 minutes or until softened and translucent. Add carrots, red pepper and yellow pepper; sauté for 3 to 4 minutes or until softened. Add farro and sauté for 1 minute.
3. Stir in bouquet garni, tomatoes with juice, lentils, cayenne, broth and wine. Close the lid and reset for the Regular cycle. Set a timer for 45 minutes. (Or reset for the Brown Rice cycle and set a timer for 1¾ hours.)
4. When the timer sounds, check to make sure lentils are tender. If necessary, continue cooking, checking for doneness every 5 minutes. Switch to the Keep Warm cycle. Let stand for 10 minutes, then discard bouquet garni and serve immediately, garnished with parsley.

Variation

Lentil and Barley Stew: Substitute barley for the farro and increase the cooking time in step 3 by 10 minutes.

White Bean Stew

Makes 4 to 6 servings

This filling stew has become a sophisticated addition to many an Italian restaurant. And with plenty of protein and fiber, it's good for both the body and the soul!

Tips

Although cooking this stew on the Brown Rice cycle takes an hour longer, it's worth it for the superior results.

For information about rice cooker sizes, see page 13.

• **Large rice cooker; fuzzy logic or on/off**

2 tbsp	extra virgin olive oil	30 mL
4	cloves garlic, minced	4
½ cup	finely chopped onion	125 mL
3 tbsp	ground cumin	45 mL
1 tbsp	ground turmeric	15 mL
½ tsp	freshly ground black pepper	2 mL
6	potatoes, peeled and cut into eighths	6
2	cans (each 14 to 19 oz/398 to 540 mL) cannellini (white kidney) beans, drained and rinsed	2
1 cup	wheat berries, rinsed and drained	250 mL
4 cups	vegetable or chicken broth	1 L
	Salt	
	Finely chopped fresh parsley	

1. Set the rice cooker for the Quick Cook or Regular cycle. When the bottom of the bowl gets hot, add oil and swirl to coat. Sauté garlic and onion for about 3 minutes or until onion is softened and translucent. Add cumin, turmeric and pepper; sauté for 1 minute.

2. Stir in potatoes, beans, wheat berries and broth. Close the lid and reset for the Regular cycle. Set a timer for 45 minutes. (Or reset for the Brown Rice cycle and set a timer for 1¾ hours.)

3. When the timer sounds, check to make sure wheat berries are tender. If necessary, continue cooking, checking for doneness every 5 minutes. Season to taste with salt. Serve immediately, garnished with parsley.

Variation

Barley and White Bean Stew: Substitute barley for the wheat berries.

Indonesian Curried Bean Stew

Makes 4 servings

With three types of beans, peanut butter and fiery spices, this stew provides so much flavor and so many nutrients, you won't miss the meat!

Tips

Use crunchy peanut butter for a crunchier texture.

For information about rice cooker sizes, see page 13.

● **Medium to large rice cooker; fuzzy logic or on/off**

2 tbsp	extra virgin olive oil	30 mL
2	cloves garlic, minced	2
1 cup	finely chopped red onion	250 mL
1 tbsp	curry powder	15 mL
1 tbsp	ground ginger	15 mL
1 tsp	ground cumin	5 mL
6 tbsp	smooth peanut butter	90 mL
1	green bell pepper, finely chopped	1
1	can (14 to 19 oz/398 to 540 mL) red kidney beans, drained and rinsed	1
1	can (14 to 19 oz/398 to 540 mL) black beans, drained and rinsed	1
1	can (14 to 19 oz/398 to 540 mL) chickpeas, drained and rinsed	1
1	can (14 oz/398 mL) diced tomatoes, with juice	1
2 tsp	salt	10 mL
1/4 tsp	freshly ground black pepper	1 mL
3 cups	water	750 mL

1. Set the rice cooker for the Quick Cook or Regular cycle. When the bottom of the bowl gets hot, add oil and swirl to coat. Sauté garlic and red onion for about 3 minutes or until onion is softened and translucent. Add curry powder, ginger, cumin and peanut butter; sauté for 1 minute, stirring thoroughly to break up peanut butter. Add green pepper and sauté for 1 minute.

2. Stir in kidney beans, black beans, chickpeas, tomatoes with juice, salt, pepper and water. Close the lid and reset for the Regular cycle. Set a timer for 30 minutes.

3. When the timer sounds, switch to the Keep Warm cycle. Let stand for 10 to 15 minutes, then serve immediately.

Chickpea and Eggplant Stew

Makes 4 servings

You'll want to make extra of this delicious stew. It's wonderful served over couscous.

Tip

You may substitute ½ tsp (2 mL) ground cinnamon for the cinnamon stick.

• **Medium to large rice cooker; fuzzy logic or on/off**

1	eggplant, peeled and cut into cubes	1
2 tsp	salt, divided	10 mL
3	cloves garlic, minced	3
2	carrots, cut into rounds	2
1	can (14 to 19 oz/398 to 540 mL) chickpeas, drained and rinsed	1
2 cups	chopped tomatoes	500 mL
1 cup	finely chopped onion	250 mL
1 cup	chopped celery	250 mL
¾ cup	rinsed drained canned red kidney beans	175 mL
1	bay leaf	1
1	2-inch (5 mL) cinnamon stick	1
2 tsp	ground cumin	10 mL
1 tsp	chili powder	5 mL
¼ tsp	freshly ground black pepper	1 mL
3 cups	chicken or vegetable broth	750 mL
¾ cup	tomato paste	175 mL

1. In a colander, toss eggplant with 1 tsp (5 mL) of the salt; let drain for 20 minutes, then pat dry.
2. In the rice cooker bowl, combine eggplant, garlic, carrots, chickpeas, tomatoes, onion, celery, kidney beans, bay leaf, cinnamon stick, cumin, chili powder, the remaining salt, pepper, broth and tomato paste. Set the rice cooker for the Regular cycle and set a timer for 40 minutes.
3. When the timer sounds, check to make sure vegetables are tender. If necessary, continue cooking, checking for doneness every 5 minutes. Switch to the Keep Warm cycle and let stand, stirring occasionally, for at least 10 minutes or up to 1 hour. Discard bay leaf and cinnamon stick. Serve hot.

Variation

Moroccan Stew with Lamb: After step 1, set the rice cooker for the Quick Cook or Regular cycle. When the bottom of the bowl gets hot, add 1 tbsp (15 mL) extra virgin olive oil and swirl to coat. Add 8 oz (250 g) ground lamb and 2 cloves garlic, minced. Sauté, breaking lamb up with the back of a spoon, for 4 to 5 minutes or until lamb is no longer pink. Stir in the remaining ingredients (omitting the 3 cloves garlic) and continue with step 2.

Butternut Squash Stew

Makes 3 to 4 servings

What better way to get your kids (or anyone) to eat their veggies than this rich stew? For you wine connoisseurs, I suggest pairing it with a Grüner Veltliner for a blissful union of flavors.

Tips

For the best results, toast the amaranth in a dry skillet over medium-high heat for 5 minutes before cooking it.

For information about rice cooker sizes, see page 13.

• Medium to large rice cooker; fuzzy logic or on/off

2 tbsp	extra virgin olive oil	30 mL
2	cloves garlic, minced	2
1 cup	finely chopped white onion	250 mL
1 tsp	dried oregano	5 mL
1 tsp	ground cumin	5 mL
1/2 tsp	chili powder	2 mL
1	zucchini, cut into 3/4-inch (2 cm) cubes	1
1 cup	chopped celery	250 mL
1 cup	cubed butternut squash (3/4-inch/2 cm cubes)	250 mL
1	can (14 oz/398 mL) diced tomatoes, with juice	1
1/2 cup	amaranth (see tip, at left)	125 mL
1 tsp	salt	5 mL
1/4 tsp	freshly ground black pepper	1 mL
1 cup	vegetable or chicken broth	250 mL

1. Set the rice cooker for the Quick Cook or Regular cycle. When the bottom of the bowl gets hot, add oil and swirl to coat. Sauté garlic and onion for about 3 minutes or until onion is softened and translucent. Add oregano, cumin and chili powder; sauté for 1 minute. Add zucchini, celery and squash; sauté for 3 to 4 minutes or until softened.
2. Stir in tomatoes with juice, amaranth, salt, pepper and broth. Close the lid and reset for the Regular cycle. Set a timer for 30 minutes.
3. When the timer sounds, check to make sure amaranth is tender. If necessary, continue cooking, checking for doneness every 5 minutes. Switch to the Keep Warm cycle. Let stand for 10 minutes, then serve immediately.

Variations

Add 2 tbsp (30 mL) finely chopped mixed fresh herbs (such as parsley, cilantro and thyme) when you switch to the Keep Warm cycle.

Substitute yellow summer squash (yellow zucchini) for the zucchini, or use a combination of the two.

Berry Breakfast Risotto (page 43)

Red Lentil and Red Rice Patties with Aïoli (page 60)

Moroccan Bean Dip (page 72)

Israeli Couscous Summer Chopped Salad (page 98)

Chinese Black Rice Salad with Orange and Avocado (page 84)

Tuscan Wheat Berry Soup (page 117)

Shrimp Corn and Quinoa Soup (page 130)

Wild Rice and Pork Stew (page 157)

Spicy Fish Stew with Quinoa

Makes 4 servings

This punchy stew is chock full of nutritious foods, including veggies, quinoa and fish, and the fresh flavors of citrus and cilantro make it a dish to die for. For a heavenly combo, pair it with your favorite Chablis or Riesling.

Tips

For a spicier stew, increase the amount of hot pepper flakes to taste.

The easiest way to grate lemon zest is with a rasp grater, such as a Microplane.

Although cooking this stew on the Brown Rice cycle takes an hour longer, it's worth it for the superior results.

● **Medium to large rice cooker; fuzzy logic or on/off**

2 tbsp	extra virgin olive oil	30 mL
2	cloves garlic, minced	2
½ cup	finely chopped onion	125 mL
1	red bell pepper, finely chopped	1
1	zucchini, diced	1
1	tomato, diced	1
1 cup	chopped celery	250 mL
1	can (14 oz/398 mL) diced tomatoes, with juice	1
1 cup	quinoa, rinsed and drained	250 mL
1 tsp	salt	5 mL
½ tsp	freshly ground black pepper	2 mL
¾ tsp	hot pepper flakes	3 mL
2 cups	fish stock or chicken broth	500 mL
1 lb	skinless white fish (such as sole, halibut or tilapia), cut into 2-inch (1 cm) pieces	500 g
½ cup	finely chopped fresh cilantro	125 mL
1 tsp	finely grated lemon zest	5 mL
	Additional finely chopped fresh cilantro	

1. Set the rice cooker for the Quick Cook or Regular cycle. When the bottom of the bowl gets hot, add oil and swirl to coat. Sauté garlic and onion for about 3 minutes or until onion is softened and translucent. Add red pepper, zucchini, fresh tomato and celery; sauté for 3 to 4 minutes or until softened.
2. Stir in canned tomatoes with juice, quinoa, salt, black pepper, hot pepper flakes and stock. Close the lid and reset for the Regular cycle. Set a timer for 30 minutes. (Or reset for the Brown Rice cycle and set a timer for 1 hour and 30 minutes.)
3. When the timer sounds, stir in fish, cilantro and lemon zest. Set the timer for 10 minutes.
4. When the timer sounds, check to make sure quinoa is tender and fish is opaque and flakes easily when tested with a fork. If necessary, continue cooking, checking for doneness every 3 minutes. Switch to the Keep Warm cycle. Let stand for 15 minutes. Serve immediately, garnished with cilantro.

Variation

Spicy Fish Stew with Millet: Substitute toasted millet (see tip, page 116) for the quinoa.

Stacy's Barley Cioppino

Makes 4 servings

The nutty flavor of barley adds a twist on this traditional Italian seafood stew, inspired by my friend Stacy's recipe. It tastes even better a day later. Serve with crusty bread.

Tips

It's best to buy mussels the day you are preparing this dish. Discard any with broken or cracked shells. If you find any mussels that are slightly open, they should close when you tap them sharply. If they do not, they are dead, and you should discard them.

To clean clams and mussels and debeard mussels, use a scrub brush or a toothbrush and scrub shell under cool running water to remove any debris or barnacles. Sharply pull any "beard" out of the lower edge of the mussel shell; use a small sharp knife if it proves to be stubborn. Rinse again under cool water.

The finished stew can be stored in an airtight container in the refrigerator for up to 24 hours. Reheat in the rice cooker on the Quick Cook or Regular cycle, stirring occasionally, until boiling.

• Large rice cooker; fuzzy logic or on/off

1/4 cup	butter	60 mL
3	cloves garlic, minced	3
1 cup	finely chopped onion	250 mL
2	cans (each 14 oz/398 mL) stewed tomatoes, drained and coarsely chopped	2
1/2 cup	pearl barley, rinsed and drained	125 mL
2	bay leaves	2
1 tsp	salt	5 mL
3/4 tsp	hot pepper flakes	3 mL
1/2 tsp	dried thyme	2 mL
1/2 tsp	dried oregano	2 mL
1/2 tsp	freshly ground black pepper	2 mL
4 cups	chicken broth, divided	1 L
1 cup	dry white wine	250 mL
1/2 cup	clam juice	125 mL
2 tbsp	tomato paste	30 mL
12	large shrimp, peeled and deveined	12
12	small clams, scrubbed	12
12	mussels, scrubbed and debearded (see tips, at left)	12
12 oz	bay scallops	375 g
1/4 cup	finely chopped fresh parsley	60 mL
3 tbsp	finely chopped fresh basil	45 mL

1. Set the rice cooker for the Quick Cook or Regular cycle. When the bottom of the bowl gets hot, add butter and let it melt. Sauté garlic and onion for about 3 minutes or until onion is softened and translucent.
2. Stir in tomatoes, barley, bay leaves, salt, hot pepper flakes, thyme, oregano, black pepper, 2 cups (500 mL) of the broth, wine, clam juice and tomato paste. Close the lid and reset for the Regular cycle. Set a timer for 50 minutes.
3. When the timer sounds, add the remaining broth. When stew returns to a boil, add shrimp, clams, mussels and scallops. Set the timer for 5 minutes.
4. When the timer sounds, switch to the Keep Warm cycle. Stir in parsley and basil. Let stand for 15 minutes or until clams and mussels open. Discard any clams and mussels that do not open.
5. Divide cioppino among warmed serving bowls. Serve immediately.

Mexican Seafood Stew

Makes 6 servings

Once you try this Mexican tradition, you will surely embrace it as one of your own. The smoky flavor of the chipotle peppers and the hint of beer combine with seafood and spice to create a truly satisfying stew. Serve with warm flour tortillas to sop up every last delicious drop. And if you have a beer left over, how about a toast to your superb cooking skills?

Tips

Increase the amount of chipotle peppers in adobo sauce if you're seeking greater heat.

Add fresh or canned clams or mussels, or any other seafood, to this dish. Add fresh seafood in step 3 and canned seafood when you switch to the Keep Warm cycle.

For information about rice cooker sizes, see page 13.

● **Large rice cooker; fuzzy logic or on/off**

2 tbsp	extra virgin olive oil	30 mL
2	cloves garlic, minced	2
1 cup	finely chopped onion	250 mL
2 tsp	dried cumin	10 mL
2 tsp	dried oregano	10 mL
1 cup	chopped celery	250 mL
1 cup	chopped green bell pepper	250 mL
1 cup	chopped red bell pepper	250 mL
1	can (14 oz/398 mL) white or yellow hominy, drained and rinsed	1
2 tbsp	minced seeded canned chipotle peppers in adobo sauce	30 mL
1 tsp	salt	5 mL
½ tsp	freshly ground black pepper	2 mL
1	bottle (12 oz/341 mL) lager beer (such as Corona or Tecate)	1
4 cups	chicken broth	1 L
12 oz	medium shrimp, peeled and deveined	375 g
12 oz	bay scallops	375 g
8 oz	skinless white fish (such as cod or halibut), cut into bite-size pieces	250 g
½ cup	finely chopped fresh cilantro	125 mL
2 tbsp	freshly squeezed lime juice	30 mL

1. Set the rice cooker for the Quick Cook or Regular cycle. When the bottom of the bowl gets hot, add oil and swirl to coat. Sauté garlic and onion for about 3 minutes or until onion is softened and translucent. Add cumin and oregano; sauté for 1 minute. Add celery, green pepper and red pepper; sauté for 3 to 4 minutes or until softened.

2. Stir in hominy, chipotles, salt, pepper, beer and broth. Close the lid and reset for the Regular cycle. Set a timer for 20 minutes.

3. When the timer sounds, add shrimp, scallops, fish, cilantro and lime juice. Set the timer for 10 minutes.

4. When the timer sounds, check to make sure shrimp are pink and opaque, scallops are firm and fish is opaque and flakes easily when tested with a fork. If necessary, continue cooking, checking for doneness every 3 minutes. Switch to the Keep Warm cycle. Let stand for 10 to 15 minutes, then serve immediately.

Spicy Chicken and Brown Rice Stew

Makes 4 to 6 servings

You'll never go back to run-of-the-mill chicken and rice soup once you've tried this twist on what the doctor ordered. The kick of the spices and the rich, nutty flavor of the brown rice bring a whole new meaning to chicken soup for the soul.

Tips

You may use boneless skinless chicken breasts for this recipe, but the thighs are more tender.

Increase the amount of hot pepper flakes to taste if you like more heat.

Although cooking this stew on the Brown Rice cycle takes an hour longer, it's worth it for the superior results.

● **Large rice cooker; fuzzy logic or on/off**

2 tbsp	extra virgin olive oil	30 mL
2	cloves garlic, minced	2
½ cup	finely chopped onion	125 mL
8 oz	boneless skinless chicken thighs, cut into ½-inch (1 cm) pieces	250 g
2 tsp	salt, divided	10 mL
1 tsp	chili powder	5 mL
1 tsp	ground cumin	5 mL
1 tsp	dried oregano	5 mL
1 tsp	sweet paprika	5 mL
¼ tsp	freshly ground black pepper	1 mL
1	small red bell pepper, finely chopped	1
1	carrot, diced	1
1½ cups	long-grain brown rice, rinsed and drained	375 mL
¾ tsp	hot pepper flakes	3 mL
4 cups	chicken broth	1 L
1 cup	dry white wine	250 mL
1 tbsp	tomato paste	15 mL
	Finely chopped fresh cilantro	

1. Set the rice cooker for the Quick Cook or Regular cycle. When the bottom of the bowl gets hot, add oil and swirl to coat. Sauté garlic and onion for about 3 minutes or until onion is softened and translucent. Add chicken, 1 tsp (5 mL) of the salt, chili powder, cumin, oregano, paprika and pepper; sauté for 4 to 5 minutes or until chicken is lightly browned on all sides. Add red pepper and carrot; sauté for 1 minute.

2. Stir in rice, the remaining salt, hot pepper flakes, broth, wine and tomato paste. Close the lid and reset for the Regular cycle. Set a timer for 40 minutes. (Or reset for the Brown Rice cycle and set a timer for 1 hour and 40 minutes.)

3. When the timer sounds, check to make sure rice is tender and juices run clear when chicken is pierced. If necessary, continue cooking, checking for doneness every 5 minutes. Switch to the Keep Warm cycle. Let stand for 10 minutes, then serve immediately, garnished with cilantro.

Chicken Paprikash

Makes 6 servings

I hope you're "Hungary," because this saucy dish will have you coming back for seconds. Considered a comfort food, paprikash goes best with egg noodles.

Tip

To bring out a pleasantly nutty aroma, toast the millet in a dry skillet over medium heat for 5 minutes before adding it to the rice cooker. (This is not necessary, but it's a nice touch if you have the time.)

Hungarian Sweet Paprika

Hungarian sweet paprika is a red powder made by grinding dried red bell peppers. It has a full pepper flavor, without heat. The color varies from bright orangey red to deep red, depending on the peppers used. Paprika deteriorates quickly, so purchase it in small quantities and store it in an airtight container, away from sunlight.

- **Medium to large rice cooker; fuzzy logic or on/off**

3 tbsp	extra virgin olive oil	45 mL
2 cups	finely chopped onions	500 mL
8 oz	boneless skinless chicken thighs, cut into ¾-inch (2 cm) pieces	250 g
2 tbsp	Hungarian sweet paprika	30 mL
2 tsp	salt	10 mL
½ tsp	freshly ground black pepper	5 mL
⅔ cup	millet (see tip, at left)	150 mL
2½ cups	chicken broth	625 mL
¼ cup	white wine	60 mL
1 cup	sour cream	250 mL

1. Set the rice cooker for the Quick Cook or Regular cycle. When the bottom of the bowl gets hot, add oil and swirl to coat. Sauté onions for about 3 minutes or until softened and translucent. Add chicken, paprika, salt and pepper; sauté for 4 to 5 minutes or until chicken is lightly browned on all sides.

2. Stir in millet, broth and wine. Close the lid and reset for the Regular cycle. Set a timer for 40 minutes.

3. When the timer sounds, check to make sure millet is tender and juices run clear when chicken is pierced. If necessary, continue cooking, checking for doneness every 5 minutes. Switch to the Keep Warm cycle. Stir in sour cream. Let stand for 15 minutes, then serve immediately.

Variation

Chicken Paprikash with Quinoa: Substitute drained rinsed quinoa for the millet (but don't toast it).

Southwestern Chicken Stew

Makes 6 servings

The Southwest is famous for its red-hued landscapes and powerful energy, and this wonderful stew captures both elements. The chicken, corn, beans and potatoes, enhanced by the flavors of jalapeño and chipotle, make for a hearty dish that will satisfy your appetite and recharge your soul. The tortilla chips add a delightful, crispy crunch.

Tips

Chipotle chile powder adds a wonderful hot, smoky flavor to this dish. Look for it in the spice aisle at the grocery store.

For convenience, you can use store-bought tortilla chips.

To crush the tortilla chips, place them in a sealable food storage bag, seal and crush with a mallet or rolling pin.

• **Large rice cooker; fuzzy logic or on/off**

2 tbsp	extra virgin olive oil	30 mL
2	cloves garlic, minced	2
1 cup	finely chopped onion	250 mL
8 oz	boneless skinless chicken thighs, cut into 1-inch (2.5 cm) pieces	250 g
1	jalapeño pepper, seeded and minced	1
1 tsp	chipotle chile powder	5 mL
¾ tsp	dried cumin	3 mL
½ tsp	dried oregano	2 mL
1	can (14 oz/398 mL) black beans, drained and rinsed	1
1 lb	red-skinned potatoes, cut into 1-inch (2.5 cm) pieces	500 g
1 cup	fresh or thawed frozen corn kernels	250 mL
1 tsp	salt	5 mL
1½ cups	chicken broth	375 mL
½ cup	finely chopped fresh cilantro	125 mL
½ cup	crushed Baked Tortilla Chips (see recipe, opposite)	125 mL
1 tbsp	freshly squeezed lime juice	15 mL
	Sour cream	

1. Set the rice cooker for the Quick Cook or Regular cycle. When the bottom of the bowl gets hot, add oil and swirl to coat. Sauté garlic and onion for about 3 minutes or until onion is softened and translucent. Add chicken, jalapeño, chile powder, cumin and oregano; sauté for 4 to 5 minutes or until chicken is lightly browned on all sides.

2. Stir in beans, potatoes, corn, salt and broth. Close the lid and reset for the Regular cycle. Set a timer for 30 minutes.

3. When the timer sounds, check to make sure potatoes are tender and juices run clear when chicken is pierced. If necessary, continue cooking, checking for doneness every 5 minutes. Switch to the Keep Warm cycle. Stir in cilantro, tortilla chips and lime juice. Let stand for 10 minutes, then serve immediately, garnished with sour cream.

Baked Tortilla Chips

Makes 36 chips

To add a homemade touch, try making your own tortilla chips. Because they're baked in the oven, rather than fried, they're a nice lighter alternative.

- **Preheat oven to 350°F (180°C)**
- **2 large baking sheets**

6	6-inch (15 cm) corn tortillas (preferably white)	6
2 tsp	vegetable oil	10 mL
	Fine sea salt	

1. Brush both sides of tortillas with oil. Stack tortillas and cut into sixths. Spread pieces out in a single layer on baking sheets and season to taste with salt.
2. Bake in preheated oven for 12 to 15 minutes, rotating the baking sheets once and switching their positions in the oven, until golden brown and crisp. Let cool.

Posole Nuevo

Makes 8 servings

In Mexico, families eat this spicy stew as a ceremonial dish to celebrate life's blessings. It's also renowned as a hangover cure. Whatever your reasons for serving it, you're sure to enjoy its unmatched flavor.

Tips

For a milder version of this dish, use jalapeño peppers in place of the serrano peppers.

For information about rice cooker sizes, see page 13.

- **Large rice cooker; fuzzy logic or on/off**
- **Blender or food processor**

2	dried pasilla chile peppers, stemmed and seeded	2
	Boiling water	
5½ cups	chicken broth, divided	1.375 mL
1 tsp	salt	5 mL
4	serrano chile peppers, seeded and chopped	4
2	cloves garlic, minced	2
2	cans (each 15 oz/426 mL) white hominy, drained and rinsed	2
1½ lbs	boneless skinless chicken thighs, cut into 2-inch (5 cm) pieces	750 g
2 cups	finely chopped onions	500 mL
1	bay leaf	1
2 tbsp	ground cumin	30 mL
2 tsp	dried oregano (preferably Mexican)	10 mL
1 tbsp	finely chopped fresh parsley	15 mL
1 tbsp	finely chopped fresh cilantro	15 mL
¼ cup	freshly squeezed lime juice	60 mL
	Additional finely chopped fresh cilantro	
	Warm corn tortillas	
	Sliced cabbage, sliced radishes and chopped onion	
	Lime wedges	

1. In a bowl, soak pasilla chile peppers in boiling water for 30 minutes. Drain and cut into ½-inch (1 cm) pieces.
2. In blender, combine pasilla chile peppers and 2 cups (500 mL) of the broth; purée until smooth.
3. In the rice cooker bowl, combine chile purée, serrano peppers, garlic, hominy, chicken, onions, bay leaf, cumin, oregano and the remaining broth. Set the rice cooker for the Regular cycle. Set a timer for 50 minutes.
4. When the timer sounds, check to make sure juices run clear when chicken is pierced. If necessary, continue cooking, checking for doneness every 5 minutes. Switch to the Keep Warm cycle. Discard bay leaf. Stir in parsley, cilantro and lime juice.
5. Ladle into soup bowls and garnish with cilantro. Serve with tortillas, cabbage, radishes, onion and lime wedges.

Bayou Stew with Andouille Sausage

Makes 4 to 6 servings

I love the spice of the andouille sausage and the freshness of the okra in this savory, gumbo-like stew. I especially love to eat it with a hunk of warm cornbread (see recipe, page 171). Yum!

Tip

Herbes de Provence is a blend of herbs commonly used in France. It's readily available at grocery stores, but to make your own, combine 3 tbsp (45 mL) dried marjoram, 3 tbsp (45 mL) dried thyme, 3 tbsp (45 mL) dried savory, 1 tsp (5 mL) dried basil, 1 tsp (5 mL) dried rosemary, ½ tsp (2 mL) dried sage and ½ tsp (2 mL) fennel seeds. Store in an airtight container in a cool, dark pantry or cupboard.

• Medium to large rice cooker; fuzzy logic or on/off

2 tbsp	extra virgin olive oil	30 mL
4	boneless skinless chicken thighs, cut into ½-inch (1 cm) pieces	4
8 oz	andouille sausage, cut diagonally into ¼-inch (0.5 cm) thick slices	250 g
1 tbsp	butter	15 mL
2	cloves garlic, minced	2
1 cup	finely chopped onion	250 mL
1 tsp	herbes de Provence (see tip, at left)	5 mL
½ tsp	freshly ground black pepper	2 mL
½ tsp	freshly ground white pepper	2 mL
½ tsp	cayenne pepper	2 mL
½ tsp	dry mustard	2 mL
½ tsp	salt	2 mL
½ cup	thinly sliced celery	125 mL
½ cup	sliced trimmed okra	125 mL
1	can (14 oz/398 mL) diced tomatoes, drained	1
1½ cups	long-grain white rice, rinsed and drained	375 mL
5 cups	chicken broth	1.25 L

1. Set the rice cooker for the Quick Cook or Regular cycle. When the bottom of the bowl gets hot, add oil and swirl to coat. Sauté chicken and sausage for 5 to 7 minutes or until chicken is no longer pink inside. Using a slotted spoon, transfer chicken and sausage to a plate lined with paper towels and set aside.

2. Add butter to the rice cooker bowl and let it melt. Sauté garlic and onion for about 3 minutes or until onion is softened and translucent. Add herbes de Provence, black pepper, white pepper, cayenne, mustard and salt; sauté for 1 minute. Add celery and okra; sauté for 4 to 5 minutes or until softened.

3. Stir in tomatoes, rice and broth. Close the lid and reset for the Regular cycle. Set a timer for 30 minutes.

4. When the timer sounds, check to make sure rice is tender. If necessary, continue cooking, checking for doneness every 5 minutes. Switch to the Keep Warm cycle. Stir in reserved chicken and sausage. Let stand for 10 minutes, then serve immediately.

Chicken Bog Stew

Makes 4 servings

A gem of coastal South Carolinian cuisine, chicken bog stew has its very own festival in that state. Close your eyes and, with each hearty spoonful, you can envision the marsh grasses swaying in the Carolina ocean breezes.

Tips

For intensified flavor, add 1 tsp (5 mL) seasoned salt (such as Lawry's) with the other seasonings.

For information about rice cooker sizes, see page 13.

● **Medium to large rice cooker; fuzzy logic or on/off**

4	boneless skinless chicken thighs	4
8 oz	smoked Italian sausage, cut diagonally into ¼-inch (0.5 cm) thick slices	250 g
½ cup	finely chopped onion	125 mL
1 tbsp	dried Italian seasoning	15 mL
2 tsp	salt	10 mL
1 tsp	freshly ground black pepper	5 mL
1 tsp	garlic powder	5 mL
1 tsp	granulated sugar	5 mL
¼ tsp	sweet paprika	1 mL
⅛ tsp	ground turmeric	0.5 mL
⅛ tsp	onion powder	0.5 mL
3½ cups	water	875 mL
¼ cup	butter	60 mL
1 cup	long-grain white rice, rinsed and drained	250 mL

1. In the rice cooker bowl, combine chicken, sausage, onion, Italian seasoning, salt, pepper, garlic powder, sugar, paprika, turmeric, onion powder, water and butter. Set the rice cooker for the Regular cycle. Set a timer for 45 minutes.
2. When the timer sounds, check to make sure juices run clear when chicken is pierced. If necessary, continue cooking, checking for doneness every 5 minutes. Using a slotted spoon, transfer chicken to a cutting board and sausage to a plate.
3. Add rice to the rice cooker bowl and swirl to combine. Close the lid and reset for the Regular cycle. Set the timer for 30 minutes.
4. Meanwhile, shred chicken and set aside.
5. When the timer sounds, check to make sure rice is tender. If necessary, continue cooking, checking for doneness every 5 minutes. Switch to the Keep Warm cycle. Stir in reserved chicken and sausage. Let stand for 10 minutes, then serve immediately.

Tex-Mex Turkey Stew

Makes 4 to 6 servings

I absolutely love the flavor and texture wild rice contributes to this recipe, and how well it combines with the Tex-Mex flavors. Fresh cilantro adds the perfect finishing touch.

Tip

Although cooking this stew on the Brown Rice cycle takes an hour longer, it's worth it for the superior results.

• Medium to large rice cooker; fuzzy logic or on/off

1 tbsp	extra virgin olive oil	15 mL
1 cup	finely chopped onion	250 mL
1 tsp	dried oregano	5 mL
1 tsp	ground cumin	5 mL
1 lb	ground turkey	500 g
2	cans (each 4 oz/114 mL) chopped mild green chiles	2
2 cups	fresh or thawed frozen white corn kernels	500 mL
1 cup	wild rice, rinsed and drained	250 mL
3¾ cups	chicken broth	925 mL
1½ cups	shredded Monterey Jack cheese	375 mL
	Finely chopped fresh cilantro	

1. Set the rice cooker for the Quick Cook or Regular cycle. When the bottom of the bowl gets hot, add oil and swirl to coat. Sauté onion for about 3 minutes or until softened and translucent. Add oregano and cumin; sauté for 1 minute. Add turkey and sauté, breaking it up with the back of a spoon, for 4 to 5 minutes or until no longer pink.

2. Add chiles, corn, wild rice and broth. Close the lid and reset for the Regular cycle. Set a timer for 55 minutes. (Or reset for the Brown Rice cycle and set a timer for 1 hour and 55 minutes.)

3. When the timer sounds, check to make sure wild rice is tender. If necessary, continue cooking, checking for doneness every 5 minutes. Serve immediately, garnished with cheese and cilantro.

Variation

For a vegetarian version of this recipe, replace the ground turkey with 12 oz (375 g) of a soy-based meat product, such as Yves veggie ground chicken. Use vegetable broth instead of chicken broth.

Black-Eyed Pea, Turkey and Swiss Chard Stew

Makes 3 to 4 servings

Two of the earth's healthiest foods, beans and greens, combine with ground turkey to create this mouthwatering concoction. Though it's typically served as a winter dish, this Greek-style stew can be enjoyed all year long.

Swiss Chard

Swiss chard is a leafy vegetable that is part of the beet family. It has shiny, green ribbed leaves, with stems that range from white to yellow to red. It has a slightly bitter taste if eaten raw, but this bitterness fades after cooking.

● **Medium rice cooker; fuzzy logic or on/off**

1 cup	dried black-eyed peas	250 mL
2 tbsp	extra virgin olive oil	30 mL
1 cup	finely chopped red onion	250 mL
8 oz	ground turkey	250 g
	Salt and freshly ground black pepper	
1	can (14 oz/398 mL) diced tomatoes, with juice	1
Pinch	hot pepper flakes	Pinch
4 cups	chicken or vegetable broth	1 L
2 tbsp	tomato paste	30 mL
1	bunch Swiss chard (green leaves only), coarsely chopped (about 5 cups/1.25 L)	1

1. Sort, rinse, soak and drain peas (see pages 32–33).
2. Set the rice cooker for the Quick Cook or Regular cycle. When the bottom of the bowl gets hot, add oil and swirl to coat. Sauté red onion for about 3 minutes or until softened and translucent. Add turkey, 1 tsp (5 mL) salt and $\frac{1}{4}$ tsp (1 mL) black pepper; sauté, breaking turkey up with the back of a spoon, for 4 to 5 minutes or until turkey is no longer pink.
3. Stir in peas, tomatoes with juice, hot pepper flakes, broth and tomato paste. Close the lid and reset for the Regular cycle. Set a timer for 1 hour.
4. When the timer sounds, check to make sure peas are tender. If necessary, continue cooking, checking for doneness every 5 minutes. Stir in Swiss chard and let stand for 10 to 15 minutes or until wilted. Season to taste with salt and black pepper. Serve immediately.

Variation

Substitute dried lima beans for the black-eyed peas.

Wild Rice and Pork Stew

Makes 4 to 6 servings

The nutty flavor of wild rice and aromatic fennel bring great depth to this autumnal stew, and it's a breeze to put together. Serve it with buttered rye bread and enjoy!

Tips

Toasting fennel seeds intensifies their flavor. Toast them in a dry skillet over medium-high heat, stirring constantly, for about 3 minutes or until fragrant. Immediately transfer to a spice grinder and let cool, then grind to a fine powder.

Try using a wild rice blend, such as Lundberg Farms.

Although cooking this stew on the Brown Rice cycle takes an hour longer, it's worth it for the superior results.

• **Medium to large rice cooker; fuzzy logic or on/off**

2 tbsp	extra virgin olive oil	30 mL
1/2 cup	finely chopped onion	125 mL
1 lb	boneless pork shoulder blade (butt) roast, cut into 2- by 1-inch (5 by 2.5 cm) pieces	500 g
2 tsp	salt, divided	10 mL
1/2 tsp	fennel seeds, toasted and ground (see tip, at left)	2 mL
1/2 tsp	chili powder	2 mL
1/4 tsp	ground cumin	1 mL
1/4 tsp	freshly ground black pepper	1 mL
3 1/2 cups	chicken broth	875 mL
2	tomatoes, diced	2
1	can (14 oz/398 mL) diced tomatoes, with juice	1
1	bay leaf	1
1 cup	wild rice, rinsed and drained	250 mL
1/4 cup	chopped green onions (green and white parts)	60 mL

1. Set the rice cooker for the Quick Cook or Regular cycle. When the bottom of the bowl gets hot, add oil and swirl to coat. Sauté onion for about 3 minutes or until softened and translucent. Add pork, 1 tsp (5 mL) salt, fennel seeds, chili powder, cumin and pepper; sauté for 10 minutes or until pork is browned on all sides.

2. Stir in broth. Close the lid and reset for the Regular cycle. Set a timer for 45 minutes.

3. When the timer sounds, check to make sure pork is fork-tender. If necessary, continue cooking, checking for doneness every 5 minutes. Using a slotted spoon, transfer pork to a cutting board.

4. Add fresh tomatoes, canned tomatoes with juice, bay leaf, rice and the remaining salt to the rice cooker bowl. Close the lid and reset for the Regular cycle. Set the timer for 55 minutes. (Or reset for the Brown Rice cycle and set a timer for 1 hour and 55 minutes.)

5. Meanwhile, shred pork and transfer to a plate. Cover and refrigerate.

6. When the timer sounds, check to make sure rice is tender. If necessary, continue cooking, checking for doneness every 5 minutes. Switch to the Keep Warm cycle. Stir in shredded pork and green onions. Let stand for 15 minutes, then serve immediately.

Beef Bourguignon

Makes 4 to 6 servings

This hearty stew is easy to make but tastes like you spent all day in the kitchen. Although it began as a peasant dish, it has become a go-to recipe for many in haute cuisine. Serve your favorite Burgundy or Merlot alongside, for a marriage made in heaven!

Tips

If you don't have cheesecloth to make a bouquet garni, simply add the herbs, clove and garlic separately. Just remember to remove them before serving.

For information about rice cooker sizes, see page 13.

• **Medium to large rice cooker; fuzzy logic or on/off**

2	fresh parsley sprigs	2
1	large bay leaf	1
1	whole clove	1
1	clove garlic, smashed	1
1¼ tsp	dried thyme	6 mL
1 lb	boneless beef top round, trimmed and cut into 1½-inch (4 cm) cubes	500 g
1 tbsp	cornstarch	15 mL
2 tbsp	extra virgin olive oil, divided	30 mL
1 tbsp	butter	15 mL
1 cup	thinly sliced onion	250 mL
¼ cup	all-purpose flour	60 mL
1½ cups	beef broth	375 mL
½ cup	dry red wine	125 mL
1 tbsp	tomato paste	15 mL
½ cup	sliced mushrooms	125 mL
½ cup	pearl barley, rinsed and drained	125 mL
½ cup	sliced carrots (cut into rounds)	125 mL
¼ cup	diced tomato	60 mL
½ tsp	salt	2 mL
¼ tsp	freshly ground black pepper	1 mL
	Fresh thyme leaves	

1. Tie parsley, bay leaf, clove, garlic and dried thyme in a square of cheesecloth, making a bouquet garni. Set aside.
2. Pat beef dry with paper towels. Place in a large sealable food storage bag, add cornstarch, seal and toss to coat.
3. Set the rice cooker for the Quick Cook or Regular cycle. When the bottom of the bowl gets hot, add 1 tbsp (15 mL) oil and butter and let butter melt. Add dredged beef and sauté for 4 to 5 minutes or until browned on all sides. Using a slotted spoon, transfer beef to a plate and set aside.
4. Add the remaining oil to the rice cooker bowl. Sauté onion for about 3 minutes or until onion is softened and translucent. Sprinkle with flour and sauté for 1 minute.

Tips

I like to use a robust red wine, such as Burgundy, for this stew.

For an alcohol-free version of this recipe, increase the beef broth to 1¾ cups (425 mL) and omit the red wine.

5. Gradually stir in broth, wine and tomato paste; cook, stirring, for 1 minute or until thickened. Stir in bouquet garni, reserved beef and any accumulated juices, mushrooms, barley, carrots, tomato, salt and pepper. Close the lid and reset for the Regular cycle. When stew comes to a boil, set a timer for 12 minutes.

6. When the timer sounds, reset the machine for the Keep Warm cycle. Set a timer for 1 hour and 15 minutes.

7. When the timer sounds, check to make sure barley and beef are tender. If necessary, continue cooking, checking for doneness every 5 minutes. Discard bouquet garni. Serve immediately, garnished with fresh thyme.

Lamb, Couscous and Lentil Stew

Makes 4 servings

Couscous and lentils go together like peas and carrots, like Champagne and strawberries, like bread and butter — you get the picture. This stew is a great way to enjoy them.

Tip

Preserved lemon is a condiment that is common in North African cuisine, and especially Moroccan cuisine. It is also known as "country lemon." To make it, lemons are pickled in a brine of water, lemon juice and salt. The resulting flavor is mildly tart but intensely lemony. It can be found at Middle Eastern markets and specialty shops.

• Large rice cooker; fuzzy logic or on/off

2 tbsp	extra virgin olive oil	30 mL
3	cloves garlic, minced	3
1 cup	finely chopped onion	250 mL
1	2-inch (5 cm) cinnamon stick	1
½ tsp	ground cumin	2 mL
½ tsp	ground coriander	2 mL
1 lb	ground lamb	500 g
1 cup	finely chopped red bell pepper	250 mL
1½ cups	dried green lentils, sorted and rinsed	375 mL
½ cup	Israeli couscous	125 mL
2 tbsp	chopped dried apricots	30 mL
1 tsp	salt	5 mL
¼ tsp	freshly ground black pepper	1 mL
	Minced peel of 1 preserved lemon (see tip, at left)	
3½ cups	chicken broth	875 mL
½ cup	dry white wine	125 mL
1	can (28 oz/796 mL) tomatoes, drained	1

1. Set the rice cooker for the Quick Cook or Regular cycle. When the bottom of the bowl gets hot, add oil and swirl to coat. Sauté garlic and onion for about 3 minutes or until onion is softened and translucent. Add cinnamon stick, cumin and coriander; sauté for 1 minute. Add lamb and sauté, breaking it up with the back of a spoon, for 4 to 5 minutes or until no longer pink. Add red pepper and sauté for 2 minutes.

2. Stir in lentils, couscous, apricots, salt, pepper, lemon peel, broth and wine. Stir in tomatoes, breaking them up with your fingers as you add them. Close the lid and reset for the Regular cycle. Set a timer for 40 minutes.

3. When the timer sounds, check to make sure lentils are tender. If necessary, continue cooking, checking for doneness every 5 minutes. Switch to the Keep Warm cycle. Let stand for 10 minutes, then discard cinnamon stick and serve immediately.

Variation

Substitute ground turkey (preferably dark meat) for the lamb.

Spicy Vegetarian Chili

Makes 6 to 8 servings

Chili is a great way to go vegetarian while never missing the carnivorous life. In this one, the spices and chipotle peppers lend a smoky heat that will light you up, in a good way! Increase the amount of hot pepper flakes if you like more heat. Serve topped with sour cream and garnished with shredded Cheddar cheese and finely chopped fresh cilantro.

Tips

If you're not serving vegetarians, add 2 cups (500 mL) diced cooked chicken for more protein.

For information about rice cooker sizes, see page 13.

• Large rice cooker; fuzzy logic or on/off

2 tbsp	extra virgin olive oil	30 mL
2	cloves garlic, minced	2
1 cup	finely chopped onion	250 mL
1 tbsp	dried oregano	15 mL
1 tbsp	chili powder	15 mL
2 tsp	ground cumin	10 mL
1 tsp	salt	5 mL
½ tsp	freshly ground black pepper	2 mL
½ tsp	hot pepper flakes (or to taste)	2 mL
1	large carrot, cut into rounds	1
1 cup	chopped green bell pepper	250 mL
1 cup	chopped red bell pepper	250 mL
½ cup	chopped celery	125 mL
1	can (14 oz/398 mL) red kidney beans, drained and rinsed	1
1	can (14 oz/398 mL) black beans, drained and rinsed	1
1	can (28 oz/796 mL) diced tomatoes, with juice	1
¾ cup	millet	175 mL
2 tbsp	minced seeded canned chipotle peppers in adobo sauce	30 mL
2 cups	vegetable broth	500 mL

1. Set the rice cooker for the Quick Cook or Regular cycle. When the bottom of the bowl gets hot, add oil and swirl to coat. Sauté garlic and onion for about 3 minutes or until onion is softened and translucent. Add oregano, chili powder, cumin, salt, black pepper and hot pepper flakes; sauté for 1 minute. Add carrot, green pepper, red pepper and celery; sauté for 3 to 4 minutes or until softened.

2. Stir in kidney beans, black beans, tomatoes with juice, millet, chipotle peppers and broth. Close the lid and reset for the Regular cycle. Set a timer for 40 minutes.

3. When the timer sounds, check to make sure millet is tender. If necessary, continue cooking, checking for doneness every 5 minutes. Switch to the Keep Warm cycle. Let stand, stirring occasionally, for at least 15 minutes or up to 1 hour.

Lentil Chili

Makes 4 to 6 servings

This is one of those very well-rounded recipes: easy to throw together, delightfully flavorful and super-good for you. Who can argue with that?

Tip

If tomato purée is not available, substitute ⅓ cup (75 mL) tomato paste combined with ⅓ cup (75 mL) water.

- **Medium to large rice cooker; fuzzy logic or on/off**

2 tbsp	extra virgin olive oil	30 mL
2	cloves garlic, minced	2
1	jalapeño pepper, seeded and minced	1
½ cup	finely chopped onion	125 mL
1 tbsp	ground cumin	15 mL
1 tsp	dried oregano	5 mL
1 tsp	chipotle chile powder	5 mL
1 tsp	salt	5 mL
¼ tsp	freshly ground black pepper	1 mL
1 cup	dried brown or green lentils, sorted and rinsed	250 mL
4 cups	chicken or vegetable broth	1 L
½ cup	tomato purée (see tip, at left)	125 mL
½ cup	chopped green onions (white and green parts)	125 mL
	Additional chopped green onion	

1. Set the rice cooker for the Quick Cook or Regular cycle. When the bottom of the bowl gets hot, add oil and swirl to coat. Sauté garlic, jalapeño pepper and onion for about 3 minutes or until onion is softened and translucent. Add cumin, oregano, chile powder, salt and pepper; sauté for 1 minute.
2. Stir in lentils, broth and tomato purée. Close the lid and reset for the Regular cycle. Set a timer for 50 minutes.
3. When the timer sounds, check to make sure lentils are tender. If necessary, continue cooking, checking for doneness every 5 minutes. Switch to the Keep Warm cycle. Stir in green onions. Let stand, stirring occasionally, for at least 10 minutes or up to 1 hour. Serve hot, garnished with green onions.

Black Bean Quinoa Chili

Makes 6 to 8 servings

Very low in fat and high in protein, this chili tastes insanely good considering its health benefits. Plus, it's easy to make — you can't go wrong.

Tip
Although cooking this chili on the Brown Rice cycle takes an hour longer, it's worth it for the superior results.

- **Large rice cooker; fuzzy logic or on/off**

2 tbsp	extra virgin olive oil	30 mL
1 cup	finely chopped onion	250 mL
2 tbsp	finely chopped fresh parsley	30 mL
1 tbsp	dried oregano	15 mL
1 tbsp	chili powder	15 mL
2 tsp	ground cumin	10 mL
½ tsp	salt	2 mL
½ tsp	freshly ground black pepper	2 mL
1	green bell pepper, finely chopped	1
1	jalapeño pepper, seeded and minced	1
1 cup	chopped celery	250 mL
2	tomatoes, diced	2
1 cup	diced carrots	250 mL
2	cans (each 14 to 19 oz/398 to 540 mL) black beans, drained and rinsed	2
1	can (28 oz/796 mL) crushed tomatoes	1
1 cup	quinoa, rinsed and drained	250 mL
2 cups	water	500 mL
	Chopped green onions (white and green parts)	
	Sour cream	
	Cubed avocado	

1. Set the rice cooker for the Quick Cook or Regular cycle. When the bottom of the bowl gets hot, add oil and swirl to coat. Sauté onion for about 3 minutes or until softened and translucent. Add parsley, oregano, chili powder, cumin, salt and pepper; sauté for 1 minute. Add green pepper, jalapeño and celery; sauté for 3 to 4 minutes or until softened. Add diced tomatoes and carrots; sauté for 3 minutes.

2. Stir in beans, crushed tomatoes, quinoa and water. Close the lid and reset for the Regular cycle. Set a timer for 45 minutes. (Or reset for the Brown Rice cycle and set a timer for 1 hour and 45 minutes.)

3. When the timer sounds, check to make sure quinoa is tender. If necessary, continue cooking, checking for doneness every 5 minutes. Switch to the Keep Warm cycle. Let stand for 15 minutes, stirring occasionally, then serve immediately, garnished with green onions, with sour cream and avocado on the side.

Hearty Bean and Barley Chili

Makes 8 servings

True to its name, this filling vegetarian chili is the perfect remedy for a chilling winter evening. I don't always think of putting chili and wine together, but this one pairs well with Shiraz.

Tips

To avoid tearing up when you're chopping onions, try refrigerating the onions for 30 minutes first, and don't cut the root off.

For information about rice cooker sizes, see page 13.

- **Large rice cooker; fuzzy logic or on/off**
- **Blender or food processor**

1½ cups	dried pinto beans	375 mL
2 tbsp	extra virgin olive oil	30 mL
2	cloves garlic, minced	2
1 cup	finely chopped onion	250 mL
2 tsp	ground cumin	10 mL
2 tsp	chili powder	10 mL
1 tsp	dried oregano	5 mL
1 tsp	salt	5 mL
½ tsp	freshly ground black pepper	2 mL
2	carrots, diced	2
2 cups	chopped celery	500 mL
1	bay leaf	1
4½ cups	water or vegetable broth	1.125 L
4	dried mild New Mexico chile peppers, stemmed and seeded	4
	Boiling water	
2 cups	vegetable broth	500 mL
1	can (28 oz/796 mL) diced tomatoes, drained	1
½ cup	pearl barley, rinsed and drained	125 mL
½ tsp	granulated sugar	2 mL
1 tbsp	cider vinegar	15 mL

1. Sort, rinse, soak and drain beans (see pages 32–33).
2. Set the rice cooker for the Quick Cook or Regular cycle. When the bottom of the bowl gets hot, add oil and swirl to coat. Sauté garlic and onion for about 3 minutes or until onion is softened and translucent. Add cumin, chili powder, oregano, salt and pepper; sauté for 1 minute. Add carrot and celery; sauté for 3 to 4 minutes or until softened.
3. Stir in soaked beans, bay leaf and water. Close the lid and reset for the Regular cycle. Set a timer for 45 minutes.

4. Meanwhile, soak chile peppers in boiling water for 30 minutes. Drain and cut into $\frac{1}{4}$-inch (0.5 cm) pieces.

5. In blender, combine chile peppers and broth; purée until smooth.

6. When the timer sounds, stir in chile purée, tomatoes and barley. Set the timer for 45 minutes.

7. When the timer sounds, check to make sure barley is tender. If necessary, continue cooking, checking for doneness every 5 minutes. Switch to the Keep Warm cycle. Stir in sugar and vinegar. Let stand for 15 minutes, stirring occasionally, then serve immediately.

Quinoa Chicken Chili

Makes 6 to 8 servings

Depth of flavor makes this chili a sure fave. The smoky chipotle pepper and the deep cocoa flavor are a winning combo.

Tips

To peel garlic quickly, place a large, wide knife (such as a chef's knife) over the clove and hit it hard — but not too hard. The garlic should crack a bit, making it easy to remove the peel.

Try sprinkling garlic cloves with a tiny bit of salt before mincing. The salt absorbs a little of the liquid, so the garlic won't stick to your knife.

You can use your favorite chili powder blend or one from a single source, such as ancho or New Mexico chiles.

• Large rice cooker; fuzzy logic or on/off

2 tbsp	extra virgin olive oil	30 mL
2	cloves garlic, minced	2
1 cup	finely chopped onion	250 mL
1	small zucchini, seeded and chopped	1
1 cup	chopped orange bell pepper	250 mL
8 oz	boneless skinless chicken thighs, cut into bite-size pieces	250 g
2 tbsp	chili powder	30 mL
1 tbsp	ground cumin	15 mL
1 tsp	dried oregano	5 mL
1 tsp	unsweetened cocoa powder	5 mL
1 tsp	salt	5 mL
1/2 tsp	freshly ground black pepper	2 mL
1/2 tsp	ground cinnamon	2 mL
1	can (14 to 19 oz/398 to 540 mL) black beans, drained and rinsed	1
1	can (14 to 19 oz/398 to 540 mL) red kidney beans, drained and rinsed	1
1	can (28 oz/796 mL) crushed tomatoes	1
1 cup	quinoa, rinsed and drained	250 mL
1 tbsp	minced seeded canned chipotle pepper in adobo sauce	15 mL
2 cups	chicken broth	500 mL
	Sour cream or Greek-style plain yogurt	
	Chopped fresh cilantro	

1. Set the rice cooker for the Quick Cook or Regular cycle. When the bottom of the bowl gets hot, add oil and swirl to coat. Sauté garlic and onion for about 3 minutes or until onion is softened and translucent. Add zucchini and orange pepper; sauté for 3 to 4 minutes or until softened. Add chicken, chili powder, cumin, oregano, cocoa powder, salt, pepper and cinnamon; sauté for 4 to 5 minutes or until chicken is lightly browned on all sides.

Although cooking this chili on the Brown Rice cycle takes an hour longer, it's worth it for the superior results.

For information about rice cooker sizes, see page 13.

2. Stir in black beans, kidney beans, tomatoes, quinoa, chipotle pepper and broth. Close the lid and reset for the Regular cycle. Set a timer for 40 minutes. (Or reset for the Brown Rice cycle and set a timer for 1 hour and 40 minutes.)

3. When the timer sounds, check to make sure quinoa is tender and juices run clear when chicken is pierced. If necessary, continue cooking, checking for doneness every 5 minutes. Switch to the Keep Warm cycle. Let stand for 15 minutes, stirring occasionally, then serve immediately, topped with sour cream and garnished with cilantro.

Variation

Quinoa Pork Chili: Replace the chicken with 1 lb (500 g) pork tenderloin, cut into $1/2$-inch (1 cm) pieces. In step 3, make sure pork is tender.

Dylan's Favorite Chili

Makes 6 servings

This is my son's favorite chili and got rave reviews from parents and youngsters alike when I served it recently at his birthday party. It incorporates the perfect blend of flavors, and works well with toasted tortilla strips!

Tips

Increase the amount of cayenne pepper for more heat in this dish.

For the best flavor, toast whole cumin and coriander seeds in a dry skillet over medium-high heat, stirring constantly, for about 3 minutes or until fragrant. Immediately transfer to a spice grinder and let cool, then grind to a fine powder.

● **Large rice cooker; fuzzy logic or on/off**

2 tbsp	extra virgin olive oil	30 mL
1	clove garlic, minced	1
1 cup	finely chopped onion	250 mL
3	poblano peppers, seeded and ribs removed, finely diced (about 1½ cups/375 mL)	3
1 lb	ground pork or chicken	500 g
1 tsp	salt	5 mL
1 tsp	ground cumin	5 mL
¾ tsp	dried oregano	3 mL
½ tsp	ground coriander	2 mL
½ tsp	freshly ground black pepper	2 mL
¼ tsp	cayenne pepper	1 mL
1 cup	chopped celery	250 mL
2	cans (14 to 19 oz/398 to 540 mL) white beans (such as cannellini or white kidney), drained and rinsed	2
1	can (15 oz/426 mL) white or yellow hominy, drained and rinsed	1
4 cups	chicken broth	1 L
	Sour cream	
	Finely chopped fresh cilantro	
	Lime wedges	

1. Set the rice cooker for the Quick Cook or Regular cycle. When the bottom of the bowl gets hot, add oil and swirl to coat. Sauté garlic and onion for about 3 minutes or until onion is softened and translucent. Add poblano peppers, pork, salt, cumin, oregano, coriander, black pepper and cayenne; sauté, breaking pork up with the back of a spoon, for 4 to 5 minutes or until pork is no longer pink. Add celery and sauté for 2 minutes.

2. Stir in beans, hominy and broth. Close the lid and reset for the Regular cycle. Set a timer for 45 minutes.

3. When the timer sounds, switch to the Keep Warm cycle. Let stand for 10 minutes, stirring occasionally, then serve immediately, topped with sour cream and garnished with cilantro, with lime wedges on the side.

White Turkey Chili with Chipotle

Makes 4 to 5 servings

This chili is a big winner at our house on game night. The canned beans make it super-easy and convenient.

Tips

The combination of chipotle chile powder and canned chipotles adds extra smokiness and texture to this dish.

Anaheim peppers are a mild chile pepper. If you want to add some heat to this dish, use jalapeños or serranos.

For information about rice cooker sizes, see page 13.

- **Medium to large rice cooker; fuzzy logic or on/off**
- **Blender or food processor**

2 tbsp	extra virgin olive oil	30 mL
1	clove garlic, minced	1
1 cup	finely chopped onion	250 mL
1 lb	ground turkey	500 g
½	Anaheim pepper, seeded and minced	½
2 tsp	ground cumin	10 mL
1 tsp	chipotle chile powder	5 mL
1 tsp	salt	5 mL
¼ tsp	freshly ground black pepper	1 mL
3	cans (each 14 to 19 oz/398 to 540 mL) cannellini (white kidney) beans, drained, reserving ½ cup (125 mL) liquid, and rinsed	3
1½ tsp	minced seeded canned chipotle pepper in adobo sauce	7 mL
1¼ cups	chicken broth, divided	300 mL
½ cup	Greek-style plain yogurt	125 mL
	Shredded Monterey Jack cheese	
	Finely chopped fresh cilantro	

1. Set the rice cooker for the Quick Cook or Regular cycle. When the bottom of the bowl gets hot, add oil and swirl to coat. Sauté garlic and onion for about 3 minutes or until onion is softened and translucent. Add turkey, Anaheim pepper, cumin, chile powder, salt and pepper; sauté, breaking turkey up with the back of a spoon, for 4 to 5 minutes or until turkey is no longer pink.

2. Add two-thirds of the beans, reserved bean liquid, chipotle pepper and ½ cup (125 mL) of the broth. Close the lid and reset for the Regular cycle. Set a timer for 45 minutes.

3. Meanwhile, in blender, combine the remaining beans and broth; purée until smooth.

4. When the timer sounds, switch to the Keep Warm cycle. Stir in bean purée and yogurt. Let stand for 10 minutes, stirring occasionally, then serve immediately, garnished with cheese and cilantro.

Game Day Chili

Makes 8 servings

Kick off a crowd-pleasing afternoon with your favorite team and this delicious bean-free chili. The turkey, millet and jalapeño make such a zesty combination, no one will realize how healthy it is. Serve it with cornbread (see recipe, opposite).

Tips

Chipotle chile powder adds a wonderful hot, smoky flavor to this dish. Look for it in the spice aisle at the grocery store.

For information about rice cooker sizes, see page 13.

• Large rice cooker; fuzzy logic or on/off

2 tbsp	extra virgin olive oil	30 mL
1	clove garlic, minced	1
1 cup	finely chopped onion	250 mL
2 tbsp	chili powder	30 mL
1 tsp	ground cumin	5 mL
1 tsp	salt	5 mL
¾ tsp	chipotle chile powder	3 mL
¼ tsp	freshly ground black pepper	1 mL
2 lbs	ground turkey	1 kg
1	jalapeño pepper, seeded and minced	1
1 cup	chopped green bell pepper	250 mL
1	can (14 oz/398 mL) diced tomatoes, with juice	1
1 cup	millet	250 mL
1 tbsp	cornmeal	15 mL
2¼ cups	beef broth	550 mL
1 tbsp	tomato paste	15 mL
	Sour cream or Greek-style plain yogurt	
	Sliced green onions (white and green parts)	
	Shredded Cheddar cheese	

1. Set the rice cooker for the Quick Cook or Regular cycle. When the bottom of the bowl gets hot, add oil and swirl to coat. Sauté garlic and onion for about 3 minutes or until onion is softened and translucent. Add chili powder, cumin, salt, chipotle chile powder and pepper; sauté for 1 minute. Add turkey, jalapeño and green pepper; sauté, breaking turkey up with the back of a spoon, for 4 to 5 minutes or until turkey is no longer pink.

2. Stir in tomatoes with juice, millet, cornmeal, broth and tomato paste. Close the lid and reset for the Regular cycle. Set a timer for 45 minutes.

3. When the timer sounds, check to make sure millet is tender. If necessary, continue cooking, checking for doneness every 5 minutes. Switch to the Keep Warm cycle. Let stand for 15 minutes, stirring occasionally, then serve immediately, topped with sour cream and garnished with green onions and cheese.

Cornbread

Makes 4 servings

Nothing beats cornbread fresh from the oven, especially when it's paired with a hearty chili or stew.

- **Preheat oven to 425°F (220°C)**
- **9-inch (23 cm) square metal baking pan, greased**

1¾ cups	cornmeal	425 mL
¾ cup	all-purpose flour	175 mL
2 tsp	baking powder	10 mL
1 tsp	salt	5 mL
1	large egg	1
1½ cups	milk	375 mL
¼ cup	melted butter	60 mL

1. In a medium bowl, whisk together cornmeal, flour, baking powder and salt.
2. In another bowl, whisk together egg, milk and butter until blended. Add to the cornmeal mixture and stir just until moistened. Pour into prepared baking pan.
3. Bake in preheated oven for 22 to 25 minutes or until a tester inserted in the center comes out clean. Let cool in pan on a wire rack for 20 minutes. Serve warm.

Bacon and Wheat Berry Chili

Makes 8 servings

The pop of the wheat berries and the potency of the bacon make this chili powerfully flavorful. You can't find a spoon big enough!

Tips

Although cooking this chili on the Brown Rice cycle takes an hour longer, it's worth it for the superior results.

For information about rice cooker sizes, see page 13.

• **Large rice cooker; fuzzy logic or on/off**

3	slices bacon, finely chopped	3
1 cup	finely chopped onion	250 mL
1 tbsp	chili powder	15 mL
1 tsp	dried oregano	5 mL
1 tsp	ground cumin	5 mL
½ tsp	freshly ground black pepper	2 mL
1	can (14 to 19 oz/398 to 540 mL) black beans, drained and rinsed	1
2 cups	wheat berries, rinsed and drained	500 mL
5 cups	chicken or vegetable broth	1.25 L
1 tsp	salt	5 mL
⅓ cup	tomato paste	75 mL
	Sour cream or Greek-style plain yogurt	
	Sliced green onions (white and green parts)	
	Shredded Cheddar cheese	

1. Set the rice cooker for the Quick Cook or Regular cycle. When the bottom of the bowl gets hot, sauté bacon until crisp. Drain off all but 1 tbsp (15 mL) fat. Add onion and sauté for about 3 minutes or until softened and translucent. Add chili powder, oregano, cumin and pepper; sauté for 1 minute.

2. Stir in beans, wheat berries and broth. Close the lid and reset for the Regular cycle. Set a timer for 1¼ hours. (Or reset for the Brown Rice cycle. Set a timer for 2¼ hours.)

3. When the timer sounds, check to make sure wheat berries are tender. If necessary, continue cooking, checking for doneness every 5 minutes. Stir in salt and tomato paste. Set the timer for 10 minutes.

4. When the timer sounds, switch to the Keep Warm cycle. Let stand for 15 minutes, then serve immediately, topped with sour cream and garnished with green onions and cheese.

Variation

Substitute spelt, Kamut or farro for the wheat berries.

Chili con Carne

Makes 4 to 6 servings

This is not your average chili recipe — but it sure should be! The complex flavors make it a ribbon winner.

Tip

Apple wood bacon is smoked over apple wood embers (wood made from various apple trees) and imparts a richer flavor than regular bacon. You can substitute regular bacon if you wish.

• Medium to large rice cooker; fuzzy logic or on/off

1½ cups	dried red kidney beans	375 mL
3	strips apple wood bacon (see tip, at left), diced	3
1 cup	finely chopped onion	250 mL
1 lb	ground beef (preferably round)	500 g
½	jalapeño pepper, seeded and minced	½
1 cup	chopped green bell pepper	250 mL
1	bay leaf	1
1 tbsp	chili powder	15 mL
1 tsp	chipotle chile powder	5 mL
Pinch	cayenne pepper	Pinch
Pinch	ground cloves	Pinch
1	can (8 oz/227 oz) tomato sauce	1
1 cup	beef broth	250 mL
1	can (14 oz/398 mL) whole tomatoes, with juice	1
	Salt and freshly ground black pepper	
	Finely chopped red onion	
	Shredded Cheddar cheese	

1. Sort, rinse, soak and drain kidney beans (see pages 32–33).
2. Set the rice cooker for the Quick Cook or Regular cycle. When the bottom of the bowl gets hot, sauté bacon until crisp. Drain off all but 1 tbsp (15 mL) fat. Add onion and sauté for about 3 minutes or until softened and translucent. Add beef, jalapeño and green pepper; sauté, breaking beef up with the back of a spoon, for 4 to 5 minutes or until beef is no longer pink.
3. Add soaked beans, bay leaf, chili powder, chipotle chile powder, cayenne, cloves, tomato sauce and broth. Stir in tomatoes with juice, breaking tomatoes up with your fingers as you add them. Close the lid and reset for the Regular cycle. Set a timer for 1½ hours.
4. When the timer sounds, check to make sure beans are tender. If necessary, continue cooking, checking for doneness every 5 minutes. Switch to the Keep Warm cycle. Let stand for 10 minutes, stirring occasionally. Season to taste with salt and black pepper. Serve immediately, garnished with red onion and cheese.

Variation

Substitute ground turkey for the beef.

Wild Rice Chili with Beef

Makes 4 to 5 servings

Throwing tradition out the window only improves on the tradition in this case. I love the unique, nutty flavor the wild rice adds to this one-of-a-kind chili.

Tips

You can use your favorite chili powder blend or one from a single source, such as ancho or New Mexico chiles.

For more intense flavor, use fire-roasted diced tomatoes.

Although cooking this chili on the Brown Rice cycle takes an hour longer, it's worth it for the superior results.

For information about rice cooker sizes, see page 13.

- **Medium to large rice cooker; fuzzy logic or on/off**

2 tbsp	extra virgin olive oil	30 mL
2	cloves garlic, minced	2
1 cup	finely chopped onion	250 mL
1 tsp	dried oregano	5 mL
1 tsp	chili powder	5 mL
½ tsp	ground cumin	2 mL
1 lb	ground beef (preferably round or sirloin)	500 g
2	cans (each 14 to 19 oz/398 to 540 mL) red kidney beans, drained and rinsed	2
1	can (14 oz/398 mL) diced tomatoes, with juice	1
¾ cup	wild rice, rinsed and drained	175 mL
1	can (5½ oz/156 mL) tomato paste	1
3¼ cups	beef broth	800 mL
	Sour cream or Greek-style plain yogurt	
	Finely chopped red onion	
	Shredded Cheddar cheese	

1. Set the rice cooker for the Quick Cook or Regular cycle. When the bottom of the bowl gets hot, add oil and swirl to coat. Sauté garlic and onion for about 3 minutes or until onion is softened and translucent. Add oregano, chili powder and cumin; sauté for 1 minute. Add beef and sauté, breaking it up with the back of a spoon, for 4 to 5 minutes or until no longer pink.

2. Stir in beans, tomatoes with juice, wild rice, tomato paste and broth. Close the lid and reset for the Regular cycle. Set a timer for 55 minutes. (Or reset for the Brown Rice cycle and set a timer for 1 hour and 55 minutes.)

3. When the timer sounds, check to make sure wild rice is tender. If necessary, continue cooking, checking for doneness every 5 minutes. Switch to the Keep Warm cycle. Let stand for 15 minutes, stirring occasionally, then serve immediately, topped with sour cream and garnished with red onion and cheese.

Variation

Wild Rice Chili with Chicken: Substitute ground chicken for the ground beef.

Main Dishes and One-Pot Meals

Fragrant Vegetable Stir-Fry on Forbidden Black Rice

Makes 3 to 4 servings

Stir-fry is a favorite in my house, and this colorful dish is even more tempting when served on forbidden rice.

Tip

To clean bok choy, separate the layers and place them in a sink filled with cool water. Swish bok choy in the water to remove dirt, which can be prevalent.

Bok Choy

Bok choy is a Chinese cabbage with a loose head of dark green leaves and thick white stems. It has a light, somewhat sweet flavor and crisp texture. Bok choy is used in soups and stir-fries, appetizers and main dishes and has been cultivated in China for centuries. You can find bok choy at Asian markets and well-stocked supermarkets.

• Medium rice cooker; fuzzy logic or on/off

1 cup	forbidden black rice, rinsed and drained	250 mL
1¾ cups	water	425 mL
1 tbsp	cornstarch	15 mL
1 tbsp	cold water	15 mL
¼ cup	vegetable oil	60 mL
1	clove garlic, minced	1
2 tsp	minced gingerroot	10 mL
1½ cups	diagonally sliced bok choy, with leaves (½-inch/1 cm slices)	375 mL
½ cup	thinly sliced mushrooms	125 mL
½ cup	thinly sliced red bell pepper	125 mL
¼ cup	drained canned bamboo shoots	60 mL
1 tsp	salt	5 mL
½ cup	chicken or vegetable broth	125 mL
2	green onions (white and green parts), cut into 2-inch (5 cm) pieces	2
½ cup	snow peas, blanched (see tip, page 84)	125 mL
2 tbsp	oyster sauce	30 mL

1. In the rice cooker bowl, combine rice and water. Set the rice cooker for the Regular or Brown Rice cycle. At the end of the cycle, hold rice on the Keep Warm cycle.
2. In a small bowl, combine cornstarch and cold water. Set aside.
3. In a wok or large nonstick skillet, heat oil over medium-high heat. Stir-fry garlic and ginger for about 1 minute or until fragrant. Add bok choy and stir-fry for 1 minute. Add mushrooms, red pepper and bamboo shoots; stir-fry for 1 minute. Stir in salt and broth; bring to a boil. Stir in cornstarch mixture and cook, stirring, for about 10 seconds or until thickened. Add green onions, peas and oyster sauce; stir-fry for 30 seconds.
4. Fluff rice with a wooden spoon or plastic paddle and scoop onto serving plates or into bowls. Top with vegetable stir-fry. Serve immediately.

Variation

Substitute any non-glutinous rice, such as Italian Black Venere, brown kalijira or long-grain brown rice.

Southeast Asian Vegetables with Tofu

Makes 4 to 6 servings

My grandmother used to say that eating root vegetables and squash during the winter builds internal energy that will be used throughout the rest of the year. This hearty soup will certainly get you through the afternoon or evening on a cold day, and it also tastes great cold if things warm up.

Tips

If you like heat, leave the seeds in when you're mincing the chile pepper. For less heat, remove them. If you like your dishes really hot, you can increase the amount of chile peppers, but beware, as this variety packs a punch.

Make sure to blot the tofu with paper towels so you're not adding any excess liquid to this dish.

You can use pumpkin or any type of winter squash in place of the butternut squash.

• **Large rice cooker; fuzzy logic or on/off**

1	can (14 oz/400 mL) coconut milk	1
1½ cups	chicken or vegetable broth	375 mL
1 tbsp	soy sauce	15 mL
1 tbsp	fish sauce (nam pla)	15 mL
1 tsp	Thai chili sauce (such as Sriracha)	5 mL
½ tsp	salt	2 mL
¼ tsp	freshly ground white pepper	1 mL
2	sweet potatoes, peeled and cut into 2-inch (5 cm) chunks	2
1	bunch green onions (white and green parts), cut into 1-inch (2.5 cm) pieces	1
1	stalk lemongrass, bottom 6 inches (15 cm) only, bulb and tough outer leaves removed), bruised with a mallet	1
1	Thai chile pepper, minced (see tip, at left)	1
2 cups	chopped butternut squash (2-inch/5 cm chunks)	500 mL
¾ cup	halved stemmed shiitake mushrooms	175 mL
½ cup	pearl barley	125 mL
½ cup	diced firm tofu, blotted (see tip, at left)	125 mL
¼ cup	coarsely chopped fresh cilantro	60 mL
¼ cup	coarsely chopped salted peanuts	60 mL

1. In a medium bowl, whisk together coconut milk, broth, soy sauce, fish sauce and chili sauce. Season with salt and pepper.

2. In the rice cooker bowl, combine sweet potatoes, green onions, lemongrass, chile pepper, squash, mushrooms and barley. Pour coconut milk mixture over top. Set the rice cooker for the Regular cycle and set a timer for 30 minutes.

3. When the timer sounds, check to make sure vegetables and barley are tender. If necessary, continue cooking, checking for doneness every 5 minutes. Switch to the Keep Warm cycle and stir in tofu. Close the lid and let stand for 15 minutes, then serve immediately, garnished with cilantro and peanuts.

Variation

Substitute farro for the barley and set the timer for 40 minutes.

Tofu and Edamame Stir-Fry

Makes 4 servings

This vegetarian dish will surprise even meat lovers with its flavor. The firm tofu combined with the brown rice makes a healthy and hearty meal.

Tips

Tofu comes packaged as extra-firm, firm, medium and soft (silken). Extra-firm and firm hold up well for grilling, sautéing and in stir-fries, while medium and soft are preferred when you want a creamier texture, such as for vegetarian lasagna and desserts.

To cook the frozen shelled edamame, simply follow the package directions, then drain and let cool.

For information about rice cooker sizes, see page 13.

• Medium rice cooker; fuzzy logic or on/off

1	package (16 oz/454 g) firm tofu	1
1 cup	brown jasmine rice, rinsed and drained	250 mL
2 cups	water	500 mL
2 tbsp	soy sauce	30 mL
1 tbsp	dry sherry	15 mL
1 tbsp	water	15 mL
1 tsp	toasted sesame oil	5 mL
3 tbsp	hoisin sauce	45 mL
3 tbsp	freshly squeezed lime juice	45 mL
1 tsp	sambal oelek or other hot Asian chili sauce	5 mL
3 tbsp	vegetable oil, divided	45 mL
1	clove garlic, minced	1
1 tsp	minced gingerroot	5 mL
3	small tomatoes, each cut into 6 wedges	3
1 cup	frozen shelled edamame, cooked	250 mL

1. Cut tofu in half lengthwise. Cut each half into 8 rectangles. Arrange rectangles on a baking sheet lined with paper towels and top with more paper towels and another baking sheet. Weight down with canned goods or a skillet. Refrigerate for at least 20 minutes or overnight.

2. In the rice cooker bowl, combine rice and 2 cups (500 mL) water. Set the rice cooker for the Regular or Brown Rice cycle. At the end of the cycle, hold rice on the Keep Warm cycle.

3. Transfer tofu to a shallow dish. In a bowl, whisk together soy sauce, sherry, 1 tbsp (15 mL) water and sesame oil; pour over tofu.

4. In a small bowl, combine hoisin sauce, lime juice and chili sauce. Set aside.

5. Remove tofu from marinade. In a medium nonstick skillet, heat 1 tbsp (15 mL) vegetable oil over medium-high heat. Pan-fry tofu for 1 to 2 minutes per side or until browned on both sides. Transfer to a plate.

6. In a wok or large nonstick skillet, heat the remaining vegetable oil over medium-high heat. Stir-fry garlic and ginger for 1 minute or until fragrant. Add tofu, tomatoes and edamame; stir-fry for 1 minute. Add reserved hoisin mixture and stir-fry for 30 seconds.

7. Fluff rice with a wooden spoon or plastic paddle and scoop onto serving plates or into bowls. Top with tofu stir-fry. Serve immediately.

Thai Fish Curry on Jasmine Rice

Makes 4 servings

There are hundreds of different kinds of curry, but I like this one because the red curry sauce gives the fish a delicious tangy flavor.

Tip

Tamarind paste is the tart pulp that surrounds the seeds of the tamarind pod. It is used much like lemon — to provide acid — and is commonly added to grilling glazes, barbecue sauces and curries. It can be found at Asian markets. If you can't find tamarind paste, you may substitute lemon or lime juice mixed with a bit of brown sugar.

Coconut Milk

Coconut milk adds a delicious flavor to rice and is used in many Thai, Southeast Asian, West African, West Indian and Hawaiian recipes. It contains essential vitamins, minerals and antioxidants that supply a host of benefits to the human body, including strengthening bones and promoting healthy brain development. Because it's non-dairy, it's wonderful for lactose-free diets.

- **Medium rice cooker; fuzzy logic or on/off**
- **Blender or food processor**

1½ cups	Thai jasmine rice, rinsed and drained	375 mL
2¼ cups	water	550 mL
2 tsp	ground cumin	10 mL
2 tsp	ground coriander	10 mL
1 tsp	minced gingerroot	5 mL
1 cup	coconut milk	250 mL
¼ cup	tamarind paste (see tip, at left)	60 mL
¼ cup	fish sauce (nam pla)	60 mL
2 tsp	Thai red curry paste	10 mL
2	lime leaves, minced (optional)	2
1½ lbs	skinless swordfish or red snapper, cut into 1-inch (2.5 cm) cubes	750 g
½ cup	sliced mushrooms	125 mL
½ cup	finely chopped fresh cilantro	125 mL
2 tbsp	packed brown sugar	30 mL
1 cup	diced seeded tomato	250 mL
	Fresh cilantro sprigs	
	Lime wedges	

1. In the rice cooker bowl, combine rice and water. Set the rice cooker for the Regular cycle. At the end of the cycle, hold rice on the Keep Warm cycle.
2. In blender, combine cumin, coriander, ginger, coconut milk, tamarind paste, fish sauce and curry paste; purée until smooth.
3. Pour sauce into a wok or large nonstick skillet and add lime leaves (if using). Bring to a boil over high heat. Add fish, mushrooms, chopped cilantro and brown sugar; reduce heat to medium, cover and simmer for 6 to 8 minutes or until fish is opaque and flakes easily when tested with a fork. Gently stir in tomato and simmer for 2 to 3 minutes or until tender.
4. Fluff rice with a wooden spoon or plastic paddle and scoop into deep serving bowls. Top with fish curry and garnish with cilantro sprigs and lime wedges. Serve immediately.

Brazilian Rice with Scallops

Makes 4 servings

I love to travel through my cooking, and this dish brings Carnivale in Rio right to your plate. The explosion of colors and flavors makes it one of my favorites.

Tips

Increase the amount of hot pepper flakes if you're seeking more heat.

To toast slivered almonds, spread them in a single layer on an ungreased baking sheet and bake in a 350°F (180°C) oven, stirring occasionally, for 10 to 15 minutes or until golden. Immediately transfer to a bowl and let cool.

- **Medium rice cooker; fuzzy logic or on/off**

3 tbsp	extra virgin olive oil, divided	45 mL
½ cup	finely chopped onion	125 mL
¼ tsp	ground cumin	1 mL
1	can (14 to 19 oz/398 to 540 mL) black beans, drained and rinsed	1
1 cup	long-grain white rice, rinsed and drained	250 mL
1 tsp	salt	5 mL
¼ tsp	freshly ground black pepper	1 mL
¼ tsp	hot pepper flakes	1 mL
1½ cups	chicken broth or fish stock	375 mL
8 oz	bay scallops	250 g
1 cup	chopped papaya (½-inch/1 cm chunks)	250 mL
¼ cup	finely chopped fresh cilantro	60 mL
¼ cup	slivered almonds, toasted (see tip, at left)	60 mL
	Grated lemon zest	
2 tbsp	freshly squeezed lemon juice	30 mL
	Chopped green onions (green and white parts)	

1. Set the rice cooker for the Quick Cook or Regular cycle. When the bottom of the bowl gets hot, add 2 tbsp (30 mL) oil and swirl to coat. Sauté onion for about 3 minutes or until softened and translucent. Add cumin and sauté for 1 minute.
2. Stir in beans, rice, salt, black pepper, hot pepper flakes and broth. Close the lid and reset for the Regular cycle.
3. When the machine switches to the Keep Warm cycle, stir in scallops, papaya, cilantro, almonds, lemon juice and the remaining oil. Close the lid and let steam for 15 minutes or until scallops are firm. Serve immediately, garnished with lemon zest and green onions.

Variation

Brazilian Rice with Shrimp: Substitute 8 oz (250 g) shrimp, peeled and deveined, for the scallops.

Shrimp Jambalaya

Makes 4 to 6 servings

Put on some jazz and get cooking with this tasty version of New Orleans jambalaya. The taste will really get your toes tapping!

Tips

Use andouille sausage for a spicier kick to this dish.

For information about rice cooker sizes, see page 13.

• Large rice cooker; fuzzy logic or on/off

2 tbsp	extra virgin olive oil	30 mL
1	clove garlic, minced	1
$\frac{1}{2}$ cup	finely chopped onion	125 mL
$\frac{1}{4}$ cup	finely chopped celery	60 mL
$\frac{1}{4}$ cup	finely chopped green bell pepper	60 mL
$\frac{1}{4}$ cup	finely chopped red bell pepper	60 mL
1 cup	long-grain white rice, rinsed and drained	250 mL
1 tsp	dried oregano	5 mL
1 tsp	dried thyme	5 mL
1 tsp	salt	5 mL
$\frac{1}{2}$ tsp	cayenne pepper	2 mL
$\frac{1}{4}$ tsp	freshly ground black pepper	1 mL
1	bay leaf	1
1 cup	chicken broth	250 mL
$\frac{3}{4}$ cup	white wine	175 mL
$\frac{3}{4}$ cup	tomato sauce	175 mL
8 oz	medium shrimp, peeled and deveined	250 g
4 oz	smoked pork or turkey kielbasa sausage, cut diagonally into $\frac{1}{4}$-inch (0.5 cm) thick slices	125 g
$\frac{1}{4}$ cup	finely chopped fresh flat-leaf (Italian) parsley, divided	60 mL

1. Set the rice cooker for the Quick Cook or Regular cycle. When the bottom of the bowl gets hot, add oil and swirl to coat. Sauté garlic and onion for about 3 minutes or until onion is softened and translucent. Add celery, green pepper and red pepper; sauté for 2 minutes. Add rice, oregano, thyme, salt, cayenne and pepper; sauté for 3 minutes.
2. Stir in bay leaf, broth, wine and tomato sauce. Close the lid and reset for the Regular cycle. Set a timer for 10 minutes.
3. When the timer sounds, stir in shrimp and kielbasa. Close the lid and continue cooking.
4. When the machine switches to the Keep Warm cycle, discard bay leaf. Stir in half the parsley and let stand for 10 minutes. Fluff rice with a wooden spoon or plastic paddle. Serve immediately, garnished with the remaining parsley.

Stir-Fried Shrimp with Asparagus on Long-Grain Rice

Makes 4 servings

I often serve this classic stir-fry dish to my family. My kids love the flavor, but they make their dad eat all the asparagus tips!

Tips

Soaking shrimp in salted water adds a clean, bright flavor to Asian shrimp dishes.

For information about rice cooker sizes, see page 13.

> ● **Medium rice cooker; fuzzy logic or on/off**

1 cup	long-grain white rice, rinsed and drained	250 mL
1½ cups	water	375 mL
2¼ tsp	salt, divided	11 mL
6 cups	warm water	1.5 L
1 lb	large shrimp, peeled and deveined (see tip, at left)	500 g
4 tsp	cornstarch, divided	20 mL
⅛ tsp	freshly ground white pepper	0.5 mL
½ tsp	toasted sesame oil	2 mL
1 tbsp	cold water	15 mL
2 tbsp	oyster sauce	30 mL
3 tbsp	vegetable oil, divided	45 mL
1	clove garlic, minced	1
1 lb	asparagus, tough ends removed, cut into 2-inch (5 cm) pieces	500 g
1	small onion, thinly sliced	1
1 cup	sliced shiitake mushrooms	250 mL
6	canned baby corn cobs	6
½ cup	chicken or vegetable broth	125 mL

1. In the rice cooker bowl, combine rice and 1½ cups (375 mL) water. Set the rice cooker for the Regular cycle. At the end of the cycle, hold rice on the Keep Warm cycle.
2. In a bowl, dissolve 2 tsp (10 mL) of the salt in warm water. Add shrimp, swirl and let stand for 5 minutes. Rinse shrimp, drain and pat dry with paper towels.
3. In a medium bowl, toss shrimp with 1 tsp (5 mL) of the cornstarch, pepper and sesame oil. Set aside.
4. In a small bowl, combine the remaining cornstarch, cold water and oyster sauce. Set aside.

5. In a wok or large nonstick skillet, heat 2 tbsp (30 mL) vegetable oil over medium-high heat. Stir-fry shrimp and garlic for about 2 minutes or until shrimp turn pink. Remove from wok and set aside.

6. Add the remaining oil to the wok. Stir-fry asparagus for 2 minutes. Add onion, mushrooms and corn; stir-fry for 1 minute. Add broth and bring to a boil. Cover and cook for 1 minute. Stir in cornstarch mixture and cook, stirring, for about 10 seconds or until thickened. Return shrimp to the wok, along with the remaining salt; stir-fry for 1 minute.

7. Fluff rice with a wooden spoon or plastic paddle and scoop onto serving plates or into bowls. Top with shrimp stir-fry. Serve immediately.

Japanese Rice with Shrimp

Makes 4 servings

The combination of the delicate shrimp and the flavorful rice creates a delicious and uniquely Japanese taste that always delights my guests. Serve it with some green tea and chopsticks, and you'll feel like you're in Tokyo.

Tips

You can buy powdered dashi mix at Asian markets, but I suggest making it from scratch, as it's simple and the taste will be superior. If you can't find either the powdered mix or the bonito shavings you need to make dashi, you can substitute fish stock.

For information about rice cooker sizes, see page 13.

• Medium to large rice cooker; fuzzy logic or on/off

1 cup	Japanese-style medium-grain japonica rice (such as Calrose)	250 mL
2½ cups	dashi (see recipe, opposite)	625 mL
3 tbsp	soy sauce	45 mL
2 tbsp	mirin	30 mL
½ tsp	toasted sesame oil	2 mL
1 tbsp	vegetable oil	15 mL
2	green onions (white part only), finely chopped	2
2 tsp	minced gingerroot	10 mL
½ cup	finely chopped red bell pepper	125 mL
½ cup	thinly sliced snow peas	125 mL
1 lb	large shrimp, peeled and deveined	500 g
	Thinly sliced green onions (green part only)	

1. Place rice in a bowl and add enough cool water to cover by 1 inch (2.5 cm); let soak for 30 minutes. Rinse and drain (see page 20).
2. In a small bowl, combine dashi, soy sauce, mirin and sesame oil. Set aside.
3. Set the rice cooker for the Quick Cook or Regular cycle. When the bottom of the bowl gets hot, add vegetable oil and swirl to coat. Sauté green onions and ginger for about 2 minutes or until onions are softened.
4. Stir in soaked rice, dashi mixture and red pepper. Close the lid and reset for the Regular cycle.
5. When the machine switches to the Keep Warm cycle, stir in peas. Place shrimp on top of rice mixture, pressing them in slightly. Close the lid and let steam for 15 minutes or until shrimp are pink and opaque. Serve immediately, garnished with green onions.

Dashi

Dashi is a Japanese broth that serves as the base of many Japanese dishes, including soups, dipping sauces and simmered dishes.

Tip
Bonito shavings (*katsuobushi*) are available at Asian markets.

3¼ cups	water	800 mL
4 tsp	bonito shavings (dried fish flakes)	20 mL

1. In a deep pot, heat water over medium heat. Just before the water boils, add bonito shavings. When the water boils, skim off any foam that rises to the surface. Remove from heat and strain broth through a paper towel.

Thai Curry with Shrimp

Makes 4 servings

This recipe, which I discovered on a moped trip through the villages of northern Thailand with my husband, has a lightness and subtle sweetness I'd never experienced before, thanks to the perfect blend of ingredients.

Tips

If fresh lemongrass in not available, you may use frozen lemongrass (available at Asian markets) or 1 tsp (5 mL) lemongrass purée in a tube (available in the produce section of well-stocked grocery stores).

When mincing the chile pepper, remove the seeds for less heat or leave them in for more heat.

For information about rice cooker sizes, see page 13.

• **Medium to large rice cooker; fuzzy logic or on/off**

2 tbsp	vegetable oil	30 mL
2	cloves garlic, minced	2
1	shallot, minced	1
1 tbsp	minced gingerroot	15 mL
1/4 tsp	ground coriander	1 mL
1/4 tsp	ground turmeric	1 mL
1 tbsp	Thai red curry paste	15 mL
1	stalk lemongrass, tender inner white bulb only, finely minced	1
1	red Thai chile pepper, minced (see tip, at left)	1
1 1/4 cups	brown jasmine rice, rinsed and drained	300 mL
1 tbsp	packed brown sugar	15 mL
2 cups	coconut milk	500 mL
1 1/2 cups	water	375 mL
1 1/2 tbsp	fish sauce (nam pla)	22 mL
1 1/2 lbs	medium shrimp, peeled and deveined	750 g
1/4 cup	finely chopped fresh cilantro	60 mL
	Salt and freshly ground white pepper	

1. Set the rice cooker for the Quick Cook or Regular cycle. When the bottom of the bowl gets hot, add oil and swirl to coat. Sauté garlic, shallot and ginger for about 2 minutes or until shallot is softened and translucent. Add coriander, turmeric and curry paste; sauté for 2 minutes.
2. Stir in lemongrass, chile pepper, rice, brown sugar, coconut milk, water and fish sauce. Close the lid and reset for the Regular or Brown Rice cycle.
3. When the machine switches to the Keep Warm cycle, stir in shrimp. Close the lid and let steam for 15 minutes or until shrimp are pink and opaque. Season to taste with salt and white pepper. Serve immediately, garnished with cilantro.

Paella

Makes 4 to 6 servings

I am a big fan of fish and shellfish, so I love making paella because I can add all the things I really like to it and no one can say a thing — except to ask for more!

Tips

If you don't have clam juice, substitute fish stock or use more chicken broth.

You can use any combination of fresh seafood in this dish.

Saffron

Saffron is a spice derived from the flower of the saffron crocus. Despite its bitter raw taste and hay-like smell, saffron imparts a rich golden color and unique, subtle flavor to dishes. It takes over 13,000 saffron threads to weigh one ounce so it's understandably the most expensive spice in the world. Fortunately, a little goes a long way.

• **Large rice cooker; fuzzy logic or on/off**

1/2 tsp	crushed saffron threads	2 mL
1/4 cup	hot water	60 mL
3 tbsp	extra virgin olive oil	45 mL
3	cloves garlic, minced	3
1 cup	finely chopped onion	250 mL
6 oz	boneless skinless chicken thighs, cut into 1/2-inch (1 cm) pieces	175 g
2	cooked sweet Italian sausages, cut into 1/4-inch (0.5 cm) thick slices	2
1	red bell pepper, finely chopped	1
3 cups	Valencia rice, rinsed and drained	750 mL
3/4 cup	chopped seeded tomato	175 mL
1 1/2 tsp	salt	7 mL
2 3/4 cups	chicken broth	675 mL
2 cups	clam juice	500 mL
8 oz	bay scallops	250 g
1/2 cup	fresh or thawed frozen peas	125 mL
1 tbsp	finely chopped fresh cilantro	15 mL
1 tbsp	finely chopped fresh parsley	15 mL
12	medium shrimp, peeled and deveined, with tails on	12
	Lemon wedges	

1. In a measuring cup or small bowl, combine saffron threads and hot water; set aside to steep.
2. Set the rice cooker for the Quick Cook or Regular cycle. When the bottom of the bowl gets hot, add oil and swirl to coat. Sauté garlic and onion for about 3 minutes or until onion is softened and translucent. Add chicken and sausages; sauté for 4 to 5 minutes or until chicken is lightly browned on all sides. Add red pepper and sauté for 1 minute.
3. Stir in saffron-infused water, rice, tomato, salt, broth and clam juice. Close the lid and reset for the Regular cycle.
4. When the machine switches to the Keep Warm cycle, stir in scallops, peas, cilantro and parsley. Place shrimp on top of rice mixture, pressing them in slightly, with the tails sticking up. Close the lid and let steam for 15 minutes or until shrimp are pink and opaque. Serve immediately, garnished with lemon wedges.

Southwestern Paella with Cilantro Cream

Makes 6 servings

Cilantro cream and toasted pine nuts make a truly blissful garnish for this aromatic chicken and sausage paella. It's great all year round for lunch, dinner or a late-night supper — I even love it for breakfast (with just a bit of extra sour cream)!

Tips

To toast pine nuts, place them in a dry skillet over medium heat and cook, stirring, for about 5 minutes or until browned and fragrant. Immediately transfer to a bowl and let cool.

For information about rice cooker sizes, see page 13.

• **Large rice cooker; fuzzy logic or on/off**

2 tbsp	extra virgin olive oil	30 mL
1	clove garlic, minced	1
1 cup	thinly sliced onion	250 mL
1¼ lbs	boneless skinless chicken thighs, cut into 1-inch (2.5 cm) pieces	625 g
2 cups	Valencia rice, rinsed and drained	500 mL
2 tbsp	minced seeded canned chipotle peppers in adobo sauce	30 mL
1 tsp	smoked paprika	5 mL
1 tsp	salt	5 mL
¼ tsp	freshly ground black pepper	1 mL
4 cups	chicken broth	1 L
1 cup	diagonally sliced andouille sausage (¼-inch/0.5 cm thick slices)	250 mL
1	red bell pepper, thinly sliced	1
2 tbsp	finely chopped fresh cilantro	30 mL
1 cup	sour cream	250 mL
2 tbsp	toasted pine nuts (see tip, at left)	30 mL
	Lime wedges	

1. Set the rice cooker for the Quick Cook or Regular cycle. When the bottom of the bowl gets hot, add oil and swirl to coat. Sauté garlic and onion for about 3 minutes or until onion is softened and translucent. Add chicken and sauté for 4 to 5 minutes or until lightly browned on all sides. Using a slotted spoon, transfer chicken to a plate.

2. Stir rice, chipotle peppers, paprika, salt, pepper and broth into the rice cooker bowl. Layer chicken, sausage and red pepper on top. Close the lid and reset for the Regular cycle.

3. When the machine switches to the Keep Warm cycle, let stand for 10 minutes.

4. Meanwhile, in a small bowl, combine cilantro and sour cream.

5. Serve paella immediately, topped with cilantro cream and garnished with pine nuts and lime wedges.

Quinoa Paella

Makes 4 servings

This paella gets its sublime nutty taste, as well as a nutrient boost, from the quinoa. But the clam juice, mussels and saffron give it a burst of flavor that's straight from Valencia. Try it with a full-bodied Spanish red wine — or better yet, make it the center of your tapas party!

Tips

Sliced andouille sausage would be a nice accompaniment to this dish.

Although cooking this dish on the Brown Rice cycle takes an hour longer, it's worth it for the superior results.

To blanch fresh peas, bring a small saucepan of water to a boil over high heat. Add peas and boil for 1 minute or until bright green and tender-crisp. Using a slotted spoon, transfer peas to a bowl of ice water and let cool completely. Drain.

- **Large rice cooker; fuzzy logic or on/off**

½ tsp	crushed saffron threads	2 mL
¼ cup	hot water	60 mL
2 tbsp	extra virgin olive oil	30 mL
2	cloves garlic, minced	2
1 cup	finely chopped red onion	250 mL
1 cup	chopped red bell pepper	250 mL
2 cups	quinoa, rinsed and drained	500 mL
1 tsp	salt	5 mL
¼ tsp	freshly ground black pepper	1 mL
2 cups	chicken or vegetable broth	500 mL
¾ cup	clam juice	175 mL
1 lb	mussels, scrubbed and debearded (see tips, page 146)	500 g
1 cup	blanched fresh or thawed frozen peas (see tip, at left)	250 mL
8 oz	medium shrimp, peeled and deveined	250 g

1. In a measuring cup or small bowl, combine saffron threads and hot water; set aside to steep.
2. Set the rice cooker for the Quick Cook or Regular cycle. When the bottom of the bowl gets hot, add oil and swirl to coat. Sauté garlic and red onion for about 3 minutes or until onion is softened and translucent. Add red pepper and sauté for 1 minute. Add quinoa and sauté for 2 minutes.
3. Stir in saffron-infused water, salt, pepper, broth and clam juice. Close the lid and reset for the Regular cycle. Set a timer for 30 minutes. (Or reset for the Brown Rice cycle and set a timer for 1½ hours.)
4. When the timer sounds, check to make sure quinoa is tender. If necessary, continue cooking, checking for doneness every 5 minutes. Stir in mussels. Close the lid and set the timer for 10 minutes.
5. When the timer sounds, switch to the Keep Warm cycle. Stir in peas. Place shrimp on top of rice mixture, pressing them in slightly. Close the lid and let steam for 15 minutes or until shrimp are pink and opaque. Discard any mussels that haven't opened. Serve immediately.

Variation

You can use any combination of fresh seafood in this dish.

Asian-Style Paella

Makes 4 to 5 servings

This is my Asian twist on a classic Spanish favorite. It is easy to make and simply delicious to eat. Your friends will think you slaved for hours, and I'll never tell.

Tips

You can buy powdered dashi mix at Asian markets, but I suggest making it from scratch (see page 185), as it's simple and the taste will be superior. If you can't find either the powdered mix or the bonito shavings you need to make dashi, you can substitute fish stock.

Chinese sausage (*lap cheong*) is a sweet dried or preserved sausage that is used in many dishes all over China. You can find it at Asian markets. I like to buy extra to keep on hand in my freezer because it's so versatile and tasty. Substitute another type of cooked sweet sausage, or omit it from the recipe, if *lap cheong* isn't available.

- **Medium to large rice cooker; fuzzy logic or on/off**

2 tbsp	extra virgin olive oil	30 mL
2	cloves garlic, minced	2
1 cup	finely chopped onion	250 mL
1/2 cup	mixed sliced Asian mushrooms (such as enoki and shiitake)	125 mL
2 cups	Valencia rice, rinsed and drained	500 mL
4 cups	dashi (see tip, at left)	1 L
2 tbsp	soy sauce	30 mL
1 tbsp	mirin	15 mL
1 cup	fresh or thawed frozen peas	250 mL
12 to 15	mussels, scrubbed and debearded (see tips, page 146)	12 to 15
4 oz	squid, mantle cut into rings, tentacles quartered	125 g
4 oz	Chinese sausage (see tip, at left), cut into 1/2-inch (1 cm) slices	125 g

1. Set the rice cooker for the Quick Cook or Regular cycle. When the bottom of the bowl gets hot, add oil and swirl to coat. Sauté garlic and onion for about 3 minutes or until onion is softened and translucent. Add mushrooms and sauté for 3 minutes.
2. Stir in rice, dashi, soy sauce and mirin. Close the lid and reset for the Regular cycle. Set a timer for 20 minutes.
3. When the timer sounds, stir in peas, mussels, squid and sausage. Close the lid and continue cooking.
4. When the machine switches to the Keep Warm cycle, let stand for 10 minutes. Discard any mussels that haven't opened. Serve immediately.

Variation

Substitute 12 to 15 little neck clams for the mussels. If fresh clams aren't available, you can use two 5-oz (142 g) cans of baby clams, drained and rinsed.

Arroz con Pollo

Makes 4 to 6 servings

Arroz con pollo (literally rice with chicken) is a traditional Latin dish and a speedy one-pot meal that's perfect for weekdays or even for guests. I love how the red and green bell peppers pop among the beautifully hued saffron rice. Serve with a tossed green salad and a pitcher of sangria. Olé!

● **Large rice cooker; fuzzy logic or on/off**

¼ tsp	crushed saffron threads	1 mL
¼ cup	hot water	60 mL
3 tbsp	extra virgin olive oil	45 mL
2	cloves garlic, minced	2
1 cup	finely chopped onion	250 mL
1 lb	boneless skinless chicken thighs, cut into ½-inch (1 cm) pieces	500 g
1	can (14 oz/398 mL) diced tomatoes, with juice	1
2 cups	long-grain white rice, rinsed and drained	500 mL
1 cup	finely chopped red bell pepper	250 mL
1 cup	finely chopped green bell pepper	250 mL
1	bay leaf	1
2 tsp	ground cumin	10 mL
1 tsp	salt	5 mL
½ tsp	freshly ground black pepper	2 mL
2¾ cups	chicken broth	675 mL
1 cup	fresh or thawed frozen peas	250 mL
½ cup	small pimento-stuffed olives, rinsed and drained	125 mL

1. In a measuring cup or small bowl, combine saffron threads and hot water; set aside to steep.
2. Set the rice cooker for the Quick Cook or Regular cycle. When the bottom of the bowl gets hot, add oil and swirl to coat. Sauté garlic and onion for about 3 minutes or until onion is softened and translucent. Add chicken and sauté for 4 to 5 minutes or until lightly browned on all sides.
3. Stir in saffron-infused water, tomatoes with juice, rice, red pepper, green pepper, bay leaf, cumin, salt, pepper and broth. Close the lid and reset for the Regular cycle.
4. When the machine switches to the Keep Warm cycle, stir in peas and olives. Close the lid and let steam for 10 minutes. Discard bay leaf. Fluff rice with a wooden spoon or plastic paddle. Serve immediately.

Variations

For a smoky flavor, add 3 slices of bacon, cooked crisp and crumbled, when the machine switches to the Keep Warm cycle.

For a spicier dish, add ½ cup (125 mL) chopped cured chorizo sausage with the broth.

Cuban-Style Chicken

Makes 4 to 5 servings

This dish tastes so authentic, even native Cubans will be begging for more. My husband liked it so much he lit a cigar afterwards.

Tips

The easiest way to grate lime zest is with a rasp grater, such as a Microplane.

Also called Jamaica pepper, allspice is the dried unripe berry of the pimento plant. It is popular in Caribbean cuisine. If you don't have allspice, you can use a mixture of equal parts ground cinnamon, cloves, nutmeg and black pepper.

Saffron has a shelf life of about 6 months. It's customary to wrap it in foil and then store it in an airtight jar or container.

For information about rice cooker sizes, see page 13.

● **Large rice cooker; fuzzy logic or on/off**

Marinade

2 tbsp	finely chopped fresh cilantro	30 mL
1½ tsp	finely chopped fresh thyme	7 mL
1½ tsp	finely grated lime zest	7 mL
1 tsp	minced seeded jalapeño pepper	5 mL
1 tsp	Hungarian sweet paprika	5 mL
1 tsp	salt	5 mL
1 tsp	freshly ground black pepper	5 mL
½ tsp	ground cumin	2 mL
½ tsp	dried oregano	2 mL
Pinch	ground allspice	Pinch
2 tbsp	freshly squeezed lime juice	30 mL
2 tbsp	extra virgin olive oil	30 mL
4 to 5	bone-in, skin-on chicken thighs (about 2¼ lbs/1.125 kg)	4 to 5
¼ tsp	crushed saffron threads	1 mL
¼ cup	hot water	60 mL
	Extra virgin olive oil	
4 oz	cooked Spanish chorizo or Cajun andouille sausage, cut into ¼-inch (0.5 cm) thick slices	125 g
2	cloves garlic, minced	2
1 cup	finely chopped onion	250 mL
½ cup	chopped red bell pepper	125 mL
1	tomato, diced	1
1½ cups	long-grain white rice, rinsed and drained	375 mL
1	bay leaf	1
1 tsp	Hungarian sweet paprika	5 mL
2¼ cups	chicken broth	550 mL
¼ cup	drained canned whole pimientos, cut into thin strips	60 mL
¼ cup	coarsely chopped fresh cilantro	60 mL
	Lime wedges	

1. *Marinade:* In a bowl, whisk together cilantro, thyme, lime zest, jalapeño, paprika, salt, pepper, cumin, oregano, allspice, lime juice and oil.

Tip

To avoid tearing up when you're chopping onions, try refrigerating the onions for 30 minutes first, and don't cut the root off.

2. Place chicken in a large sealable plastic bag and add marinade. Seal and turn several times to coat chicken. Refrigerate, turning occasionally, for at least 4 hours or up to 1 day. Using tongs, transfer chicken to a plate, allowing excess marinade to drip back into bag. Reserve marinade.

3. In a measuring cup or small bowl, combine saffron threads and hot water; set aside to steep.

4. Set the rice cooker for the Quick Cook or Regular cycle. When the bottom of the bowl gets hot, add 2 tbsp (30 mL) oil and swirl to coat. Cook chicken, in batches if necessary, for about 3 minutes per side or until browned on both sides, adding oil as needed between batches. Transfer to a plate and set aside.

5. Add chorizo to the rice cooker bowl and sauté for 3 minutes. Add garlic, onion and red pepper; sauté for about 3 minutes or until onion is softened and translucent.

6. Stir in reserved marinade, saffron-infused water, tomato, rice, bay leaf, paprika and broth. Close the lid and reset for the Regular cycle. When the mixture comes to a boil, arrange chicken on top of rice mixture. Sprinkle pimientos on top of chicken. Close the lid and continue cooking.

7. When the machine switches to the Keep Warm cycle, check to make sure juices run clear when chicken is pierced. If necessary, reset for the Regular cycle and check for doneness every 5 minutes. Let stand for 10 minutes. Discard bay leaf. Serve immediately, garnished with cilantro and lime wedges.

Chicken with Fresh Mint and Basil

Makes 4 servings

This simply prepared dish takes me right back to my honeymoon in Chiang Mai. The combination of fresh mint, coconut milk, Thai basil and chiles is magical.

Tip

Be careful when handling chile peppers. They contain oils that can burn your skin and especially your eyes. Wear rubber gloves or try generously greasing your fingers with shortening.

Serrano Peppers

The serrano pepper is a smaller version of the jalapeño but is said to be five times as hot! Serranos have thin walls, so they don't need to be charred, steamed or peeled before use. They are perfect for salsas, sauces, relishes and garnishes, and taste great when roasted. They are commonly used in Thai and Mexican dishes.

• **Medium rice cooker; fuzzy logic or on/off**

1 cup	Thai jasmine rice, rinsed and drained	250 mL
¾ cup	coconut milk	175 mL
¾ cup	water	175 mL
3 tbsp	vegetable oil	45 mL
4	cloves garlic, minced	4
3	shallots, thinly sliced	3
2	serrano chile peppers, seeded and cut into thin strips	2
¾ cup	packed fresh Thai basil leaves, thinly sliced, divided	175 mL
1 lb	boneless skinless chicken breasts, cut into ½-inch (1 cm) pieces	500 g
2 tbsp	granulated sugar	30 mL
Pinch	freshly ground white pepper	Pinch
3 tbsp	fish sauce (nam pla)	45 mL
2 tbsp	water	30 mL
¼ cup	packed fresh mint leaves	60 mL

1. In the rice cooker bowl, combine rice, coconut milk and water. Set the rice cooker for the Regular cycle. At the end of the cycle, hold rice on the Keep Warm cycle.
2. In a wok or large nonstick skillet, heat oil over medium-high heat. Stir-fry garlic and shallots for about 2 minutes or until shallots are softened and translucent. Add serrano peppers and two-thirds of the basil; stir-fry for 1 minute or until basil wilts. Add chicken and stir-fry for 3 minutes. Add sugar, pepper, fish sauce and water; stir-fry for about 2 minutes or until sauce bubbles and thickens. Add mint and the remaining basil; stir-fry for 5 to 10 seconds.
3. Fluff rice with a wooden spoon or plastic paddle and scoop onto serving plates or into bowls. Top with chicken stir-fry. Serve immediately.

Variations

Shrimp with Fresh Mint and Basil on Thai Jasmine Rice: Substitute 1 lb (500 g) medium shrimp, peeled and deveined, for the chicken breasts.

For a spicier version of this dish, replace the serrano peppers with 1 Thai chile pepper, sliced, with seeds, or add 1 tsp (5 mL) Thai chili sauce (such as Sriracha).

Chicken and Chickpea Tagine

Makes 6 servings

I love chicken thighs, and this meal is a tasty and easy way to prepare them so that there are no leftovers. The mix of spices and dried apricots gives it a great flavor and texture.

Tip

If dried apricots aren't available, you can substitute ¼ cup (60 mL) apricot jam.

Cumin

Cumin is a smoky, aromatic spice that can add a kick to your dishes. It is often used in Middle Eastern, Eastern European and Mexican cuisines and is a key ingredient in Indian curries.

● Large rice cooker; fuzzy logic or on/off

2 tbsp	extra virgin olive oil	30 mL
1¼ lbs	boneless skinless chicken thighs, cut into 1-inch (2.5 cm) pieces	625 g
1	clove garlic, minced	1
1 cup	finely chopped onion	250 mL
1 tsp	minced gingerroot	5 mL
1 cup	diced tomato	250 mL
½ cup	chopped dried apricots	125 mL
1 tbsp	ground cumin	15 mL
1½ tsp	ground coriander	7 mL
½ tsp	ground cinnamon	2 mL
1 tsp	salt	5 mL
¼ tsp	freshly ground black pepper	1 mL
2 cups	rinsed drained canned chickpeas	500 mL
1 cup	coarse bulgur	250 mL
1¾ cups	chicken broth	425 mL
¼ cup	finely chopped fresh parsley	60 mL

1. Set the rice cooker for the Quick Cook or Regular cycle. When the bottom of the bowl gets hot, add oil and swirl to coat. Sauté chicken for 4 to 5 minutes or until lightly browned on all sides. Using a slotted spoon, transfer chicken to a plate.
2. Add garlic, onion and ginger to the rice cooker bowl and sauté for about 3 minutes or until onion is softened and translucent. Add tomato, apricots, cumin, coriander, cinnamon, salt and pepper; sauté for 2 minutes.
3. Stir in chickpeas, bulgur and broth. Close the lid and reset for the Regular cycle. Set a timer for 20 minutes.
4. When the timer sounds, arrange chicken on top of chickpea mixture and set the timer for 20 minutes.
5. When the timer sounds, check to make sure bulgur is tender and juices run clear when chicken is pierced. If necessary, continue cooking, checking for doneness every 5 minutes. Switch to the Keep Warm cycle and let stand for 10 minutes, then serve immediately, garnished with parsley.

Chicken Tikka Masala on Basmati Rice

Makes 4 servings

You don't need a tandoori oven for this dish, just a rice cooker for the long-grained basmati, which serves as an excellent base for the rich but light tikka masala. Pungent herbs mixed with jalapeño pepper and Greek-style yogurt make the ideal marinade for the tender chunks of chicken.

Tips

If you can't find Greek-style yogurt, you can substitute regular plain yogurt.

Toasting fennel seeds intensifies their flavor. Toast them in a dry skillet over medium-high heat, stirring constantly, for about 3 minutes or until fragrant. Immediately transfer to a spice grinder and let cool, then grind to a fine powder.

For information about rice cooker sizes, see page 13.

- Medium rice cooker; fuzzy logic or on/off
- Baking sheet, lined with parchment paper and brushed with ghee

Chicken

1 tbsp	minced gingerroot	15 mL
2 tsp	fennel seeds, toasted and ground (see tip, at left)	10 mL
2 tsp	ground cumin	10 mL
2 tsp	cayenne pepper	10 mL
1 tsp	ground cinnamon	5 mL
1 tsp	ground cardamom	5 mL
	Salt and freshly ground black pepper	
1½ cups	Greek-style plain yogurt	375 mL
1 tbsp	freshly squeezed lemon juice	15 mL
6	boneless skinless chicken thighs	6
2 tbsp	ghee (see recipe, page 203)	30 mL

Rice

1 cup	white basmati rice, rinsed and drained	250 mL
1½ cups	water	375 mL
¼ tsp	salt	1 mL

Sauce

2 tbsp	ghee	30 mL
1	clove garlic, minced	1
1	jalapeño pepper, seeded and finely chopped	1
2 tsp	ground cumin	10 mL
2 tsp	sweet paprika	10 mL
1 tsp	salt	5 mL
1	can (8 oz/227 mL) tomato sauce	1
1 cup	heavy or whipping (35%) cream	250 mL
	Finely chopped fresh cilantro	

1. *Chicken:* In a large bowl, whisk together ginger, fennel seeds, cumin, cayenne, cinnamon, cardamom, 1 tsp (5 mL) salt, ½ tsp (2 mL) black pepper, yogurt and lemon juice. Add chicken and turn to coat. Cover and refrigerate for at least 8 hours or up to 12 hours.

2. *Rice:* In the rice cooker bowl, combine rice, water and salt. Set the rice cooker for the Regular cycle. At the end of the cycle, hold rice on the Keep Warm cycle.

3. *Sauce:* In a large nonstick skillet, heat ghee over medium heat. Sauté garlic and jalapeño for 1 minute. Add cumin, paprika, salt, tomato sauce and cream; reduce heat and simmer for about 20 minutes or until thickened.

4. Meanwhile, preheat broiler. Remove chicken from marinade, wiping off and discarding excess marinade. Brush chicken with ghee and sprinkle with salt and pepper. Arrange on prepared baking sheet. Broil for about 4 minutes per side or until golden brown on both sides and juices run clear when chicken is pierced. Transfer chicken to a cutting board and let rest for 5 minutes. Cut into 1-inch (2.5 cm) thick slices. Add chicken to sauce and simmer for 10 minutes.

5. Fluff rice with a wooden spoon or plastic paddle and scoop onto serving plates or into bowls. Top with chicken and garnish with cilantro. Serve immediately.

Variation

Substitute white kalijira rice for the basmati rice.

Hainanese-Style Chicken

Makes 6 servings

I first tried this light and tasty dish in Singapore and absolutely had to recreate it at home. The skinless chicken is low in fat but loaded with flavor.

Tips

Chinese rice wine is also called Shaoxing, named after a famous wine-making city in China. It has typically been aged for more than 10 years and can be found in Asian markets and liquor stores. You may substitute dry sherry.

For information about rice cooker sizes, see page 13.

- **Large rice cooker; fuzzy logic or on/off**
- **Blender or food processor**

4 to 5	cloves garlic, lightly smashed	4 to 5
4	1/4-inch (0.5 cm) slices gingerroot	4
3	boneless skinless chicken thighs	3
3	boneless skinless chicken breasts	3
6 cups	water	1.5 L
1 tbsp	Chinese rice wine (see tip, at left)	15 mL
1 tbsp	soy sauce	15 mL
2 cups	long-grain white rice, rinsed and drained	500 mL
	Fresh cilantro leaves	
	Sliced green onions (white and green parts) and cucumber	

Chili Garlic Dipping Sauce

4	cloves garlic, smashed	4
2 tbsp	minced gingerroot	30 mL
1/2 tsp	salt	2 mL
2 tbsp	sambal oelek or other hot Asian chili sauce	30 mL
2 tsp	freshly squeezed lime juice	10 mL

Seasoned Soy Sauce

1 1/2 tbsp	granulated sugar	22 mL
1 tsp	minced garlic	5 mL
1/3 cup	soy sauce	75 mL
1 tbsp	vegetable or canola oil	15 mL
1 tsp	sesame oil	5 mL

1. In a medium saucepan, combine garlic to taste, ginger, chicken thighs, chicken breasts, water, wine and soy sauce. Bring to a boil over high heat. Reduce heat and simmer for 15 to 20 minutes or until juices run clear when chicken thighs are pierced and chicken breasts are no longer pink inside (thighs cook more quickly than breasts, so check the thighs at 15 minutes and remove pieces as necessary when cooked). Using a slotted spoon, transfer chicken to a plate, cover and refrigerate. Reserve broth.
2. In the rice cooker bowl, combine rice and 3 cups (750 mL) reserved broth. Close the lid and set for the Quick Cook or Regular cycle.

Sambal Oelek

A *sambal* is a chili sauce used as a condiment in Indian and Asian cooking. Sambal oelek is a common sambal composed of fiery red chile peppers, vinegar and salt. It can be found at well-stocked grocery stores and Asian markets.

3. *Chili Garlic Dipping Sauce:* In blender, combine garlic, ginger, salt, 1/4 cup (60 mL) reserved broth, chili sauce and lime juice; process until smooth. Set aside.

4. *Seasoned Soy Sauce:* In a small bowl, whisk together sugar, garlic, soy sauce, 3 tbsp (45 mL) reserved broth, vegetable oil and sesame oil until well blended. Set aside.

5. When the machine switches to the Keep Warm cycle, arrange chicken on top of rice. Close the lid and let steam for 15 minutes. Transfer chicken to a cutting board and cut each piece crosswise into 5 or 6 slices.

6. Place a scoop of rice on each of 6 plates and arrange chicken alongside. Spoon seasoned soy sauce over chicken. Garnish with cilantro, green onions and cucumber. Serve immediately, with dipping sauce on the side.

Malaysian Clay Pot

Makes 4 servings

This recipe is traditionally made in a clay pot, a centuries-old Asian cooking method that harmoniously melds flavors together. My rice cooker version replicates this time-honored technique and makes a great family meal for a busy weeknight. Serve with steamed vegetables.

Tips

Serve this dish in a ceramic "clay pot" bowl, available at Asian kitchenware stores.

For information about rice cooker sizes, see page 13.

● **Medium to large rice cooker; fuzzy logic or on/off**

1 tbsp	minced gingerroot	15 mL
1 tsp	granulated sugar	5 mL
1 tsp	cornstarch	5 mL
1 tbsp	soy sauce	15 mL
1 tsp	toasted sesame oil	5 mL
6 oz	boneless skinless chicken thighs, cut into $\frac{1}{2}$-inch (1 cm) pieces	175 g
1	sweet chicken or turkey sausage, cut diagonally into $\frac{1}{4}$-inch (0.5 cm) thick slices	1
2 tbsp	peanut or corn oil	30 mL
$\frac{1}{2}$ cup	chopped green onions (white part only)	125 mL
2 cups	long-grain white rice, rinsed and drained	500 mL
1 tsp	salt	5 mL
3 cups	chicken broth	750 mL
	Chopped green onions (green and white parts)	

1. In a large bowl, combine ginger, sugar, cornstarch, soy sauce and sesame oil. Add chicken and sausage, tossing to coat. Cover and refrigerate for 30 minutes.
2. Set the rice cooker for the Quick Cook or Regular cycle. When the bottom of the bowl gets hot, add peanut oil and swirl to coat. Sauté green onions for about 2 minutes or until softened. Add chicken and sausage; sauté for 4 to 5 minutes or until chicken is lightly browned on all sides.
3. Stir in rice, salt and broth. Close the lid and reset for the Regular cycle.
4. When the machine switches to the Keep Warm cycle, let steam for 10 minutes. Fluff rice with a wooden spoon or plastic paddle. Serve immediately, garnished with green onions.

Variation

Malaysian Clay Pot with Pork and Rice: Substitute 8 oz (250 g) pork tenderloin, cut into $\frac{1}{2}$-inch (1 cm) pieces, for the chicken thighs.

Ginger Chicken Stir-Fry

Makes 4 servings

This simple stir-fry is so flavorful, my kids gobble up the red pepper, straw mushrooms and sugar snap peas without even realizing they're eating something healthy.

Tip

To blanch sugar snap peas, bring a small saucepan of water to a boil over high heat. Add peas and boil for 1 minute or until tender-crisp. Using a slotted spoon, transfer peas to a bowl of ice water and let cool completely. Drain well.

Straw Mushrooms

Straw mushrooms are happy-looking mushrooms that appear to be wearing hats. They are grown in Asia and are available at Asian markets. They are wonderful to have on hand in your pantry for stir-fries and soups.

- **Medium rice cooker; fuzzy logic or on/off**

1 cup	Jasmati rice, rinsed and drained	250 mL
2 cups	water	500 mL
2 tsp	salt, divided	10 mL
1 tsp	cornstarch	5 mL
1/4 tsp	freshly ground white pepper	1 mL
1	large egg white	1
1 tsp	soy sauce	5 mL
3	boneless skinless chicken breasts, cut into 1/2-inch (1 cm) slices	3
2 tbsp	cornstarch	30 mL
1/2 tsp	granulated sugar	2 mL
1/4 cup	cold water	60 mL
2 tbsp	oyster sauce	30 mL
3 tbsp	vegetable oil	45 mL
2	cloves garlic, minced	2
1 tbsp	minced gingerroot	15 mL
1/2 cup	rinsed drained canned straw mushrooms	125 mL
1/2 cup	rinsed drained canned sliced water chestnuts	125 mL
1/2 cup	thinly sliced red bell pepper	125 mL
1/4 cup	chicken broth	60 mL
2 tsp	dry white wine	10 mL
1/2 cup	trimmed sugar snap peas, blanched	125 mL

1. In the rice cooker bowl, combine rice and water. Set the rice cooker for the Regular cycle. At the end of the cycle, hold rice on the Keep Warm cycle.

2. In a small bowl, combine 1 tsp (5 mL) of the salt, 1 tsp (5 mL) cornstarch, pepper, egg white and soy sauce. Add chicken and stir to coat. Cover and refrigerate for 30 minutes.

3. In another small bowl, combine 2 tbsp (30 mL) cornstarch, sugar, cold water and oyster sauce. Set aside.

4. In a wok or large nonstick skillet, heat oil over medium-high heat. Stir-fry garlic and ginger for about 1 minute or until fragrant. Add mushrooms, water chestnuts and the remaining salt; stir-fry for 1 minute. Stir in chicken, red pepper, broth and wine; cover and cook for 2 minutes. Stir in cornstarch mixture and stir-fry until sauce thickens. Add peas and stir-fry for 30 seconds.

5. Fluff rice with a wooden spoon or plastic paddle and scoop onto serving plates or into bowls. Top with chicken stir-fry.

Bombay Turkey

Makes 4 servings

I love to serve this dish in the fall, when the combination of crisp apple, squash and yellow peppers seems to match the colors of the season. Enjoy!

Tips

To avoid tearing up when you're chopping onions, try refrigerating the onions for 30 minutes first, and don't cut the root off.

For information about rice cooker sizes, see page 13.

● **Medium to large rice cooker; fuzzy logic or on/off**

2 tbsp	ghee (see recipe, opposite)	30 mL
1 tbsp	curry powder	15 mL
1 tsp	salt	5 mL
1/2 tsp	garam masala	2 mL
1/2 tsp	ground cumin	2 mL
1/4 tsp	freshly ground black pepper	1 mL
1 lb	lean ground turkey	500 g
1 cup	finely chopped onion	250 mL
1/2	yellow bell pepper, finely chopped	1/2
1 cup	pearl barley	250 mL
1 cup	diced acorn or butternut squash	250 mL
1/2 cup	diced Granny Smith or other tart apple	125 mL
2 cups	chicken broth	500 mL

1. Set the rice cooker for the Quick Cook or Regular cycle. When the bottom of the bowl gets hot, add ghee and swirl to coat. Sauté curry powder, salt, garam masala, cumin and pepper for 1 minute. Add turkey and onion; sauté, breaking turkey up with the back of a spoon, for 4 to 5 minutes or until turkey is no longer pink.

2. Stir in yellow pepper, barley, squash, apple and broth. Close the lid and reset for the Regular cycle. Set a timer for 40 minutes.

3. When the timer sounds, check to make sure barley is tender. If necessary, continue cooking, checking for doneness every 5 minutes. Switch to the Keep Warm cycle and let stand for 10 minutes, then serve immediately.

Variation

Bombay Chicken: Substitute lean ground chicken for the turkey.

Ghee

Ghee **is the Sanskrit word for a highly clarified butter made of cow or water buffalo milk. Because of its high smoking point, ghee does not burn easily.**

1 lb	unsalted butter, cut into chunks	454 g

1. In a medium saucepan, heat butter over medium-high heat until it comes to a boil, 2 to 3 minutes. Reduce heat to medium. As it continues cooking, the butter will form a foam, which will then disappear. Cook until a second foam forms on top and butter turns golden, 7 to 8 minutes. Brown milk solids will be in bottom of pan.

2. Gently pour through a fine-mesh sieve or cheesecloth into a heatproof container. Let cool. Store at room temperature in an airtight container, keeping it free from moisture, for up to 1 month.

Turkey Quinoa Picadillo

Makes 4 servings

Good friends picked up this hearty recipe at a *paladeres* (home restaurant) in Havana and shared it with us when they returned home. I've been making it ever since. The mix of ginger, garlic, raisins, cilantro and jalapeño gives the broth a distinct Caribbean flavor.

Tip

For the best flavor, toast whole cumin seeds in a skillet over medium-high heat, stirring constantly, for about 3 minutes or until fragrant. Immediately transfer to a spice grinder and let cool, then grind to a fine powder.

• **Medium to large rice cooker; fuzzy logic or on/off**

2 tbsp	extra virgin olive oil	30 mL
3	cloves garlic, minced	3
1	jalapeño pepper, seeded and minced	1
1 cup	finely chopped onion	250 mL
1 tbsp	minced gingerroot	15 mL
1 lb	lean ground turkey	500 g
1	poblano pepper, seeded and finely diced	1
2 tsp	chili powder	10 mL
1 tsp	ground cumin (see tip, at left)	5 mL
1 tsp	dried oregano	5 mL
1	can (14 oz/398 mL) diced tomatoes, with juices	1
1 cup	quinoa, rinsed and drained	250 mL
1 tsp	salt	5 mL
¼ tsp	freshly ground black pepper	1 mL
1¾ cups	chicken broth	425 mL
¼ cup	raisins	60 mL
3 tbsp	finely chopped fresh cilantro	45 mL
12	6-inch (15 cm) flour or corn tortillas, warmed	12

1. Set the rice cooker for the Quick Cook or Regular cycle. When the bottom of the bowl gets hot, add oil and swirl to coat. Sauté garlic, jalapeño, onion and ginger for about 3 minutes or until onion is softened and translucent. Add turkey and sauté, breaking it up with the back of a spoon, for 4 to 5 minutes or until no longer pink. Add poblano pepper, chili powder, cumin and oregano; sauté for 2 minutes.
2. Stir in tomatoes with juice, quinoa, salt, pepper and broth. Close the lid and reset for the Regular or Brown Rice cycle.
3. When the machine switches to the Keep Warm cycle, stir in raisins. Close the lid and let stand for 10 minutes. Sprinkle with cilantro.
4. Scoop picadillo into warm tortillas and serve immediately.

Variations

Vegetarian Picadillo: Substitute 12 oz (375 g) soy-based meat product (such as Yves veggie ground chicken) for the ground turkey and replace the chicken broth with vegetable broth.

Substitute toasted millet (see tip, page 116) for the quinoa.

Barley and Sesame Pork Stir-Fry

Makes 4 servings

Barley is a wonderfully nutritious grain that takes this stir-fry to the next level. I particularly love the finishing crunch of the toasted sesame seeds!

Tips

Cornstarch is a key marinating ingredient in Asian dishes, as it seals in the meat's juices, making it tender and juicy. It's also combined with cold water to form a slurry that creates velvety Chinese gravies. You may substitute tapioca starch for the cornstarch.

To blanch snow peas, bring a small saucepan of water to a boil over high heat. Add trimmed peas and boil for 1 minute or until tender-crisp. Using a slotted spoon, transfer peas to a bowl of ice water and let cool completely. Drain well.

5 tsp	cornstarch, divided	25 mL
1 tsp	salt	5 mL
1/2 tsp	granulated sugar	2 mL
Pinch	freshly ground white pepper	Pinch
2 tsp	toasted sesame oil, divided	10 mL
1 tsp	soy sauce	5 mL
1 lb	pork tenderloin, cut into thin 2- by 1-inch (5 by 2.5 cm) slices	500 g
1 tbsp	cold water	15 mL
1/4 cup	vegetable oil	60 mL
2	cloves garlic, minced	2
2	cans (each 8 oz/227 mL) straw mushrooms, drained and rinsed	2
1	can (8 1/2 oz/241 mL) sliced bamboo shoots, drained and rinsed	1
1 cup	cooked pearl barley (see page 27)	250 mL
1 tbsp	dark soy sauce (see tip, page 211)	15 mL
1/4 cup	chicken broth	60 mL
3	green onions (white and green parts), cut into 2-inch (5 cm) pieces	3
1/2 cup	snow peas, blanched (see tip, at left)	125 mL
1 tsp	sambal oelek or other hot Asian chili sauce	5 mL
1 tsp	toasted sesame seeds (see tip, page 54)	5 mL

1. In a medium bowl, combine 2 tsp (10 mL) of the cornstarch, salt, sugar, pepper, 1 tsp (5 mL) of the sesame oil and soy sauce. Add pork and toss to coat. Cover and refrigerate for 20 minutes.

2. In a small bowl, combine the remaining cornstarch and cold water. Set aside.

3. In a wok or large nonstick skillet, heat vegetable oil over medium-high heat. Add pork mixture and garlic; stir-fry for about 3 minutes or until pork is no longer pink. Add mushrooms, bamboo shoots, barley, soy sauce and the remaining sesame oil; stir-fry for 1 minute. Add broth and bring to a boil. Stir in cornstarch mixture and stir-fry for about 10 seconds or until sauce thickens. Add green onions, peas and chili sauce; stir-fry for 30 seconds. Serve immediately, garnished with sesame seeds.

Pork and Lentil Cassoulet

Makes 4 servings

I fell in love with this
dish at a small Provençal
café in St. Remy on a
winter night. It was
accompanied by a
spinach and pear salad,
a crusty baguette, a
pungent red wine and
a roaring fireplace.
I could have stayed
there forever.

Tip
You may substitute fresh
rosemary and thyme,
but use double the
quantity.

● **Large rice cooker; fuzzy logic or on/off**

2 tbsp	extra virgin olive oil	30 mL
2	cloves garlic, minced	2
1 cup	thinly sliced onion	250 mL
1 lb	boneless pork shoulder blade (butt) roast, trimmed and cut into ½-inch (1 cm) cubes	500 g
1	can (14 oz/398 mL) diced tomatoes, with juice	1
2 cups	sliced parsnips (½-inch/1 cm slices)	500 mL
1 cup	thinly sliced celery	250 mL
¾ cup	dried green lentils, sorted and rinsed	175 mL
1 tsp	salt	5 mL
1 tsp	dried rosemary	5 mL
½ tsp	dried thyme	2 mL
¼ tsp	freshly ground black pepper	1 mL
1½ cups	beef broth	375 mL
1	fresh rosemary sprig	1

1. Set the rice cooker for the Quick Cook or Regular cycle. When the bottom of the bowl gets hot, add oil and swirl to coat. Sauté garlic and onion for about 3 minutes or until onion is softened and translucent. Add pork and sauté for 4 to 5 minutes or until browned on all sides.
2. Stir in tomatoes with juice, parsnips, celery, lentils, salt, dried rosemary, thyme, pepper and broth. Close the lid and reset for the Regular cycle. When mixture comes to a boil, set a timer for 12 minutes.
3. When the timer sounds, reset for the Keep Warm cycle and set the timer for 1 hour and 15 minutes.
4. When the timer sounds, check to make sure lentils and pork are tender. If necessary, continue cooking, checking for doneness every 5 minutes. Serve immediately, garnished with rosemary sprig.

Variation
Lamb and Lentil Cassoulet: Substitute boneless lamb shoulder cubes for the pork.

Dirty Rice

Makes 4 to 5 servings

Dirty rice is a traditional Cajun dish that gets its name from its "dirty" appearance. In some regions of the South, it's called "rice dressing." The richness of the bacon and pork make it a meal in itself. This dish was inspired by my friend Ryan's recent trip to New Orleans.

Tip

For information about rice cooker sizes, see page 13.

• Large rice cooker; fuzzy logic or on/off

6	slices bacon, diced	6
8 oz	ground pork	250 g
	Salt and freshly ground black pepper	
2	cloves garlic, minced	2
1 cup	finely chopped onion	250 mL
1 cup	chopped celery	250 mL
2 cups	long-grain white rice, rinsed and drained	500 mL
½ cup	finely chopped green bell pepper	125 mL
½ cup	finely chopped red bell pepper	125 mL
2 tsp	chipotle chile powder	10 mL
2 tsp	ground cumin	10 mL
1 tsp	dried oregano	5 mL
3 cups	chicken broth	750 mL
¼ cup	finely chopped fresh chives	60 mL
	Additional finely chopped fresh chives	

1. Set the rice cooker for the Quick Cook or Regular cycle. When the bottom of the bowl gets hot, sauté bacon for about 5 minutes or until slightly crisp. Transfer bacon to a plate and drain off all but 1 tbsp (15 mL) fat.
2. Add pork to the rice cooker bowl and sprinkle with salt and pepper. Sauté, breaking pork up with the back of a spoon, for 4 to 5 minutes or until no longer pink. Using a slotted spoon, transfer to the plate with the bacon.
3. Add garlic and onion to the rice cooker bowl; sauté for about 3 minutes or until onion is softened and translucent. Add celery and sauté for 3 minutes.
4. Stir in rice, green pepper, red pepper, 2 tsp (10 mL) salt, chile powder, cumin, oregano and broth. Close the lid and reset for the Regular cycle.
5. When the machine switches to the Keep Warm cycle, stir in bacon, pork and chives. Close the lid and let stand for 10 minutes. Fluff rice with a wooden spoon or plastic paddle. Serve immediately, garnished with chives.

Variation

For a more authentic take on this dish, add 1 cup (250 mL) minced chicken or duck livers at the end of step 3 and cook for about 4 minutes or until tender. The liver is what really makes this rice look "dirty."

Louisiana Red Beans

Makes 3 to 4 servings

When paired with rice, this Creole recipe creates a piquant stand-alone meal guaranteed to be a frequent request. To really bring out the spice, try serving it with a red Zinfandel.

Tips

Ham hocks are a cut of pork from the ankle joint of a pig. They contribute a lot of flavor to soups and stews. You can find them at some grocery stores and at Asian and Latin markets.

For information about rice cooker sizes, see page 13.

• Large rice cooker; fuzzy logic or on/off

1 cup	dried red kidney beans	250 mL
2 tbsp	extra virgin olive oil, divided	30 mL
½ cup	finely chopped onion	125 mL
2 cups	andouille or other spicy sausage, cut diagonally into ¼-inch (0.5 cm) thick slices	500 mL
1	green bell pepper, finely chopped	1
1	stalk celery, finely chopped	1
2	smoked ham hocks (see tip, at left)	2
1	bay leaf	1
1 tsp	finely chopped fresh oregano	5 mL
½ tsp	salt	2 mL
Pinch	cayenne pepper	Pinch
4 cups	water	1 L
	Chopped green onions (white and green parts)	

1. Sort, rinse, soak and drain beans (see pages 32–33).
2. Set the rice cooker for the Quick Cook or Regular cycle. When the bottom of the bowl gets hot, add 1 tbsp (15 mL) oil and swirl to coat. Sauté onion for about 3 minutes or until softened and translucent. Add sausage and sauté for 4 to 5 minutes or until lightly browned. Add green pepper and celery; sauté for 30 seconds.
3. Stir in soaked beans, ham hocks, bay leaf, oregano, salt, cayenne and water. Close the lid and reset for the Regular cycle. Set a timer for 1½ hours.
4. When the timer sounds, check to make sure beans are tender. If necessary, continue cooking, checking for doneness every 5 minutes. Discard ham hocks and bay leaf. Drizzle with the remaining oil. Serve immediately, garnished with green onions.

Farro, Broccoli and Pancetta Stir-Fry

Makes 4 to 6 servings

Not just another stir-fry, this one will wow your family. The combination of pancetta, fresh ginger, red pepper and garlic is superb, but the oyster sauce is the magical secret ingredient.

Tips

Chinese rice wine is also called Shaoxing, named after a famous wine-making city in China. It has typically been aged for more than 10 years and can be found in Asian markets and liquor stores. You may substitute dry sherry.

To blanch broccoli florets, bring a small saucepan of water to a boil over high heat. Add broccoli and boil for 3 minutes or until bright green and tender-crisp. Using a slotted spoon, transfer broccoli to a bowl of ice water and let cool completely. Drain well.

$\frac{1}{4}$ tsp	cornstarch	1 mL
$\frac{1}{4}$ cup	chicken broth	60 mL
1 tbsp	Chinese rice wine (see tip, at left)	15 mL
1 tsp	soy sauce	5 mL
$2\frac{1}{2}$ tbsp	vegetable oil, divided	37 mL
4 oz	finely chopped pancetta	125 g
1	clove garlic, minced	1
1 tbsp	minced gingerroot	15 mL
2 cups	broccoli florets, blanched (see tip, at left)	500 mL
$1\frac{1}{2}$ cups	cooked farro (see page 27)	375 mL
1 cup	chopped red bell pepper	250 mL
1 tbsp	oyster sauce	15 mL

1. In a small bowl, combine cornstarch, broth, wine and soy sauce. Set aside.

2. In a wok or large nonstick skillet, heat $\frac{1}{2}$ tbsp (7 mL) oil over medium-high heat. Stir-fry pancetta for 1 minute or until starting to brown. Add garlic, ginger and the remaining oil; stir-fry for about 1 minute or until fragrant. Add broccoli, farro, red pepper and oyster sauce; stir-fry for 2 minutes. Serve immediately.

Variation

Wheat Berry, Broccoli and Pancetta Stir-Fry: Substitute cooked wheat berries for the farro.

Beef Biryani

Makes 4 to 5 servings

Across the Middle East and Asia, biryani is a popular dish with a blend of exotic spices and aromatic flavors. In my version, I use tenderloin to really make the beef stand out.

Garam Masala

Garam masala is a spice blend commonly used in Indian cuisine. It typically includes ground coriander, cumin, ginger, cardamom, cinnamon and cloves. It can be found in well-stocked grocery stores and Indian markets.

• Medium to large rice cooker; fuzzy logic or on/off

3 tbsp	ghee (see recipe, page 203), divided (approx.)	45 mL
1 tbsp	garam masala	15 mL
1 tsp	ground cumin	5 mL
1/2 tsp	ground turmeric	2 mL
1 1/2 lbs	beef tenderloin or boneless top sirloin, trimmed and cut into 1-inch (2.5 cm) cubes	750 g
2	cloves garlic, minced	2
1	onion, thinly sliced	1
2 tsp	minced gingerroot	10 mL
1 1/2 cups	white basmati rice, rinsed and drained	375 mL
3 cups	beef or chicken broth	750 mL
1 tsp	salt	5 mL

1. Set the rice cooker for the Quick Cook or Regular cycle. When the bottom of the bowl gets hot, add 1 tbsp (15 mL) ghee and swirl to coat. Sauté garam masala, cumin and turmeric for 30 seconds. Add beef, in two batches, and cook, stirring occasionally, for 4 to 5 minutes or until browned all over, adding 1 tbsp (15 mL) more ghee as necessary between batches. Using a slotted spoon, transfer beef to a plate.

2. Add the remaining ghee to the rice cooker bowl. Sauté garlic, onion and ginger for about 3 minutes or until onion is softened and translucent. Add rice and sauté for 2 minutes. Flatten rice and place beef on top. Carefully pour in broth and sprinkle with salt. Close the lid and reset for the Regular cycle.

3. When the machine switches to the Keep Warm cycle, let stand for 10 minutes. Serve immediately.

Beef Donburi on Japanese Rice

Makes 4 servings

In North America, donburi may not be as famous as sushi, sashimi, ramen or teriyaki, but it is hugely popular all over Japan. Donburi consists of a bowl of hot cooked rice, on top of which you put various fish, meats and/or vegetables.

Tips

I like to put beef in the freezer for about 30 minutes before slicing it. It makes it a lot easier to cut.

Dark soy sauce has been aged longer than regular soy sauce and contains molasses and some cornstarch, so it is darker and has a more full-bodied flavor. It is also less salty. Look for it at Asian markets. You can substitute regular soy sauce if you can't find dark.

"Julienne" is a culinary term for a preparation in which food is cut into long, thin strips similar to matchsticks.

- **Medium rice cooker; fuzzy logic or on/off**

1 cup	Japanese-style medium-grain japonica rice (such as Calrose)	250 mL
1/2 tsp	minced garlic	2 mL
4 tsp	granulated sugar, divided	20 mL
4 tsp	mirin, divided	20 mL
1 tsp	dark soy sauce (see tip, at left)	5 mL
8 oz	beef tenderloin or boneless top sirloin, thinly sliced across the grain	250 g
2 tbsp	vegetable oil	30 mL
1/4	onion, thinly sliced	1/4
6	mushrooms, sliced	6
1/2	small carrot, julienned (see tip, at left)	1/2
3/4 cup	dashi (see recipe, page 185)	175 mL
2	green onions (white and green parts), cut into 2-inch (5 cm) pieces	2
1 tbsp	sake	15 mL
2	large eggs, lightly beaten	2

1. Place rice in a bowl and add enough cool water to cover by 1 inch (2.5 cm); let soak for 30 minutes. Rinse and drain (see page 20).

2. In a medium bowl, combine garlic, 2 tsp (10 mL) of the sugar, 2 tsp (10 mL) of the mirin and soy sauce. Add beef and toss to coat. Cover and marinate for 10 minutes.

3. In the rice cooker bowl, combine rice and 1 1/3 cups (325 mL) water. Set the rice cooker for the Regular cycle. At the end of the cycle, hold rice on the Keep Warm cycle.

4. In a wok or large nonstick skillet, heat oil over medium-high heat. Stir-fry onion for about 3 minutes or until softened and translucent. Add beef mixture, mushrooms and carrot; stir-fry for about 3 minutes or until beef is browned on all sides. Add dashi and bring to a boil. Add green onions, the remaining sugar, the remaining mirin and sake; reduce heat to medium-low and cook for 3 minutes. Pour eggs on top (do not stir). Cover and cook for 2 minutes.

5. Fluff rice with a wooden spoon or plastic paddle and scoop into deep serving bowls. Top with donburi. Serve immediately.

Variation

Pork Donburi: Substitute pork tenderloin for the beef tenderloin.

Lamb Vindaloo on Kalijira Rice

Makes 4 servings

Kalijira rice was once reserved for royalty and for holiday celebrations because it's so expensive in India. But it is such a perfect accompaniment to so many dishes, including this spicy, scrumptious lamb vindaloo, made flavorful by a wide array of fragrant spices.

Tips

Kalijira is a miniature version of basmati rice. If it's not available, you can substitute white or brown basmati.

This dish is quite spicy. If you like less heat, reduce the amount of cayenne pepper.

For information about rice cooker sizes, see page 13.

● **Medium rice cooker; fuzzy logic or on/off**

Lamb

3	cloves garlic, minced	3
3 tbsp	grated gingerroot	45 mL
1 tbsp	ground coriander	15 mL
1 tbsp	ground cumin	15 mL
1 tbsp	ground cardamom	15 mL
1 tbsp	ground cloves	15 mL
1 tbsp	chili powder	15 mL
1 tbsp	cayenne pepper	15 mL
1 tbsp	ground turmeric	15 mL
1 tbsp	granulated sugar	15 mL
2 tsp	salt	10 mL
2 tsp	freshly ground black pepper	10 mL
1 tsp	dried mustard	5 mL
1 cup	Greek-style plain yogurt	250 mL
¾ cup	white wine vinegar	175 mL
2 lbs	lamb shoulder, trimmed and cut into 1-inch (2.5 cm) cubes	1 kg

Rice

1 cup	white kalijira rice, rinsed and drained	250 mL
⅛ tsp	salt	0.5 mL
1½ cups	water	375 mL
1 tbsp	butter	15 mL

Sauce

¼ cup	ghee (see recipe, page 203)	60 mL
4	tomatoes, cored, seeded and finely diced	4
1	serrano chile pepper, seeded and finely chopped	1
2 cups	finely chopped onions	500 mL
	Naan (Indian flatbread)	
	Raita (see recipe, page 249)	

1. *Lamb:* In a large bowl, whisk together garlic, ginger, coriander, cumin, cardamom, cloves, chili powder, cayenne, turmeric, sugar, salt, pepper, mustard, yogurt and vinegar. Add lamb and toss to coat. Cover and refrigerate for at least 8 hours or overnight.

2. *Rice:* In the rice cooker bowl, combine rice, salt, water and butter. Set the rice cooker for the Regular cycle. At the end of the cycle, hold rice on the Keep Warm cycle.

3. *Sauce:* Meanwhile, in a large nonstick skillet, heat ghee over medium-high heat. Sauté tomatoes, serrano pepper and onions for 4 to 5 minutes or until tender. Add lamb mixture and simmer, stirring occasionally, for 30 minutes or until sauce is thickened and lamb is fork-tender.

4. Fluff rice with a wooden spoon or plastic paddle and scoop onto serving plates or into bowls. Top with lamb mixture. Serve immediately, with naan and raita.

Variation

Replace the lamb with boneless skinless chicken thighs and, in step 3, cook for 15 to 20 minutes or until juices run clear when chicken is pierced. Or use boneless beef top round and cook for 30 minutes or until beef is fork-tender.

Persian-Style Lamb with Rice

Makes 6 to 8 servings

My Persian friend Mary loved this dish so much when I served it to her that I had to promise not to tell her mom! The combination of rice and lentils gives it a great texture.

Tips

Try using a 1-inch (2.5 cm) cinnamon stick in place of the ground cinnamon. Just make sure to remove it before serving.

For information about rice cooker sizes, see page 13.

- **Large rice cooker; fuzzy logic or on/off**

2 cups	white basmati rice, rinsed and drained	500 mL
1 cup	dried green or brown lentils, sorted and rinsed	250 mL
4½ cups	beef or chicken broth	1.125 L
1½ lbs	boneless lamb loin, trimmed and cut into 1-inch (2.5 cm) pieces	750 g
	Salt and freshly ground black pepper	
2 tbsp	extra virgin olive oil	30 mL
½ tsp	ground cinnamon	2 mL
½ tsp	ground cardamom	2 mL
½ tsp	ground cumin	2 mL
1 cup	finely chopped onion	250 mL
¾ cup	golden raisins	175 mL
¼ cup	pine nuts or slivered almonds	60 mL
	Sour cream or yogurt	
	Cucumbers, radish, basil and mint	

1. In the rice cooker bowl, combine rice, lentils and broth. Set the rice cooker for the Regular cycle.
2. Meanwhile, sprinkle lamb with salt and pepper. In a large nonstick skillet, heat oil over medium-high heat. Sauté lamb, cinnamon, cardamom and cumin for 6 to 8 minutes or until lamb is no longer pink inside. Add onion and sauté for about 3 minutes or until softened and translucent. Add raisins and pine nuts; sauté for 2 minutes. Turn off heat, cover and keep warm while rice finishes cooking.
3. When the rice cooker switches to the Keep Warm cycle, stir in lamb mixture. Close the lid and let stand for 10 minutes. Season to taste with salt and pepper. Serve immediately.

Variation

Persian-Style Beef with Rice: Substitute beef tenderloin for the lamb.

Mongolian Lamb on Bhutanese Red Rice

Makes 3 to 4 servings

With its complex, nutty and earthy flavor, Bhutanese red rice is the perfect accompaniment to big-flavor foods like this hearty lamb dish fit for a Mongolian warrior–sized appetite!

Tips

Look for Bhutanese red rice at gourmet stores and online. If you can't find it, substitute red cargo rice or regular red rice.

You can substitute top sirloin beef or pork tenderloin for the lamb if you wish, but lamb is a great companion to Bhutanese red rice.

● **Medium rice cooker; fuzzy logic or on/off**

1 lb	boneless lamb leg or shoulder, trimmed	500 g
1 tsp	cornstarch	5 mL
1 tsp	granulated sugar	5 mL
½ tsp	salt, divided	2 mL
Pinch	freshly ground white pepper	Pinch
¼ cup	vegetable oil, divided	60 mL
4 tsp	soy sauce, divided	20 mL
1 cup	Bhutanese red rice, rinsed and drained	250 mL
1½ cups	water	375 mL
2	cloves garlic, minced	2
2 tsp	minced gingerroot	10 mL
1	green onion (white and green parts), cut into 2-inch (5 cm) pieces	1

1. Cut lamb with the grain into 2-inch (5 cm) strips. Cut strips across the grain into ⅛-inch (3 mm) slices.

2. In a medium bowl, combine cornstarch, sugar, ¼ tsp (1 mL) of the salt, pepper, 1 tbsp (15 mL) of the oil and 1 tsp (5 mL) of the soy sauce. Add lamb and toss to coat. Cover and refrigerate for at least 1 hour or up to 24 hours.

3. In the rice cooker bowl, combine rice, the remaining salt and water. Set the rice cooker for the Regular or Brown Rice cycle. At the end of the cycle, hold rice on the Keep Warm cycle.

4. In a wok or large nonstick skillet, heat the remaining oil over medium-high heat. Stir-fry garlic and ginger for about 1 minute or until fragrant. Add lamb mixture and stir-fry for 3 minutes. Stir in the remaining soy sauce. Add green onion and stir-fry for 30 seconds.

5. Fluff rice with a wooden spoon or plastic paddle and scoop onto serving plates or into bowls. Top with lamb stir-fry. Serve immediately.

Brown Basmati Fried Rice with Ginger and Edamame

Makes 4 to 5 servings

Fried rice never looked so good — or was so good for you! This colorful dish features the benefits of nutritious soybeans and fresh ginger.

Tips

To cook the frozen shelled edamame, simply follow the package directions, then drain and let cool.

To blanch fresh corn kernels, bring a small saucepan of water to a boil over high heat. Add corn and boil for 1 to 2 minutes or until tender-crisp. Using a slotted spoon, transfer corn to a bowl of ice water and let cool completely. Drain.

Make sure to blot the tofu well with paper towels; otherwise, the fried rice could get mushy.

4	large eggs	4
1 tsp	salt	5 mL
Pinch	freshly ground white pepper	Pinch
4 tbsp	vegetable oil, divided	60 mL
4	cloves garlic, minced	4
2 tbsp	minced gingerroot	30 mL
6 cups	cooked brown basmati rice (see page 20), cooled	1.5 L
1/4 tsp	freshly ground white pepper	1 mL
3 tbsp	soy sauce	45 mL
12 oz	firm tofu, cut into 1/4-inch (0.5 cm) cubes and blotted (see tip, at left)	375 g
1 1/2 cups	finely chopped red bell pepper	375 mL
1 1/2 cups	frozen shelled edamame, cooked (see tip, at left)	375 mL
1 cup	blanched fresh or thawed frozen corn kernels (see tip, at left)	250 mL
6	green onions (white and green parts), chopped	6

1. In a medium bowl, whisk together eggs, salt and pinch of white pepper.
2. In a wok, heat 1 tbsp (15 mL) oil over medium heat. Cook eggs, stirring, until set but still moist. Transfer eggs to a plate. Wash and thoroughly dry wok.
3. In the wok, heat 1 tbsp (15 mL) oil over medium-high heat. Stir-fry garlic and ginger for about 2 minutes or until fragrant. Add the remaining oil. Add rice and stir-fry for 1 minute. Stir in 1/4 tsp (1 mL) white pepper and soy sauce. Add tofu, red pepper, edamame and corn; stir-fry for 2 minutes. Return eggs to the wok and add green onions; stir-fry for 30 seconds.

Fried Forbidden Black Rice with Shrimp

Makes 4 to 5 servings

Anything that's forbidden tastes better, right? Just ask Eve. This protein-rich dish makes a deliciously satisfying entrée for the most thrill-seeking of appetites.

Tips

White pepper is the milder cousin of black pepper. It is preferred in Chinese cooking for aesthetic reasons, as there are no black flecks in the finished dish.

Use heart-healthy canola oil in any recipe that calls for vegetable oil.

To blanch fresh peas, bring a small saucepan of water to a boil over high heat. Add peas and boil for 1 minute or until bright green and tender-crisp. Using a slotted spoon, transfer peas to a bowl of ice water and let cool completely. Drain.

4	large eggs	4
5 tsp	salt, divided	25 mL
	Freshly ground white pepper	
3 tbsp	vegetable oil, divided	45 mL
2 tbsp	chicken broth	30 mL
2 tbsp	Chinese rice wine (see tip, page 209) or dry sherry	30 mL
2 tsp	soy sauce	10 mL
2 tsp	toasted sesame oil	10 mL
6 cups	cooked forbidden black rice (see page 20), cooled	1.5 L
2 cups	cubed cooked shrimp (1/2-inch/1 cm cubes)	500 mL
1 cup	blanched fresh or thawed frozen peas	250 mL
1 cup	finely chopped green onions (white parts only)	250 mL
	Chopped green onions (green and white parts)	

1. In a medium bowl, whisk together eggs, 1 tsp (5 mL) salt and a pinch of pepper.
2. In a wok, heat 1 tbsp (15 mL) oil over medium heat. Cook eggs, stirring, until set but still moist. Transfer eggs to a plate. Wash and thoroughly dry wok.
3. In a small bowl, combine the remaining salt, 1/8 tsp (0.5 mL) pepper, broth, rice wine, soy sauce and sesame oil. Set aside.
4. In the wok, heat the remaining oil over medium-high heat. Stir-fry rice for 1 minute. Stir in broth mixture. Add shrimp and peas; stir-fry for 1 minute. Return eggs to the wok and add finely chopped white parts of green onions; stir-fry for 30 seconds. Serve hot, garnished with chopped green onions.

Variation

Substitute cooled cooked wheat berries (see page 27) for the rice.

Farro and Shrimp, Fried Rice–Style

Makes 4 to 5 servings

This twist on classic fried rice uses nutty and nutrient-rich farro in such an innovative and delicious way, your family won't know the difference. Rice is nice, but farro is the star here.

Tips

Pancetta would also be great in this dish in place of the ham.

Increase the amount of hot curry powder if you're a heat seeker.

To blanch fresh peas, bring a small saucepan of water to a boil over high heat. Add peas and boil for 1 minute or until bright green and tender-crisp. Using a slotted spoon, transfer peas to a bowl of ice water and let cool completely. Drain.

4	large eggs	4
1 tsp	salt	4 mL
Pinch	freshly ground white pepper	Pinch
4 tbsp	vegetable oil, divided	60 mL
4	cloves garlic, minced	4
2 tbsp	minced gingerroot	30 mL
4 tsp	hot curry powder	20 mL
2 tsp	hot pepper flakes	10 mL
6 cups	cooked farro (see page 27), cooled	1.5 L
1/4 cup	soy sauce	60 mL
1 1/2 cups	cubed cooked shrimp (1/2-inch/1 cm cubes)	375 mL
1 1/2 cups	cubed smoked ham (1/2-inch/1 cm cubes)	375 mL
1 cup	blanched fresh or thawed frozen peas	250 mL
1 cup	finely chopped red bell pepper	250 mL
6	green onions (white and green parts), chopped	6
4 tsp	toasted sesame oil	20 mL
1/4 cup	finely chopped fresh cilantro	60 mL

1. In a medium bowl, whisk together eggs, salt and pepper.
2. In a wok, heat 1 tbsp (15 mL) oil over medium heat. Cook eggs, stirring, until set but still moist. Transfer eggs to a plate. Wash and thoroughly dry wok.
3. In the wok, heat 1 tbsp (15 mL) oil over medium-high heat. Add garlic, ginger, curry powder and hot pepper flakes; stir-fry for about 1 minute or until fragrant. Add the remaining oil. Add farro and stir-fry for 1 minute. Stir in soy sauce. Add shrimp, ham, peas and red pepper; stir-fry for 2 minutes. Return eggs to the wok and add green onions and sesame oil; stir-fry for 30 seconds. Serve hot, garnished with cilantro.

Thai Pineapple Fried Rice

Makes 4 to 6 servings

This indulgence is like taking a vacation right at your dinner table. The signature dish of Thailand marries tangy and sweet flavors into one vibrant, satisfying meal.

Tips

The pineapple shell makes for a fabulous presentation, but if whole pineapple isn't available, simply prepare this dish using 2 cups (500 mL) diced fresh or drained canned pineapple.

Add 1 tsp (5 mL) Thai chili sauce (such as Sriracha) for a spicy fried rice.

1	whole pineapple	1
4	large eggs	4
1 tbsp	salt, divided	15 mL
Pinch	freshly ground white pepper	Pinch
3 tbsp	vegetable oil, divided	45 mL
6 cups	cooked Thai jasmine rice (see page 20), cooled	1.5 L
1/4 cup	fish sauce (nam pla)	60 mL
2 tbsp	soy sauce	30 mL
2 cups	cubed cooked chicken breast (1/2-inch/1 cm cubes)	500 mL
2 cups	cubed cooked shrimp (1/2-inch/1 cm cubes)	500 mL
1 cup	fresh or thawed frozen peas	250 mL
1/2 cup	finely chopped fresh cilantro	125 mL
1/2 cup	finely chopped fresh mint	125 mL
	Additional finely chopped fresh cilantro	

1. Cut pineapple in half lengthwise and cut the fruit from the middle, leaving shell halves intact. Cut out the eyes and core. Set shell halves aside. Dice the fruit. Dry diced pineapple with paper towels and set aside.

2. In a medium bowl, whisk together eggs, 1 tsp (5 mL) of the salt and pepper.

3. In a wok or large nonstick skillet, heat 1 tbsp (15 mL) oil over medium heat. Cook eggs, stirring, until set but still moist. Transfer eggs to a plate. Wash and thoroughly dry wok.

4. In the wok, heat the remaining oil over medium-high heat. Stir-fry rice for 2 minutes. Stir in fish sauce and soy sauce. Add chicken, shrimp, peas and the remaining salt; stir-fry for 2 minutes. Return eggs to the wok and add pineapple, cilantro and mint; stir-fry for 30 seconds.

5. Scoop fried rice into the pineapple shells and garnish with cilantro.

Variation

Substitute cooled cooked forbidden black rice (see page 20) for the jasmine rice.

Chicken and Asparagus Fried Rice

Makes 5 to 6 servings

This quick and easy recipe is a surefire way to please any dinner guest. I enjoy the leftovers as a delicious next-day lunch!

Tips

To blanch asparagus, bring a small saucepan of water to a boil over high heat. Add asparagus and boil for 2 to 4 minutes or until bright green and tender-crisp. Using a slotted spoon, transfer asparagus to a bowl of ice water and let cool completely. Drain well, then chop.

Any leftover cooked meat works well in this recipe.

4	large eggs	4
1 tbsp	salt, divided	15 mL
Pinch	freshly ground white pepper	Pinch
4 tbsp	vegetable oil, divided	60 mL
12	spears asparagus, tough ends removed, blanched (see tip, at left) and chopped	12
1 cup	drained small canned mushrooms	250 mL
6 cups	cooked long-grain white rice (see page 20), cooled	1.5 L
¼ cup	soy sauce	60 mL
2 cups	bean sprouts	500 mL
4 cups	cubed cooked chicken breast (½-inch/1 cm cubes)	1 L
4	green onions (white and green parts), chopped	4
	Additional chopped green onions	

1. In a medium bowl, whisk together eggs, 1 tsp (5 mL) salt and pepper.
2. In a wok, heat 1 tbsp (15 mL) oil over medium heat. Cook eggs, stirring, until set but still moist. Transfer eggs to a plate. Wash and thoroughly dry wok.
3. In the wok, heat 1 tbsp (15 mL) oil over medium-high heat. Add asparagus, mushrooms and the remaining salt; stir-fry for 2 minutes. Add the remaining oil. Add rice and stir-fry for 1 minute. Stir in soy sauce. Add bean sprouts and stir-fry for 1 minute. Return eggs to the wok and add chicken and green onions; stir-fry for 30 seconds. Serve hot, garnished with green onions.

Beef Kimchi Fried Rice (*Bokumbap*)

Makes 4 servings

Kimchi is Korea's most beloved and well-known food, and it flourishes in recipes that allow its fiery nature to shine. The fried egg and sirloin provide a hearty balance to the spice of this authentic, satisfying dish.

Tip

The Korean government named kimchi (or kim chee) a national treasure. A basic recipe for kimchi consists of cabbage and vegetables pickled in a solution of garlic, salt and red chili peppers. It's available at Asian markets and some grocery stores.

6 tbsp	vegetable oil, divided	90 mL
1 lb	ground beef (preferably sirloin)	500 g
4	cloves garlic, minced	4
1 cup	finely chopped onion	250 mL
6 cups	cooked Japanese-style medium-grain japonica rice (see page 20), cooled	1.5 L
2 cups	kimchi (see tip, at left), cut into bite-size pieces if necessary	500 mL
1 tsp	salt	5 mL
Pinch	freshly ground white pepper	Pinch
¼ cup	soy sauce	60 mL
4	green onions (white and green parts), chopped	4
2 tbsp	sambal oelek or other hot Asian chili sauce	30 mL
4	large eggs	4

1. In a wok or large nonstick skillet, heat 2 tbsp (30 mL) oil over medium-high heat. Add beef and cook, breaking it up with the back of a spoon, for 4 to 5 minutes or until no longer pink. Add garlic and onion; sauté for about 3 minutes or until onion is softened and translucent.

2. Add 3 tbsp (45 mL) oil to the wok. Add rice and stir-fry for 1 minute. Add kimchi, salt, pepper and soy sauce; stir-fry for 1 minute. Add green onions and sambal oelek; stir-fry for 30 seconds. Remove from heat.

3. In a small nonstick skillet, heat the remaining oil over medium heat. Fry eggs until desired yolk texture is achieved. Transfer to a plate.

4. Divide fried rice among four plates and place a fried egg on top of each.

Variation

Substitute ground pork for the beef.

Ten-Ingredient Fried Rice

Makes 3 to 4 servings

No ingredient left behind! This dish is perfect for fried rice lovers who can't decide what to throw in the wok. You really can have it all, and eat it too!

Tips

For a uniform look, cut the cooked shrimp and meats into 1/2-inch (1 cm) cubes.

This is a great dish to make on Thursday nights, when you can throw all your leftovers from the week into the wok.

2	large eggs	2
1 1/2 tsp	salt, divided	7 mL
Pinch	freshly ground white pepper	Pinch
4 tbsp	vegetable oil, divided	60 mL
4 cups	cooked long-grain white rice (see page 20), cooled	1 L
3 tbsp	soy sauce	45 mL
2 cups	bean sprouts	500 mL
1/2 cup	finely chopped red bell pepper	125 mL
1/2 cup	cubed cooked shrimp (see tip, at left)	125 mL
1/2 cup	cubed cooked chicken breast	125 mL
1/2 cup	cubed cooked beef	125 mL
1/4 cup	cubed smoked ham	60 mL
1/4 cup	cubed Chinese barbecued pork	60 mL
2	green onions (white and green parts), chopped	2
	Additional chopped green onions (white and green parts)	

1. In a medium bowl, whisk together eggs, 1/2 tsp (2 mL) of the salt and pepper.
2. In a wok or large nonstick skillet, heat 1 tbsp (15 mL) oil over medium heat. Cook eggs, stirring, until set but still moist. Transfer eggs to a plate. Wash and thoroughly dry wok.
3. In the wok, heat 2 tbsp (30 mL) oil over medium-high heat. Stir-fry rice for 1 minute. Stir in soy sauce. Add bean sprouts and red pepper; stir-fry for 1 minute. Add the remaining oil. Add shrimp, chicken, beef, pork and the remaining salt; stir-fry for 1 minute. Return eggs to the wok and add green onions; stir-fry for 30 seconds. Serve hot, garnished with green onions.

Risottos and Pilafs

Risotto Milanese

Makes 4 to 6 servings

Legend has it that risotto Milanese dates back to 1574, when a stained-glass artisan, Zafferano, added the saffron he used for his paintings to his daughter's wedding risotto. It became (and still is) the talk of the town!

Tips

If you don't have saffron, omit the hot water, increase the chicken broth to 3 cups (750 mL) and replace the saffron with 2 tsp (10 mL) ground turmeric, adding it with the broth.

This risotto will hold on the Keep Warm cycle for about 1 hour, but you'll need to add ¼ cup (60 mL) more broth for a creamy consistency. Wait until you're ready to serve before folding in the Parmesan, seasoning and garnishing.

- **Medium to large rice cooker; fuzzy logic (preferred) or on/off**

1 tsp	crushed saffron threads	5 mL
¼ cup	hot water	60 mL
2 tbsp	extra virgin olive oil	30 mL
5 tsp	butter, divided	25 mL
1	onion, finely chopped	1
1 cup	Arborio rice	250 mL
¼ cup	white wine	60 mL
2¾ cups	chicken broth	675 mL
½ cup	freshly grated Parmesan cheese	125 mL
	Salt and freshly ground black pepper	
	Additional freshly grated Parmesan cheese	

1. In a measuring cup or small bowl, combine saffron threads and hot water; set aside to steep.

2. Set the rice cooker for the Quick Cook or Regular cycle. When the bottom of the bowl gets hot, add oil and 1 tbsp (15 mL) butter and let butter melt. Sauté onion for about 3 minutes or until softened and translucent.

3. Stir in rice until completely coated. Sauté for about 4 minutes or until rice is mostly translucent and only a dot of white remains. Stir in wine and cook for 3 to 4 minutes or until evaporated. Stir in saffron-infused water and broth. Close the lid and reset for the Porridge or Regular cycle. Set a timer for 25 minutes. Stir two or three times while the risotto is cooking.

4. When the timer sounds, check to make sure risotto is al dente. If necessary, continue cooking, checking for doneness every 5 minutes. Fold in the remaining butter. Fold in Parmesan. Season to taste with salt and pepper. Serve immediately, garnished with Parmesan.

Asian-Style Risotto

Makes 4 to 6 servings

Inspired by my recent trip to Los Angeles' Little Tokyo, this fusion take on traditional risotto combines the creaminess of Arborio rice with the delicate texture of Asian mushrooms and the sublime flavors of sake and dashi.

Tips

Enoki mushrooms are delicately flavored and are widely used in Japanese and fusion cooking. You can find them at well-stocked grocery stores and at Asian markets and specialty stores.

This risotto will hold on the Keep Warm cycle for about 1 hour, but you'll need to add ¼ cup (60 mL) more dashi for a creamy consistency. Wait until you're ready to serve before seasoning and garnishing.

- **Medium to large rice cooker; fuzzy logic (preferred) or on/off**

2 tbsp	extra virgin olive oil	30 mL
2	cloves garlic, minced	2
½ cup	chopped green onions (white part only)	125 mL
1 cup	sliced mixed Asian mushrooms (such as enoki and shiitake)	250 mL
1 cup	Arborio rice	250 mL
¼ cup	sake	60 mL
2¾ cups	dashi (see recipe, page 185) or fish stock	675 mL
1 tbsp	soy sauce	15 mL
	Freshly ground white pepper	
	Additional soy sauce	
	Thinly sliced green onions (white and green parts)	

1. Set the rice cooker for the Quick Cook or Regular cycle. When the bottom of the bowl gets hot, add oil and swirl to coat. Sauté garlic and green onions for about 3 minutes or until onions are softened. Add mushrooms and sauté for 3 minutes.

2. Stir in rice until completely coated. Sauté for about 4 minutes or until mostly translucent and only a dot of white remains. Stir in sake and cook for 3 to 4 minutes or until evaporated. Stir in dashi. Close the lid and reset for the Porridge or Regular cycle. Set a timer for 25 minutes. Stir two or three times while the risotto is cooking.

3. When the timer sounds, check to make sure risotto is al dente. If necessary, continue cooking, checking for doneness every 5 minutes. Fold in soy sauce. Season to taste with white pepper and more soy sauce. Serve immediately, garnished with green onions.

Artichoke Risotto

Makes 4 to 6 servings

It doesn't get much more Italian than artichoke risotto. And the rice cooker technique means it will turn out perfectly every time!

Tips

If you want to use frozen baby artichokes instead of fresh, thaw and blot them dry with a paper towel. In step 1, sauté them for 4 to 5 minutes or until tender, then continue with step 2.

This risotto will hold on the Keep Warm cycle for about 1 hour, but you'll need to add ¼ cup (60 mL) more broth for a creamy consistency. Wait until you're ready to serve before folding in the Parmesan and seasoning.

For information about rice cooker sizes, see page 13.

- **Medium to large rice cooker; fuzzy logic (preferred) or on/off**

2 tsp	extra virgin olive oil	10 mL
12	baby artichokes, trimmed (see box, opposite) and quartered	12
2 tbsp	extra virgin olive oil	30 mL
5 tsp	butter, divided	25 mL
2 tbsp	minced shallots	30 mL
1 cup	Arborio rice	250 mL
¼ cup	white wine	60 mL
3 cups	chicken broth	750 mL
½ cup	freshly grated Parmesan cheese	125 mL
	Salt and freshly ground black pepper	
	Additional freshly grated Parmesan cheese	

1. In a nonstick skillet, heat 2 tsp (10 mL) oil over medium-high heat. Sauté artichokes for about 8 minutes or until tender. Remove from heat and set aside.

2. Set the rice cooker for the Quick Cook or Regular cycle. When the bottom of the bowl gets hot, add 2 tbsp (30 mL) oil and 1 tbsp (15 mL) butter and let butter melt. Sauté shallots for about 3 minutes or until softened and translucent.

3. Stir in rice until completely coated. Sauté for about 4 minutes or until mostly translucent and only a dot of white remains. Stir in artichokes. Stir in wine and cook for 3 to 4 minutes or until evaporated. Stir in broth. Close the lid and reset for the Porridge or Regular cycle. Set a timer for 25 minutes. Stir two or three times while the risotto is cooking.

4. When the timer sounds, check to make sure risotto is al dente. If necessary, continue cooking, checking for doneness every 5 minutes. Fold in the remaining butter. Fold in Parmesan. Season to taste with salt and pepper. Serve immediately, with additional Parmesan on the side.

When buying baby artichokes, look for tight, compact heads and freshly cut stem ends.

How to Trim a Baby Artichoke

1. Using a serrated knife, cut off the spiky top third of the artichoke and discard the trimmings.
2. Pull back each dark outer leaf and snap it off at the base until you reach the tender, pale green inner leaves.
3. Use a vegetable peeler to remove the tough outer layers around the stem until you reach the pale layer underneath.
4. Leave the stem attached. With a paring knife, cut off the tough bottom $\frac{1}{4}$ inch (0.5 cm) of the stem.
5. Use the paring knife to trim any remaining dark green or tough parts around the edge and underside of the artichoke and stem until it is smooth and uniformly pale in color.
6. Rub the cleaned baby artichoke with the cut side of a lemon half and use immediately. Or place it in 4 cups (1 L) water mixed with the juice of 2 lemons (which will prevent browning), cover and store in the refrigerator for up to 2 days. Drain well before quartering and sautéing.

Butternut Squash and Ginger Risotto

Makes 4 to 6 servings

Fragrant ginger and sweet winter squash make this risotto dish the perfect indulgence. Butternut squash is an excellent source of nutrients, and kids love it!

Tips

To save time, you can buy packages of butternut squash that has been cleaned and cut into chunks.

This risotto will hold on the Keep Warm cycle for about 1 hour, but you'll need to add ¼ cup (60 mL) more broth for a creamy consistency. Wait until you're ready to serve before folding in the Parmesan, seasoning and garnishing.

• **Medium to large rice cooker; fuzzy logic (preferred) or on/off**

2 tbsp	extra virgin olive oil	30 mL
5 tsp	butter, divided	25 mL
1 cup	finely chopped onion	250 mL
2 tbsp	minced gingerroot	30 mL
2 cups	chopped butternut squash (½-inch/1 cm chunks)	500 mL
1 cup	Arborio rice	250 mL
¼ cup	white wine	60 mL
3 cups	chicken broth	750 mL
½ cup	freshly grated Parmesan cheese	125 mL
	Salt and freshly ground black pepper	
	Ground cinnamon	
	Additional freshly grated Parmesan cheese	

1. Set the rice cooker for the Quick Cook or Regular cycle. When the bottom of the bowl gets hot, add oil and 1 tbsp (15 mL) butter and let butter melt. Sauté onion and ginger for about 3 minutes or until onion is softened and translucent. Add squash and sauté for 6 to 8 minutes or until tender.

2. Stir in rice until completely coated. Sauté for about 4 minutes or until mostly translucent and only a dot of white remains. Stir in wine and cook for 3 to 4 minutes or until evaporated. Stir in broth. Close the lid and reset for the Porridge or Regular cycle. Set a timer for 25 minutes. Stir two or three times while the risotto is cooking.

3. When the timer sounds, check to make sure risotto is al dente. If necessary, continue cooking, checking for doneness every 5 minutes. Fold in the remaining butter. Fold in Parmesan. Season to taste with salt and pepper. Serve immediately, dusted with cinnamon and garnished with Parmesan.

Summer Squash Risotto

Makes 4 to 6 servings

True to its name, this zesty and colorful risotto is perfect for a light summer evening meal, along with a lemon pepper chicken or pork roast.

Tips

Rosé wine adds a light and summery feel to this dish, but any dry white wine will do.

You may use regular lemons if Meyer lemons aren't available.

This risotto will hold on the Keep Warm cycle for about 1 hour, but you'll need to add ¼ cup (60 mL) more broth for a creamy consistency. Wait until you're ready to serve before folding in the Parmesan, seasoning and garnishing.

- **Medium to large rice cooker; fuzzy logic (preferred) or on/off**

2 tbsp	extra virgin olive oil	30 mL
5 tsp	butter, divided	25 mL
3 tbsp	minced shallots	45 mL
½ cup	diced zucchini	125 mL
½ cup	diced yellow summer squash (yellow zucchini)	125 mL
1 cup	Arborio rice	250 mL
¼ cup	rosé wine (see tip, at left)	60 mL
3 cups	chicken broth	750 mL
1 tbsp	finely chopped fresh basil	15 mL
½ cup	freshly grated Parmesan cheese	125 mL
1 tsp	finely grated Meyer lemon zest (see tip, at left)	5 mL
1 tbsp	freshly squeezed Meyer lemon juice	15 mL
	Salt and freshly ground black pepper	
	Additional freshly grated Parmesan cheese	

1. Set the rice cooker for the Quick Cook or Regular cycle. When the bottom of the bowl gets hot, add oil and 1 tbsp (15 mL) butter and let butter melt. Sauté shallots for about 3 minutes or until softened and translucent. Add zucchini and squash; sauté for 2 minutes.

2. Stir in rice until completely coated. Sauté for about 4 minutes or until mostly translucent and only a dot of white remains. Stir in wine and cook for 3 to 4 minutes or until evaporated. Stir in broth. Close the lid and reset for the Porridge or Regular cycle. Set a timer for 20 minutes. Stir two or three times while the risotto is cooking.

3. When the timer sounds, stir in basil. Set the timer for 5 minutes.

4. When the timer sounds, check to make sure risotto is al dente. If necessary, continue cooking, checking for doneness every 5 minutes. Fold in the remaining butter. Fold in Parmesan, lemon zest and lemon juice. Season to taste with salt and pepper. Serve immediately, garnished with Parmesan.

Zucchini Blossom and Prosecco Risotto

Makes 4 to 6 servings

Brilliant gold zucchini blossoms make this risotto a treat for the eyes as well as the taste buds. It's the ideal recipe for a romantic meal. Save some Prosecco to toast your feast!

Tips

Zucchini blossoms are the flowers located at the end of the zucchini. With their golden-orange hue, they are a delicate and beautiful summertime treat. Zucchini blossoms can be found at farmers' markets and specialty gourmet shops during the summer (and sometimes into fall and winter).

This risotto will hold on the Keep Warm cycle for about 1 hour, but you'll need to add $\frac{1}{4}$ cup (60 mL) more broth for a creamy consistency. Wait until you're ready to serve before folding in the Parmesan, seasoning, drizzling with Prosecco and oil, and garnishing.

- **Medium to large rice cooker; fuzzy logic (preferred) or on/off**

3 tbsp	extra virgin olive oil, divided	45 mL
5 tsp	butter, divided	25 mL
1 cup	finely chopped onion	250 mL
1 cup	Arborio rice	250 mL
$\frac{1}{2}$ cup	Prosecco	125 mL
4 cups	chicken broth	1 L
10	zucchini blossoms, stems and pistils removed, thinly sliced (see tip, at left)	10
$\frac{1}{2}$ cup	freshly grated Parmesan cheese	125 mL
	Salt and freshly ground black pepper	
1 tbsp	Prosecco	15 mL
	Finely chopped fresh parsley	
	Additional freshly grated Parmesan cheese	

1. Set the rice cooker for the Quick Cook or Regular cycle. When the bottom of the bowl gets hot, add 2 tbsp (30 mL) oil and 1 tbsp (15 mL) butter and let butter melt. Sauté onion for about 3 minutes or until softened and translucent.

2. Stir in rice until completely coated. Sauté for about 4 minutes or until mostly translucent and only a dot of white remains. Stir in $\frac{1}{2}$ cup (125 mL) Prosecco and cook for 3 to 4 minutes or until evaporated. Stir in broth. Close the lid and reset for the Porridge or Regular cycle. Set a timer for 20 minutes. Stir two or three times while the risotto is cooking.

3. When the timer sounds, fold in zucchini blossoms. Set the timer for 5 minutes.

4. When the timer sounds, check to make sure risotto is al dente. If necessary, continue cooking, checking for doneness every 5 minutes. Fold in the remaining butter. Fold in Parmesan. Season to taste with salt and pepper. Drizzle with 1 tbsp (15 mL) Prosecco and the remaining oil. Serve immediately, garnished with parsley. Serve additional Parmesan on the side.

Bulgur Risotto with Asparagus and Watercress

Makes 4 to 6 servings

The chewy bulgur in this dish provides a great texture contrast to the flavorful asparagus and watercress.

Tips

To blanch asparagus, bring a small saucepan of water to a boil over high heat. Add asparagus and boil for 2 to 4 minutes or until bright green and tender-crisp. Using a slotted spoon, transfer asparagus to a bowl of ice water and let cool completely. Drain well, then chop.

This risotto will hold on the Keep Warm cycle for about 1 hour, but you'll need to add ¼ cup (60 mL) more broth for a moist consistency. Wait until you're ready to serve before folding in the Parmesan, seasoning and garnishing.

• **Medium to large rice cooker; fuzzy logic (preferred) or on/off**

2 tbsp	extra virgin olive oil	30 mL
5 tsp	butter, divided	25 mL
2	cloves garlic, minced	2
1 cup	finely chopped onion	250 mL
1 cup	coarse bulgur	250 mL
2 cups	vegetable broth or water	500 mL
1	sprig fresh thyme	1
12	spears asparagus, tough ends removed, blanched (see tip, at left) and cut into 1-inch (2.5 cm) pieces	12
¾ cup	trimmed watercress	175 mL
2 tbsp	finely chopped fresh tarragon	30 mL
1 tbsp	finely chopped fresh thyme	15 mL
½ cup	freshly grated Parmesan cheese	125 mL
	Salt and freshly ground black pepper	
	Additional freshly grated Parmesan cheese	

1. Set the rice cooker for the Quick Cook or Regular cycle. When the bottom of the bowl gets hot, add oil and 1 tbsp (15 mL) butter and let butter melt. Sauté garlic and onion for about 3 minutes or until onion is softened and translucent.

2. Stir in bulgur until completely coated. Sauté for 3 minutes. Stir in broth and thyme sprig. Close the lid and reset for the Porridge or Regular cycle. Set a timer for 30 minutes. Stir two or three times while the risotto is cooking.

3. When the timer sounds, check to make sure bulgur is tender. If necessary, continue cooking, checking for doneness every 5 minutes. Fold in asparagus, watercress, tarragon, chopped thyme and the remaining butter. Close the lid and let stand for 1 minute to wilt the watercress. Discard thyme sprig. Fold in Parmesan. Season to taste with salt and pepper. Serve immediately, with additional Parmesan on the side.

Variation

For more protein, add 1 cup (250 mL) chopped grilled chicken or grilled shrimp with the asparagus.

Farro Risotto with Fava Beans and Zucchini

Makes 4 to 6 servings

This dish is brimming with veggie goodness and is so tasty that it's sure to become a fava-rite in your house.

Tips

Although farro is a whole grain, it is sometimes placed in the pasta aisle at health food and specialty shops. It can also be ordered online from a variety of sources.

When shopping for fava beans, select small pods; those that bulge with beans are past their prime.

This risotto will hold on the Keep Warm cycle for about 1 hour, but you'll need to add ¼ cup (60 mL) more broth for a creamy consistency. Wait until you're ready to serve before folding in the Parmesan, seasoning and garnishing.

- **Medium to large rice cooker; fuzzy logic (preferred) or on/off**

3 tbsp	extra virgin olive oil	45 mL
2	cloves garlic, minced	2
1	onion, finely chopped	1
1 cup	diced zucchini	250 mL
1½ cups	farro, rinsed and drained	375 mL
¼ cup	white wine	60 mL
3 cups	chicken or vegetable broth	750 mL
2 cups	fresh or thawed frozen shelled fava beans, blanched if fresh (see tip, page 109)	500 mL
½ cup	freshly grated Parmesan cheese	125 mL
	Salt and freshly ground black pepper	
	Additional freshly grated Parmesan cheese	

1. Set the rice cooker for the Quick Cook or Regular cycle. When the bottom of the bowl gets hot, add oil and swirl to coat. Sauté garlic and onion for about 3 minutes or until onion is softened and translucent. Add zucchini and sauté for 2 minutes.
2. Stir in farro until completely coated. Sauté for 5 minutes. Stir in wine and cook for 3 to 4 minutes or until evaporated. Stir in broth. Close the lid and reset for the Porridge or Regular cycle. Set a timer for 20 minutes. Stir two or three times while the risotto is cooking.
3. When the timer sounds, fold in beans. Set the timer for 5 minutes.
4. When the timer sounds, check to make sure farro is tender. If necessary, continue cooking, checking for doneness every 5 minutes. Fold in Parmesan. Season to taste with salt and pepper. Serve immediately, garnished with Parmesan.

Variation

For a more traditional risotto dish, substitute 1 cup (250 mL) Arborio rice for the farro and sauté it in step 2 for about 4 minutes or until mostly translucent and only a dot of white remains.

Quinoa Risotto with Mushrooms and Thyme

Makes 4 to 6 servings

This dish is delicious and yet so quick and easy to make. We all love thyme, especially saving it!

Tips

Use any fresh mushrooms you have on hand for this dish. Clean them with a damp paper towel. Remember never to soak fresh mushrooms, as they'll absorb too much water and become mushy.

This risotto will hold on the Keep Warm cycle for about 1 hour, but you'll need to add ¼ cup (60 mL) more broth for a creamy consistency. Wait until you're ready to serve before folding in the Parmesan, seasoning and garnishing.

- **Medium to large rice cooker; fuzzy logic (preferred) or on/off**

2 tbsp	extra virgin olive oil	30 mL
5 tsp	butter, divided	25 mL
2	cloves garlic, minced	2
1 cup	finely chopped onion	250 mL
8 oz	cremini mushrooms, sliced	250 g
6 oz	shiitake mushrooms, sliced	175 g
3 tbsp	finely chopped fresh thyme, divided	45 mL
1½ cups	quinoa, rinsed and drained	375 mL
¼ cup	white wine	60 mL
3 cups	chicken or vegetable broth	750 mL
¼ cup	freshly grated Parmesan cheese	60 mL
	Salt and freshly ground black pepper	
	Additional freshly grated Parmesan cheese	

1. Set the rice cooker for the Quick Cook or Regular cycle. When the bottom of the bowl gets hot, add oil and 1 tbsp (15 mL) butter and let butter melt. Sauté garlic and onion for about 3 minutes or until onion is softened and translucent. Add cremini mushrooms, shiitake mushrooms and thyme; sauté for about 6 minutes or until tender.

2. Stir in quinoa until completely coated. Sauté for 3 minutes. Stir in wine and cook for 3 to 4 minutes or until evaporated. Stir in broth. Close the lid and reset for the Porridge or Regular cycle. Set a timer for 18 minutes. Stir two or three times while the risotto is cooking.

3. When the timer sounds, check to make sure quinoa is tender. If necessary, continue cooking, checking for doneness every 5 minutes. Fold in the remaining butter. Fold in Parmesan. Season to taste with salt and pepper. Serve immediately, garnished with Parmesan.

Variation

Substitute toasted millet (see tip, page 254) for the quinoa.

Quinoa and Goat Cheese Risotto

Makes 4 to 6 servings

Goat cheese is one of my absolute favorite cheeses, and I'm not alone. Your friends and family will love this quinoa risotto.

Tips

The easiest way to zest citrus fruit is with a rasp grater, such as a Microplane.

This risotto will hold on the Keep Warm cycle for about 1 hour, but you'll need to add ¼ cup (60 mL) more broth for a creamy consistency. Wait until you're ready to serve before folding in the goat cheese, seasoning and garnishing.

For information about rice cooker sizes, see page 13.

- **Medium to large rice cooker; fuzzy logic (preferred) or on/off**

2 tbsp	extra virgin olive oil	30 mL
5 tsp	butter, divided	25 mL
2	cloves garlic, minced	2
1 cup	finely chopped onion	250 mL
1½ cups	quinoa, rinsed and drained	375 mL
¼ cup	white wine	60 mL
3 cups	chicken or vegetable broth	750 mL
1 cup	packed baby spinach, coarsely chopped	250 mL
4 oz	goat cheese, crumbled	125 g
	Salt and freshly ground black pepper	
	Freshly grated Parmesan cheese	
	Chopped fresh parsley	
	Grated lemon zest	

1. Set the rice cooker for the Quick Cook or Regular cycle. When the bottom of the bowl gets hot, add oil and 1 tbsp (15 mL) butter and let butter melt. Sauté garlic and onion for about 3 minutes or until onion is softened and translucent.

2. Stir in quinoa until completely coated. Sauté for 3 minutes. Stir in wine and cook for 3 to 4 minutes or until evaporated. Stir in broth. Close the lid and reset for the Porridge or Regular cycle. Set a timer for 15 minutes. Stir two or three times while the risotto is cooking.

3. When the timer sounds, fold in spinach. Set the timer for 3 minutes.

4. When the timer sounds, check to make sure quinoa is tender. If necessary, continue cooking, checking for doneness every 5 minutes. Fold in the remaining butter. Fold in goat cheese. Season to taste with salt and pepper. Serve immediately, garnished with Parmesan, parsley and lemon zest.

Variation

For a burst of tangy flavor, add ¼ cup (60 mL) thinly sliced sun-dried tomatoes with the spinach.

Risi e Bisi

Makes 4 to 6 servings

The name of this classic Venetian dish literally means "rice and peas." It's as fun to eat as it is to say!

Tips

For the ultimate convenience, I like to use a 1-quart (1 L) box of ready-to-use organic chicken broth for this recipe.

To blanch fresh peas, bring a small saucepan of water to a boil over high heat. Add peas and boil for 1 minute or until bright green and tender-crisp. Using a slotted spoon, transfer peas to a bowl of ice water and let cool completely. Drain.

This risotto will hold on the Keep Warm cycle for about 1 hour, but you'll need to add 1/4 cup (60 mL) more broth for a creamy consistency. Wait until you're ready to serve before folding in the Parmesan, seasoning and drizzling with oil.

- **Medium to large rice cooker; fuzzy logic (preferred) or on/off**

3 tbsp	extra virgin olive oil, divided	45 mL
5 tsp	butter, divided	25 mL
1 cup	finely chopped onion	250 mL
1 cup	Arborio rice	250 mL
1/2 cup	white wine	125 mL
4 cups	chicken broth	1 L
1 cup	blanched fresh or thawed frozen peas (see tip, at left)	250 mL
1/2 cup	freshly grated Parmesan cheese	125 mL
	Salt and freshly ground black pepper	
	Additional freshly grated Parmesan cheese	

1. Set the rice cooker for the Quick Cook or Regular cycle. When the bottom of the bowl gets hot, add 2 tbsp (30 mL) olive oil and 1 tbsp (15 mL) butter and let butter melt. Sauté onion for about 3 minutes or until softened and translucent.

2. Stir in rice until completely coated. Sauté for about 4 minutes or until mostly translucent and only a dot of white remains. Stir in wine and cook for 3 to 4 minutes or until evaporated. Stir in broth. Close the lid and reset for the Porridge or Regular cycle. Set a timer for 20 minutes. Stir two or three times while the risotto is cooking.

3. When the timer sounds, fold in peas. Set the timer for 5 minutes.

4. When the timer sounds, check to make sure risotto is al dente. If necessary, continue cooking, checking for doneness every 5 minutes. Fold in the remaining butter. Fold in Parmesan. Season to taste with salt and pepper. Drizzle with the remaining oil. Serve immediately, with additional Parmesan on the side.

Variation

For a heartier dish, add 1 cup (250 mL) diced pancetta with the Parmesan.

Kidney Bean Risotto

Makes 4 to 6 servings

Think outside the chili! Kidney beans prove versatile in this Italian version of beans and rice.

Tips

To toast cashews, spread them in a single layer on a baking sheet. Bake in a 350°F (180°C) oven, stirring often, for 7 to 10 minutes or until light brown and fragrant. Immediately transfer to a bowl and let cool. To toast pine nuts, see tip on page 188.

This risotto will hold on the Keep Warm cycle for about 1 hour, but you'll need to add ¼ cup (60 mL) more broth for a creamy consistency. Wait until you're ready to serve before seasoning and garnishing.

- **Medium to large rice cooker; fuzzy logic (preferred) or on/off**

3 tbsp	extra virgin olive oil	45 mL
2	cloves garlic, minced	2
1 cup	finely chopped onion	250 mL
½ cup	diced celery	125 mL
1 cup	Arborio rice	250 mL
¼ cup	white wine	60 mL
3 cups	chicken or vegetable broth	750 mL
1	can (14 to 19 oz/398 to 540 mL) red kidney beans, drained and rinsed	1
1 cup	diced zucchini	250 mL
½ cup	cashews or pine nuts, toasted (see tip, at left)	125 mL
3 tbsp	finely chopped fresh parsley	45 mL
	Salt and freshly ground black pepper	
	Additional finely chopped fresh parsley	

1. Set the rice cooker for the Quick Cook or Regular cycle. When the bottom of the bowl gets hot, add oil and swirl to coat. Sauté garlic and onion for about 3 minutes or until onion is softened and translucent. Add celery and sauté for 2 minutes.
2. Stir in rice until completely coated. Sauté for about 4 minutes or until mostly translucent and only a dot of white remains. Stir in wine and cook for 3 to 4 minutes or until evaporated. Stir in broth. Close the lid and reset for the Porridge or Regular cycle. Set a timer for 20 minutes. Stir two or three times while the risotto is cooking.
3. When the timer sounds, fold in beans, zucchini, cashews and parsley. Set the timer for 5 minutes.
4. When the timer sounds, check to make sure risotto is al dente. If necessary, continue cooking, checking for doneness every 5 minutes. Season to taste with salt and pepper. Serve immediately, garnished with parsley.

Variation

Substitute 1½ cups (375 mL) farro for the Arborio rice and sauté it in step 2 for 5 minutes.

Lobster Risotto

Makes 4 to 6 servings

Lobster risotto is one of the most decadent and delightful ways to spoil your dinner guests — and yourself! Go easy on the cheese to really let the lobster and the truffle oil take the spotlight.

Tips

Substitute 2 cups (500 mL) chopped cooked monkfish for a more economical version of this dish using "poor man's lobster."

This risotto will hold on the Keep Warm cycle for about 1 hour, but you'll need to add ¼ cup (60 mL) more broth for a creamy consistency. Wait until you're ready to serve before folding in the Parmesan, seasoning and garnishing.

- **Medium to large rice cooker; fuzzy logic (preferred) or on/off**

1 lb	fresh or thawed frozen lobster tails	500 g
2 tbsp	white or black truffle oil or extra virgin olive oil	30 mL
5 tsp	butter, divided	25 mL
1	onion, finely chopped	1
1 cup	Arborio rice	250 mL
1 tbsp	finely chopped fresh thyme	15 mL
¼ cup	brandy or dry red wine	60 mL
3 cups	chicken broth	750 mL
¼ cup	finely chopped fresh chives	60 mL
½ cup	freshly grated Parmesan cheese	125 mL
	Salt and freshly ground black pepper	
	Additional finely chopped fresh chives	
	Additional freshly grated Parmesan cheese	

1. Bring a medium saucepan of salted water to a boil over medium-high heat. Add lobster tails and boil for 8 to 10 minutes or until shells curl and meat turns white. Transfer lobster to a bowl of cold water and let cool.

2. Set the rice cooker for the Quick Cook or Regular cycle. When the bottom of the bowl gets hot, add truffle oil and 1 tbsp (15 mL) butter and let butter melt. Sauté onion for about 3 minutes or until softened and translucent.

3. Stir in rice and thyme until completely coated. Sauté for about 4 minutes or until rice is mostly translucent and only a dot of white remains. Stir in brandy and cook for 3 to 4 minutes or until evaporated. Stir in broth. Close the lid and reset for the Porridge or Regular cycle. Set a timer for 25 minutes. Stir two or three times while the risotto is cooking.

4. Meanwhile, drain lobster. Remove meat from shells and cut into ½-inch (1 cm) pieces.

5. When the timer sounds, check to make sure risotto is al dente. If necessary, continue cooking, checking for doneness every 5 minutes. Fold in lobster, chives and the remaining butter. Fold in Parmesan. Season to taste with salt and pepper. Serve immediately, garnished with chives. Serve additional Parmesan on the side.

Lemony Risotto with Shrimp

Makes 4 to 6 servings

I love the refreshing burst of lemon in this dish, and it's a fantastic recipe to make when fresh corn is in season. Vibrant pink shrimp make it a colorful dish for entertaining. Serve with a mixed green salad for an easy, breezy dinner.

Tips

To blanch fresh corn kernels, bring a small saucepan of water to a boil over high heat. Add corn and boil for 1 to 2 minutes or until tender-crisp. Using a slotted spoon, transfer corn to a bowl of ice water and let cool completely. Drain.

Try using Meyer lemons for the juice and zest.

This risotto will hold on the Keep Warm cycle for about 1 hour, but you'll need to add ¼ cup (60 mL) more broth for a creamy consistency. Wait until you're ready to serve before folding in the Parmesan, seasoning and garnishing.

- **Medium to large rice cooker; fuzzy logic (preferred) or on/off**

2 tbsp	extra virgin olive oil	30 mL
5 tsp	butter, divided	25 mL
1 cup	finely chopped onion	250 mL
1 tbsp	finely grated lemon zest	15 mL
1 cup	Arborio rice	250 mL
¼ cup	white wine	60 mL
3 cups	chicken broth	750 mL
12	medium shrimp, peeled and deveined	12
1 cup	blanched fresh or thawed frozen corn kernels (see tip, at left)	250 mL
3 tbsp	freshly squeezed lemon juice	45 mL
½ cup	freshly grated Parmesan cheese	125 mL
	Salt and freshly ground black pepper	
	Finely chopped fresh parsley	
	Lemon wedges	
	Additional freshly grated Parmesan cheese	

1. Set the rice cooker for the Quick Cook or Regular cycle. When the bottom of the bowl gets hot, add oil and 1 tbsp (15 mL) butter and let butter melt. Sauté onion for about 3 minutes or until softened and translucent. Stir in lemon zest.

2. Stir in rice until completely coated. Sauté for about 4 minutes or until mostly translucent and only a dot of white remains. Stir in wine and cook for 3 to 4 minutes or until evaporated. Stir in broth. Close the lid and reset for the Porridge or Regular cycle. Set a timer for 20 minutes. Stir two or three times while the risotto is cooking.

3. When the timer sounds, fold in shrimp, corn and lemon juice. Set the timer for 5 minutes.

4. When the timer sounds, check to make sure risotto is al dente and shrimp are pink and opaque. If necessary, continue cooking, checking for doneness every 5 minutes. Fold in the remaining butter. Fold in Parmesan. Season to taste with salt and pepper. Serve immediately, garnished with parsley and lemon wedges. Serve additional Parmesan on the side.

Variation

Substitute 1 cup (250 mL) chopped grilled chicken for the shrimp, adding it with the Parmesan.

Fontina Chicken Risotto

Makes 4 to 6 servings

Italian cheeses take center stage in this lovely risotto dish, supported by flavorful diced chicken breast. Together, these ingredients steal the show. *Bellissimo!*

Tips

You may use a sprig of thyme instead of chopped. Just remember to remove it before serving.

This risotto will hold on the Keep Warm cycle for about 1 hour, but you'll need to add ¼ cup (60 mL) more broth for a creamy consistency. Wait until you're ready to serve before folding in the chicken, Parmesan and fontina, seasoning and garnishing.

For information about rice cooker sizes, see page 13.

- **Medium to large rice cooker; fuzzy logic (preferred) or on/off**

2 tbsp	extra virgin olive oil	30 mL
5 tsp	butter, divided	25 mL
1 cup	finely chopped onion	250 mL
1 cup	Arborio rice	250 mL
1 tbsp	finely chopped fresh thyme	15 mL
¼ cup	white wine	60 mL
3 cups	chicken broth	750 mL
1 cup	diced cooked chicken breast	250 mL
½ cup	freshly grated Parmesan cheese	125 mL
½ cup	shredded fontina cheese	125 mL
	Salt and freshly ground black pepper	
¼ cup	finely chopped fresh parsley	60 mL
	Additional shredded fontina cheese	
	Additional freshly grated Parmesan cheese	

1. Set the rice cooker for the Quick Cook or Regular cycle. When the bottom of the bowl gets hot, add oil and 1 tbsp (15 mL) butter and let butter melt. Sauté onion for about 3 minutes or until softened and translucent.

2. Stir in rice and thyme until completely coated. Sauté for about 4 minutes or until rice is mostly translucent and only a dot of white remains. Stir in wine and cook for 3 to 4 minutes or until evaporated. Stir in broth. Close the lid and reset for the Porridge or Regular cycle. Set a timer for 25 minutes. Stir two or three times while the risotto is cooking.

3. When the timer sounds, check to make sure risotto is al dente. If necessary, continue cooking, checking for doneness every 5 minutes. Fold in the remaining butter. Fold in chicken, Parmesan and fontina. Season to taste with salt and pepper. Serve immediately, garnished with parsley and fontina. Serve additional Parmesan on the side.

Variations

Substitute 1½ cups (375 mL) quinoa for the Arborio rice and sauté it in step 2 for 3 minutes.

Replace the fontina cheese with Havarti or Gruyère.

Pancetta and Pea Risotto

Makes 4 to 6 servings

I love the saltiness of the pancetta coupled with delicate peas in this wonderful recipe. It's a flavor combination that just naturally goes together.

Tips

Pancetta is an Italian dry-cured meat similar to bacon (though bacon is smoked, not cured). You can substitute bacon in this risotto, but you may want to blanch it first to eliminate its smoky flavor. To do so, cook bacon in boiling water for 4 minutes; drain and pat dry.

To blanch fresh peas, bring a small saucepan of water to a boil over high heat. Add peas and boil for 1 minute or until bright green and tender-crisp. Using a slotted spoon, transfer peas to a bowl of ice water and let cool completely. Drain.

This risotto will hold on the Keep Warm cycle for about 1 hour, but you'll need to add ¼ cup (60 mL) more broth for a creamy consistency. Wait until you're ready to serve before folding in the Parmesan and seasoning.

- **Medium to large rice cooker; fuzzy logic (preferred) or on/off**

2 tbsp	extra virgin olive oil	30 mL
5 tsp	butter, divided	25 mL
1 cup	finely chopped onion	250 mL
4 oz	pancetta, diced	125 g
1 cup	Arborio rice	250 mL
¼ cup	white wine	60 mL
3 cups	chicken broth	750 mL
1 cup	blanched fresh or thawed frozen peas (see tip, at left)	250 mL
½ cup	freshly grated Parmesan cheese	125 mL
	Salt and freshly ground black pepper	
	Additional freshly grated Parmesan cheese	

1. Set the rice cooker for the Quick Cook or Regular cycle. When the bottom of the bowl gets hot, add oil and 1 tbsp (15 mL) butter and let butter melt. Sauté onion for about 3 minutes or until softened and translucent. Add pancetta and sauté for about 5 minutes or until golden brown.

2. Stir in rice until completely coated. Sauté for about 4 minutes or until mostly translucent and only a dot of white remains. Stir in wine and cook for 3 to 4 minutes or until evaporated. Stir in broth. Close the lid and reset for the Porridge or Regular cycle. Set a timer for 20 minutes. Stir two or three times while the risotto is cooking.

3. When the timer sounds, fold in peas. Set the timer for 5 minutes.

4. When the timer sounds, check to make sure risotto is al dente. If necessary, continue cooking, checking for doneness every 5 minutes. Fold in the remaining butter. Fold in Parmesan. Season to taste with salt and pepper. Serve immediately, with additional Parmesan on the side.

Variation

Substitute fatty prosciutto for the pancetta.

Chili Con Carne (page 173)

Arroz con Pollo (page 191)

Bombay Turkey (page 202)

Lemony Risotto with Shrimp (page 238)

Brown Basmati Fried Rice with Ginger and Edamame (page 216)

Crab Dumplings (page 316)

Quinoa Banana Chocolate Cake (page 354)

Rocky Road Polenta Pudding (page 369)

Italian Sausage and Mushroom Risotto

Makes 4 to 6 servings

My husband couldn't believe this dish was made in a rice cooker! The richness of the sausage, combined with lush portobellos and accented with fresh herbs and Madeira, make this a soul-satisfying dish to serve on a chilly night.

Tips

You may substitute port, sherry or dry vermouth for the Madeira. If you prefer to omit the wine altogether, add an additional ¼ cup (60 mL) chicken broth.

This risotto will hold on the Keep Warm cycle for about 1 hour, but you'll need to add ¼ cup (60 mL) more broth for a creamy consistency. Wait until you're ready to serve before folding in the Parmesan and salt and garnishing.

- **Medium to large rice cooker; fuzzy logic (preferred) or on/off**

1 tbsp	extra virgin olive oil	15 mL
5 tsp	butter, divided	25 mL
3 tbsp	minced shallots	45 mL
8 oz	sweet Italian sausage, casings removed, crumbled into small pieces	250 g
8 oz	baby portobello mushrooms, sliced	250 g
1 tsp	finely chopped fresh thyme	5 mL
1 tsp	finely chopped fresh oregano	5 mL
1 cup	Arborio rice	250 mL
¼ cup	Madeira (see tip, at left)	60 mL
3 cups	chicken broth	750 mL
½ cup	freshly grated Parmesan cheese	125 mL
1 tsp	salt	5 mL
	Additional freshly grated Parmesan cheese	

1. Set the rice cooker for the Quick Cook or Regular cycle. When the bottom of the bowl gets hot, add oil and 1 tbsp (15 mL) butter and let butter melt. Sauté shallots for about 3 minutes or until softened and translucent. Add sausage and sauté, breaking it up with the back of a spoon, for 4 to 5 minutes or until no longer pink. Add mushrooms, thyme and oregano; sauté for 3 minutes.

2. Stir in rice until completely coated. Sauté for about 4 minutes or until mostly translucent and only a dot of white remains. Stir in Madeira and cook for 3 to 4 minutes or until evaporated. Stir in broth. Close the lid and reset for the Porridge or Regular cycle. Set a timer for 25 minutes. Stir two or three times while the risotto is cooking.

3. When the timer sounds, check to make sure risotto is al dente. If necessary, continue cooking, checking for doneness every 5 minutes. Fold in the remaining butter. Fold in Parmesan and salt. Serve immediately, garnished with Parmesan.

Variation

Use a variety of mushrooms, such as a mixture of cremini, shiitake, wood ear and morels, in this dish.

Moroccan Rice Pilaf with Saffron

Makes 3 to 4 servings

Did you know that saffron is the world's most expensive spice? But it's well worth it. Try this pilaf with spiced pork chops for a complete meal.

Tip

For information about rice cooker sizes, see page 13.

● **Medium rice cooker; fuzzy logic or on/off**

1 tsp	crushed saffron threads	5 mL
¼ cup	hot water	60 mL
2 tbsp	butter	30 mL
1 tbsp	extra virgin olive oil	15 mL
1	clove garlic, minced	1
½ cup	finely chopped onion	125 mL
1 tsp	minced gingerroot	5 mL
2	2-inch (5 cm) cinnamon sticks	2
¼ tsp	ground turmeric	1 mL
¼ tsp	ground cumin	1 mL
½	carrot, finely chopped	½
½	red bell pepper, finely chopped	½
1 cup	long-grain white rice, rinsed and drained	250 mL
¼ cup	fresh or thawed frozen peas	60 mL
½ tsp	salt	2 mL
1½ cups	chicken broth	375 mL
¼ cup	finely chopped fresh cilantro	60 mL
	Additional finely chopped fresh cilantro	

1. In a measuring cup or small bowl, combine saffron threads and hot water; set aside to steep.
2. Set the rice cooker for the Quick Cook or Regular cycle. When the bottom of the bowl gets hot, add butter and oil and let butter melt. Sauté garlic, onion, ginger, cinnamon sticks, turmeric and cumin for about 3 minutes or until onion is softened and translucent.
3. Stir in carrot, red pepper and rice; cook, stirring occasionally, until rice is evenly coated and hot (3 to 4 minutes in an on/off machine or 8 to 10 minutes in a fuzzy logic machine). Stir in saffron-infused water, peas, salt and broth. Close the lid and reset for the Regular cycle.
4. When the machine switches to the Keep Warm cycle, sprinkle with cilantro. Close the lid and let stand for 15 minutes. Fluff rice with a wooden spoon or plastic paddle, stirring in cilantro. Discard cinnamon sticks. Serve immediately or hold on the Keep Warm cycle for up to 1 hour. Serve garnished with cilantro.

Variation

Add diced cooked chicken, shrimp or beef to this dish to make it a complete meal.

Rice, Raisin and Herb Pilaf

Makes 3 to 4 servings

This rice pilaf is an explosion of flavors. The combination of sweet raisins, crunchy pine nuts and cool mint is a great example of successful culinary symbiosis.

Tip

Try using jumbo golden raisins in this dish for visual appeal and more flavor. You may want to increase the amount of lemon juice slightly to balance the enhanced sweetness.

• Medium rice cooker; fuzzy logic or on/off

2 tbsp	butter	30 mL
1 tbsp	extra virgin olive oil	15 mL
1/2 cup	finely chopped onion	125 mL
1 cup	long-grain white rice, rinsed and drained	250 mL
1/4 cup	pine nuts	60 mL
1/2 cup	golden raisins	125 mL
1/2 tsp	salt	2 mL
1/4 tsp	ground allspice	1 mL
1 3/4 cups	chicken broth	425 mL
2 tbsp	freshly squeezed lemon juice	30 mL
2 tbsp	finely chopped fresh mint	30 mL
2 tbsp	finely chopped fresh dill	30 mL

1. Set the rice cooker for the Quick Cook or Regular cycle. When the bottom of the bowl gets hot, add butter and oil and let butter melt. Sauté onion for about 3 minutes or until softened and translucent.

2. Stir in rice and pine nuts; cook, stirring occasionally, until rice is evenly coated and hot (3 to 4 minutes in an on/off machine or 8 to 10 minutes in a fuzzy logic machine). Stir in raisins, salt, allspice, broth and lemon juice. Close the lid and reset for the Regular cycle.

3. When the machine switches to the Keep Warm cycle, sprinkle with mint and dill. Close the lid and let stand for 10 minutes. Fluff rice with a wooden spoon or plastic paddle, stirring in herbs. Serve immediately or hold on the Keep Warm cycle for up to 1 hour.

Green Pilaf with Pine Nuts

Makes 3 to 4 servings

Nutritionally, this can serve as a great stand-alone dish. Working with the other ingredients, the nuts and rice offer up a healthy dose of protein, and a double portion offers a full serving of vegetables!

Tip

You may substitute 1/3 cup (75 mL) drained thawed frozen baby spinach for the fresh. Squeeze out liquid with your hands and a kitchen towel before adding the spinach to the rice cooker.

• Medium rice cooker; fuzzy logic or on/off

2 tbsp	butter	30 mL
1 tbsp	extra virgin olive oil	15 mL
1/2 cup	finely chopped onion	125 mL
2	cloves garlic, minced	2
1 1/2 cups	long-grain brown rice, rinsed and drained	375 mL
1/2 cup	pine nuts	125 mL
1/2 tsp	salt	2 mL
2 1/2 cups	chicken or vegetable broth	625 mL
2 tbsp	freshly squeezed lemon juice	30 mL
1 1/2 cups	packed baby spinach, shredded	375 mL
3 tbsp	finely chopped fresh mint	45 mL
3 tbsp	finely chopped fresh flat-leaf (Italian) parsley	45 mL

1. Set the rice cooker for the Quick Cook, Regular or Brown Rice cycle. When the bottom of the bowl gets hot, add butter and oil and let butter melt. Sauté onion for about 3 minutes or until softened and translucent.

2. Stir in garlic, rice and pine nuts; cook, stirring occasionally, until rice is evenly coated and hot (3 to 4 minutes in an on/off machine or 8 to 10 minutes in a fuzzy logic machine). Stir in salt, broth and lemon juice. Close the lid and reset for the Regular or Brown Rice cycle.

3. When the machine switches to the Keep Warm cycle, sprinkle with spinach, mint and parsley. Close the lid and let stand for 10 minutes. Fluff rice with a wooden spoon or plastic paddle, stirring in spinach and herbs. Serve immediately.

Almond Rice Pilaf

Makes 3 to 4 servings

Slivered almonds are one of my favorite ways to jazz up the flavor of a dish and squeeze in extra nutrition. This is a no-fail, versatile recipe that goes with any meal!

Tip

For information about rice cooker sizes, see page 13.

● Medium rice cooker; fuzzy logic or on/off

2 tbsp	butter	30 mL
2 tbsp	minced shallots	30 mL
1 cup	long-grain white rice, rinsed and drained	250 mL
½ cup	sliced mushrooms (such as cremini)	125 mL
½ cup	slivered almonds	125 mL
½ tsp	salt	2 mL
1¾ cups	chicken broth	425 mL
	Toasted slivered almonds	

1. Set the rice cooker for the Quick Cook or Regular cycle. When the bottom of the bowl gets hot, add butter and let it melt. Sauté shallots for about 3 minutes or until softened and translucent.
2. Stir in rice, mushrooms and almonds; cook, stirring occasionally, until rice is evenly coated and hot (3 to 4 minutes in an on/off machine or 8 to 10 minutes in a fuzzy logic machine). Stir in salt and broth. Close the lid and reset for the Regular cycle.
3. When the machine switches to the Keep Warm cycle, let stand for 15 minutes. Fluff rice with a wooden spoon or plastic paddle. Serve immediately or hold on the Keep Warm cycle for up to 1 hour. Serve garnished with toasted almonds.

Variations

Substitute 1 cup (250 mL) white basmati rice for the long-grain white rice.

Substitute chopped cashews or pecans — or any tree nut you like — for the almonds.

Orange Pistachio Pilaf

Makes 3 to 4 servings

This zesty pilaf tastes as good as it looks. The sweet flavors in this side dish work well with a roasted chicken and a somewhat bitter veggie, such as sautéed chicory.

Tips

Room-temperature oranges, lemons and limes yield more juice than those that are refrigerated. Use your palm to roll citrus fruit around on the countertop a few times before squeezing.

For more pronounced orange flavor, try adding 1 tsp (5 mL) citrus-infused orange oil with the orange juice. Boyajian makes a wonderful array of infused oils, available at specialty and gourmet stores.

● **Medium rice cooker; fuzzy logic or on/off**

2 tbsp	butter	30 mL
1 tbsp	extra virgin olive oil	15 mL
1/2 cup	finely chopped onion	125 mL
2	cloves garlic, minced	2
1/2	red bell pepper, finely chopped	1/2
1 cup	long-grain white rice, rinsed and drained	250 mL
1	bay leaf	1
1 tsp	finely grated orange zest	5 mL
1/2 tsp	salt	2 mL
1 1/4 cups	chicken broth	300 mL
1/2 cup	freshly squeezed orange juice	125 mL
	Coarsely chopped pistachios	

1. Set the rice cooker for the Quick Cook or Regular cycle. When the bottom of the bowl gets hot, add butter and oil and let butter melt. Sauté onion for about 3 minutes or until softened and translucent.

2. Stir in garlic, red pepper and rice; cook, stirring occasionally, until rice is evenly coated and hot (3 to 4 minutes in an on/off machine or 8 to 10 minutes in a fuzzy logic machine). Stir in bay leaf, orange zest, salt, broth and orange juice. Close the lid and reset for the Regular cycle.

3. When the machine switches to the Keep Warm cycle, let stand for 15 minutes. Fluff rice with a wooden spoon or plastic paddle. Discard bay leaf. Serve immediately or hold on the Keep Warm cycle for up to 1 hour. Serve garnished with pistachios.

Variation

Substitute wild rice for the long-grain white rice and increase the broth to 3 1/2 cups (875 mL).

Zucchini, Tomato and Rice Pilaf

Makes 6 to 8 servings

This colorful pilaf is a great low-cal option and is simply delicious. Because it uses common ingredients, it's an extremely versatile side dish. Be sure to bookmark this one!

Tips

If you prefer, you can use 1¾ cups (425 mL) diced fresh tomatoes or halved cherry tomatoes in place of the canned tomatoes.

For information about rice cooker sizes, see page 13.

● **Medium rice cooker; fuzzy logic or on/off**

2 tbsp	butter	30 mL
1 tbsp	extra virgin olive oil	15 mL
1 cup	finely chopped onion	250 mL
2 cups	long-grain white rice, rinsed and drained	500 mL
½ cup	finely diced zucchini	125 mL
½ cup	finely chopped yellow bell pepper	125 mL
1	can (14 oz/398 mL) diced tomatoes, with juice	1
¾ tsp	salt	3 mL
2¼ cups	chicken broth	550 mL

1. Set the rice cooker for the Quick Cook or Regular cycle. When the bottom of the bowl gets hot, add butter and oil and let butter melt. Sauté onion for about 3 minutes or until softened and translucent.

2. Stir in rice, zucchini and yellow pepper; cook, stirring occasionally, until rice is evenly coated and hot (3 to 4 minutes in an on/off machine or 8 to 10 minutes in a fuzzy logic machine). Stir in tomatoes with juice, salt and broth. Close the lid and reset for the Regular cycle.

3. When the machine switches to the Keep Warm cycle, let stand for 10 minutes. Fluff rice with a wooden spoon or plastic paddle. Serve immediately or hold on the Keep Warm cycle for up to 1 hour.

Variations

Use a combination of red, green and yellow peppers to add colorful vibrancy to this dish.

To make this dish a complete meal, add cooked shrimp when the machine switches to the Keep Warm cycle.

Curried Rice Pilaf

Makes 3 to 4 servings

Who says you can't be both sweet and spicy? This palatable pilaf is a perfect blend of flavors. Serve it with braised lamb for a flawless meal.

Tip

Curry powder is readily available at grocery stores, but it's quick and easy to make your own. In a food processor, combine 2 tbsp (30 mL) ground cumin, 2 tbsp (30 mL) ground coriander, 2 tsp (10 mL) ground turmeric, 1/2 tsp (2 mL) hot pepper flakes, 1/2 tsp (2 mL) mustard seed and 1/2 tsp (2 mL) ground ginger; process to a fine powder. Store in an airtight container for up to 2 years.

• Medium rice cooker; fuzzy logic or on/off

2 tbsp	butter	30 mL
1 tbsp	extra virgin olive oil	15 mL
1/2 cup	finely chopped onion	125 mL
1/2 cup	golden raisins	125 mL
2 tsp	curry powder (see tip, at left)	10 mL
1 cup	long-grain white rice, rinsed and drained	250 mL
1/3 cup	pine nuts	75 mL
1	bay leaf	1
1/2 tsp	salt	2 mL
1 3/4 cups	chicken broth	425 mL

1. Set the rice cooker for the Quick Cook or Regular cycle. When the bottom of the bowl gets hot, add butter and oil and let butter melt. Sauté onion, raisins and curry powder for about 3 minutes or until onion is softened and translucent.

2. Stir in rice and pine nuts; cook, stirring occasionally, until rice is evenly coated and hot (3 to 4 minutes in an on/off machine or 8 to 10 minutes in a fuzzy logic machine). Stir in bay leaf, salt and broth. Close the lid and reset for the Regular cycle.

3. When the machine switches to the Keep Warm cycle, let stand for 10 minutes. Fluff rice with a wooden spoon or plastic paddle. Discard bay leaf. Serve immediately or hold on the Keep Warm cycle for up to 1 hour.

Basmati Rice Pilaf with Indian Spices

**Makes 3 to
4 servings**

Its nuanced flavor and
pleasing fragrance
make this side dish
a hit for any crowd.
Serve it with spiced
grilled shrimp and a
bottle of Sauvignon
Blanc for a delicious,
well-rounded meal.

Tips

You can use ½ tsp
(2 mL) ground
cardamom instead of
the cardamom pods.

Store-bought hot
Indian mango chutney
(available at specialty
and Indian markets)
would be a wonderful
accompaniment to
this dish.

• Medium rice cooker; fuzzy logic or on/off

2 tbsp	butter	30 mL
1 tbsp	extra virgin olive oil	15 mL
½ cup	finely chopped onion	125 mL
1 cup	white basmati rice, rinsed and drained	250 mL
4	green cardamom pods	4
4	whole cloves	4
1	2-inch (5 cm) cinnamon stick	1
½ tsp	coriander seeds, crushed	2 mL
¼ tsp	ground ginger	1 mL
1	bay leaf	1
½ tsp	salt	2 mL
1¾ cups	chicken broth	425 mL
	Raita (see recipe, below)	

1. Set the rice cooker for the Quick Cook or Regular cycle. When the bottom of the bowl gets hot, add butter and oil and let butter melt. Sauté onion for about 3 minutes or until softened.
2. Stir in rice, cardamom, cloves, cinnamon, coriander seeds and ginger; cook, stirring occasionally, until rice is evenly coated and hot (3 to 4 minutes in an on/off machine or 8 to 10 minutes in a fuzzy logic machine). Stir in bay leaf, salt and broth. Close the lid and reset for the Regular cycle.
3. When the machine switches to the Keep Warm cycle, let stand for 10 minutes. Fluff rice with a wooden spoon or plastic paddle. Discard bay leaf, cardamom pods, cloves and cinnamon stick. Serve immediately or hold on the Keep Warm cycle for up to 1 hour. Serve dolloped with raita.

Raita

**Makes about
1½ cups (375 mL)**

This light, smooth and
creamy yogurt sauce,
made with refreshing
mint and cucumber,
is used in many
Indian dishes.

½	cucumber, peeled, seeded and chopped	½
2 tbsp	chopped fresh mint	30 mL
½ tsp	ground cumin	2 mL
⅛ tsp	chili powder	0.5 mL
1 cup	plain yogurt	250 mL
	Salt and freshly ground black pepper	

1. In a small bowl, combine cucumber, mint, cumin, chili powder and yogurt. Season to taste with salt and pepper. Cover and refrigerate for 30 minutes before serving.

Wild Rice Pilaf with Goat Cheese and Figs

Makes 3 to 4 servings

This is a fabulously light side dish for any meal. The unique flavor of goat cheese and the touch of sweetness brought by the figs make it a delightfully decadent pilaf.

Tip

Dried figs are perfect for people who want to satisfy their sweet tooth without gaining fat.

● **Medium rice cooker; fuzzy logic or on/off**

2 tbsp	butter	30 mL
1 tbsp	extra virgin olive oil	15 mL
2 tbsp	minced shallots	30 mL
1 cup	wild rice, rinsed and drained	250 mL
½ tsp	salt	2 mL
3½ cups	chicken broth	875 mL
¼ cup	chopped dried figs	60 mL
¼ cup	dried cranberries	60 mL
¼ cup	crumbled goat cheese	60 mL
	Finely chopped fresh parsley	

1. Set the rice cooker for the Quick Cook, Regular or Brown Rice cycle. When the bottom of the bowl gets hot, add butter and oil and let butter melt. Sauté shallots for about 3 minutes or until softened and translucent.

2. Stir in wild rice and cook, stirring occasionally, until evenly coated and hot (3 to 4 minutes in an on/off machine or 8 to 10 minutes in a fuzzy logic machine). Stir in salt and broth. Close the lid and reset for the Regular or Brown Rice cycle.

3. When the machine switches to the Keep Warm cycle, sprinkle with figs and cranberries. Close the lid and let stand for 10 minutes. Sprinkle with goat cheese. Fluff rice with a wooden spoon or plastic paddle, stirring in fruit and goat cheese. Serve immediately, garnished with parsley.

Turkish Bulgur and Chickpea Pilaf

Makes 4 to 6 servings

Although it sounds exotic, this pilaf is surprisingly simple to make, tastes great and is good for you. The savory substitution of bulgur for rice will do your heart and your digestive system good.

Tip

For information about rice cooker sizes, see page 13.

● **Medium rice cooker; fuzzy logic or on/off**

2 tbsp	butter	30 mL
1 tbsp	extra virgin olive oil	15 mL
½ cup	finely chopped onion	125 mL
½	red bell pepper, finely chopped	½
2 cups	coarse bulgur	500 mL
1	can (14 oz/398 mL) diced tomatoes, with juice	1
1	can (14 to 19 oz/398 to 540 mL) chickpeas, drained and rinsed	1
1 tsp	salt	5 mL
1½ cups	chicken or vegetable broth	375 mL
	Finely chopped fresh parsley	

1. Set the rice cooker for the Quick Cook, Regular or Brown Rice cycle. When the bottom of the bowl gets hot, add butter and oil and let butter melt. Sauté onion for about 3 minutes or until softened and translucent.
2. Stir in red pepper and bulgur; cook, stirring occasionally, until bulgur is evenly coated and hot (3 to 4 minutes in an on/off machine or 8 to 10 minutes in a fuzzy logic machine). Stir in tomatoes with juice, chickpeas, salt and broth. Close the lid and reset for the Regular or Brown Rice cycle.
3. When the machine switches to the Keep Warm cycle, let stand for 10 minutes. Fluff bulgur with a wooden spoon or plastic paddle. Serve immediately or hold on the Keep Warm cycle for up to 1 hour. Serve garnished with parsley.

Caribbean Pilaf with Red Quinoa

Makes 3 to 4 servings

This zesty pilaf bursts with tropical flavors. Both sweet and savory, it will leave a lasting impression.

Tips

Red quinoa is available at some health food and specialty stores, as well as online. It's fine to use regular quinoa in this dish, but red quinoa adds a vibrant and festive flair. You could also try using black quinoa.

Use whatever chile peppers you have on hand, such as jalapeño or even half a habanero.

To toast almonds, spread them in a single layer on a baking sheet. Bake in a 325°F (160°C) oven for 5 to 10 minutes or until light brown and fragrant. Stir frequently to ensure even toasting.

- **Preheat oven to 350°F (180°C)**
- **Medium rice cooker; fuzzy logic or on/off**

2 tbsp	extra virgin olive oil	30 mL
½ cup	finely chopped green onions (white part only)	125 mL
½	red bell pepper, finely chopped	½
1 cup	red quinoa (see tip, at left), rinsed and drained	250 mL
1	serrano chile pepper, seeded and minced	1
½ tsp	salt	2 mL
1¾ cups	chicken or vegetable broth	425 mL
¼ cup	unsweetened shredded coconut	60 mL
1	mango, finely chopped	1
½ cup	sliced almonds, toasted (see tip, at left)	125 mL
¼ cup	dried cranberries	60 mL
3 tbsp	finely chopped fresh cilantro	45 mL
¼ cup	freshly squeezed lime juice	60 mL
1 tbsp	balsamic vinegar	15 mL
	Thinly sliced green onions (green and white parts)	

1. Set the rice cooker for the Quick Cook, Regular or Brown Rice cycle. When the bottom of the bowl gets hot, add oil and swirl to coat. Sauté green onions for about 3 minutes or until softened.

2. Stir in red pepper and quinoa; cook, stirring occasionally, until quinoa is evenly coated and hot (3 to 4 minutes in an on/off machine or 8 to 10 minutes in a fuzzy logic machine). Stir in serrano pepper, salt and broth. Close the lid and reset for the Regular or Brown Rice cycle.

3. Meanwhile, spread coconut in a thin layer on a baking sheet and bake in preheated oven, stirring occasionally, for 10 minutes or until lightly browned.

4. When the machine switches to the Keep Warm cycle, let stand for 10 minutes. Sprinkle with mango, almonds, cranberries, cilantro, lime juice and vinegar. Fluff quinoa with a wooden spoon or plastic paddle, stirring in the added ingredients. Serve immediately or hold on the Keep Warm cycle for up to 1 hour. Serve garnished with toasted coconut and green onions.

Quinoa Pilaf with Pine Nuts and Mint

Makes 4 to 6 servings

Quinoa is known as the mother of all grains, and this pilaf showcases its versatility. The cool relationship of the toasted pine nuts and fresh mint will make even a quinoa first-timer a regular customer.

Tips

To peel garlic quickly, place a large, wide knife (such as a chef's knife) over the clove and hit it hard — but not too hard. The garlic should crack a bit, making it easy to remove the peel.

Try sprinkling garlic cloves with a tiny bit of salt before mincing. The salt absorbs a little of the liquid, so the garlic won't stick to your knife.

• Medium rice cooker; fuzzy logic or on/off

2 tbsp	butter	30 mL
2 tbsp	extra virgin olive oil, divided	30 mL
1	clove garlic, minced	1
½	onion, finely chopped	½
1	red bell pepper, finely chopped	1
1½ cups	quinoa, rinsed and drained	375 mL
½ tsp	salt	2 mL
2 cups	chicken or vegetable broth	500 mL
¼ cup	pine nuts, toasted (see tip, page 273)	60 mL
3 tbsp	finely chopped fresh basil	45 mL
2 tbsp	finely chopped fresh mint	30 mL
1 tbsp	finely chopped fresh chives	15 mL
	Finely chopped fresh parsley	

1. Set the rice cooker for the Quick Cook, Regular or Brown Rice cycle. When the bottom of the bowl gets hot, add butter and 1 tbsp (15 mL) oil and let butter melt. Sauté garlic and onion for about 3 minutes or until onion is softened and translucent.

2. Stir in red pepper and quinoa; cook, stirring occasionally, until rice is evenly coated and hot (3 to 4 minutes in an on/off machine or 8 to 10 minutes in a fuzzy logic machine). Stir in salt and broth. Close the lid and reset for the Regular or Brown Rice cycle.

3. When the machine switches to the Keep Warm cycle, drizzle with the remaining oil and sprinkle with pine nuts, basil, mint and chives. Close the lid and let stand for 10 minutes. Fluff quinoa with a wooden spoon or plastic paddle, stirring in oil, pine nuts and herbs. Serve immediately or hold on the Keep Warm cycle for up to 1 hour. Serve garnished with parsley.

Variation

Substitute toasted millet (see tip, page 254) for the quinoa.

Triple-Grain Pilaf

Makes 4 to 6 servings

The three grains in this recipe contribute great texture and a mild, nutty flavor that is pleasing to the palate, making the use of spices unnecessary.

Tips

To bring out a pleasantly nutty aroma, toast the millet in a dry skillet over medium heat, stirring constantly, for 5 minutes before adding it to the rice cooker. (This is not necessary, but it's a nice touch if you have the time.)

For information about rice cooker sizes, see page 13.

• Medium rice cooker; fuzzy logic or on/off

3 tbsp	butter	45 mL
1 cup	finely chopped green onions (white part only)	250 mL
1 cup	basmati rice, rinsed and drained	250 mL
½ cup	quinoa, rinsed and drained	125 mL
½ cup	millet (see tip, at left)	125 mL
¾ tsp	salt	3 mL
2½ cups	chicken broth	625 mL
	Chopped green onions (white and green parts)	

1. Set the rice cooker for the Quick Cook, Regular or Brown Rice cycle. When the bottom of the bowl gets hot, add butter and let it melt. Sauté green onions for about 3 minutes or until softened.

2. Stir in rice, quinoa and millet; cook, stirring occasionally, until grains are evenly coated and hot (3 to 4 minutes in an on/off machine or 8 to 10 minutes in a fuzzy logic machine). Stir in salt and broth. Close the lid and reset for the Regular or Brown Rice cycle.

3. When the machine switches to the Keep Warm cycle, let stand for 15 minutes. Fluff rice with a wooden spoon or plastic paddle. Serve immediately or hold on the Keep Warm cycle for up to 1 hour. Serve garnished with green onions.

Split Pea Pilaf

Makes 3 to 4 servings

I love this Indian-inspired, piquant pilaf. The combination of flavors and zippy spices make it oh-so-appetizing, especially with a spicy chicken dish and a glass of Pinot Grigio.

Tip

Black mustard seeds are commonly used in Indian cooking and are the most pungent of all mustard seeds. They are tiny and sometimes have a slightly reddish hue. They can be hard to find, so if they're not available, substitute brown mustard seeds or simply omit them.

• Medium rice cooker; fuzzy logic or on/off

2 tbsp	ghee (see recipe, page 203)	30 mL
1 cup	finely chopped onion	250 mL
1 tsp	curry powder	5 mL
1 tsp	ground cumin	5 mL
1 tsp	black mustard seeds (see tip, at left)	5 mL
¼ tsp	hot pepper flakes	1 mL
Pinch	ground turmeric	Pinch
1 cup	white basmati rice, rinsed and drained	250 mL
¼ cup	dried yellow split peas, sorted and rinsed	60 mL
½ tsp	salt	2 mL
2¼ cups	vegetable broth or water	550 mL
	Plain yogurt	

1. Set the rice cooker for the Quick Cook or Regular cycle. When the bottom of the bowl gets hot, add ghee and swirl to coat. Sauté onion, curry powder, cumin, mustard seeds, hot pepper flakes and turmeric for about 3 minutes or until onion is softened and translucent.
2. Stir in rice and split peas; cook, stirring occasionally, until rice is evenly coated and hot (3 to 4 minutes in an on/off machine or 8 to 10 minutes in a fuzzy logic machine). Stir in salt and broth. Close the lid and reset for the Regular cycle.
3. When the machine switches to the Keep Warm cycle, let stand for 10 minutes. Fluff rice with a wooden spoon or plastic paddle. Serve immediately or hold on the Keep Warm cycle for up to 3 hours. Serve dolloped with yogurt.

Variation

Substitute dried red lentils for the split peas.

Andouille Sausage Pilaf

Makes 3 to 4 servings

Reminiscent of jambalaya, this spicy pilaf works well alone. Or, for a true Cajun treat, try it with blackened shrimp and skillet cornbread.

Tip

Add more sausage to this recipe for a bigger kick!

Andouille Sausage

Andouille sausage originated in France and was brought to Louisiana by French immigrants. It is a coarse-grained smoked meat made with pork, pepper, onions, wine and seasonings. Cajun andouille sausage is the spiciest variety. It's great to keep some on hand in your freezer, as it adds so much flavor to a variety of dishes.

• **Medium rice cooker; fuzzy logic or on/off**

2 tbsp	butter	30 mL
1 tbsp	extra virgin olive oil	15 mL
½ cup	finely chopped onion	125 mL
1	small red bell pepper, finely chopped	1
4 oz	Cajun andouille sausage (or other spicy sausage), cut diagonally into ¼-inch (0.5 cm) thick slices	125 g
1 cup	long-grain white rice, rinsed and drained	250 mL
¼ cup	fresh or thawed frozen peas	60 mL
¾ tsp	salt	3 mL
1¾ cups	chicken broth	425 mL
	Finely chopped fresh parsley	

1. Set the rice cooker for the Quick Cook or Regular cycle. When the bottom of the bowl gets hot, add butter and oil and let butter melt. Sauté onion for about 3 minutes or until softened and translucent.

2. Stir in red pepper, sausage and rice; cook, stirring occasionally, until rice is evenly coated and hot (3 to 4 minutes in an on/off machine or 8 to 10 minutes in a fuzzy logic machine). Stir in peas, salt and broth. Close the lid and reset for the Regular cycle.

3. When the machine switches to the Keep Warm cycle, let stand for 15 minutes. Fluff rice with a wooden spoon or plastic paddle. Serve immediately, garnished with parsley.

Side Dishes

Herbed Rice

Makes 3 to 4 servings

Mixed herbs give this dish a fresh, light flavor that works wonderfully with grilled meat.

Tips

If you're planning to hold the rice on the Keep Warm cycle, wait until just before serving to stir in the herbs.

Use any combination of your favorite herbs.

I like to keep small pots of fresh herbs in my kitchen, allowing me to snip off what I need for dishes created at the peak of freshness.

- **Medium rice cooker; fuzzy logic or on/off**

1 cup	long-grain white rice, rinsed and drained	250 mL
1/4 tsp	salt	1 mL
1 1/2 cups	chicken broth	375 mL
1 1/2 tsp	finely chopped fresh mint	7 mL
1 1/2 tsp	finely chopped fresh dill	7 mL
1 1/2 tsp	finely chopped fresh thyme	7 mL
2 tbsp	butter	30 mL
	Additional finely chopped fresh mint	

1. In the rice cooker bowl, combine rice, salt and broth. Set the rice cooker for the Regular cycle.
2. When the machine switches to the Keep Warm cycle, stir in mint, dill, thyme and butter. Close the lid and let stand for 10 minutes. Fluff rice with a wooden spoon or plastic paddle. Serve immediately or hold on the Keep Warm cycle for up to 3 hours (see tip, at left). Serve garnished with mint.

Variation

Herbed Farro: Substitute farro for the rice and increase the broth to 2 1/2 cups (625 mL). Set the rice cooker for the Brown Rice cycle.

Coriander Rice

Makes 3 to 4 servings

This delightfully aromatic rice is perfect with Indian dishes such as curries or tandoori meats.

Tips

For the best flavor, toast whole coriander seeds in a skillet over medium-high heat, stirring constantly, for about 3 minutes or until fragrant. Immediately transfer to a spice grinder and let cool, then grind to a fine powder.

Air, light and heat are the enemies of spices, so store them in airtight containers in a drawer or cupboard — never over the stove.

• Medium rice cooker; fuzzy logic or on/off

2 tbsp	butter	30 mL
½ cup	finely chopped onion	125 mL
1 tbsp	coriander seeds, coarsely crushed (see tip, at left)	15 mL
1 cup	white basmati rice, rinsed and drained	250 mL
½ tsp	salt	2 mL
1½ cups	water	375 mL
3	3- by 1-inch (7.5 by 2.5 cm) strips lemon peel	3

1. Set the rice cooker for the Quick Cook or Regular cycle. When the bottom of the bowl gets hot, add butter and let it melt. Sauté onion and coriander seeds for about 3 minutes or until onion is softened and translucent.

2. Stir in rice, salt and water. Place lemon peel on top. Close the lid and reset for the Regular cycle.

3. When the machine switches to the Keep Warm cycle, let stand for 10 minutes. Fluff rice with a wooden spoon or plastic paddle. Discard lemon peel. Serve immediately or hold on the Keep Warm cycle for up to 3 hours.

Confetti Rice

Makes 3 to 4 servings

Confetti rice is a colorful dish made of common ingredients you may already have in the fridge and pantry. It's easy to make, but the results look impressive!

Tips

For easier cleanup, try coating the bottom of the rice cooker bowl with nonstick cooking spray before adding the rice and other ingredients.

For information about rice cooker sizes, see page 13.

• **Medium rice cooker; fuzzy logic or on/off**

1 cup	long-grain white rice, rinsed and drained	250 mL
1/4 cup	finely chopped red bell pepper	60 mL
1/4 cup	finely chopped green bell pepper	60 mL
1/4 cup	finely chopped yellow bell pepper	60 mL
1/4 tsp	dried oregano	1 mL
1/4 tsp	salt	1 mL
1/8 tsp	freshly ground black pepper	0.5 mL
1 1/2 cups	chicken broth	375 mL
1/2 cup	fresh or thawed frozen peas	125 mL
2 tbsp	finely chopped fresh parsley	30 mL

1. In the rice cooker bowl, combine rice, red pepper, green pepper, yellow pepper, oregano, salt, pepper and broth. Set the rice cooker for the Regular cycle.
2. When the machine switches to the Keep Warm cycle, stir in peas. Close the lid and let stand for 10 minutes. Fluff rice with a wooden spoon or plastic paddle. Serve immediately or hold on the Keep Warm cycle for up to 1 hour. Serve garnished with parsley.

Variations

For a complete meal, add chopped cooked chicken or shrimp with the peas.

For a more nutritious dish, use long-grain brown rice and increase the broth to 2 cups (500 mL). Set the rice cooker for the Brown Rice cycle.

Rice Almandine

Makes 3 to 4 servings

Rice almandine is a wonderfully versatile side dish with great flavor and texture. It complements just about any entrée!

Tip

Unless your mushrooms are extremely dirty, you can simply wipe them with a damp paper towel to clean them. If you need to wash them, rinse them in a colander and wipe them dry with a paper towel. Never soak fresh mushrooms, as they'll absorb too much water.

Almonds

Roasted almonds tend to be harder in texture than other nuts because a lot of moisture is removed during the dry-roasting process. Therefore, natural almonds are better for cooking and baking. Almonds can also be used as a great alternative to bread crumbs.

• Medium rice cooker; fuzzy logic or on/off

4 tbsp	butter, divided	60 mL
½ cup	mushrooms (such as cremini or shiitake), sliced	125 mL
1 cup	long-grain white rice, rinsed and drained	250 mL
½ tsp	salt	2 mL
1½ cups	chicken or vegetable broth	375 mL
½ cup	toasted sliced almonds (see tip, page 252)	125 mL
¼ cup	fresh or thawed frozen peas	60 mL
	Additional toasted sliced almonds	

1. Set the rice cooker for the Quick Cook or Regular cycle. When the bottom of the bowl gets hot, add 2 tbsp (30 mL) butter and let it melt. Sauté mushrooms for about 2 minutes or until softened.
2. Stir in rice, salt, broth and the remaining butter. Close the lid and reset for the Regular cycle.
3. When the machine switches to the Keep Warm cycle, stir in almonds and peas. Close the lid and let stand for 10 minutes. Fluff rice with a wooden spoon or plastic paddle. Serve immediately or hold on the Keep Warm cycle for up to 1 hour. Serve garnished with almonds.

Variation

Substitute wild rice for the white rice and increase the broth to 3 cups (750 mL).

Parmesan Rice

Makes 3 to 4 servings

This is such an easy recipe you'll be making it by heart in no time.

Tips

A cheese labeled "Parmesan" is essentially a cheese that imitates the recipe for Parmigiano-Reggiano but is made outside of the approved Italian regions. Either Parmesan or Parmigiano-Reggiano is suitable for this dish.

If you're planning to hold the rice on the Keep Warm cycle, wait until just before serving to stir in the Parmesan.

Parmigiano-Reggiano

According to Italian law, a cheese cannot be called Parmigiano-Reggiano unless it is made using a specific recipe and production method within the provinces of Parma, Reggio-Emilia, Modena or specific regions in the provinces of Bologna and Mantua. This law ensures the flavor and quality of Parmigiano-Reggiano cheese and upholds the integrity of this Italian treasure.

- **Medium rice cooker; fuzzy logic or on/off**

1 cup	long-grain white rice, rinsed and drained	250 mL
1/4 tsp	salt	1 mL
1 1/2 cups	chicken broth	375 mL
3 tbsp	freshly grated Parmesan cheese	45 mL
2 tbsp	butter	30 mL
1 tbsp	finely chopped fresh parsley	15 mL

1. In the rice cooker bowl, combine rice, salt and broth. Set the rice cooker for the Regular cycle.
2. When the machine switches to the Keep Warm cycle, let stand for 10 minutes. Fold in Parmesan and butter. Fluff rice with a wooden spoon or plastic paddle. Serve immediately or hold on the Keep Warm cycle for up to 1 hour (see tip, at left). Serve garnished with parsley.

Parmesan Brown Rice

Makes 3 to 4 servings

Devastatingly simple, yet just plain delicious, this side dish complements a broad range of main dishes.

Tips

To toast walnut halves, spread nuts in a single layer on a baking sheet. Bake in a 350°F (180°C) oven, stirring often, for 5 to 10 minutes or until light brown and fragrant. Immediately transfer to a bowl and let cool before chopping.

If you're planning to hold the rice on the Keep Warm cycle, wait until just before serving to stir in the walnuts, Parmesan and parsley.

- **Medium rice cooker; fuzzy logic or on/off**

1 cup	long-grain brown rice, rinsed and drained	250 mL
¼ tsp	salt	1 mL
2 cups	water or vegetable broth	500 mL
½ cup	walnut halves, toasted (see tip, at left) and coarsely chopped	125 mL
¼ cup	freshly grated Parmesan cheese	60 mL
¼ cup	finely chopped fresh parsley	60 mL
	Additional finely chopped fresh parsley	

1. In the rice cooker bowl, combine rice, salt and water. Set the rice cooker for the Regular or Brown Rice cycle.
2. When the machine switches to the Keep Warm cycle, let stand for 10 minutes. Fold in walnuts, Parmesan and parsley. Fluff rice with a wooden spoon or plastic paddle. Serve immediately or hold on the Keep Warm cycle for up to 1 hour (see tip, at left). Serve garnished with parsley.

Variations

Substitute brown basmati rice for the long-grain brown rice.

Replace the walnut halves with hazelnuts.

Citrus Rice

Makes 3 to 4 servings

This side dish will delight the senses. The basmati rice, accented by citrus and fresh mint, smells as wonderful as it tastes.

Tips

For a more nutritious version, use brown basmati rice.

The easiest way to zest citrus fruit is with a rasp grater, such as a Microplane.

If you're planning to hold the rice on the Keep Warm cycle, wait until just before serving to stir in the mint, lime zest and orange zest.

• Medium rice cooker; fuzzy logic or on/off

1 cup	white basmati rice, rinsed and drained	250 mL
1/4 tsp	salt	1 mL
1 1/2 cups	vegetable or chicken broth	375 mL
1 1/2 tbsp	finely chopped fresh mint	22 mL
1 tsp	finely grated lime zest	5 mL
1 tsp	finely grated orange zest	5 mL
2 tbsp	butter	30 mL
	Additional finely chopped fresh mint	

1. In the rice cooker bowl, combine rice, salt and broth. Set the rice cooker for the Regular cycle.
2. When the machine switches to the Keep Warm cycle, stir in mint, lime zest, orange zest and butter. Close the lid and let stand for 10 minutes. Fluff rice with a wooden spoon or plastic paddle. Serve immediately or hold on the Keep Warm cycle for up to 3 hours (see tip, at left). Serve garnished with mint.

Variation

For a more intense citrus flavor, drizzle with 1 tsp (5 mL) blood orange–infused olive oil just before serving.

Pineapple Lime Rice

Makes 3 to 4 servings

Sweet pineapple and citrus make this the perfect side dish for a summer barbecue. Blackened mahi mahi tacos or ginger lime chicken skewers would especially complement its flavors.

Tips

For enhanced pineapple flavor, substitute unsweetened pineapple juice for the water.

If you're planning to hold the rice on the Keep Warm cycle, wait until just before serving to stir in the cilantro and lime zest.

● **Medium rice cooker; fuzzy logic or on/off**

1 cup	long-grain white rice, rinsed and drained	250 mL
¼ tsp	salt	1 mL
1 cup	finely chopped fresh pineapple (or canned crushed pineapple, with juice)	250 mL
¾ cup	coconut milk	175 mL
¾ cup	water	175 mL
¼ cup	finely chopped fresh cilantro	60 mL
¼ cup	finely chopped green onions (white and green parts)	60 mL
½ tsp	finely grated lime zest	2 mL
2 tbsp	butter	30 mL
1 tbsp	freshly squeezed lime juice	15 mL

1. In the rice cooker bowl, combine rice, salt, pineapple, coconut milk and water. Set the rice cooker for the Regular cycle.

2. When the machine switches to the Keep Warm cycle, stir in cilantro, green onions, lime zest, butter and lime juice. Close the lid and let stand for 10 minutes. Fluff rice with a wooden spoon or plastic paddle. Serve immediately or hold on the Keep Warm cycle for up to 1 hour (see tip, at left).

Caribbean Yellow Rice

Makes 6 to 8 servings

Yellow rice is a popular Caribbean dish that is a great complement to Cuban pork or garlic lemon chicken.

Tips

Sazón with annatto is a spice blend used in Caribbean cooking. It is available at Latin markets.

For information about rice cooker sizes, see page 13.

- **Medium rice cooker; fuzzy logic or on/off**

2 tbsp	extra virgin olive oil	30 mL
1 cup	sofrito (see recipe, opposite)	250 mL
1	packet (2 oz/56 g) sazón with annatto (see tip, at left)	1
1	can (14 to 19 oz/398 to 540 mL) pink beans, drained and rinsed	1
2 cups	long-grain white rice, rinsed and drained	500 mL
1 tsp	salt	5 mL
¼ tsp	freshly ground black pepper	1 mL
4 cups	chicken broth	1 L

1. Set the rice cooker for the Quick Cook or Regular cycle. When the bottom of the bowl gets hot, add oil and swirl to coat. Sauté sofrito for 1 minute.
2. Stir in sazón, beans, rice, salt, pepper and broth. Close the lid and reset for the Regular cycle.
3. When the machine switches to the Keep Warm cycle, let stand for 10 minutes. Fluff rice with a wooden spoon or plastic paddle. Serve immediately or hold on the Keep Warm cycle for up to 1 hour.

Variation

For a complete meal, add 1 cup (250 mL) cooked bay scallops when the machine switches to the Keep Warm cycle.

Sofrito

Makes about 1 cup (250 mL)

Sofrito is a savory sauce traditionally made of tomatoes, onion, garlic, bell peppers and spices. It is often used as a cooking base and can be added to soups and stews as a first-step ingredient for authentic Latino cooking. Sofrito adds freshness, herbal notes and a flavorful boost to your dishes.

Tip

Refrigerate unused sofrito in an airtight container for up to 1 week.

2 tbsp	extra virgin olive oil	30 mL
10	cherry tomatoes, finely chopped	10
4 to 5	cloves garlic, minced	4 to 5
1	green bell pepper, finely chopped	1
1	large onion, finely chopped	1
1	bay leaf	1
Pinch	ground cumin	Pinch
Pinch	dried oregano	Pinch
¼ cup	dry sherry	60 mL
	Salt	

1. In a large nonstick skillet, heat oil over medium-high heat. Sauté tomatoes, garlic, green pepper, onion, bay leaf, cumin and oregano for 4 to 5 minutes or until vegetables are softened. Stir in sherry, reduce heat and simmer, stirring occasionally, for 15 to 20 minutes to blend the flavors. Season to taste with salt.

Jamaican Rice with Peas

Makes 6 to 8 servings

Jamaicans often refer to beans as "peas," which is what gives this Caribbean-inspired beans and rice recipe its name. The creaminess of the coconut milk and the heat from the habanero pair well with jerk chicken as a main dish.

Tip

To bruise a green onion, lay it flat on a cutting board and crush it slightly with a meat mallet or the side of a large knife or cleaver.

The Scoville Scale

The Scoville scale (developed by Wilbur Scoville) measures the heat of chile peppers in units from 500 to 500,000. Scotch bonnet peppers and habaneros rank as the hottest peppers on earth, tipping the scale at anywhere from 100,000 to 500,000 Scoville units. By comparison, the jalapeño weighs in at just 5,000 to 10,000.

• Medium rice cooker; fuzzy logic or on/off

4	green onions, bruised (see tip, at left) and bent slightly to fit in rice cooker	4
3	sprigs fresh thyme	3
2	cloves garlic, minced	2
1	Scotch bonnet pepper or habanero chile pepper	1
1	can (14 to 19 oz/398 to 540 mL) pigeon peas, kidney beans or navy beans, drained and rinsed	1
2 cups	long-grain white rice, rinsed and drained	500 mL
½ tsp	salt	2 mL
3 cups	coconut milk	750 mL
	Thinly sliced green onions (green part only)	
	Lime wedges	

1. In the rice cooker bowl, combine bruised green onions, thyme sprigs, garlic, Scotch bonnet pepper, peas, rice, salt and coconut milk. Set the rice cooker for the Regular cycle.

2. When the machine switches to the Keep Warm cycle, let stand for 10 minutes. Fluff rice with a wooden spoon or plastic paddle. Discard green onions, thyme sprigs and hot pepper. Serve immediately or hold on the Keep Warm cycle for up to 1 hour. Serve garnished with sliced green onions, with lime wedges on the side.

Mexicali Rice

Makes 4 to 6 servings

This zesty recipe, influenced by Mexican cuisine, is tasty yet low in fat.

Tips

Thanks to the combination of black beans, corn and rice, this dish could be a meal on its own. As a meal, it makes 2 to 3 servings.

For information about rice cooker sizes, see page 13.

● Large rice cooker; fuzzy logic or on/off

2 tbsp	extra virgin olive oil	30 mL
1 cup	finely chopped onion	250 mL
1	serrano chile pepper, seeded and minced	1
1	red bell pepper, finely chopped	1
1	can (14 to 19 oz/398 to 540 mL) black beans, drained and rinsed	1
2 cups	long-grain white rice, rinsed and drained	500 mL
1 cup	fresh or thawed frozen corn kernels	250 mL
1½ tbsp	ground cumin	22 mL
1 tbsp	chili powder	15 mL
2 tsp	finely grated orange zest	10 mL
1½ tsp	salt	7 mL
2 cups	chicken broth	500 mL
1 cup	freshly squeezed orange juice	250 mL
3 tbsp	freshly squeezed lime juice	45 mL
½ cup	finely chopped fresh cilantro	125 mL
	Additional finely chopped fresh cilantro	

1. Set the rice cooker for the Quick Cook or Regular cycle. When the bottom of the bowl gets hot, add oil and swirl to coat. Sauté onion for about 3 minutes or until softened and translucent.

2. Stir in serrano pepper, red pepper, beans, rice, corn, cumin, chili powder, orange zest, salt, broth, orange juice and lime juice. Close the lid and reset for the Regular cycle.

3. When the machine switches to the Keep Warm cycle, stir in cilantro. Close the lid and let stand for 10 minutes. Fluff rice with a wooden spoon or plastic paddle. Serve immediately, garnished with cilantro.

Brazilian-Style Rice

Makes 3 to 4 servings

This simple recipe is the main side dish served throughout Brazil. It's wonderful with Brazilian *churrasco* (grilled meats) and *Caipirinhas* (Brazilian-style Mojitos).

Tip

To avoid tearing up when you're chopping onions, try refrigerating the onions for 30 minutes first, and don't cut the root off.

• **Medium rice cooker; fuzzy logic or on/off**

2 tbsp	extra virgin olive oil	30 mL
1	clove garlic, minced	1
2 tbsp	finely chopped onion	30 mL
1 cup	long-grain white rice, rinsed and drained	250 mL
¼ tsp	salt	1 mL
1½ cups	water	375 mL

1. Set the rice cooker for the Quick Cook or Regular cycle. When the bottom of the bowl gets hot, add oil and swirl to coat. Sauté garlic and onion for about 3 minutes or until onion is softened and translucent.
2. Stir in rice, salt and water. Close the lid and reset for the Regular cycle.
3. When the machine switches to the Keep Warm cycle, let stand for 10 minutes. Fluff rice with a wooden spoon or plastic paddle. Serve immediately or hold on the Keep Warm cycle for up to 1 hour.

Spanish Rice

Makes 3 to 4 servings

This easy rice dish is sure to jazz up any number of meals. It's particularly fantastic alongside Mexican entrées.

Tips

To make this dish even faster and easier, omit the diced tomatoes and increase the tomato paste to 4 tsp (20 mL).

For information about rice cooker sizes, see page 13.

● **Medium rice cooker; fuzzy logic or on/off**

2 tbsp	extra virgin olive oil	30 mL
1	clove garlic, minced	1
½ cup	finely chopped onion	125 mL
1 cup	long-grain white rice, rinsed and drained	250 mL
¾ cup	diced tomatoes	175 mL
½ tsp	salt	2 mL
Pinch	dried oregano	Pinch
1½ cups	chicken or vegetable broth	375 mL
2 tsp	tomato paste	10 mL

1. Set the rice cooker for the Quick Cook or Regular cycle. When the bottom of the bowl gets hot, add oil and swirl to coat. Sauté garlic and onion for about 3 minutes or until onion is softened and translucent.
2. Stir in rice, tomatoes, salt, oregano, broth and tomato paste. Close the lid and reset for the Regular cycle.
3. When the machine switches to the Keep Warm cycle, let stand for 10 minutes. Fluff rice with a wooden spoon or plastic paddle. Serve immediately or hold on the Keep Warm cycle for up to 1 hour.

Green Spanish Rice (*Arroz Verde*)

Makes 3 to 4 servings

This pretty side dish goes well with a variety of Mexican entrées. It gets its green color from the fresh parsley and cilantro.

Tips

I recommend wearing rubber gloves when you're handling chile peppers; otherwise, the juices may burn your skin. And there's nothing worse than accidentally rubbing your eye after handling a chile pepper without gloves!

If you're planning to hold the rice on the Keep Warm cycle, wait until just before serving to stir in the herbs.

● **Medium rice cooker; fuzzy logic or on/off**

1 tbsp	butter	15 mL
1	clove garlic, minced	1
½ cup	finely chopped onion	125 mL
1	jalapeño pepper, seeded and minced	1
1 cup	long-grain rice, rinsed and drained	250 mL
1 tsp	ground cumin	5 mL
¼ tsp	salt	1 mL
1½ cups	chicken broth	375 mL
¼ cup	finely chopped fresh cilantro	60 mL
¼ cup	finely chopped fresh parsley	60 mL
	Additional finely chopped fresh cilantro and parsley	

1. Set the rice cooker for the Quick Cook or Regular cycle. When the bottom of the bowl gets hot, add butter and let it melt. Sauté garlic and onion for about 3 minutes or until onion is softened and translucent.
2. Stir in jalapeño, rice, cumin, salt and broth. Close the lid and reset for the Regular cycle.
3. When the machine switches to the Keep Warm cycle, stir in cilantro and parsley. Close the lid and let stand for 10 minutes. Fluff rice with a wooden spoon or plastic paddle. Serve immediately or hold on the Keep Warm cycle for up to 1 hour (see tip, at left). Serve garnished with cilantro and parsley.

Variation

For a complete meal, add 1 cup (250 mL) shredded cooked pork when the machine switches to the Keep Warm cycle.

Turkish Rice

Makes 3 to 4 servings

The best things in life are often the simplest. It takes only a few ingredients to create the deliciously distinct flavor of this fragrant rice dish.

Tips

If you don't have a cinnamon stick, you can use ½ tsp (2 mL) ground cinnamon.

To toast pine nuts, place them in a dry skillet over medium heat and cook, stirring, for about 5 minutes or until browned and fragrant. Immediately transfer to a bowl and let cool.

Pine Nuts

Pine nuts (pignolas) are small, oblong, cream-colored nuts gathered from pine trees. They can be eaten raw but are usually roasted or toasted, which cuts down on their somewhat bitter aftertaste. Shelled pine nuts can deteriorate rapidly, becoming rancid within a few weeks (or even days in warm, humid conditions); however, they can be stored in the freezer for up to 9 months.

• Medium rice cooker; fuzzy logic or on/off

1 cup	long-grain white rice, rinsed and drained	250 mL
2	whole cloves	2
1	2-inch (5 cm) cinnamon stick	1
¼ tsp	ground allspice	1 mL
¼ tsp	ground nutmeg	1 mL
¼ tsp	salt	1 mL
1½ cups	chicken broth	375 mL
2 tbsp	butter	30 mL
	Toasted pine nuts (see tip, at left)	

1. In the rice cooker bowl, combine rice, cloves, cinnamon, allspice, nutmeg, salt and broth. Set the rice cooker for the Regular cycle.

2. When the machine switches to the Keep Warm cycle, let stand for 10 minutes. Fold in butter. Fluff rice with a wooden spoon or plastic paddle. Discard cloves and cinnamon stick. Serve immediately or hold on the Keep Warm cycle for up to 1 hour. Serve garnished with pine nuts.

Variation

Add 2 tbsp (30 mL) finely chopped fresh mint and 2 tbsp (30 mL) finely chopped fresh parsley when the machine switches to the Keep Warm cycle. (If you're planning to hold the rice on the Keep Warm cycle, wait until just before serving to stir in the herbs.)

Persian-Style Rice

Makes 3 to 4 servings

Turmeric is known to be a powerful healer, which only increases the list of pros for this attractive green dish, which goes well with chicken or fish.

Tips

When shopping for fava beans, select small pods; those that bulge with beans are past their prime. Two pounds (500 g) of unshelled beans yields about 1 cup (250 mL) shelled.

To prepare and blanch fava beans, remove the beans from their pods. Bring a small saucepan of water to a boil over high heat. Add beans and boil for 1 minute or until tender-crisp. Using a slotted spoon, transfer beans to a bowl of ice water and let cool completely. Remove the tough outer skins from the beans by pinching the skin between your thumb and forefinger; discard skins.

If you're planning to hold the rice on the Keep Warm cycle, wait until just before serving to stir in the herbs.

• Medium rice cooker; fuzzy logic or on/off

1 cup	long-grain white rice, rinsed and drained	250 mL
½ cup	fresh or thawed frozen shelled fava beans, blanched if fresh (see tips, at left)	125 mL
1	2-inch (5 cm) cinnamon stick	1
1 tsp	ground turmeric	5 mL
¼ tsp	salt	1 mL
1½ cups	vegetable or chicken broth	375 mL
1 tbsp	finely chopped fresh cilantro	15 mL
1 tbsp	finely chopped fresh parsley	15 mL
1 tbsp	finely chopped fresh dill	15 mL
	Additional finely chopped fresh parsley	

1. In the rice cooker bowl, combine rice, beans, cinnamon stick, turmeric, salt and broth. Set the rice cooker for the Regular cycle.
2. When the machine switches to the Keep Warm cycle, stir in cilantro, parsley and dill. Close the lid and let stand for 10 minutes. Fluff rice with a wooden spoon or plastic paddle. Discard cinnamon stick. Serve immediately or hold on the Keep Warm cycle for up to 1 hour (see tip, at left). Serve garnished with parsley.

Variation

Persian-Style Rice with Lentils: Add ½ cup (125 mL) dried green lentils, sorted and rinsed, in step 1 and increase the broth to 2 cups (500 mL).

Red Curry Rice

Makes 3 to 4 servings

Spice up a cold winter evening with a Thai chicken dish served with this red curry rice recipe. The subtle essence of jasmine rice combined with the other sweet and spicy ingredients is a winner!

Tips

For more heat, increase the curry paste to 1 tbsp (15 mL).

For information about rice cooker sizes, see page 13.

For information about rice cooker sizes, see page 13.

● **Medium rice cooker; fuzzy logic or on/off**

1½ tsp	packed brown sugar	7 mL
1½ cups	coconut milk	375 mL
2 tsp	Thai red curry paste	10 mL
1½ tsp	fish sauce (nam pla)	7 mL
1 cup	Thai jasmine rice, rinsed and drained	250 mL

1. In a small bowl, whisk together brown sugar, coconut milk, curry paste and fish sauce until brown sugar dissolves and curry paste is blended.
2. In the rice cooker bowl, combine brown sugar mixture and rice. Set the rice cooker for the Regular cycle.
3. When the machine switches to the Keep Warm cycle, let stand for 10 minutes. Fluff rice with a wooden spoon or plastic paddle. Serve immediately or hold on the Keep Warm cycle for up to 1 hour.

Variation

For a complete meal, add 1 cup (250 mL) cubed firm tofu and ½ cup (125 mL) julienned red bell pepper with the rice.

Saffron Rice

Makes 3 to 4 servings

No single ingredient could possibly replace saffron, which is what gives this recipe its unique flavor. To offset the slightly bitter taste of saffron, pair this dish with a medium-bodied white wine, such as Riesling.

Tips

Saffron has a shelf life of about 6 months. It's customary to wrap it in foil and then store it in an airtight jar or container.

For information about rice cooker sizes, see page 13.

● **Medium rice cooker; fuzzy logic or on/off**

½ tsp	crushed saffron threads	2 mL
¼ cup	hot water	60 mL
1 cup	long-grain white rice, rinsed and drained	250 mL
¼ tsp	salt	1 mL
1¼ cups	chicken broth	300 mL

1. In a measuring cup or small bowl, combine saffron threads and hot water; let steep for 10 minutes.
2. In the rice cooker bowl, combine saffron-infused water, rice, salt and broth. Set the rice cooker for the Regular cycle.
3. When the machine switches to the Keep Warm cycle, let stand for 10 minutes. Fluff rice with a wooden spoon or plastic paddle. Serve immediately or hold on the Keep Warm cycle for up to 3 hours.

Fragrant Lemongrass Rice

Makes 3 to 4 servings

Lemongrass is frequently used in Thai cuisine. While you're preparing and cooking this dish, citrus scents permeate the air, tantalizing the taste buds.

Tip

You may use frozen lemongrass (available at Asian markets) or 1 tbsp (15 mL) minced lemongrass in a tube (sold in the produce department of grocery stores) if fresh is unavailable.

● Medium rice cooker; fuzzy logic or on/off

1	stalk lemongrass	1
1 cup	Thai jasmine rice, rinsed and drained	250 mL
2	bay leaves	2
1/2 tsp	ground turmeric	2 mL
Pinch	salt	Pinch
1 1/2 cups	coconut milk	375 mL

1. Peel away the tough outer leaves of the lemongrass. Cut the remaining stalk into 3-inch (7.5 cm) pieces and bruise several times with a mallet.
2. In the rice cooker bowl, combine lemongrass, rice, bay leaves, turmeric, salt and coconut milk. Set the rice cooker for the Regular cycle.
3. When the machine switches to the Keep Warm cycle, let stand for 10 minutes. Fluff rice with a wooden spoon or plastic paddle. Discard bay leaves and lemongrass. Serve immediately or hold on the Keep Warm cycle for up to 1 hour.

Variation

Substitute forbidden black rice for the jasmine rice and increase the coconut milk to 1¾ cups (425 mL). Set the rice cooker for the Brown Rice cycle.

Five-Ingredient Japanese Rice (*Takikomi Gohan*)

Makes 6 to 8 servings

In Japan, *takikomi gohan* is a popular dish to serve in autumn.

Tips

You may use rehydrated dried mushrooms in place of fresh in this dish. To rehydrate, soak ½ oz (14 g) dried mushrooms in hot water for 30 minutes; drain and squeeze out liquid before using. Remove and discard stems, and cut caps into thin slices.

You can buy powdered dashi mix at Asian markets, but I suggest making it from scratch (see page 185), as it's simple and the taste will be superior.

• **Medium rice cooker; fuzzy logic or on/off**

2 cups	Japanese-style medium-grain japonica rice (such as Calrose)	500 mL
3	boneless skinless chicken thighs, cut into ½-inch (1 cm) pieces	3
2	carrots, diced	2
1 cup	mixed Asian mushrooms (such as shiitake or enoki), stemmed and sliced	250 mL
½ cup	drained canned thinly sliced bamboo shoots	125 mL
¼ tsp	salt	1 mL
2½ cups	dashi (see tip, at left) or chicken broth	625 mL
2 tbsp	soy sauce	30 mL
1 tbsp	sake	15 mL
1 tbsp	mirin	15 mL
	Finely grated lemon zest	

1. Place rice in a bowl and add enough cool water to cover by 1 inch (2.5 cm); let soak for 30 minutes. Rinse and drain (see page 20).
2. In the rice cooker bowl, combine soaked rice, chicken, carrots, mushrooms, bamboo shoots, salt, dashi, soy sauce, sake and mirin. Set the rice cooker for the Regular cycle.
3. When the machine switches to the Keep Warm cycle, let stand for 10 minutes. Fluff rice with a wooden spoon or plastic paddle. Serve immediately, garnished with lemon zest.

Indonesian Spiced Coconut Rice

Makes 3 to 4 servings

The slightly sweet flavors in this rice dish pair well with curries or Thai barbecued chicken.

Tips

For a lighter version of this recipe, replace half the coconut milk with water.

If you're planning to hold the rice on the Keep Warm cycle, wait until just before serving to stir in the cilantro.

For information about rice cooker sizes, see page 13.

• **Medium rice cooker; fuzzy logic or on/off**

1 cup	long-grain white rice, rinsed and drained	250 mL
1 tsp	ground coriander	5 mL
1 tsp	ground cumin	5 mL
1/4 tsp	salt	1 mL
1 1/2 cups	coconut milk	375 mL
1/4 cup	finely chopped fresh cilantro	60 mL
1 1/2 tsp	freshly squeezed lemon juice	7 mL

1. In the rice cooker bowl, combine rice, coriander, cumin, salt and coconut milk. Set the rice cooker for the Regular cycle.
2. When the machine switches to the Keep Warm cycle, stir in cilantro and lemon juice. Close the lid and let stand for 10 minutes. Fluff rice with a wooden spoon or plastic paddle. Serve immediately or hold on the Keep Warm cycle for up to 1 hour (see tip, at left).

Variation

Substitute red cargo rice for the long-grain white rice and increase the coconut milk to 2 cups (500 mL). Set the rice cooker for the Brown Rice cycle.

Balinese Fried Rice (*Nasi Goreng*)

Makes 3 to 4 servings

Nasi goreng, the national dish of Indonesia, was praised by U.S. President Barack Obama during his 2010 visit to the region. The banana leaves add an elegant touch and are sure to wow even the most influential dinner guests.

Tips

Indonesians typically use banana leaves as plates. You may buy fresh or frozen banana leaves at Asian and Latin markets. They are also wonderful for steaming fish.

Add more chili powder to taste if you like a spicier dish.

2 tbsp	vegetable oil, divided	30 mL
2	cloves garlic, minced	2
1 cup	finely chopped onion	250 mL
2 tsp	chili powder	10 mL
1½ cups	cooked long-grain white rice (see page 20), cooled	375 mL
½ tsp	salt	2 mL
⅛ tsp	freshly ground white pepper	0.5 mL
⅛ tsp	packed dark brown sugar	0.5 mL
2 tsp	dark soy sauce (see tip, page 211)	10 mL
	Banana leaves	
	Chopped green onions (white and green parts)	

1. In a wok or large nonstick skillet, heat 1 tbsp (15 mL) oil over medium-high heat. Stir-fry garlic, onion and chili powder for about 3 minutes or until onion is softened and translucent. Add the remaining oil. Add rice and stir-fry for 1 minute. Add salt, pepper, brown sugar and soy sauce; stir-fry for 30 seconds.
2. Wipe banana leaves clean with a damp paper towel. Lay leaves on a serving platter. Mound rice on top of leaves. Serve hot, garnished with green onions.

Variations

Place a fried egg on top of the rice before serving. In Indonesia, this is called *nasi goreng istimewa,* which means "special fried rice."

Add 1 cup (250 mL) chopped cooked meat or seafood to this dish, stir-frying it for 1 minute after the rice.

Wild Rice with Cranberries and Pecans

Makes 3 to 4 servings

This dish is a great addition to any Thanksgiving meal. The sweetness of the berries and apricots meshes well with the crunchy pecans and the luxurious nutty flavor of the wild rice.

Tips

Lundberg Farms makes a wild rice/ brown rice blend that works wonderfully in this recipe.

If you're planning to hold the wild rice on the Keep Warm cycle, wait until just before serving to stir in the dried fruit and parsley.

• Medium rice cooker; fuzzy logic or on/off

4 tbsp	butter, divided	60 mL
½ cup	finely chopped onion	125 mL
½ cup	pecan halves, coarsely chopped	125 mL
1 cup	wild rice or wild rice/brown rice blend, rinsed and drained	250 mL
¼ tsp	salt	1 mL
3 cups	chicken or vegetable broth	750 mL
¼ cup	finely chopped dried apricots	60 mL
¼ cup	dried cranberries	60 mL
¼ cup	finely chopped fresh parsley	60 mL
	Additional finely chopped fresh parsley	

1. Set the rice cooker for the Quick Cook, Regular or Brown Rice cycle. When the bottom of the bowl gets hot, add 2 tbsp (30 mL) butter and let it melt. Sauté onion and pecans for about 3 minutes or until onion is softened and translucent.
2. Stir in wild rice, salt, broth and the remaining butter. Close the lid and reset for the Regular or Brown Rice cycle.
3. When the machine switches to the Keep Warm cycle, stir in apricots, cranberries and parsley. Close the lid and let stand for 10 minutes. Fluff wild rice with a wooden spoon or plastic paddle. Serve immediately or hold on the Keep Warm cycle for up to 1 hour (see tip, at left). Serve garnished with parsley.

Variation

Substitute pearl barley for the wild rice.

Barley and Wild Rice with Dried Cherries

Makes 3 to 4 servings

The sweetness of the cherries and orange juice in this dish make it a perfect complement to lamb chops or pork chops.

Tips

Lundberg Farms makes a wild rice/brown rice blend that works wonderfully in this recipe.

Dried cranberries are a good substitute for dried cherries in this dish.

If you're planning to hold the barley and wild rice on the Keep Warm cycle, wait until just before serving to stir in the cherries, walnuts and parsley.

- **Medium rice cooker; fuzzy logic or on/off**

¾ cup	dried cherries	175 mL
1 cup	freshly squeezed orange juice	250 mL
2 tbsp	butter	30 mL
½ cup	finely chopped onion	125 mL
¾ cup	pearl barley, rinsed and drained	175 mL
¼ cup	wild rice or wild rice/brown rice blend, rinsed and drained	60 mL
½ tsp	salt	2 mL
3½ cups	chicken or vegetable broth	875 mL
1 tbsp	minced shallots	15 mL
1 tbsp	freshly squeezed lemon juice	15 mL
⅓ cup	extra virgin olive oil	75 mL
1 cup	walnut halves, toasted (see tip, page 263) and coarsely chopped	250 mL
¼ cup	chopped fresh parsley	60 mL
	Additional chopped fresh parsley	
	Additional walnuts halves, toasted and coarsely chopped	

1. Place cherries in a small bowl and pour orange juice over top. Set aside.
2. Set the rice cooker for the Quick Cook, Regular or Brown Rice cycle. When the bottom of the bowl gets hot, add butter and let it melt. Sauté onion for about 3 minutes or until softened and translucent.
3. Stir in barley, wild rice, salt and broth. Close the lid and reset for the Regular or Brown Rice cycle.
4. Meanwhile, drain cherries, reserving ⅓ cup (75 mL) orange juice. In a bowl, combine reserved orange juice, shallots and lemon juice. Gradually whisk in oil until well blended. Set aside.
5. When the machine switches to the Keep Warm cycle, stir in cherries, walnuts and parsley. Close the lid and let stand for 10 minutes. Fluff grains with a wooden spoon or plastic paddle. Drizzle orange juice mixture over top. Serve immediately or hold on the Keep Warm cycle for up to 1 hour (see tip, at left). Serve garnished with parsley and walnuts.

Curried Bulgur with Tomatoes

Makes 4 servings

The pungent richness of the curry in this dish is perfectly complemented by the sweetness of the corn and sweet potato.

Tip

To blanch fresh corn kernels, bring a small saucepan of water to a boil over high heat. Add corn and boil for 1 to 2 minutes or until tender-crisp. Using a slotted spoon, transfer corn to a bowl of ice water and let cool completely. Drain.

Curry Powder

Curry powder is not a single spice but a blend of Indian spices with nearly limitless variations. English cooks wanted to recreate the beloved Indian flavors they had come to adore during colonial rule, so they invented this clever spice blend. The curry powder available today is relatively mild. If you want a spicier dish, opt for a hot curry powder blend.

• Medium rice cooker; fuzzy logic or on/off

2 tbsp	toasted sesame oil	30 mL
½ cup	finely chopped onion	125 mL
1 cup	coarse bulgur	250 mL
1 tbsp	curry powder	15 mL
1 cup	diced peeled sweet potato	250 mL
½ cup	diced tomato	125 mL
1 tsp	salt	5 mL
¼ tsp	freshly ground black pepper	1 mL
2 cups	chicken or vegetable broth	500 mL
½ cup	blanched fresh or thawed frozen corn kernels (see tip, at left)	125 mL

1. Set the rice cooker for the Quick Cook, Regular or Brown Rice cycle. When the bottom of the bowl gets hot, add oil and swirl to coat. Sauté onion for about 3 minutes or until softened and translucent. Add bulgur and curry powder; sauté for 30 seconds.

2. Stir in sweet potato, tomato, salt, pepper and broth. Close the lid and reset for the Regular or Brown Rice cycle.

3. When the machine switches to the Keep Warm cycle, stir in corn. Close the lid and let stand for 10 minutes. Serve immediately or hold on the Keep Warm cycle for up to 1 hour.

Variation

Substitute roasted halved cherry tomatoes for the diced tomato. To roast, place halved tomatoes on a baking sheet, sprinkle the cut side with salt and freshly ground black pepper and roast in a 350°F (180°C) oven for 20 to 30 minutes or until softened and slightly blackened. Fold into bulgur when the machine switches to the Keep Warm cycle.

Couscous with Butternut Squash

Makes 4 to 6 servings

The golden hue of the squash makes this a beautiful dish to serve in autumn or winter, when butternut squash is at its peak. I like to serve it with roast pork loin and a full-bodied Cabernet.

Tip

Freshly grated nutmeg is more aromatic than pre-ground and adds a wonderful depth of flavor to butternut squash. To grate fresh nutmeg, scrape it against the finest holes of a box grater or use a rasp grater, such as a Microplane.

• **Medium rice cooker; fuzzy logic or on/off**

2 tbsp	extra virgin olive oil	30 mL
2	cloves garlic, minced	2
1	onion, finely chopped	1
1 tbsp	minced gingerroot	15 mL
2 cups	couscous	500 mL
1 cup	diced butternut squash	250 mL
¾ cup	golden raisins	175 mL
½ tsp	salt	2 mL
2 cups	water or vegetable broth	500 mL
2 tbsp	finely chopped fresh parsley	30 mL
½ tsp	grated nutmeg (see tip, at left)	2 mL
	Additional finely chopped fresh parsley	

1. Set the rice cooker for the Quick Cook or Regular cycle. When the bottom of the bowl gets hot, add oil and swirl to coat. Sauté garlic, onion and ginger for about 3 minutes or until onion is softened and translucent.
2. Stir in couscous, squash, raisins, salt and broth. Close the lid and reset for the Regular cycle.
3. When the machine switches to the Keep Warm cycle, stir in parsley and nutmeg. Close the lid and let stand for 10 minutes. Fluff couscous with a wooden spoon or plastic paddle. Serve immediately, garnished with parsley.

Variation

For added texture and protein, fold in ½ cup (125 mL) crumbled goat cheese when the machine switches to the Keep Warm cycle.

Moroccan Couscous

Makes 4 to 6 servings

This couscous provides complex flavors with simple ingredients. Sweet and fragrant, this one is a crowd pleaser!

Tip

To toast slivered almonds, spread them in a single layer on an ungreased baking sheet and bake in a 350°F (180°C) oven, stirring occasionally, for 10 to 15 minutes or until golden. Immediately transfer to a bowl and let cool.

• Medium rice cooker; fuzzy logic or on/off

2 cups	couscous	500 mL
1/3 cup	finely chopped dried dates	75 mL
1/3 cup	finely chopped dried apricots	75 mL
1/3 cup	golden raisins	75 mL
1	2-inch (5 cm) cinnamon stick	1
1/2 tsp	salt	2 mL
2 cups	vegetable broth	500 mL
1/3 cup	butter	75 mL
1/2 cup	slivered almonds, toasted (see tip, at left)	125 mL

1. In the rice cooker bowl, combine couscous, dates, apricots, raisins, cinnamon stick, salt, broth and butter. Set the rice cooker for the Regular cycle.
2. When the machine switches to the Keep Warm cycle, let stand for 10 minutes. Fluff couscous with a wooden spoon or plastic paddle. Discard cinnamon stick. Serve immediately, garnished with almonds.

Variations

Moroccan Saffron Couscous: In a measuring cup or small bowl, combine 1/2 tsp (2 mL) crushed saffron threads and 1/4 cup (60 mL) hot water; let steep for 10 minutes. Add with the couscous. Reduce the broth to 1 3/4 cups (425 mL).

Substitute dried currants for the apricots.

Toasted pine nuts also work well in place of the almonds.

Israeli Couscous with Mint and Feta Cheese

Makes 4 to 6 servings

I love the flavors in Greek salad and wanted to recreate them in a side dish. Serve with a simple grilled fish for a quick and light dinner. Pair with Pinot Grigio.

Tips

English cucumbers are waxless, so they don't require peeling. If you want to substitute regular cucumbers, peel them before chopping.

Try using seasoned feta cheese, such as roasted garlic–flavor.

English Cucumbers

English cucumbers are generally sweeter, longer and thinner than regular cucumbers. They have very small seeds and are often said to be "seedless." Although more expensive, they are excellent for salads and cooking because of their sweet flavor.

• **Medium rice cooker; fuzzy logic or on/off**

2	cloves garlic, minced, divided	2
½ tsp	finely grated lemon zest	2 mL
4 tbsp	extra virgin olive oil, divided	60 mL
2 tbsp	freshly squeezed lemon juice	30 mL
1½ cups	Israeli couscous	375 mL
1 tsp	salt	5 mL
3 cups	chicken or vegetable broth	750 mL
1	English cucumber, finely chopped	1
1 cup	crumbled feta cheese	250 mL
½ cup	coarsely chopped fresh mint	125 mL
	Additional coarsely chopped fresh mint	

1. In a small bowl, whisk together half the minced garlic, lemon zest, 2 tbsp (30 mL) oil and lemon juice. Set aside.
2. Set the rice cooker for the Quick Cook or Regular cycle. When the bottom of the bowl gets hot, add the remaining oil and swirl to coat. Add couscous and sauté for 3 minutes. Add the remaining garlic and sauté for 2 minutes or until couscous is golden brown.
3. Stir in salt and broth. Close the lid and reset for the Regular cycle.
4. When the machine switches to the Keep Warm cycle, stir in cucumber. Close the lid and let stand for 10 minutes. Fluff couscous with a wooden spoon or plastic paddle. Add feta and mint, tossing to coat. Drizzle reserved dressing over top. Serve immediately, garnished with mint.

Variation

Substitute 1 cup (250 mL) pearl barley for the Israeli couscous.

Israeli Couscous with Sugar Snap Peas

Makes 4 to 6 servings

Israeli couscous is considered a dish for children in Israel, but in the rest of the world, kids of all ages enjoy its unique shape and texture. The brightness of the lemon juice and zest make this version a real winner.

Tips

String sugar snap peas by beginning at the tip and pulling it down. If peas are very young, you can omit this step. Cut off stem ends and leave whole.

To blanch sugar snap peas, bring a small saucepan of water to a boil over high heat. Add peas and boil for 1 minute or until tender-crisp. Using a slotted spoon, transfer peas to a bowl of ice water and let cool completely. Drain well.

- **Medium rice cooker; fuzzy logic or on/off**

1	clove garlic, minced	1
½ tsp	finely grated lemon zest	2 mL
4 tbsp	extra virgin olive oil, divided	60 mL
2 tbsp	freshly squeezed lemon juice	30 mL
1	onion, finely chopped	1
1½ cups	Israeli couscous	375 mL
1 tsp	salt	5 mL
3 cups	chicken or vegetable broth	750 mL
3 cups	trimmed sugar snap peas, blanched (see tip, at left) and cut diagonally into ½-inch (1 cm) pieces	750 mL
½ cup	finely grated Parmesan cheese	125 mL
⅓ cup	finely chopped fresh chives	75 mL
	Additional finely grated Parmesan cheese and finely chopped fresh chives	

1. In a small bowl, whisk together garlic, lemon zest, 2 tbsp (30 mL) oil and lemon juice. Set aside.
2. Set the rice cooker for the Quick Cook or Regular cycle. When the bottom of the bowl gets hot, add the remaining oil and swirl to coat. Add onion and couscous; sauté for about 5 minutes or until couscous is golden brown.
3. Stir in salt and broth. Close the lid and reset for the Regular cycle.
4. When the machine switches to the Keep Warm cycle, stir in peas, Parmesan and chives. Close the lid and let stand for 5 minutes. Fluff couscous with a wooden spoon or plastic paddle. Drizzle reserved dressing over top. Serve immediately, garnished with Parmesan and chives.

Variation

Substitute 2 cups (500 mL) chopped blanched asparagus for the sugar snap peas.

Israeli Couscous with Pancetta

Makes 4 to 6 servings

The distinctive flavor of pancetta enhances the flavors in couscous as nothing else can. Although pancetta is often called "Italian bacon," its essence is really one of a kind.

Tip

Grape tomatoes are a hybrid strain with enhanced sweetness and a delicate shape. If grape tomatoes aren't available, cherry tomatoes are a fine substitute.

● **Medium rice cooker; fuzzy logic or on/off**

2 tbsp	extra virgin olive oil	30 mL
4 oz	pancetta, diced	125 g
1½ cups	Israeli couscous	375 mL
2 tbsp	minced shallots	30 mL
½ tsp	salt	2 mL
3 cups	chicken or vegetable broth	750 mL
1 cup	grape tomatoes, quartered	250 mL
1 cup	fresh or thawed frozen peas	250 mL
	Finely chopped fresh parsley	

1. Set the rice cooker for the Quick Cook or Regular cycle. When the bottom of the bowl gets hot, add oil and swirl to coat. Sauté pancetta, couscous and shallots for about 5 minutes or until pancetta and couscous are golden brown.
2. Stir in salt and broth. Close the lid and reset for the Regular cycle.
3. When the machine switches to the Keep Warm cycle, stir in tomatoes and peas. Close the lid and let stand for 10 minutes. Serve immediately, garnished with parsley.

Farro with Pistachios

Makes 3 to 4 servings

I love to serve this hearty side dish when vegetarian guests are over. The saltiness of the pistachios pairs wonderfully with the sweetness of the raisins.

Tips

If you're planning to hold the farro on the Keep Warm cycle, wait until just before serving to stir in the raisins, pistachios and parsley.

For information about rice cooker sizes, see page 13.

• Medium rice cooker; fuzzy logic or on/off

2 tbsp	extra virgin olive oil	30 mL
1	clove garlic, minced	1
½ cup	finely chopped onion	125 mL
1 cup	farro, rinsed and drained	250 mL
½ tsp	salt	2 mL
2 cups	vegetable or chicken broth	500 mL
¼ cup	golden raisins	60 mL
¼ cup	salted roasted pistachios, chopped	60 mL
¼ cup	finely chopped fresh parsley	60 mL
	Additional finely chopped fresh parsley	

1. Set the rice cooker for the Quick Cook, Regular or Brown Rice cycle. When the bottom of the bowl gets hot, add oil and swirl to coat. Sauté garlic and onion for about 3 minutes or until onion is softened and translucent.
2. Stir in farro, salt and broth. Close the lid and reset for the Regular or Brown Rice cycle.
3. When the machine switches to the Keep Warm cycle, stir in raisins, pistachios and parsley. Close the lid and let stand for 10 minutes. Fluff farro with a wooden spoon or plastic paddle. Serve immediately or hold on the Keep Warm cycle for up to 1 hour (see tip, at left). Serve garnished with parsley.

Kasha Varnishkes with Caramelized Onions

Makes 6 to 8 servings

Kasha varnishkes are a traditional Eastern European Jewish dish. The merry mixture of kasha, bow tie pasta, mushrooms and caramelized onions makes this a truly satisfying accompaniment to any meal.

Tips

To achieve caramelized onions that melt in your mouth, you'll want to cut thin slices from the root end to the stem end.

To help brown the onions, you may add the sugar at the beginning of cooking in step 4.

• Large rice cooker; fuzzy logic or on/off

3	large eggs, beaten	3
1½ cups	kasha	375 mL
2 tbsp	butter	30 mL
½ cup	mixed mushrooms (such as shiitake, cremini and chanterelle)	125 mL
	Salt and freshly ground black pepper	
4 cups	water	1 L
¾ cup	bow tie egg pasta	175 mL
2 tbsp	extra virgin olive oil	30 mL
2	onions, thinly sliced (see tip, at left)	2
¼ tsp	granulated sugar	1 mL

1. In a medium bowl, combine eggs and kasha. Spread out on a baking sheet and let dry for 15 minutes.

2. Set the rice cooker for the Quick Cook, Regular or Brown Rice cycle. When the bottom of the bowl gets hot, add butter and let it melt. Sauté mushrooms for about 3 minutes or until softened. Stir in kasha mixture and cook, stirring occasionally, for about 5 minutes or until kasha is dry and toasty.

3. Stir in 1 tsp (5 mL) salt, a pinch of pepper and water. Sprinkle pasta evenly on top. Close the lid and reset for the Regular or Brown Rice cycle. Set a timer for 30 minutes.

4. Meanwhile, in a medium nonstick skillet, heat oil over medium-high heat. Add onions, stirring to coat with oil, and cook, stirring often, for 10 minutes. Sprinkle with ½ tsp (2 mL) salt and sugar. Transfer onions to a baking sheet covered with paper towels and blot liquid.

5. When the timer sounds, stir in caramelized onions. Close the lid and cook for 5 minutes. Check to make sure kasha is tender. If necessary, continue cooking, checking for doneness every 5 minutes. Fluff kasha with a wooden spoon or plastic paddle. Season to taste with salt and pepper. Serve immediately.

Millet Cauliflower Mash

Makes 4 servings

Millet, quite possibly the first cereal grain known to man, offers outstanding health benefits, such as lowering cholesterol and reducing the risks of cancer. Pairing it with super-nutritious cauliflower makes for an extremely healthy and tasty side dish.

Tip

To bring out a pleasantly nutty aroma, toast the millet in a dry skillet over medium heat, stirring constantly, for 5 minutes before adding it to the rice cooker. (This is not necessary, but it's a nice touch if you have the time.)

- **Medium rice cooker; fuzzy logic or on/off**

2 tbsp	extra virgin olive oil	30 mL
1	clove garlic, minced	1
1/2 cup	finely chopped onion	125 mL
2 cups	chopped cauliflower florets	500 mL
1 cup	millet	250 mL
1/4 tsp	salt	1 mL
3 cups	chicken or vegetable broth	750 mL
3/4 cup	shredded Cheddar cheese	175 mL
1/4 cup	whole or 2% milk	60 mL
2 tbsp	butter	30 mL
	Salt and freshly ground black pepper	
	Finely chopped fresh parsley	

1. Set the rice cooker for the Quick Cook or Regular cycle. When the bottom of the bowl gets hot, add oil and swirl to coat. Sauté garlic and onion for about 3 minutes or until onion is softened and translucent.
2. Stir in cauliflower, millet, salt and broth. Close the lid and reset for the Regular cycle.
3. When the machine switches to the Keep Warm cycle, let stand for 10 minutes. Transfer to a large bowl and add cheese, milk and butter; mash with a potato masher. Season to taste with salt and pepper. Serve immediately, garnished with parsley.

Variation

For enhanced flavor, add about 1 tbsp (15 mL) roasted garlic paste when mashing.

Polenta-Style Quinoa

Makes 3 to 4 servings

This simple quinoa side dish has a creamy texture that resembles polenta. It is quite easy to make, but not lacking in flavor by any means.

Tips

Fresh herbs are much easier to handle if they're dry. After rinsing them, thoroughly pat them dry with a paper towel. If you're handling a large amount, use a salad spinner to dry them.

If you're planning to hold the quinoa on the Keep Warm cycle, wait until just before serving to stir in the Parmesan and herbs.

For information about rice cooker sizes, see page 13.

• Medium rice cooker; fuzzy logic or on/off

1 cup	quinoa, rinsed and drained	250 mL
	Salt	
2 cups	chicken or vegetable broth	500 mL
¼ cup	freshly grated Parmesan cheese	60 mL
2 tbsp	chopped mixed fresh herbs (such as thyme, parsley and rosemary)	30 mL
1 tbsp	butter	15 mL
	Freshly ground black pepper	
	Finely chopped fresh parsley	

1. In the rice cooker bowl, combine quinoa, $\frac{1}{2}$ tsp (2 mL) salt and broth. Set the rice cooker for the Regular or Brown Rice cycle.

2. When the machine switches to the Keep Warm cycle, stir in Parmesan, herbs and butter. Close the lid and let stand for 10 minutes. Serve immediately or hold on the Keep Warm cycle for up to 1 hour (see tip, at left). Stir again before serving. Season to taste with salt and pepper. Serve immediately, garnished with parsley.

Variation

Substitute toasted millet (see tip, page 291) for the quinoa.

Quinoa Creamed Spinach

Makes 3 to 4 servings

This creamy dish is a great way to sneak vegetables into your kids' diet — plus, you get protein from the quinoa.

Tips

Quinoa flakes can be found in natural food and specialty food stores, usually near the dried cereals. You can also purchase them online.

To blanch fresh corn kernels, bring a small saucepan of water to a boil over high heat. Add corn and boil for 1 to 2 minutes or until tender-crisp. Using a slotted spoon, transfer corn to a bowl of ice water and let cool completely. Drain.

Freshly grated nutmeg is more aromatic than pre-ground and adds a wonderful depth of flavor to this dish. To grate fresh nutmeg, scrape it against the finest holes of a box grater or use a rasp grater, such as a Microplane.

• Medium rice cooker; fuzzy logic or on/off

2 tbsp	extra virgin olive oil	30 mL
2	cloves garlic, minced	2
1 cup	quinoa flakes (see tip, at left)	250 mL
1/2 tsp	salt	2 mL
3 cups	chicken or vegetable broth	750 mL
1 1/2 cups	packed baby spinach, coarsely chopped	375 mL
3/4 cup	blanched fresh or thawed frozen sweet corn kernels (see tip, at left)	175 mL
1 tbsp	butter	15 mL
1/4 tsp	grated nutmeg (see tip, at left)	1 mL

1. Set the rice cooker for the Quick Cook, Regular or Brown Rice cycle. When the bottom of the bowl gets hot, add oil and swirl to coat. Sauté garlic for about 1 minute or until fragrant.
2. Stir in quinoa, salt and broth. Close the lid and reset for the Regular or Brown Rice cycle.
3. When the machine switches to the Keep Warm cycle, stir in spinach, corn and butter. Close the lid and let stand for 10 minutes. Serve immediately, sprinkled with nutmeg.

Wheat Berries with Wild Mushrooms

Makes 4 to 6 servings

This healthy yet flavorful side dish goes well with roasted fish. It incorporates a complementary blend of spices, and the wheat berries provide fiber.

Tips

If fresh herbs aren't available, you can use dried; simply double the amount.

Tamari is made with more soybeans than soy sauce, resulting in a smoother, more balanced, more complex flavor. It is available at well-stocked grocery stores and Asian markets.

If you're planning to hold the wheat berries on the Keep Warm cycle, wait until just before serving to stir in the herbs and lemon zest.

● **Medium to large rice cooker; fuzzy logic or on/off**

1 tbsp	extra virgin olive oil	15 mL
1 tbsp	butter	15 mL
1	clove garlic, minced	1
½ cup	finely chopped onion	125 mL
1 cup	mixed mushrooms (such as shiitake and cremini), sliced	250 mL
¼ cup	red wine	60 mL
1 cup	wheat berries, rinsed and drained	250 mL
3 cups	chicken or vegetable broth	750 mL
2 tbsp	tamari (see tip, at left)	30 mL
1 tsp	finely chopped fresh thyme	5 mL
1 tsp	finely chopped fresh rosemary	5 mL
1 tsp	finely grated lemon zest	5 mL
	Salt and freshly ground black pepper	
	Finely chopped fresh parsley	

1. Set the rice cooker for the Quick Cook, Regular or Brown Rice cycle. When the bottom of the bowl gets hot, add oil and butter and let butter melt. Sauté garlic and onion for about 3 minutes or until onion is softened and translucent. Add mushrooms and sauté for about 2 minutes or until softened. Stir in wine and cook for 3 to 4 minutes or until evaporated.
2. Stir in wheat berries, broth and tamari. Close the lid and reset for the Regular or Brown Rice cycle.
3. When the machine switches to the Keep Warm cycle, stir in thyme, rosemary and lemon zest. Close the lid and let stand for 10 minutes. Season to taste with salt and pepper. Serve immediately or hold on the Keep Warm cycle for up to 1 hour (see tip, at left). Serve garnished with parsley.

Old-Fashioned Grits

Makes 3 to 4 servings

My friends from the South say grits is the ultimate comfort food. After trying this classic, down-home recipe with a hint of thyme, you'll be a believer too — wherever you're from.

Tips

Stone-ground grits are readily available in the southern United States, but are not easy to find elsewhere. Old Mill is a great source that delivers right to your door.

If you want to remove the grit husks, combine grits with some cold water in a bowl. The husks will rise to the top and can be skimmed off. Drain grits before cooking.

If using a fuzzy logic machine, you may wish to run the Porridge cycle a second time for extra-creamy grits — but my Southern friends raved about this recipe when I used just one cycle.

- **Medium rice cooker; fuzzy logic (preferred) or on/off**

1 cup	coarse stone-ground grits (see tips, at left)	250 mL
½ tsp	salt	2 mL
3 cups	water	750 mL
¼ tsp	freshly ground black pepper	1 mL
2 tbsp	butter	30 mL
	Fresh thyme sprigs	

1. In the rice cooker bowl, combine grits, salt and water, stirring thoroughly with a wooden spoon or plastic paddle. Set the rice cooker for the Porridge or Regular cycle. Stir thoroughly two or three times while the grits are cooking.

2. When the machine switches to the Keep Warm cycle, stir in pepper and butter. Close the lid and let stand for 10 minutes, then stir thoroughly. Serve immediately or hold on the Keep Warm cycle for up to 1 hour. Serve garnished with thyme sprigs.

Variation

For creamy-style grits, replace half the water with milk (fuzzy logic machines only).

Traditional Grits with Gruyère

Makes 3 to 4 servings

Here's a scrumptiously inventive way to dress up a basic dish. The slightly salty, nutty flavor of the Gruyère is an elegant embellishment.

Tips

If you don't have Gruyère on hand, you can use any other cheese, such as Cheddar or Havarti.

For information about rice cooker sizes, see page 13.

- **Medium rice cooker; fuzzy logic (preferred) or on/off**

1 cup	coarse stone-ground grits (see tips, page 295)	250 mL
½ tsp	salt	2 mL
3 cups	water	750 mL
1 cup	shredded Gruyère cheese	250 mL
¼ tsp	freshly ground black pepper	1 mL
2 tbsp	butter	30 mL

1. In the rice cooker bowl, combine grits, salt and water, stirring thoroughly with a wooden spoon or plastic paddle. Set the rice cooker for the Porridge or Regular cycle. Stir thoroughly two or three times while the grits are cooking.

2. When the machine switches to the Keep Warm cycle, stir in cheese, pepper and butter. Close the lid and let stand for 10 minutes, then stir thoroughly. Serve immediately or hold on the Keep Warm cycle for up to 1 hour.

Creamy Grits with Butternut Squash and Goat Cheese

Makes 3 to 4 servings

Goat cheese and butternut squash lend a certain elegance to this traditional Southern dish, resulting in a plate of creamy, scrumptious goodness!

Tips

Feel free to substitute pumpkin or any other winter squash for the butternut squash.

This recipe is for fuzzy logic machines only because of the milk content. Milk tends to boil over in on/off machines, resulting in a huge mess.

You may wish to run the Porridge cycle a second time for extra-creamy grits — but my Southern friends raved about this recipe when I used just one cycle.

- **Medium rice cooker; fuzzy logic only**

1 cup	coarse stone-ground grits (see tips, page 295)	250 mL
1 tsp	salt	5 mL
1½ cups	water	375 mL
1½ cups	milk	375 mL
1 cup	diced butternut squash	250 mL
1 cup	crumbled goat cheese	250 mL
¼ tsp	freshly ground black pepper	1 mL
2 tbsp	butter	30 mL

1. In the rice cooker bowl, combine grits, salt, water and milk, stirring thoroughly with a wooden spoon or plastic paddle. Stir in squash. Set the rice cooker for the Porridge cycle. Stir thoroughly two or three times while the grits are cooking.
2. When the machine switches to the Keep Warm cycle, stir in goat cheese, pepper and butter. Close the lid and let stand for 10 minutes, then stir thoroughly. Serve immediately or hold on the Keep Warm cycle for up to 1 hour.

Variation

Add 1 cup (250 mL) coarsely chopped toasted walnuts with the goat cheese.

Grits Carbonara

Makes 3 to 4 servings

Apple wood bacon contributes so much flavor to this fabulously rich and indulgent recipe, and the texture of the peas adds complexity.

Tips

Apple wood bacon is smoked over apple wood embers (wood made from various apple trees) and imparts a richer flavor than regular bacon. You can substitute regular bacon if you wish.

For a lighter version, use $\frac{1}{4}$ cup (60 mL) reduced-fat sour cream in place of the heavy cream.

• Medium rice cooker; fuzzy logic (preferred) or on/off

2	slices apple wood bacon (see tip, at left), chopped	2
1	clove garlic, minced	1
1 cup	coarse stone-ground grits (see tips, page 295)	250 mL
$\frac{1}{2}$ tsp	salt	2 mL
3 cups	water	750 mL
$\frac{1}{2}$ cup	freshly grated Parmesan cheese	125 mL
$\frac{1}{4}$ cup	fresh or thawed frozen peas	60 mL
$\frac{1}{4}$ tsp	freshly ground black pepper	1 mL
$\frac{1}{4}$ cup	heavy or whipping (35%) cream	60 mL
$\frac{1}{4}$ cup	butter	60 mL

1. Set the rice cooker for the Quick Cook or Regular cycle. When the bottom of the rice cooker bowl gets hot, cook bacon for about 4 minutes or until lightly browned.
2. Add garlic, grits, salt and water, stirring thoroughly with a wooden spoon or plastic paddle. Close the lid and reset for the Porridge or Regular cycle. Stir thoroughly two or three times while the grits are cooking.
3. When the machine switches to the Keep Warm cycle, stir in Parmesan, peas, pepper, cream and butter. Close the lid and let stand for 10 minutes, then stir thoroughly. Serve immediately.

Grits Jambalaya

Makes 3 to 4 servings

Celebrate the flavors of New Orleans with this feisty dish that marries two classics from the Old South. I love the creaminess of the stone-ground grits paired with the punch of cayenne pepper and Cajun andouille sausage.

Tips

Double this recipe and serve it as an entrée with some crusty French bread.

Increase the cayenne pepper in this recipe if you like it hot, hot, hot.

For information about rice cooker sizes, see page 13.

● **Medium rice cooker; fuzzy logic (preferred) or on/off**

2 tbsp	extra virgin olive oil	30 mL
2	cloves garlic, minced	2
1 cup	finely chopped onion	250 mL
4 oz	Cajun andouille sausage, cut into 1/4-inch (0.5 cm) thick slices	125 g
1 cup	finely chopped green bell pepper	250 mL
1	can (14 oz/398 mL) diced tomatoes, with juice	1
1 cup	coarse stone-ground grits (see tips, page 295)	250 mL
2 tsp	cayenne pepper	10 mL
1/2 tsp	salt	2 mL
1/4 tsp	dried thyme	1 mL
2 cups	beef or chicken broth	500 mL
8 or 9	medium shrimp, peeled and deveined	8 or 9

1. Set the rice cooker for the Quick Cook or Regular cycle. When the bottom of the bowl gets hot, add oil and swirl to coat. Sauté garlic and onion for about 3 minutes or until onion is softened and translucent. Add sausage and green pepper; sauté for 3 minutes.

2. Add tomatoes with juice, grits, cayenne, salt, thyme and broth, stirring thoroughly with a wooden spoon or plastic paddle. Close the lid and reset for the Porridge or Regular cycle. Stir thoroughly two or three times while the grits are cooking.

3. When the machine switches to the Keep Warm cycle, stir in shrimp. Close the lid and let stand for 15 minutes or until shrimp are pink and opaque. Stir thoroughly. Serve immediately.

Variation

Polenta Jambalaya: Substitute coarse-grain polenta for the grits and increase the broth to 4 cups (1 L).

Cheesy Grits with Shrimp

Makes 3 to 4 servings

This recipe is a classic example of coastal South Carolinian cuisine. You may think you don't like grits, but wait until you've tried this dish!

Tips

Use apple wood–smoked bacon for added flavor.

For information about rice cooker sizes, see page 13.

- **Medium rice cooker; fuzzy logic (preferred) or on/off**

1 cup	coarse stone-ground grits (see tips, page 295)	295 mL
	Salt	
3 cups	chicken broth	750 mL
4	slices bacon	4
1 cup	shredded Cheddar cheese	250 mL
	Freshly ground black pepper	
2 tbsp	butter	30 mL
1/2 cup	finely chopped onion	125 mL
1 lb	large shrimp, peeled and deveined	500 g
3	green onions (white and green parts), chopped	3
1	clove garlic, minced	1
2 tbsp	finely chopped red bell pepper	30 mL
1 tbsp	chopped fresh parsley	15 mL
2 tsp	freshly squeezed lemon juice	10 mL
1 tsp	Worcestershire sauce	5 mL

1. In the rice cooker bowl, combine grits, 1/2 tsp (2 mL) salt and broth, stirring thoroughly with a wooden spoon or plastic paddle. Set the rice cooker for the Porridge or Regular cycle. Stir thoroughly two or three times while the grits are cooking.

2. Meanwhile, in a large nonstick skillet, cook bacon over medium-high heat for about 3 minutes or until crispy. Transfer to a cutting board and coarsely chop. Set aside. Drain off all but 1 tbsp (15 mL) fat from skillet and set aside.

3. When the machine switches to the Keep Warm cycle, stir in bacon, cheese, 1/4 tsp (1 mL) pepper and butter. Close the lid and let stand for 10 minutes.

4. Meanwhile, heat bacon fat remaining in skillet over medium-high heat until sizzling. Sauté onion for about 3 minutes or until softened and translucent. Add shrimp, green onions, garlic, red pepper, parsley, lemon juice and Worcestershire sauce; sauté for about 2 minutes or until shrimp are pink and opaque. Season to taste with salt and pepper. Remove from heat.

5. Spoon hot grits onto individual serving plates and top with shrimp mixture. Serve immediately.

Quick and Easy Polenta

Makes 3 to 4 servings

The name of the recipe says it all: quick and easy! You can throw this tasty treat together in under 30 minutes from start to finish.

- **Medium rice cooker; fuzzy logic (preferred) or on/off**

1 cup	coarse-grain yellow polenta	250 mL
½ tsp	salt	2 mL
4 cups	chicken broth or water	1 L
1 tbsp	butter	15 mL

1. In the rice cooker bowl, combine polenta, salt and broth, stirring for 15 seconds with a wooden spoon or plastic paddle. Set the rice cooker for the Porridge or Regular cycle. Stir thoroughly two or three times while the polenta is cooking.
2. When the machine switches to the Keep Warm cycle, stir in butter. Close the lid and let stand for 10 minutes. Serve immediately or hold on the Keep Warm cycle for up to 1 hour. Stir thoroughly before serving.

Variation

Italian-Style Polenta: Add ½ cup (125 mL) freshly grated Parmesan cheese with the butter.

Sliced Polenta

Makes 3 to 4 servings

Polenta was, and still is, considered to be a peasant food, but has held its own in the field of gourmet cooking since the 20th century.

Tip

Make a double batch and freeze what you don't use. I freeze the slices in dinner-sized portions and simply defrost what I need in the microwave for a quick dinner solution.

- **8- by 4-inch (20 by 10 cm) loaf pan, lined with heavy-duty plastic wrap**

3 cups	hot Quick and Easy Polenta (see recipe, above)	750 mL

1. Spoon polenta into prepared loaf pan, spreading evenly, and let cool for 15 minutes. Cover and refrigerate for 2 hours or until very firm.
2. Turn polenta out onto a cutting board. Remove plastic and cut into ½-inch (1 cm) slices.

Variation

Use one of the other polenta recipes in this chapter (pages 302 to 307) to create flavored variations.

Grilled Polenta with Wild Mushroom Ragoût

Makes 3 to 4 servings

This elegant yet savory dish is great for entertaining, as it can be paired with red, white and even sparkling wines. It's bursting with rich flavors and has become a favorite in my home.

Tips

To make this rich and savory side dish truly vegetarian, substitute vegetable broth for the chicken broth.

For information about rice cooker sizes, see page 13.

- **Medium rice cooker; fuzzy logic (preferred) or on/off**
- **8- by 4-inch (20 by 10 cm) loaf pan, lined with heavy-duty plastic wrap**

Polenta

1 cup	coarse-grain yellow polenta	250 mL
½ tsp	salt	2 mL
4 cups	chicken broth	1 L
½ cup	freshly grated Parmesan cheese	125 mL
¼ tsp	freshly ground black pepper	1 mL
1 tbsp	butter	15 mL

Wild Mushroom Ragoût

2 tbsp	butter, divided	30 mL
1 tbsp	extra virgin olive oil	15 mL
1 cup	mixed mushrooms (such as shiitake, cremini, chanterelle and morel)	250 mL
½ tsp	salt	2 mL
½ cup	dry red wine	125 mL
¼ cup	chicken or vegetable broth	60 mL

1. *Polenta:* In the rice cooker bowl, combine polenta, salt and broth, stirring for 15 seconds with a wooden spoon or plastic paddle. Set the rice cooker for the Porridge or Regular cycle. Stir thoroughly two or three times while the polenta is cooking.
2. When the machine switches to the Keep Warm cycle, stir in Parmesan, pepper and butter.
3. Spoon polenta into prepared loaf pan, spreading evenly, and let cool for 15 minutes. Cover and refrigerate for 2 hours or until very firm.
4. Turn polenta out onto a cutting board. Remove plastic and cut into ½-inch (1 cm) slices. Set aside.

Unless your mushrooms are extremely dirty, you can simply wipe them with a damp paper towel to clean them. If you need to wash them, rinse them in a colander and wipe them dry with a paper towel. Never soak fresh mushrooms, as they'll absorb too much water.

5. *Ragoût:* In a large nonstick skillet, heat 1 tbsp (15 mL) butter and oil over medium heat. Sauté mushrooms and salt for 8 to 10 minutes or until mushrooms have released their liquid. Stir in wine and cook for about 5 minutes or until reduced to a glaze. Reduce heat to medium-low and stir in broth. Cook, stirring occasionally, for 8 to 10 minutes or until tender. Remove from heat and swirl in the remaining butter. Cover and set aside.

6. Spray barbecue grill with nonstick cooking spray and heat over medium-high heat. Grill polenta slices, turning once, for 4 to 5 minutes per side or until crisp and browned on both sides, with visible grill marks.

7. Place polenta slices on warmed serving plates and top with ragoût. Serve immediately.

Variation

Serve grilled polenta with tomato coulis instead of ragoût.

Polenta Primavera

Makes 3 to 4 servings

This dish is a great option for those following a gluten-free diet. The variety of vegetables adds superb flavor and texture.

Tips

Use whatever fresh vegetables you have on hand for this everyday recipe, keeping the total amount you cook in step 1 at 3 cups (750 mL).

To blanch fresh peas, bring a small saucepan of water to a boil over high heat. Add peas and boil for 1 minute or until bright green and tender-crisp. Using a slotted spoon, transfer peas to a bowl of ice water and let cool completely. Drain.

For a lighter version, use $\frac{1}{4}$ cup (60 mL) reduced-fat sour cream in place of the heavy cream.

● Medium rice cooker; fuzzy logic (preferred) or on/off

2 tbsp	extra virgin olive oil	30 mL
2	cloves garlic, minced	2
1 cup	finely chopped onion	250 mL
$\frac{3}{4}$ cup	julienned red bell pepper (see tip, page 326)	175 mL
$\frac{3}{4}$ cup	julienned zucchini	175 mL
$\frac{3}{4}$ cup	julienned yellow summer squash (yellow zucchini)	175 mL
$\frac{3}{4}$ cup	julienned carrots	175 mL
1 cup	coarse-grain yellow polenta	250 mL
$\frac{1}{2}$ tsp	salt	2 mL
$3\frac{3}{4}$ cups	chicken or vegetable broth	925 mL
15	cherry tomatoes, halved	15
1 cup	blanched fresh or thawed frozen peas (see tip, at left)	250 mL
$\frac{1}{2}$ cup	freshly grated Parmesan cheese	125 mL
$\frac{1}{4}$ cup	heavy or whipping (35%) cream	60 mL
	Freshly ground black pepper	

1. Set the rice cooker for the Quick Cook or Regular cycle. When the bottom of the bowl gets hot, add oil and swirl to coat. Sauté garlic and onion for about 3 minutes or until onion is softened and translucent. Add red pepper, zucchini, yellow squash and carrots; sauté for 3 minutes.
2. Add polenta, salt and broth, stirring for 15 seconds with a wooden spoon or plastic paddle. Close the lid and reset for the Porridge or Regular cycle. Stir thoroughly two or three times while the polenta is cooking.
3. When the machine switches to the Keep Warm cycle, stir in tomatoes, peas, Parmesan and cream. Season to taste with pepper. Stir thoroughly and serve immediately.

Kyla's Polenta with Sun-Dried Tomatoes

Makes 3 to 4 servings

The intensity of the sun-dried tomatoes meets the distinct flavor of goat cheese for a successful merger. Pair this dish with a seafood entrée — baked tilapia, perhaps. My step-daughter Kyla loved this dish so much she packed it in her lunch for school the next day.

Tip

Goat cheese is usually sold in vacuum packs at grocery stores. If you feel like splurging, look for more expensive, but higher-quality paper-wrapped goat cheese at gourmet and specialty shops. Goat cheese is best used at room temperature.

● **Medium rice cooker; fuzzy logic (preferred) or on/off**

1 cup	coarse-grain yellow polenta	250 mL
1 tsp	salt	5 mL
4 cups	chicken or vegetable broth	1 L
¾ cup	crumbled goat cheese	175 mL
⅓ cup	thinly sliced sun-dried tomatoes	75 mL
1 tbsp	finely chopped fresh basil	15 mL
1 tbsp	butter	15 mL
	Fresh basil leaves	

1. In the rice cooker bowl, combine polenta, salt and broth, stirring for 15 seconds with a wooden spoon or plastic paddle. Set the rice cooker for the Porridge or Regular cycle. Stir thoroughly two or three times while the polenta is cooking.
2. When the machine switches to the Keep Warm cycle, stir in goat cheese, sun-dried tomatoes, chopped basil and butter. Close the lid and let stand for 10 minutes. Serve immediately, garnished with basil leaves.

Variation

Add ¼ cup (60 mL) toasted pine nuts with the goat cheese.

Roasted Red Pepper Polenta

Makes 3 to 4 servings

Roasting bell peppers brings out their natural sweetness and intensifies their flavor. In this case, the roasted peppers add a delicious oomph to polenta.

Tips

To save time, you can buy roasted red peppers in a can or jar and use 1 cup (250 mL) drained. Roland makes a wonderful product.

If you're planning to hold the polenta on the Keep Warm cycle, wait until just before serving to stir in the cilantro.

For information about rice cooker sizes, see page 13.

- • **Preheat broiler**
- • **Blender or food processor**
- • **Medium rice cooker; fuzzy logic only**

2	red bell peppers, cut in half and seeded	2
2½ cups	chicken or vegetable broth, divided	625 mL
2 tbsp	butter	30 mL
2	cloves garlic, minced	2
1 cup	finely chopped onion	250 mL
1 cup	coarse-grain yellow polenta	250 mL
1 tsp	salt	5 mL
½ tsp	cayenne pepper	2 mL
2 cups	whole milk	500 mL
1 tbsp	finely chopped fresh cilantro	15 mL
1 tbsp	freshly squeezed lemon juice	15 mL
	Freshly ground black pepper	

1. Place peppers, skin side up, on a baking sheet. Broil for 7 to 10 minutes or until skins are blackened. Immediately transfer peppers to a paper bag; close bag and let stand for 15 to 20 minutes or until peppers are cool enough to handle. Peel off skins.
2. In blender, combine peppers and ½ cup (125 mL) broth; purée until smooth. Set aside.
3. Set the rice cooker for the Quick Cook cycle. When the bottom of the bowl gets hot, add butter and let it melt. Sauté garlic and onion for about 3 minutes or until onion is softened and translucent.
4. Add polenta, salt, cayenne, milk and the remaining broth, stirring for 15 seconds with a wooden spoon or plastic paddle. Close the lid and reset for the Porridge cycle. Stir thoroughly two or three times while the polenta is cooking.
5. When the machine switches to the Keep Warm cycle, stir in puréed peppers, cilantro and lemon juice. Close the lid and let stand for 10 minutes. Season to taste with black pepper. Serve immediately or hold on the Keep Warm cycle for up to 1 hour (see tip, at left). Stir thoroughly before serving.

Golden Corn and Saffron Polenta

Makes 3 to 4 servings

A touch of bitter and a touch of sweet proves to be an ideal match in this smooth and tasty polenta, best served with a good ol' Southern dish such as fried chicken.

Tips

To blanch fresh corn kernels, bring a small saucepan of water to a boil over high heat. Add corn and boil for 1 to 2 minutes or until tender-crisp. Using a slotted spoon, transfer corn to a bowl of ice water and let cool completely. Drain.

When you're stirring the polenta while it is cooking, add a bit more water or broth if it gets too stiff.

• **Medium rice cooker; fuzzy logic (preferred) or on/off**

½ tsp	crushed saffron threads	2 mL
¼ cup	hot water	60 mL
2 tbsp	extra virgin olive oil	30 mL
2	cloves garlic, minced	2
1 cup	finely chopped onion	250 mL
1 cup	coarse-grain yellow polenta	250 mL
1 tsp	salt	5 mL
3¾ cups	chicken or vegetable broth	925 mL
1½ cups	blanched fresh or thawed frozen corn kernels (see tip, at left)	375 mL
1 tbsp	butter	15 mL
	Freshly ground black pepper	

1. In a measuring cup or small bowl, combine saffron threads and hot water; set aside to steep.
2. Set the rice cooker for the Quick Cook or Regular cycle. When the bottom of the bowl gets hot, add oil and swirl to coat. Sauté garlic and onion for about 3 minutes or until onion is softened and translucent.
3. Add saffron-infused water, polenta, salt and broth, stirring for 15 seconds with a wooden spoon or plastic paddle. Close the lid and reset for the Porridge or Regular cycle. Stir thoroughly two or three times while the polenta is cooking.
4. When the machine switches to the Keep Warm cycle, stir in corn and butter. Close the lid and let stand for 10 minutes. Season to taste with pepper. Serve immediately or hold on the Keep Warm cycle for up to 1 hour. Stir thoroughly before serving.

Variations

Roasted Corn and Saffron Polenta: Preheat barbecue grill to medium for indirect heat. Place each of 3 corn cobs on a sheet of heavy-duty foil. Drizzle with 1 tbsp (15 mL) water and spread evenly with melted butter. Wrap very tightly, so the packages will not leak. Place over unlit side and grill for 45 minutes or until tender. Let cool, then cut off kernels. Add with the butter.

To add creaminess to this dish, add ¼ cup (60 mL) heavy or whipping (35%) cream with the corn.

Lentils and Barley with Caramelized Onions

Makes 6 to 8 servings

Lentils and caramelized onions are one of the better food pairings. This hearty side dish is both delicious and nutritious!

Tips

For the best flavor, toast whole cumin seeds in a skillet over medium-high heat, stirring constantly, for about 3 minutes or until fragrant. Immediately transfer to a spice grinder and let cool, then grind to a fine powder.

Try using red or green lentils, or a combination.

To achieve caramelized onions that melt in your mouth, you'll want to cut thin slices from the root end to the stem end.

To help brown the onions, you may add the sugar at the beginning of cooking in step 3.

● **Large rice cooker; fuzzy logic or on/off**

3 tbsp	extra virgin olive oil, divided	45 mL
1	onion, finely chopped	1
1 tsp	minced garlic	5 mL
1 tsp	ground cumin (see tip, at left)	5 mL
½ cup	dried brown lentils, sorted and rinsed	125 mL
½ cup	pearl barley	125 mL
¾ tsp	salt, divided	3 mL
2¼ cups	chicken or vegetable broth	550 mL
1	onion, thinly sliced (see tip, at left)	1
¼ tsp	granulated sugar	1 mL

1. Set the rice cooker for the Quick Cook or Regular cycle. When the bottom of the bowl gets hot, add 1 tbsp (15 mL) oil and swirl to coat. Sauté chopped onion and garlic for about 3 minutes or until onion is softened and translucent. Add cumin and sauté for 1 minute.

2. Stir in lentils, barley, ½ tsp (2 mL) of the salt and broth. Close the lid and reset for the Regular cycle. Set a timer for 45 minutes.

3. Meanwhile, in a medium nonstick skillet, heat the remaining oil over medium-high heat. Add sliced onion, stirring to coat with oil, and cook for 10 minutes. Sprinkle with sugar and the remaining salt. Transfer to a baking sheet covered with paper towels and blot liquid.

4. When the timer sounds, stir in caramelized onions. Close the lid and cook for 5 minutes. Check to make sure lentils and barley are tender. If necessary, continue cooking, checking for doneness every 5 minutes. Fluff barley with a wooden spoon or plastic paddle. Serve immediately or hold on the Keep Warm cycle for up to 1 hour.

Variation

Substitute wheat berries for the barley and increase the cooking time in step 2 to 1¼ hours.

Cuban Black Beans (*Frijoles Negros*)

Makes 8 servings

Cuban food is a fusion of African, Spanish and Caribbean cuisines. This traditional dish really zips with flavor and is a snap to prepare.

Tips

I recommend wearing rubber gloves when you're handling chile peppers; otherwise, the juices may burn your skin. And there's nothing worse than accidentally rubbing your eye after handling a chile pepper without gloves!

For information about rice cooker sizes, see page 13.

- **Large rice cooker; fuzzy logic or on/off**

2 cups	dried black beans	500 mL
4 tbsp	extra virgin olive oil, divided	60 mL
4	cloves garlic, mashed with 2 tsp (10 mL) salt	4
2 cups	finely chopped onions	500 mL
2	jalapeño peppers, seeded and minced	2
1 cup	finely chopped green bell pepper	250 mL
1	bay leaf	1
1 tsp	dried oregano	5 mL
1 tsp	ground cumin	5 mL
1/2 tsp	freshly ground black pepper	2 mL
8 cups	water	2 L
1/2 cup	dry white wine (preferably Spanish)	125 mL
2 tsp	granulated sugar	10 mL
1 tbsp	white vinegar	15 mL
	Salt	
	Finely chopped fresh cilantro and white onions	

1. Sort, rinse, soak and drain beans (see pages 32–33).
2. Set the rice cooker for the Quick Cook or Regular cycle. When the bottom of the bowl gets hot, add 2 tbsp (30 mL) oil and swirl to coat. Sauté garlic and onions for about 3 minutes or until softened and translucent.
3. Stir in soaked beans, jalapeños, green pepper, bay leaf, oregano, cumin, pepper, water and wine. Close the lid and reset for the Regular cycle. Set a timer for 1 1/2 hours.
4. When the timer sounds, stir in sugar and vinegar. Check to make sure beans are tender. If necessary, continue cooking, checking for doneness every 5 minutes. Season to taste with salt. Drizzle with the remaining oil. Serve immediately, garnished with cilantro and onions.

Variation

Add a 4-oz (125 g) smoked ham hock with the beans. When the timer sounds, transfer ham hock to a cutting board. Remove the meat from the bone and discard bone, fat and skin. Cut ham into 1/2-inch (1 cm) pieces and stir back in before serving.

Orange Chipotle Black Beans

Makes 4 to 6 servings

The fresh orange flavor combines with the warm, smoky flavor of the chipotle peppers for a happy balance. Feeling extra saucy? Enjoy this side dish with a Cointreau margarita.

Tip

Queso fresco is a traditional Mexican cheese that is a common ingredient in a wide range of dishes. It is often available at well-stocked grocery stores and Latin markets.

• Large rice cooker; fuzzy logic or on/off

1 cup	dried black beans	250 mL
2 tbsp	extra virgin olive oil	30 mL
2	cloves garlic, minced	2
1/2 cup	finely chopped onion	125 mL
1	jalapeño pepper, seeded and minced	1
1 tsp	ground cumin	5 mL
3 cups	water	750 mL
2 tbsp	finely grated orange zest	30 mL
1 tsp	minced seeded canned chipotle peppers in adobo sauce	5 mL
1/4 cup	freshly squeezed orange juice	60 mL
2 tbsp	finely chopped fresh cilantro	30 mL
2 tbsp	crumbled queso fresco	30 mL

1. Sort, rinse, soak and drain beans (see pages 32–33).
2. Set the rice cooker for the Quick Cook or Regular cycle. When the bottom of the bowl gets hot, add oil and swirl to coat. Sauté garlic and onion for about 3 minutes or until onion is softened and translucent.
3. Stir in soaked beans, jalapeño, cumin and water. Close the lid and reset for the Regular cycle. Set a timer for $1\frac{1}{4}$ hours.
4. When the timer sounds, stir in orange zest, chipotle peppers and orange juice. Set the timer for 10 minutes.
5. When the timer sounds, check to make sure beans are tender. If necessary, continue cooking, checking for doneness every 5 minutes. Serve immediately, garnished with cilantro and queso fresco.

Kale and Adzuki Beans

Makes 3 to 4 servings

Adzuki beans are small, reddish-brown beans with a strong nutty and sweet flavor. They are commonly used in the macrobiotic diet.

Tips

When served over rice, this recipe can be a stand-alone meal for two people.

For information about rice cooker sizes, see page 13.

• Medium to large rice cooker; fuzzy logic or on/off

1 cup	dried adzuki beans	250 mL
2 tbsp	extra virgin olive oil	30 mL
2	cloves garlic, minced	2
4 cups	packed kale, tough stems removed, roughly chopped	1 L
1 tsp	ground cumin	5 mL
1 tsp	coriander seeds, crushed	5 mL
3 cups	water	750 mL
3 tbsp	tamari	45 mL

1. Sort, rinse, soak and drain beans (see pages 32–33).
2. Set the rice cooker for the Quick Cook or Regular cycle. When the bottom of the bowl gets hot, add oil and swirl to coat. Cook garlic and kale, stirring occasionally, for 3 to 4 minutes or until kale is wilted.
3. Stir in soaked beans, cumin, coriander seeds, water and tamari. Close the lid and reset for the Regular cycle. Set a timer for 50 minutes.
4. When the timer sounds, check to make sure beans are tender. If necessary, continue cooking, checking for doneness every 5 minutes. Serve immediately or hold on the Keep Warm cycle for up to 1 hour.

Variation

For a sweeter, richer flavor, replace half the water with coconut milk.

Tuscan-Style White Beans

Makes 4 to 6 servings

The fundamental pillar of Tuscan cuisine is simplicity, and this dish is a perfect example. For an authentic Tuscan meal, enjoy these beans with steak Florentine and a glass of Chianti.

Tip

For information about rice cooker sizes, see page 13.

- **Medium to large rice cooker; fuzzy logic or on/off**

1 cup	dried white beans, such as cannellini (white kidney) or great Northern	250 mL
1 tbsp	finely chopped fresh sage	15 mL
3 cups	water	750 mL
3 tbsp	extra-virgin olive oil, divided	45 mL
1	clove garlic, minced	1
	Salt and freshly ground black pepper	

1. Sort, rinse, soak and drain beans (see pages 32–33).
2. In the rice cooker bowl, combine beans, sage, water and 2 tbsp (30 mL) oil. Set the rice cooker for the Regular cycle and set a timer for $1\frac{1}{4}$ hours.
3. When the timer sounds, check to make sure beans are tender. If necessary, continue cooking, checking for doneness every 5 minutes. Stir in garlic. Season to taste with salt and pepper. Drizzle with the remaining oil. Serve immediately or hold on the Keep Warm cycle for up to 1 hour.

Variation

For a heartier version, stir in 1 cup (250 mL) sliced Italian sausage after the beans have been cooking for 1 hour.

Steam Cuisine

Chicken Dumplings (*Jiaozi*)

Makes
24 dumplings

These crescent-shaped dumplings are popular to prepare during the Chinese New Year. The mild flavor of ground chicken lends to their broad appeal.

Tips

Chinese rice wine is also called Shaoxing, named after a famous wine-making city in China. It has typically been aged for more than 10 years and can be found in Asian markets. You may substitute dry sherry.

Dumpling wrappers can be found in the produce section of well-stocked grocery stores or at Asian markets. They may be labeled "pot sticker wrappers" or "gyoza wrappers." Shu mei wrappers will also do the trick. You can freeze leftover wrappers in a sealable food storage bag for up to 3 months. Let come to room temperature before using.

- **Medium to large rice cooker with a steamer basket; fuzzy logic or on/off**

Dumplings

1 cup	Chinese cabbage, cut into thin strips	250 mL
2½ tsp	salt, divided	12 mL
1 lb	lean ground chicken	500 g
1	clove garlic, minced	1
½ cup	finely chopped onion	125 mL
1 tsp	minced gingerroot	5 mL
1 tsp	cornstarch	5 mL
¼ tsp	freshly ground white pepper	1 mL
2	large egg whites, lightly beaten, divided	2
1 tbsp	Chinese rice wine (see tip, at left) or dry sherry	15 mL
1 tsp	toasted sesame oil	5 mL
24	dumpling wrappers (see tip, at left)	24
	Cabbage leaves or nonstick cooking spray	

Dipping Sauce

1 tsp	finely chopped green onion (white and green parts)	5 mL
3 tbsp	soy sauce	45 mL
1 tbsp	rice vinegar	15 mL

1. *Dumplings:* In a bowl, combine cabbage and 2 tsp (10 mL) of the salt; let stand for 5 minutes. Squeeze out excess moisture.
2. In a large bowl, combine cabbage, chicken, garlic, onion, ginger, cornstarch, the remaining salt, pepper, half the egg whites, rice wine and oil.
3. Place 1 tbsp (15 mL) chicken mixture in the center of a dumpling wrapper. Using a pastry brush, moisten the outside top half perimeter of the wrapper with egg white. Lift the edges of the circle and pinch 5 pleats up, creating a pouch that encases the mixture. Pinch the top together. Repeat with the remaining chicken mixture and wrappers, keeping the filled dumplings covered with plastic wrap as you work.
4. Place 4 cups (1 L) water in the rice cooker bowl and set the rice cooker for the Regular or Steam cycle.

Tip

To freeze dumplings before they're cooked, place them on a baking sheet lined with parchment paper and place in the freezer until frozen. Transfer frozen dumplings to a large freezer bag and freeze for up to 3 months. Thaw overnight in refrigerator before steaming.

5. Line the steamer basket with cabbage leaves or spray with cooking spray. Place as many dumplings in the basket as will fit without touching each other. When the water comes to a boil, place the basket in the rice cooker. Set a timer for 12 minutes.

6. *Sauce:* Meanwhile, in a small bowl, combine green onion, soy sauce and vinegar.

7. When the timer sounds, check to make sure wrappers are tender and dumplings have reached an internal temperature of 165°F (74°C). If necessary, continue cooking, checking for doneness every 2 to 3 minutes. Transfer dumplings to a serving platter. If necessary, replenish water in rice cooker bowl, bring to a boil and steam another batch of dumplings. Serve dumplings with dipping sauce.

Variation

Pan-Fried Dumplings: After steaming dumplings, in a skillet, heat 1 tbsp (15 mL) vegetable oil over medium-high heat. Pan-fry dumplings, in batches as necessary, until bottoms are golden brown.

Crab Dumplings (*Fen Guo*)

Makes
24 dumplings

Now you can make delicious dim sum in the comfort of your own kitchen! The sumptuousness of crabmeat makes many recipes better, and these Chinese appetizers are no exception. Slightly sweet and succulent, these dumplings are an utter delight.

Tip
To freeze dumplings before they're cooked, place them on a baking sheet lined with parchment paper and place in the freezer until frozen. Transfer frozen dumplings to a large freezer bag and freeze for up to 3 months. Thaw overnight in refrigerator before steaming.

- **Medium to large rice cooker with a steamer basket; fuzzy logic or on/off**

Dumplings
1 lb	cooked white crabmeat	500 g
½ cup	chopped fresh cilantro	125 mL
2 tsp	cornstarch	10 mL
1 tsp	granulated sugar	5 mL
½ tsp	salt	2 mL
¼ tsp	freshly ground white pepper	1 mL
2	large egg whites, lightly beaten, divided	2
1 tsp	toasted sesame oil	5 mL
24	dumpling wrappers (see tip, page 314)	24
	Cabbage leaves or nonstick cooking spray	

Dipping Sauce
1 tsp	finely chopped green onion	5 mL
2 tbsp	soy sauce	30 mL
2 tbsp	balsamic vinegar	30 mL

1. *Dumplings:* In a bowl, combine crab, cilantro, cornstarch, sugar, salt, pepper, half the egg whites and oil.
2. Place 1 tbsp (15 mL) crab mixture in the center of a dumpling wrapper. Using a pastry brush, moisten the outside top half perimeter of the wrapper with egg white. Fold the wrapper in half to create a half-moon shape and seal the edges. Repeat with the remaining crab mixture and wrappers, keeping the filled dumplings covered with plastic wrap as you work.
3. Place 4 cups (1 L) water in the rice cooker bowl and set the rice cooker for the Regular or Steam cycle.
4. Line the steamer basket with cabbage leaves or spray with cooking spray. Place as many dumplings in the basket as will fit without touching each other. When the water comes to a boil, place the basket in the rice cooker. Set a timer for 12 minutes.
5. *Sauce:* Meanwhile, in a small bowl, combine green onion, soy sauce and vinegar.
6. When the timer sounds, check to make sure wrappers are tender and dumplings are hot in the center. If necessary, continue cooking, checking for doneness every 2 to 3 minutes. Transfer dumplings to a serving platter. If necessary, replenish water in rice cooker bowl, bring to a boil and steam another batch of dumplings. Serve dumplings with dipping sauce.

Spareribs with Black Beans

Makes about 12 spareribs

Blending the flavors of black beans, garlic and spareribs creates a mouth-watering combination. Mashing the beans is the hardest part of this delish dim sum dish.

Tips

You may replace the black beans with 2 tbsp (30 mL) black bean sauce, available at Asian markets and many grocery stores, and skip step 1.

For information about rice cooker sizes, see page 13.

For information about rice cooker sizes, see page 13.

● **Medium to large rice cooker with a steamer basket; fuzzy logic or on/off**

1 tbsp	fermented black beans	15 mL
	Warm water	
1 lb	pork spareribs (rib tips), fat and membranes removed, cut crosswise into 1- to 2-inch (2.5 to 5 cm) sections	500 g
½ tsp	minced gingerroot	2 mL
½ tsp	minced garlic	2 mL
1½ tsp	cornstarch	7 mL
½ tsp	salt	2 mL
⅛ tsp	freshly ground white pepper	0.5 mL
1 tbsp	vegetable oil	15 mL
2 tsp	soy sauce	10 mL
¼ tsp	toasted sesame oil	1 mL

1. Soak beans in warm water for 15 minutes; drain. Rinse beans with cold water to remove skins. Drain and transfer to a medium bowl. Mash beans.
2. Add spareribs, ginger, garlic, cornstarch, salt, pepper, vegetable oil, soy sauce and sesame oil to beans in bowl and toss to combine. Cover and refrigerate for 1 hour.
3. Transfer half the ribs and marinade onto a heatproof plate that will fit in your steamer basket. Place the plate in the basket. Cover and refrigerate the remaining ribs and marinade.
4. Place 4 cups (1 L) water in the rice cooker bowl and set the rice cooker for the Regular or Steam cycle. When the water comes to a boil, place the steamer basket in the rice cooker. Set a timer for 30 minutes.
5. When the timer sounds, check to make sure meat is fork-tender. If necessary, continue cooking, checking for doneness every 5 minutes. Transfer spareribs to a serving platter and serve warm. Replenish water in rice cooker bowl, bring to a boil, place the basket in the rice cooker and steam the remaining ribs and marinade. Serve warm.

Pork and Shrimp Shu Mei

Makes
18 shu mei

This is my mother, Leeann's, famous recipe. Adding shrimp to the traditional pork dumpling creates a brilliant gem of Chinese cuisine.

Tip

Shu mei wrappers are thinner than pot sticker or gyoza wrappers, although these wrappers are an acceptable substitute. You may also substitute square wonton wrappers, but you will need to cut off the square edges to create a round shape for shu mei.

• **Medium to large rice cooker with a steamer basket; fuzzy logic or on/off**

Dumplings

4	dried black mushrooms	4
	Hot water	
2 cups	warm water	500 mL
1½ tsp	salt, divided	7 mL
8 oz	medium shrimp, peeled and deveined	250 g
¼ cup	finely chopped onion	60 mL
2 tbsp	finely chopped carrot	30 mL
1 tsp	minced gingerroot	5 mL
1 tbsp	cornstarch	15 mL
⅛ tsp	freshly ground white pepper	0.5 mL
1	large egg white, lightly beaten	1
2 tsp	vegetable oil	10 mL
½ tsp	sesame oil	2 mL
8 oz	lean ground pork	250 g
18	shu mei wrappers (see tip, at left)	18
	Cabbage leaves or nonstick cooking spray	

Dipping Sauce

1 tsp	finely chopped green onion (white and green parts)	5 mL
½ tsp	granulated sugar	2 mL
3 tbsp	soy sauce	45 mL
1 tbsp	water	15 mL

1. *Dumplings:* Place mushrooms in a bowl and cover with hot water; let soak for 15 to 20 minutes or until soft. Rinse with cold water and drain. Squeeze out any excess water. Remove and discard stems and cut mushrooms into ¼-inch (0.5 cm) pieces.

2. In a large bowl, combine warm water and 1 tsp (5 mL) of the salt, stirring to dissolve salt. Add shrimp and swirl; let stand for 5 minutes. Drain. Rinse with cold water, drain and pat dry with paper towels. Cut shrimp into ¼-inch (0.5 cm) dice.

3. In another large bowl, combine onion, carrot, ginger, cornstarch, the remaining salt, pepper, egg white, vegetable oil and sesame oil. Add mushrooms, shrimp and pork, mixing well.

4. Place 1 tbsp (15 mL) pork mixture in the center of a shu mei wrapper and bring the edges up around the filling, forming small pleats and leaving the top open. Repeat with the remaining pork mixture and wrappers, keeping the filled dumplings covered with plastic wrap as you work.

5. Place 4 cups (1 L) water in the rice cooker bowl and set the rice cooker for the Regular or Steam cycle.

6. Line the steamer basket with cabbage leaves or spray with cooking spray. Place as many shu mei in the basket as will fit without touching each other. When the water comes to a boil, place the basket in the rice cooker. Set a timer for 12 minutes.

7. *Sauce:* Meanwhile, in a small bowl, combine green onion, sugar, soy sauce and water.

8. When the timer sounds, check to make sure wrappers are tender and dumplings have reached an internal temperature of 160°F (71°C). If necessary, continue cooking, checking for doneness every 3 minutes. Transfer shu mei to a serving platter. If necessary, replenish water in rice cooker bowl, bring to a boil and steam another batch of shu mei. Serve shu mei with dipping sauce.

Variation

Chicken and Shrimp Shu Mei: Substitute ground chicken for the pork.

Thousand Corner Shrimp Balls

Makes 28 to 30 balls

A popular Chinese New Year finger food, these shrimp balls are relatively easy to make and even easier to eat. Shrimp is served at many Chinese celebrations, as the word for "shrimp" in Chinese is *har*, which sounds like laughter. The rice coating on these shrimp balls resembles tiny corners — hence the name. If you're looking for a unique appetizer to serve at your next gathering, try these!

Tips

Chinese rice wine is also called Shaoxing, named after a famous wine-making city in China. It has typically been aged for more than 10 years and can be found in Asian markets. You may substitute dry sherry.

For information about rice cooker sizes, see page 13.

- **Medium to large rice cooker with a steamer basket; fuzzy logic or on/off**

Shrimp Balls

2 cups	warm water	500 mL
1½ tsp	salt, divided	7 mL
1 lb	small shrimp, peeled and deveined	500 g
6	canned water chestnuts, drained and minced	6
1	green onion (white part only), finely chopped	1
½ tsp	minced gingerroot	2 mL
3 tbsp	cornstarch	45 mL
½ tsp	granulated sugar	2 mL
Pinch	freshly ground white pepper	Pinch
1	large egg white, lightly beaten	1
3 tbsp	water	45 mL
1 tbsp	Chinese rice wine (see tip, at left) or dry sherry	15 mL
1 tbsp	vegetable oil	15 mL
2 tsp	toasted sesame oil	10 mL
¾ cup	glutinous white rice, soaked overnight, rinsed and drained	175 mL
	Cabbage leaves or nonstick cooking spray	

Dipping Sauce

1 cup	soy sauce	250 mL
1 tsp	toasted sesame oil	5 mL
	Chopped green onions (green part only)	

1. *Shrimp Balls:* In a large bowl, combine warm water and 1 tsp (5 mL) of the salt, stirring to dissolve salt. Add shrimp and swirl; let stand for 5 minutes. Drain. Rinse with cold water, drain and pat dry with paper towels. Finely chop shrimp.

2. In another large bowl, combine shrimp, water chestnuts, green onion, ginger, cornstarch, sugar, the remaining salt, pepper, egg white, water, rice wine, vegetable oil and sesame oil.

3. Spread rice out on a baking sheet. Form a spoonful of shrimp mixture into a 1½-inch (4 cm) ball. Roll lightly over rice. Repeat with the remaining shrimp mixture.

4. Place 4 cups (1 L) water in the rice cooker bowl and set the rice cooker for the Regular or Steam cycle.

Tips

You can make the filling for the balls a day in advance. Cover and refrigerate until ready to proceed with step 3.

Any leftover balls are wonderful when dropped into hot chicken broth. Add some snow peas and cilantro for a quick lunch.

5. Line the steamer basket with cabbage leaves or spray with cooking spray. Place as many shrimp balls in the basket as will fit without touching each other. When the water comes to a boil, place the basket in the rice cooker. Set a timer for 25 minutes.

6. *Sauce:* Meanwhile, in a small bowl, combine soy sauce and oil. Sprinkle green onions on top.

7. When the timer sounds, check to make sure rice is tender and shrimp balls are hot in the center. If necessary, continue cooking, checking for doneness every 5 minutes. Transfer shrimp balls to a serving platter. If necessary, replenish water in rice cooker bowl, bring to a boil and steam another batch of shrimp balls. Serve shrimp balls with dipping sauce.

Variation

Thousand Corner Fish Balls: Substitute 1 lb (500 g) minced fish fillet (such as rock fish) for the shrimp.

Char Siu Bao

Makes 20 bao

Char siu bao is a savory grab-and-go item popular in Cantonese cuisine. *Char siu* means "pork filling" and *bao* means "bun," so as you'd expect, tender, barbecued pork is enveloped in a soft, doughy encasement, then steamed to perfection.

Tip

The temperature of the water must be accurate — if it's too cool, it won't activate the yeast; if it's too hot, it will kill the yeast. Fill a liquid measuring cup to the 1/4 cup (60 mL) line with hot tap water and test the temperature with a kitchen thermometer. If necessary, adjust the temperature of the water until it is between 105°F and 115°F (40°C and 46°C). Add 2 tbsp (30 mL) of the water to the yeast.

- **Medium to large rice cooker with a steamer basket; fuzzy logic or on/off**
- **Twenty 2-inch (5 cm) squares of waxed paper**

Dough

1 cup	milk	250 mL
1/4 cup	granulated sugar	60 mL
1/4 tsp	salt	1 mL
1 tbsp	shortening	15 mL
1	package (1/4 oz/7 g) active dry yeast	1
2 tbsp	warm water (105°F to 115°F/40°C to 46°C)	30 mL
1	large egg white, lightly beaten	1
3 cups	all-purpose flour, plus more for kneading	750 mL

Filling

3 tbsp	vegetable oil	45 mL
2 cups	chopped barbecued pork (see tip, opposite)	500 mL
1/2 cup	chicken broth	125 mL
2 tbsp	oyster sauce	30 mL
1 tbsp	cornstarch	15 mL
1 tbsp	cold water	15 mL

1. *Dough:* In a small saucepan, scald milk over medium heat just until bubbles form around the edge and milk is steaming. Remove from heat; stir in sugar, salt and shortening until shortening is melted. Let cool to lukewarm.

2. Dissolve yeast in warm water. Stir into milk mixture, along with egg white.

3. Place flour in a large bowl. Stir in milk mixture until smooth. Stir in enough additional flour to make dough easy to handle.

4. Turn dough out onto a lightly floured surface and knead for about 4 minutes or until smooth and elastic. Place in a greased bowl and turn dough greased side up. Cover and let rise in a warm, draft-free place for 1 1/2 to 2 hours or until an indentation remains when dough is touched.

5. *Filling:* When dough is ready, heat a wok or large nonstick skillet over medium-high heat until 1 or 2 drops of water bubble and skitter when sprinkled in wok. Add oil and swirl to coat. Stir-fry pork for 30 seconds. Stir in broth and oyster sauce; bring to a boil. Combine cornstarch and cold water. Stir into pork mixture and cook, stirring, for about 10 seconds or until thickened.

Tip

It's easiest to buy barbecued pork from your nearest Chinese restaurant. If you wish to make it yourself, cut 1 lb (500 g) pork tenderloin into 1-inch (2.5 cm) slices. In a large bowl, combine $\frac{1}{2}$ clove garlic, minced, 2 tsp (10 mL) granulated sugar, $\frac{1}{2}$ tsp (2 mL) salt, $\frac{1}{3}$ cup (75 mL) ketchup, $1\frac{1}{2}$ tbsp (22 mL) hoisin sauce and $1\frac{1}{2}$ tsp (7 mL) dry sherry. Add pork, tossing to coat. Cover and refrigerate for 2 hours. Remove pork from marinade, reserving marinade, and place pork in a shallow roasting pan. Bake in a 300°F (150°C) oven for 15 minutes. Brush with reserved marinade and bake for 15 minutes or until just a hint of pink remains inside pork. Discard any remaining marinade.

6. Punch down dough and divide into 20 pieces. Place each piece on a lightly floured surface, flatten with the palm of your hand and press out into a 2-inch (5 cm) round. Place 1 tbsp (15 mL) filling in the center of a round. Gather dough up around the filling by pleating along the edges. Bring the pleats up and twist securely and firmly. Repeat with the remaining dough rounds and filling.

7. Place each filled bun on a square of waxed paper. Cover with a clean towel. Let rise in a warm, draft-free place for 1 hour or until dough springs back when touched with a finger. Remove towel.

8. Place 4 cups (1 L) water in the rice cooker bowl and set for the Regular or Steam cycle. Place as many buns (still on the waxed paper) in the steamer basket as will fit without touching each other. When the water comes to a boil, place the basket in the rice cooker. Set a timer for 10 minutes.

9. When the timer sounds, check to make sure dough is fluffy and filling is hot. If necessary, continue cooking, checking for doneness every 3 minutes. Transfer buns to a serving platter. If necessary, replenish water in rice cooker bowl, bring to a boil and steam another batch of buns.

Salmon with Ginger and Green Onions

Makes 4 to 6 servings

This is a simple, elegant dish with subtle notes of ginger and soy. It always garners rave reviews from my dinner guests, and I love making it when I am entertaining on a weekday, as it's so easy yet makes everyone feel special.

Tips

For a unique presentation, try cutting the salmon into strips and braiding them before spreading with the ginger mixture.

For information about rice cooker sizes, see page 13.

- **Medium to large rice cooker with a steamer basket; fuzzy logic or on/off**

1 tbsp	minced gingerroot, divided	15 mL
1 tsp	minced garlic	5 mL
1/2 tsp	granulated sugar	2 mL
1/2 tsp	salt	2 mL
1/4 tsp	freshly ground white pepper	1 mL
5 tbsp	vegetable oil, divided	75 mL
2 to 3 lb	skinless salmon fillet, cut into 4 to 6 pieces	1 to 1.5 kg
2 tsp	cornstarch	10 mL
2 tbsp	soy sauce	30 mL
1/2 cup	finely chopped green onions (white and green parts)	125 mL

1. In a small bowl, combine 2 tsp (10 mL) of the ginger, garlic, sugar, salt, pepper and 1 tbsp (15 mL) of the oil.
2. Rinse salmon and pat dry with paper towels. Place salmon on a heatproof plate that will fit in your steamer basket. Spread ginger mixture over top of fish and sprinkle with cornstarch. Cover and refrigerate for 30 minutes. Place plate in the steamer basket.
3. Place 4 cups (1 L) water in the rice cooker bowl and set the rice cooker for the Regular or Steam cycle. When the water comes to a boil, place the steamer basket in the rice cooker. Set a timer for 10 minutes.
4. Meanwhile, in a small saucepan, heat the remaining oil over medium-high heat. Sauté the remaining ginger until sizzling.
5. When the timer sounds, check to make sure salmon is opaque and flakes easily when tested with a fork. If necessary, continue cooking, checking for doneness every 3 minutes. Transfer salmon to a serving platter. Drizzle hot ginger oil and soy sauce over fish. Serve immediately, garnished with green onions.

Variation

Substitute orange roughy for the salmon.

Whole Fish with Garlic and Black Beans

Makes 4 servings

This recipe follows a very basic preparation to produce not-so-basic results. The mild flavor of the fish is accented by the garlicky black beans, making it easy to savor every flaky forkful.

Tips

You may replace the black beans with 2 tbsp (30 mL) black bean sauce, available at Asian markets and many grocery stores, and skip step 1.

Try using this black bean marinade on fish fillets or even chicken breasts.

• **Medium to large rice cooker with a steamer basket; fuzzy logic or on/off**

2 tbsp	fermented black beans	30 mL
2	cloves garlic, minced	2
2 tsp	minced gingerroot	10 mL
2 tsp	salt	10 mL
1/4 cup	vegetable oil	60 mL
2 tsp	soy sauce	10 mL
1/2 tsp	toasted sesame oil	2 mL
2 to 3 lb	whole sea bass or red snapper	1 to 1.5 kg
2	green onions (white and green parts), cut into 2-inch (5 cm) pieces and finely shredded lengthwise	2

1. Soak beans in warm water for 15 minutes. Rinse beans with cold water to remove skins. Drain and transfer to a small bowl. Mash beans.
2. Add garlic, ginger, salt, vegetable oil, soy sauce and sesame oil to beans and stir to combine.
3. Rinse sea bass and pat dry with paper towels. Place fish on a heatproof plate that will fit in your steamer basket and make 3 crosswise slashes on each side. Rub the cavity and outside of the fish with bean mixture. Cover and refrigerate for 40 minutes. Place plate in the steamer basket, curling fish slightly to fit, if necessary.
4. Place 4 cups (1 L) water in the rice cooker bowl and set the rice cooker for the Regular or Steam cycle. When the water comes to a boil, place the steamer basket in the rice cooker. Set a timer for 20 minutes.
5. When the timer sounds, check to make sure fish is opaque and flakes easily when tested with a fork. If necessary, continue cooking, checking for doneness every 3 minutes. Serve immediately, garnished with green onions.

Sea Bass Bibimbap

Makes 4 servings

Bibimbap is a popular Korean dish that, literally translated, means "mixed meal." At the table, pass sesame oil, rice vinegar, Korean red pepper paste and kimchi for guests to enjoy with the bibimbap.

Tips

"Julienne" is a culinary term for a preparation in which food is cut into long, thin strips similar to matchsticks.

For information about rice cooker sizes, see page 13.

● **Medium to large rice cooker with a steamer basket; fuzzy logic or on/off**

1 cup	Japanese-style medium-grain japonica rice (such as Calrose)	250 mL
8 oz	skinless sea bass fillet	250 g
	Salt and freshly ground black pepper	
1⅓ cups	water	325 mL
	Cabbage leaves or nonstick cooking spray	
1 cup	packed spinach, trimmed	250 mL
2 tbsp	vegetable oil	30 mL
4	fresh shiitake mushrooms, thinly sliced	4
1	zucchini, julienned (see tip, at left)	1
1	carrot, julienned	1
1 cup	bean sprouts	250 mL
	Sesame seeds	
2 tsp	toasted sesame oil, divided	10 mL
2	large eggs	2
1 tsp	rice vinegar	5 mL
1 tsp	Korean red pepper paste (*kochujang*) or hot Asian chili sauce (such as sambal oelek)	5 mL
	Finely chopped green onions	

1. Place rice in a bowl and add enough cool water to cover by 1 inch (2.5 cm); let soak for 30 minutes. Rinse and drain (see page 20).

2. Rinse sea bass and pat dry with paper towels. Sprinkle evenly with salt and pepper.

3. In the rice cooker bowl, combine soaked rice, 1 tsp (5 mL) salt and water. Line the steamer basket with cabbage leaves or spray with cooking spray. Place sea bass on one side of the basket. Place the basket in the rice cooker. Set the rice cooker for the Regular cycle and set a timer for 12 minutes.

4. When the timer sounds, place spinach next to the sea bass. Let the cycle complete.

5. Meanwhile, in a nonstick skillet, heat vegetable oil over medium-high heat. Sauté mushrooms, zucchini, carrot and ½ tsp (2 mL) salt for 4 minutes. Transfer to a plate and set aside.

6. In a small bowl, combine bean sprouts, ½ tsp (2 mL) salt, a pinch of sesame seeds and 1 tsp (5 mL) of the sesame oil. Set aside.

Unless your mushrooms are extremely dirty, you can simply wipe them with a damp paper towel to clean them. If you need to wash them, rinse them in a colander and wipe them dry with a paper towel. Never soak fresh mushrooms, as they'll absorb too much water.

7. When the machine switches to the Keep Warm cycle, check to make sure rice is tender and fish is opaque and flakes easily when tested with a fork. If necessary, continue cooking, checking for doneness every 3 minutes. Remove the steamer basket. Break eggs gently on top of rice, so they're lying side by side. Close the lid, reset for the Regular cycle and set a timer for 4 minutes.

8. Meanwhile, wring spinach in a kitchen towel to remove excess moisture. Slice into thin strips. In a small bowl, toss spinach with a pinch of sesame seeds, the remaining sesame oil and vinegar.

9. Flake sea bass into medium flakes and transfer to a bowl.

10. When the timer sounds, switch to the Keep Warm cycle. Arrange spinach mixture and sea bass on one side of the eggs. Close the lid and let stand for about 10 minutes or until egg whites are opaque (yolks should be runny).

11. Bring the rice cooker bowl to the table and place 1 tsp (5 mL) red pepper paste on top of the eggs. Add sautéed vegetables and bean sprout mixture. Sprinkle sesame seeds and green onions on top. After your dinner guests have admired the presentation, stir to combine and scoop rice, fish and spinach into serving bowls.

Variation

Vegetarian Bibimbap: Drain a 16-oz (454 g) package of water-packed firm tofu and cut into 4 to 6 slices. Substitute for the fish.

Coconut Fish Steamed in Banana Leaves

Makes 4 servings

This tender, exotic dish is an impressive culinary gem. It boasts the typical characteristics of Thai cuisine: sweetness, sourness, creaminess and an infusion of heat, thanks to the Thai chile.

Tips

Banana leaves are available at Asian markets. If you use frozen banana leaves, thaw them for at least 30 minutes before using.

If you can't find banana leaves, you may substitute sheets of parchment paper or foil.

Lime leaves are available at Asian markets. If you can't find them, substitute 1 tsp (5 mL) finely grated lime zest.

Instead of discarding the remaining marinade in step 5, pour it into a small saucepan and bring to a boil over high heat. Reduce heat and simmer for 12 minutes. Serve sauce in a gravy boat for guests to drizzle over their fish.

- **Food processor or blender**
- **Medium to large rice cooker with a steamer basket; fuzzy logic or on/off**
- **4 toothpicks**

1 lb	skinless red snapper or cod fillets, cut into 2-inch (5 cm) pieces	500 g
	Salt and freshly ground black pepper	
8	banana leaves (see tips, at left)	8
	Hot water	

Coconut Marinade

3	lime leaves (see tip, at left), shredded	3
2	stalks lemongrass, tender inner white bulbs only	2
2	cloves garlic	2
1	shallot	1
1	red Thai chile pepper, sliced	1
½ cup	coarsely chopped fresh basil	125 mL
1 tbsp	minced galangal or gingerroot	15 mL
2 tsp	ground coriander	10 mL
½ tsp	ground turmeric	2 mL
½ tsp	packed brown sugar	2 mL
¼ cup	coconut milk	60 mL
2 tbsp	fish sauce (nam pla)	30 mL
1 tbsp	freshly squeezed lime juice	15 mL

Rice

1 cup	Thai jasmine rice, rinsed and drained	250 mL
1 cup	coconut milk	250 mL
½ cup	water	125 mL

1. Place fish in a large bowl and sprinkle evenly with salt and pepper.
2. *Marinade:* In food processor, combine lime leaves, lemongrass, garlic, shallot, Thai chile, basil, galangal, coriander, turmeric, brown sugar, coconut milk, fish sauce and lime juice; purée until smooth.
3. Pour marinade over fish, tossing to coat evenly. Cover and refrigerate for 15 minutes.

Lemongrass

Lemongrass has a highly aromatic citrus flavor with a trace of ginger. Lemon juice (or lime juice) may be substituted for lemongrass in a pinch, but will not fully replicate its unique qualities and taste. It is best to use fresh lemongrass, which is fragrant and tightly formed. Select lemongrass that is a yellowish green color toward the lower end of the stalk, near the bulb, and a brighter green near the upper end of the stalk. Lemongrass freezes well, so if fresh is not available, check the freezer section of your local Asian grocery store, or store some at home!

4. Meanwhile, remove ribs from banana leaves and place leaves in a large bowl of hot water for 1 minute to soften and avoid tearing. Cut leaves into four 12- by 8-inch (30 by 20 cm) rectangles and four 6- by 3-inch (15 by 7.5 cm) rectangles. Place the large rectangles in front of you on a cutting board; place a smaller rectangle in the center of each, parallel to the large rectangle.

5. Using a slotted spoon, place 3 to 4 pieces of fish on each smaller rectangle and pour 1 tbsp (15 mL) marinade over the fish. Fold the sides of the large rectangle up to form a packet and secure firmly with a toothpick, taking extra care that the marinade doesn't leak. Continue until you have 4 packets. (Discard the remaining marinade or see tip, at left.) Place packets on a heatproof plate that will fit in your steamer basket. Place in the basket.

6. *Rice*: In the rice cooker bowl, combine rice, coconut milk and water. Place the steamer basket in the rice cooker. Set the rice cooker for the Regular cycle.

7. When the machine switches to the Keep Warm cycle, let stand for 10 minutes.

8. Place a scoop of rice on each of 4 serving plates and top with a fish packet. Let each guest open their own packet.

Thai-Style Steamed Fish

Makes 4 servings

This is a great recipe if you are following a low-glycemic diet. Serve it with brown basmati rice for a wholesome and hearty meal.

Tips

Make sure to pour the sauce carefully over the fish so it doesn't leak into the rice cooker bowl.

For information about rice cooker sizes, see page 13.

> • **Medium to large rice cooker with a steamer basket; fuzzy logic or on/off**

6	cloves garlic, minced	6
4	serrano chile peppers, seeded and finely chopped	4
2	stalks lemongrass, tender inner white bulbs only, minced	2
1/2 cup	chicken broth	125 mL
1/4 cup	fish sauce (nam pla)	60 mL
2 tbsp	freshly squeezed lime juice	15 mL
1 1/2 to 2 lb	whole trout	750 g to 1 lb
4	baby bok choy, halved lengthwise	4
2	stalks lemongrass	2
1/2 cup	packed fresh cilantro leaves	125 mL

1. In a medium bowl, combine garlic, serrano peppers, minced lemongrass, broth, fish sauce and lime juice, stirring until well blended.
2. Rinse trout and pat dry with paper towels. Place fish on a heatproof plate that will fit in your steamer basket and make 3 crosswise slashes on each side. Place plate in the basket, curling fish slightly to fit, if necessary. Pour garlic mixture over fish. Place bok choy on top.
3. Peel away the tough outer leaves of the lemongrass. Cut remaining stalk into 3-inch (7.5 cm) pieces and bruise several times with a mallet. Place bruised lemongrass stalks and 4 cups (1 L) water in the rice cooker bowl and set the rice cooker for the Regular or Steam cycle. When the water comes to a boil, place the steamer basket in the rice cooker. Set a timer for 20 minutes.
4. When the timer sounds, check to make sure fish is opaque and flakes easily when tested with a fork. If necessary, continue cooking, checking for doneness every 3 minutes. Serve immediately, garnished with cilantro.

Variations

Substitute a whole sea bass or tilapia for the trout.

For a spicier take on this dish, add 1 tsp (5 mL) sambal oelek or other hot Asian chili sauce with the fish sauce.

Sake-Steamed Shrimp

Makes 4 servings

The eggplant exquisitely enriches this traditional dish, which is beautifully adorned with a delicious spicy miso dressing. Creative presentation is common practice in Japanese cuisine.

Tip

White miso paste is a common Japanese seasoning made of rice, barley and a small quantity of soybeans. It is sweet, salty and earthy, with a very smooth texture due to a high rice koji content. It can be found at Asian markets.

- **Medium to large rice cooker with a steamer basket; fuzzy logic or on/off**

2 cups	sake	500 mL
1 lb	medium shrimp, with tails on, peeled and deveined	500 g
2 cups	sliced peeled Japanese eggplant (½-inch/1 cm slices)	500 mL

Spicy Miso Dressing

½ cup	granulated sugar	125 mL
½ cup	mayonnaise	125 mL
¼ cup	white miso paste (see tip, at left)	60 mL
¼ cup	mirin	60 mL
1 tbsp	soy sauce	15 mL
1 tsp	Thai chili sauce (such as Sriracha)	5 mL
1 tsp	Asian ground sesame paste or tahini	5 mL

1. Place sake in the rice cooker bowl and set the rice cooker for the Regular or Steam cycle.
2. Arrange shrimp on one side of the steamer basket and eggplant on the other. When the sake comes to a boil, place the basket in rice cooker. Set a timer for 4 minutes.
3. *Dressing:* Meanwhile, in a small bowl, combine sugar, mayonnaise, miso paste, mirin, soy sauce, chili sauce and sesame paste until well blended.
4. When the timer sounds, check to make sure shrimp are pink and opaque. If necessary, continue cooking, checking for doneness every 1 minute. Transfer shrimp and eggplant to a serving dish and drizzle with dressing. Serve immediately.

Variation

Sake-Steamed Scallops: Substitute 1 lb (500 g) bay scallops for the shrimp; cook until scallops are just firm and opaque.

Garlic Cilantro Chicken Breasts

Makes 4 servings

A touch of sweetness, along with the flavors of cilantro and citrus, makes this chicken deliciously unique. Honing perfection, the zesty cream sauce finishes off the dish.

Tips

To make ¼ cup (60 mL) lime juice, you'll need 2 to 4 medium limes. One lemon should yield enough juice for the sauce.

You may want to double the sauce recipe — my kids go crazy for it and love to drizzle it over their rice as well. It's a great way to get kids to clean their plate.

For information about rice cooker sizes, see page 13.

• **Medium to large rice cooker with a steamer basket; fuzzy logic or on/off**

6	cloves garlic, minced	6
½ cup	finely chopped fresh cilantro	125 mL
½ tsp	salt	2 mL
¼ tsp	freshly ground black pepper	1 mL
¼ cup	freshly squeezed lime juice (see tip, at left)	60 mL
1 tbsp	extra virgin olive oil	15 mL
1 tbsp	liquid honey	15 mL
4	boneless skinless chicken breasts (about 2 lbs/1 kg total)	4
1½ cups	long-grain white rice, rinsed and drained	375 mL
2 cups	water	500 mL
	Cabbage leaves or nonstick cooking spray	

Sauce

½ cup	finely chopped fresh cilantro	125 mL
1 tsp	minced garlic	5 mL
½ tsp	chili powder	2 mL
1 cup	Greek-style plain yogurt or sour cream	250 mL
3 tbsp	freshly squeezed lemon juice	45 mL

1. In a large bowl, whisk together garlic, cilantro, salt, pepper, lime juice, oil and honey until well blended. Add chicken and turn to coat. Cover and refrigerate for 30 minutes.
2. In the rice cooker bowl, combine rice and water. Line the steamer basket with cabbage leaves or spray with cooking spray. Remove chicken from marinade, discarding marinade, and place chicken in the steamer basket. Place basket in the rice cooker. Set the rice cooker for the Regular cycle.
3. *Sauce:* Meanwhile, in a small bowl, whisk cilantro, garlic, chili powder, yogurt and lemon juice.
4. When the machine switches to the Keep Warm cycle, let stand for 10 minutes. Check to make sure chicken is no longer pink inside. If necessary, let stand on the Keep Warm cycle, checking for doneness every 3 minutes. Serve chicken with a dollop of sauce on top and rice on the side.

Ginger Teriyaki Chicken Thighs

Makes 3 servings

This authentic jewel of Japanese cuisine will be a hit at the dinner table. A Sauvignon Blanc is a great match.

Tips

You may use boneless skinless chicken breasts in this dish, if you prefer. In step 5, check to make sure chicken is no longer pink inside.

For convenience, you could use 1 cup (250 mL) bottled teriyaki sauce in this recipe, but this simple sauce gets rave reviews.

Rice Vinegar

Rice vinegar is made from fermented rice or rice wine. Japanese rice vinegars tend to be milder than Chinese ones. Chinese rice vinegars range in color from clear to various shades of red and brown. Western vinegars are more acidic than Asian rice vinegars so they are not recommended as a substitute.

- **Medium to large rice cooker with a steamer basket; fuzzy logic or on/off**

1 cup	Japanese-style medium-grain japonica rice (such as Calrose)	250 mL
1	clove garlic, minced	1
1 tbsp	minced gingerroot	15 mL
3 tbsp	packed brown sugar	45 mL
1½ tsp	dry mustard	7 mL
1½ cups	soy sauce	375 mL
3¼ cups	water, divided	800 mL
3 tbsp	rice vinegar	45 mL
6	boneless skinless chicken thighs	6
	Cabbage leaves or nonstick cooking spray	
3 tbsp	cornstarch	45 mL
3 tbsp	cold water	45 mL

1. Place rice in a bowl and add enough cool water to cover by 1 inch (2.5 cm); let soak for 30 minutes. Rinse and drain (see page 20).
2. Meanwhile, in a large bowl, whisk together garlic, ginger, brown sugar, mustard, soy sauce, 1½ cups (375 mL) of the water and vinegar. Add chicken and turn to coat. Cover and refrigerate for 30 minutes.
3. In the rice cooker bowl, combine rice and the remaining water. Line the steamer basket with cabbage leaves or spray with cooking spray. Remove chicken from marinade, reserving marinade, and place chicken in the steamer basket. Place basket in the rice cooker. Set the rice cooker for the Regular cycle.
4. Meanwhile, in a small bowl, combine cornstarch and cold water. In a medium saucepan, bring reserved marinade to a boil over medium-high heat. Stir in cornstarch mixture. Reduce heat and simmer, stirring, for about 12 minutes or until sauce is thickened.
5. When the machine switches to the Keep Warm cycle, let stand for 10 minutes. Check to make sure juices run clear when chicken is pierced with a fork. If necessary, let stand on the Keep Warm cycle, checking for doneness every 3 minutes. Serve chicken with rice and teriyaki sauce on the side.

Beer-Steamed Kielbasa and Sauerkraut

Makes 4 servings

This recipe is an absolute snap and a surefire crowd pleaser. The mellow taste of the beer and the tart apple complement the traditional sausages and sauerkraut well.

Tips

I like to use a German beer, such as a Pilsner.

Fresh sauerkraut is preferred, but jarred is fine too.

● **Medium to large rice cooker with a steamer basket; fuzzy logic or on/off**

3 cups	lager beer or unsweetened apple cider	750 mL
1 lb	kielbasa, cut into 4-inch (10 cm) pieces, or bratwurst sausages	500 g
1 tbsp	fennel seeds, crushed	15 mL
1½ cups	drained sauerkraut, rinsed and squeezed dry	375 mL
1	onion, sliced	1
1	Granny Smith apple, thinly sliced	1
	Assorted mustards	
	Rye or whole-grain bread	

1. Place beer in the rice cooker bowl and set the rice cooker for the Regular or Steam cycle.
2. Place kielbasa on a heatproof plate that will fit in your steamer basket. Sprinkle crushed fennel seeds on top. Layer sauerkraut, onion and apple on top. Place the plate in the steamer basket. When the beer comes to a boil, place the basket in the rice cooker. Set a timer for 20 minutes.
3. When the timer sounds, check to make sure apple and onion are tender and kielbasa are hot in the center. If necessary, continue cooking, checking for doneness every 5 minutes. Serve sausages with assorted mustards and bread.

Baby Artichokes with Lemon Aïoli

Makes 4 servings

Lemon aïoli lends a zing to delicate, tender baby artichokes. This is a simple gourmet recipe that pairs well with a citrus chicken dish.

Tips

When buying baby artichokes, look for tight, compact heads and freshly cut stem ends.

For information about rice cooker sizes, see page 13.

- **Medium to large rice cooker with a steamer basket; fuzzy logic or on/off**

	Nonstick cooking spray	
1 lb	baby artichokes, trimmed (see box, page 227)	500 g
2	cloves garlic, minced	2
1 tsp	grated lemon zest	5 mL
¼ tsp	salt	1 mL
⅛ tsp	freshly ground black pepper	0.5 mL
¾ cup	mayonnaise	175 mL
1 tbsp	freshly squeezed lemon juice	15 mL

1. Place 4 cups (1 L) water in the rice cooker bowl and set the rice cooker for the Regular or Steam cycle.
2. Spray the steamer basket with cooking spray. Place artichokes in the basket. When the water comes to a boil, place the basket in the rice cooker. Set a timer for 15 minutes.
3. Meanwhile, in a small bowl, combine garlic, lemon zest, salt, pepper, mayonnaise and lemon juice until well blended. Set aside.
4. When the timer sounds, check to make sure artichokes are tender. If necessary, continue cooking, checking for doneness every 3 minutes. Transfer artichokes to a serving platter. Serve warm or chilled, with lemon aïoli on the side.

Asparagus Wrapped in Prosciutto

Makes 4 servings

The intense flavor of prosciutto and the crunch of asparagus results in a terrific food pairing. The creamy garlic butter sauce makes the dish even more decadent.

Prosciutto

Prosciutto is the Italian word for "ham." The curing process for prosciutto involves salting ham and then air-drying it for up to 2 years. After curing, prosciutto is cut into paper-thin, slightly transparent slices. The most popular uses for uncooked prosciutto include serving it on charcuterie plates, adding it to salads or wrapping it around vegetables or fruits, such as the popular *prosciutto e melone* (melon wrapped in prosciutto).

- **Medium to large rice cooker with a steamer basket; fuzzy logic or on/off**

1 tsp	salt	5 mL
3 cups	water	750 mL
1 tbsp	butter	15 mL
1 lb	asparagus spears, tough ends removed and ends peeled	500 g
4	thin slices prosciutto	4
	Nonstick cooking spray	
4	lemon wedges	4

Garlic Butter Sauce

2 tbsp	extra virgin olive oil	30 mL
1 tsp	butter	5 mL
1	clove garlic, minced	1

1. In the rice cooker bowl, combine salt, water and butter. Set the rice cooker for the Regular or Steam cycle.
2. Divide asparagus into 4 bunches. Wrap each bunch with a slice of prosciutto, tucking ends underneath.
3. Spray the steamer basket with cooking spray. Place asparagus bundles in the basket. When the water comes to a boil, place the basket in the rice cooker. Set a timer for 8 minutes.
4. *Sauce:* Meanwhile, in a small saucepan, heat oil and butter over medium heat. Sauté garlic for 30 seconds. Remove from heat.
5. When the timer sounds, check to make sure asparagus is tender-crisp. If necessary, continue cooking, checking for doneness every 2 minutes. Serve asparagus bundles drizzled with sauce, with lemon wedges on the side.

Broccoli, Snow Peas and Carrots with Curry Honey Sauce

Makes 4 servings

With flavors ranging from sweet to sour to spicy, these veggies make a great addition to a meal of Szechuan beef or Peking duck. Complete the trifecta with a spicy Syrah.

Tip

Add some lemon slices to the steaming water for a citrusy note.

- **Medium to large rice cooker with a steamer basket; fuzzy logic or on/off**

	Nonstick cooking spray	
1 cup	baby carrots	250 mL
1 cup	broccoli florets	250 mL
1 cup	snow peas, trimmed	250 mL

Curry Honey Sauce

1½ tsp	curry powder	7 mL
¾ cup	mayonnaise	175 mL
1½ tbsp	freshly squeezed lemon juice	22 mL
1½ tbsp	liquid honey	22 mL

1. Place 3 cups (750 mL) water in the rice cooker bowl and set the rice cooker for the Regular or Steam cycle.
2. Spray the steamer basket with cooking spray. Place carrots in the bottom of the basket. Place broccoli on top of carrots. Place snow peas on top of broccoli. When the water comes to a boil, place the basket in the rice cooker. Set a timer for 20 minutes.
3. *Sauce:* Meanwhile, in a small bowl, whisk together curry powder, mayonnaise, lemon juice and honey until well blended.
4. When the timer sounds, check to make sure vegetables are tender-crisp. If necessary, continue cooking, checking for doneness every 3 minutes. Serve immediately, with sauce on the side.

Mashed Cauliflower with Cheese

Makes 4 servings

Adding cheese is a great way to get your kids to eat their cauliflower. Tantalize them with this deceptively delicious side dish.

Tips

Mash the cauliflower mixture by hand for a coarser texture.

For information about rice cooker sizes, see page 13.

- **Medium to large rice cooker with a steamer basket; fuzzy logic or on/off**
- **Food processor or blender**

	Nonstick cooking spray	
4 cups	cauliflower florets	1 L
1/4 cup	crumbled feta cheese	60 mL
1/4 cup	softened cream cheese	60 mL
1/4 cup	heavy or whipping (35%) cream	60 mL
2 tbsp	butter	30 mL
	Salt and freshly ground black pepper	
2 tsp	extra virgin olive oil	10 mL
	Finely chopped fresh parsley	

1. Place 4 cups (1 L) water in the rice cooker bowl and set the rice cooker for the Regular or Steam cycle.
2. Spray the steamer basket with cooking spray. Place cauliflower in the basket. When the water comes to a boil, place the basket in the rice cooker. Set a timer for 6 minutes.
3. When the timer sounds, check to make sure cauliflower is tender. If necessary, continue cooking, checking for doneness every 1 minute. Transfer cauliflower to a colander, pressing down on it with a small plate to remove excess moisture.
4. In food processor, combine cauliflower, feta, cream cheese, cream and butter; pulse until smooth and creamy.
5. Transfer to a serving dish and season to taste with salt and pepper. Drizzle with oil and garnish with parsley. Serve warm.

Variations

Baked Potato–Style Mashed Cauliflower: Substitute 1 cup (250 mL) shredded Cheddar cheese and 1/4 cup (60 mL) sour cream for the feta and cream cheese. Add 2 tsp (10 mL) finely chopped fresh chives.

Substitute freshly grated Parmesan cheese for the feta.

Buttery Smashed Kohlrabi

Makes 4 servings

Kohlrabi is a derivative of the cabbage plant, but its flavor is at once milder and slightly sweeter than its kin.

Tip

For a smoother consistency, use a food processor or blender to mash the kohlrabi mixture.

• Medium to large rice cooker with a steamer basket; fuzzy logic or on/off

	Nonstick cooking spray	
1	large kohlrabi, peeled and cut into cubes (about 4 cups/1 L)	1
1	clove garlic, minced	1
¼ cup	sour cream	60 mL
2 tbsp	butter	30 mL
½ cup	whole or 2% milk (approx.)	125 mL
	Salt and freshly ground black pepper	
	Snipped fresh chives	

1. Place 4 cups (1 L) water in the rice cooker bowl and set the rice cooker for the Regular or Steam cycle.
2. Spray the steamer basket with cooking spray. Place kohlrabi in the basket. When the water comes to a boil, place the basket in the rice cooker. Set a timer for 15 minutes.
3. When the timer sounds, check to make sure kohlrabi is tender. If necessary, continue cooking, checking for doneness every 3 minutes.
4. Transfer kohlrabi to a large bowl. Add garlic, sour cream and butter; mash with a potato masher or fork, adding milk as needed, until smooth. Season to taste with salt and pepper. Serve warm, garnished with chives.

Variation

Buttery Smashed Bacon Kohlrabi: Add ½ cup (125 mL) chopped cooked bacon with the garlic.

Thai Spiced Steamed Vegetables

Makes 4 servings

I love this spicy alternative to the basic steamed veggie dish. As with many Thai recipes, the chili sauce gives these normally mellow vegetables a flavorful kick.

Tips

You may use globe eggplants in place of the Japanese eggplants.

When purchasing eggplant, make sure the skin has a glossy shine; otherwise, the eggplant will be bitter.

Japanese Eggplants

Japanese eggplants are smaller and often thinner than globe eggplants, and have thinner skins. They can be grilled, steamed, simmered or fried. Eggplants absorb oil quickly, so use extra oil when frying them. You can soak eggplants in salted water before cooking to prevent them from turning brown.

- **Medium to large rice cooker with a steamer basket; fuzzy logic or on/off**
- **Blender or food processor**

	Nonstick cooking spray	
3	baby bok choy, cut in half lengthwise	3
2	zucchini, cut into ½-inch (1 cm) thick rounds	2
2	Japanese eggplants, cut diagonally into ½-inch (1 cm) slices	2
	Thai basil leaves	

Sauce

1	bunch Thai basil, tough stems removed (about 1 cup/250 mL)	1
1	clove garlic, minced	1
2 tsp	packed brown sugar	10 mL
2 tsp	fish sauce (nam pla)	10 mL
2 tsp	toasted sesame oil	10 mL
1 tsp	sambal oelek or hot Asian chili sauce	5 mL

1. Place 3 cups (750 mL) water in the rice cooker bowl and set the rice cooker for the Regular or Steam cycle.
2. Spray the steamer basket with cooking spray. Place bok coy in the basket. Place zucchini and eggplants on top. When the water comes to a boil, place the basket in the rice cooker. Set a timer for 17 minutes.
3. *Sauce:* Meanwhile, in blender, combine basil, garlic, brown sugar, fish sauce, sesame oil and sambal oelek; purée until smooth.
4. When the timer sounds, check to make sure vegetables are tender. If necessary, continue cooking, checking for doneness every 3 minutes. Transfer vegetables to a serving bowl. Toss with sauce and garnish with basil leaves. Serve immediately.

Puréed Root Vegetables with Nutmeg and Cinnamon Dust

Makes 4 servings

When autumn arrives, I love to celebrate the season's harvest of root vegetables. The sherry truly enhances the butter in this comforting, soul-satisfying dish that will fill your kitchen with a sublime aroma.

Tips

Parsnips are a root vegetable related to the carrot, but they are paler and have a stronger, sweeter flavor.

For information about rice cooker sizes, see page 13.

- **Medium to large rice cooker with a steamer basket; fuzzy logic or on/off**
- **Food processor or blender**

	Nonstick cooking spray	
1	sweet potato, peeled and cut into 2-inch (5 cm) pieces	1
1	turnip, cut into 2-inch (5 cm) pieces	1
1	parsnip, cut into 2-inch (5 cm) pieces	1
½ tsp	ground nutmeg	2 mL
½ tsp	ground cinnamon	2 mL
½ tsp	ground ginger	2 mL
½ cup	chicken broth	125 mL
2 tbsp	butter	30 mL
1 tbsp	dry sherry	15 mL
	Salt and freshly ground black pepper	

1. Place 4 cups (1 L) water in the rice cooker bowl and set the rice cooker for the Regular or Steam cycle.
2. Spray the steamer basket with cooking spray. Place vegetables in the basket in the following order: sweet potato, turnip and parsnip. When the water comes to a boil, place the basket in the rice cooker. Set a timer for 16 minutes.
3. Meanwhile, in a small bowl, sift together nutmeg, cinnamon and ginger.
4. When the timer sounds, check to make sure vegetables are tender. If necessary, continue cooking, checking for doneness every 3 minutes.
5. In food processor, combine steamed vegetables, broth, butter and sherry; purée until smooth.
6. Transfer to a serving dish and season to taste with salt and pepper. Dust with spice mixture and serve warm.

Individual Chocolate Cakes with Banana Rum Sauce

Makes 4 servings

These indulgent cakes drenched in a bananas Foster–like sauce are absolutely scrumptious. What a perfect way to end any meal!

Tips

For buttery flavor, use butter-flavored nonstick cooking spray.

For information about rice cooker sizes, see page 13.

- **Four 4-oz (125 mL) custard cups or ramekins, sprayed with nonstick cooking spray**
- **Medium to large rice cooker with a steamer basket; fuzzy logic or on/off**

Cakes

1/3 cup	all-purpose flour	75 mL
1/4 cup	unsweetened cocoa powder	60 mL
1/8 tsp	baking powder	0.5 mL
1/8 tsp	baking soda	0.5 mL
Pinch	salt	Pinch
1 cup + 1 tbsp	granulated sugar	265 mL
1/2 cup	evaporated milk	125 mL
1/4 cup	butter	60 mL
1/4 tsp	vanilla extract	1 mL
1	large egg, well beaten	1
4	large chocolate kisses (such as Hershey's)	4

Banana Rum Sauce

1/4 cup	butter, cut into pieces	60 mL
2 tbsp	packed brown sugar	30 mL
1	ripe banana, cut into 1/4-inch (0.5 cm) slices	1
2 tbsp	light rum	30 mL

1. *Cakes:* In a large bowl, sift together flour, cocoa, baking powder, baking soda and salt. Set aside.
2. In a small saucepan, combine sugar, evaporated milk, butter and vanilla. Heat over low heat, stirring constantly, until sugar is dissolved and butter is melted. Transfer to a bowl and let cool to room temperature.
3. Add egg to milk mixture and whisk until well blended. Pour over flour mixture and whisk until well blended.
4. Fill each prepared custard cup half full with batter. Place a chocolate kiss in the center of each cup. Fill until two-thirds full with the remaining batter. Cover each cup tightly with foil. Place cups in the steamer basket.

5. Place 4 cups (1 L) water in the rice cooker bowl and set the
   rice cooker for the Regular or Steam cycle. When the water
   comes to a boil, place the basket in the rice cooker. Set a timer
   for 40 minutes.

6. *Sauce:* Meanwhile, in a small, heavy saucepan, melt butter over
   medium heat. Add brown sugar and cook, whisking, for about
   1 minute or until smooth and well combined. Add banana
   and rum; reduce heat and simmer, stirring occasionally, for
   2 minutes. Remove from heat and keep warm.

7. When the timer sounds, check to make sure a tester inserted
   in the center comes out clean. If necessary, continue cooking,
   checking for doneness every 3 minutes. Remove custard cups
   from the rice cooker and remove foil. Serve warm, with sauce
   spooned over top.

Variation

Individual Chocolate Cakes with Raspberry Coulis: In a small
saucepan, heat $1/4$ cup (60 mL) granulated sugar and 2 tbsp
(30 mL) water over medium heat, stirring until sugar is
dissolved. Transfer to a blender and add $2^1/2$ cups (625 mL)
fresh raspberries; purée until well blended. Strain through a
fine-mesh sieve. Spoon over steamed chocolate cakes in place
of the banana rum sauce.

Individual Blueberry Cheesecakes

Makes 4 servings

These rich layered delights will be an eye-catching and oh-so-delicious ending to your next dinner party. Serve them with piping hot cups of coffee.

Tips

For a graham cracker crust effect, combine ¼ cup (60 mL) crushed graham crackers and 1 tbsp (15 mL) softened butter. Press into bottom of custard cups before pouring in the cream cheese mixture.

The topping can be stored in an airtight container in the refrigerator for up to 3 days.

- **Four 4-oz (125 mL) custard cups or ramekins, sprayed with nonstick cooking spray**
- **Medium to large rice cooker with a steamer basket; fuzzy logic or on/off**

Cheesecakes

4 oz	cream cheese, softened	125 g
¼ cup	granulated sugar	60 mL
2	large eggs	2
½ cup	heavy or whipping (35%) cream	125 mL
¾ tsp	vanilla extract	3 mL

Topping

1 cup	blueberries	250 mL
¼ cup	granulated sugar	60 mL
1 tsp	cornstarch	5 mL
2 tsp	butter	10 mL
2 tsp	freshly squeezed lemon juice	10 mL

1. *Cheesecakes:* In a medium bowl, using an electric mixer, beat cream cheese and sugar until smooth. Beat in eggs, cream and vanilla until smooth.

2. Carefully pour cream cheese mixture into prepared custard cups. Cover each cup tightly with foil. Place cups in the steamer basket.

3. Place 4 cups (1 L) water in the rice cooker bowl and set the rice cooker for the Regular or Steam cycle. When the water comes to a boil, place the rack or basket in the rice cooker. Set a timer for 20 minutes.

4. *Topping:* Meanwhile, in a small saucepan, combine blueberries, sugar, cornstarch, butter and lemon juice. Bring to a boil over medium-high heat; reduce heat and simmer, stirring occasionally, for about 4 minutes or until berries break down. Let cool to room temperature, then transfer to a bowl, cover and refrigerate until ready to use.

5. When the timer sounds, check to make sure tops of cheesecakes are firm to the touch. If necessary, continue cooking, checking for doneness every 3 minutes. Remove custard cups from the rice cooker and remove foil. Let cool to room temperature, then refrigerate for 30 minutes, until chilled, or for up to 24 hours. Spread topping over cheesecakes right before serving.

Leche Flan

Makes 4 servings

This basic custard recipe, popularized by Filipino cuisine, is easy to prepare. It is a must-have dessert for any holiday gathering.

Tips

You may use sweetened condensed milk instead of whole milk in this recipe, but reduce the sugar in step 3 to 2 tbsp (30 mL).

For information about rice cooker sizes, see page 13.

- **Four 4-oz (125 mL) custard cups or ramekins, sprayed with nonstick cooking spray**
- **Medium to large rice cooker with a steamer basket; fuzzy logic or on/off**

¾ cup	granulated sugar, divided	175 mL
¼ cup	water	60 mL
1 cup	whole milk	250 mL
1	large egg	1
½ tsp	vanilla extract	2 mL

1. In a small saucepan, combine ½ cup (125 mL) of the sugar and water. Heat over medium-low heat, stirring, until sugar dissolves. Increase heat to medium and boil for about 11 minutes or until mixture thickens and turns dark golden. Carefully pour into prepared custard cups, distributing evenly.
2. In another small saucepan, bring milk to a boil over medium-high heat. Reduce heat and simmer, stirring occasionally, for 5 minutes. Cover, turn off heat and let stand on the burner for 10 minutes.
3. In a medium bowl, whisk together the remaining sugar, egg and vanilla until well blended. Gradually add boiled milk, stirring constantly.
4. Carefully pour into custard cups, on top of the caramel sauce. Cover each cup tightly with foil. Place cups in the steamer basket.
5. Place 4 cups (1 L) water in the rice cooker bowl and set the rice cooker for the Regular or Steam cycle. When the water comes to a boil, place the rack or basket in the rice cooker. Set a timer for 30 minutes.
6. When the timer sounds, remove custard cups from the rice cooker and remove foil. Let cool to room temperature, then refrigerate for 1 hour, until chilled, or for up to 24 hours.

Variation

Cuban Coconut Flan: Replace the milk with coconut milk and add 2 tbsp (30 mL) rum with the egg.

Cider-Steamed Custards

Makes 4 servings

A chilly winter evening would be the ideal time to enjoy this cinnamon-spiced treat. The apple cider perfectly enriches the flavor of the airy custard.

Tips

For a richer custard, replace the half-and-half cream with heavy or whipping (35%) cream.

For information about rice cooker sizes, see page 13.

- **Four 4-oz (125 mL) custard cups or ramekins, sprayed with nonstick cooking spray**
- **Medium to large rice cooker with a steamer basket; fuzzy logic or on/off**

½ cup	whole or 2% milk	125 mL
½ cup	half-and-half (10%) cream	125 mL
¼ cup	granulated sugar	60 mL
¼ tsp	ground cinnamon	1 mL
2	large egg yolks	2
1	large egg	1
6 cups	unsweetened apple cider, divided	1.5 L
5	3-inch (7.5 cm) cinnamon sticks, divided	5

1. In a small saucepan, bring milk and cream to a boil over medium-high heat. Reduce heat and simmer, stirring occasionally, for 5 minutes. Cover, turn off heat and let stand on the burner for 10 minutes.
2. In a medium bowl, whisk together sugar, cinnamon, egg yolks and egg until well blended. Gradually add milk mixture, stirring constantly.
3. Carefully pour into prepared custard cups. Cover each cup tightly with foil. Place cups in the steamer basket.
4. Place 4 cups (1 L) of the cider and 4 cinnamon sticks in the rice cooker bowl and set the rice cooker for the Regular or Steam cycle. When the cider comes to a boil, place the rack or basket in the rice cooker. Set a timer for 30 minutes.
5. When the timer sounds, check to make sure custards are firm and a tester inserted in the center comes out clean. If necessary, continue cooking, checking for doneness every 3 minutes. Remove custard cups from the rice cooker and remove foil. Let cool to room temperature, then refrigerate for 1 hour, until chilled, or for up to 24 hours.

Serve the hot cider used
for steaming along with
the custards, if you wish.

6. Meanwhile, in a saucepan, bring the remaining cider and
remaining cinnamon stick to a boil over medium-high
heat. Reduce heat and simmer for about 15 minutes or until
reduced to $\frac{1}{4}$ cup (60 mL). Remove cinnamon sticks and
spoon reduction over top of custards.

Variation

Spiced Cider-Steamed Custards: Tie two 3-inch (7.5 cm)
cinnamon sticks, $\frac{1}{2}$ tsp (2 mL) whole allspice and $\frac{1}{2}$ tsp
(2 mL) whole cloves in a square of cheesecloth. In a medium
saucepan, combine 4 cups (1 L) unsweetened apple cider,
$\frac{1}{4}$ cup (60 mL) packed brown sugar and spice packet. Bring to
a boil over high heat. Reduce heat and simmer for 10 minutes.
Use in place of regular cider and cinnamon sticks to steam
custards (use regular cider to make the cider reduction).

Blackberry Custards

Makes 4 servings

Custards are a deliciously light dessert, and they add an elegant touch to the menu.

Tip

For information about rice cooker sizes, see page 13.

- **Four 4-oz (125 mL) custard cups or ramekins, sprayed with nonstick cooking spray**
- **Medium to large rice cooker with a steamer basket; fuzzy logic or on/off**

Custards

8	blackberries	8
5 tbsp	granulated sugar, divided	75 mL
1/2 cup	whole milk	125 mL
1/2 cup	half-and-half (10%) cream	125 mL
2	large egg yolks	2
1	large egg	1
1/4 tsp	vanilla extract	1 mL

Topping

3/4 cup	water	175 mL
Pinch	salt	Pinch
1/2 cup	granulated sugar	125 mL
2 tbsp	all-purpose flour	30 mL
1/4 cup	crushed blackberries	60 mL
2 tbsp	butter	30 mL
1 1/2 tsp	freshly squeezed lemon juice	7 mL

1. *Custards:* Place 2 blackberries in each prepared custard cup. Sprinkle blackberries with 1 tbsp (15 mL) sugar, dividing evenly.
2. In a small saucepan, bring milk and cream to a boil over medium-high heat. Reduce heat and simmer, stirring occasionally, for 5 minutes. Cover, turn off heat and let stand on the burner for 10 minutes.
3. In a medium bowl, whisk together the remaining sugar, egg yolks, egg and vanilla until well blended. Gradually add milk mixture, stirring constantly.
4. Carefully pour into custard cups, covering the berries. Cover each cup tightly with foil. Place cups in the steamer basket.
5. Place 4 cups (1 L) water in the rice cooker bowl and set the rice cooker for the Regular or Steam cycle. When the water comes to a boil, place the rack or basket in the rice cooker. Set a timer for 30 minutes.

Tip
A red Zinfandel
alongside this
dessert would accent
the flavor of the
blackberries flawlessly.

6. *Topping:* Meanwhile, in a small saucepan, combine water and salt. Bring to a boil over medium-high heat. Stir in sugar and flour; boil, stirring constantly, for 3 to 4 minutes or until thickened. Add crushed blackberries, reduce heat and simmer, stirring occasionally, for 12 to 15 minutes or until very thick. Stir in butter and lemon juice. Remove from heat and keep warm. (Or, if serving the custards cold, let cool to room temperature, cover and refrigerate for up to 24 hours.)

7. When the timer sounds, check to make sure custards are firm and a tester inserted in the center comes out clean. If necessary, continue cooking, checking for doneness every 3 minutes. Remove custard cups from the rice cooker and remove foil. Serve warm or refrigerate for up to 24 hours. Just before serving, spoon topping over custards.

Variation

Try raspberries in place of the blackberries, or use a combination of raspberries and blackberries for a double berry treat.

Lemongrass Custards with Mango Glaze

Makes 4 servings

Borrowing flavors from Thai cuisine, this deliciously delicate custard is an impeccable conclusion to any dinner.

Tips

If fresh lemongrass is not available, you may use frozen lemongrass (available at Asian markets.)

For information about rice cooker sizes, see page 13.

- **Four 4-oz (125 mL) custard cups or ramekins, sprayed with nonstick cooking spray**
- **Medium to large rice cooker with a steamer basket; fuzzy logic or on/off**

Custards

½ cup	coconut milk	125 mL
½ cup	half-and-half (10%) cream	125 mL
2	stalks lemongrass, tender inner white bulbs only, minced	2
¼ cup	granulated sugar	60 mL
2	large egg yolks	2
1	large egg	1
1	stalk lemongrass	1

Mango Glaze

½ cup	thinly sliced mango	125 mL
½ cup	granulated sugar	125 mL
½ cup	water	125 mL
½ tsp	freshly squeezed lemon juice	2 mL
1½ tsp	cornstarch	7 mL

1. *Custards:* In a small saucepan, bring coconut milk, cream and minced lemongrass to a boil over medium-high heat. Reduce heat and simmer, stirring occasionally, for 5 minutes. Cover, turn off heat and let stand on the burner for 10 minutes. Strain through a fine-mesh strainer into a measuring cup or bowl; discard lemongrass.

2. In a medium bowl, whisk together sugar, egg yolks and egg until well blended. Gradually add coconut milk mixture, stirring constantly.

3. Carefully pour into prepared custard cups. Cover each cup tightly with foil. Place cups in the steamer basket.

4. Peel away the tough outer leaves of the lemongrass stalk. Cut remaining stalk into 3-inch (7.5 cm) pieces and bruise several times with a mallet. Place 4 cups (1 L) water and bruised lemongrass stalk in the rice cooker bowl and set the rice cooker for the Regular or Steam cycle. When the water comes to a boil, place the rack or basket in the rice cooker. Set a timer for 30 minutes.

5. *Glaze:* Meanwhile, in a small saucepan, combine mango, sugar, water and lemon juice. Heat over medium-low heat, stirring, until sugar dissolves. Increase heat to medium-high and bring to a boil, stirring constantly. Reduce heat to medium-low, add cornstarch and simmer, stirring constantly, for about 10 minutes or until thickened. Let cool to room temperature, then transfer to a bowl, cover and refrigerate until ready to use.

6. When the timer sounds, check to make sure custards are firm and a tester inserted in the center comes out clean. If necessary, continue cooking, checking for doneness every 3 minutes. Remove custard cups from the rice cooker and remove foil. Let cool to room temperature, then refrigerate for 1 hour, until chilled, or for up to 24 hours. Just before serving, spoon glaze over top.

Caramel Custards

Makes 4 servings

This dessert is popular in India. It is super-easy to make and tastes fantastic!

Tips

For a lighter touch, use half-and-half (10%) cream in place of the heavy cream.

For information about rice cooker sizes, see page 13.

- **Four 4-oz (125 mL) custard cups or ramekins, sprayed with nonstick cooking spray**
- **Medium to large rice cooker with a steamer basket; fuzzy logic or on/off**

1/4 cup	granulated sugar	60 mL
1/8 tsp	ground nutmeg	0.5 mL
3	large eggs	3
1 cup	heavy or whipping (35%) cream	250 mL
1/4 tsp	vanilla extract	1 mL

1. In a medium bowl, whisk together sugar, nutmeg, eggs, cream and vanilla until well blended.
2. Carefully pour into prepared custard cups. Cover each cup tightly with foil. Place cups in the steamer basket.
3. Place 4 cups (1 L) water in the rice cooker bowl and set the rice cooker for the Regular or Steam cycle. When the water comes to a boil, place the rack or basket in the rice cooker. Set a timer for 30 minutes.
4. When the timer sounds, check to make sure custards are firm and a tester inserted in the center comes out clean. If necessary, continue cooking, checking for doneness every 3 minutes. Remove custard cups from the rice cooker and remove foil. Let cool to room temperature, then refrigerate for 1 hour, until chilled, or for up to 24 hours.

Desserts

Quinoa Banana Chocolate Cake

Makes 6 to 8 servings

The Incas called quinoa the "mother of all grains." Which means this decadent chocolate cake is the mother of all desserts.

Tip

If you don't have baking powder, increase the baking soda to 1¼ tsp (6 mL) and add ½ tsp (2 mL) cream of tartar.

- **Preheat oven to 350°F (180°C)**
- **9-inch (23 cm) round cake pan, greased**

1 cup	all-purpose flour	250 mL
½ cup	granulated sugar	125 mL
1 tsp	baking powder	5 mL
1 tsp	baking soda	5 mL
1 tsp	ground cinnamon	5 mL
1 tsp	ground ginger	5 mL
Pinch	ground nutmeg	Pinch
3	large eggs	3
½ cup	butter, melted	125 mL
1 tsp	vanilla extract	5 mL
1½ cups	cooked quinoa (see page 27), cooled	375 mL
1 cup	semisweet chocolate chips	250 mL
1½ cups	mashed bananas	375 mL

1. In a large bowl, whisk together flour, sugar, baking powder, baking soda, cinnamon, ginger and nutmeg.
2. In a small bowl, whisk together eggs, butter and vanilla until combined. Add to flour mixture and stir until just combined. Stir in quinoa and chocolate chips. Stir in bananas. Pour into prepared pan.
3. Bake in preheated oven for 35 to 45 minutes or until a tester inserted in the center comes out clean. Let cool completely in pan on a wire rack.

Grits Pie with Strawberries and Whipped Cream

Makes 6 to 8 servings

Grits are an unexpected base for a dessert, but deliver down-home goodness. Adding strawberries and an easy pie crust creates a luscious treat. Don't be surprised when guests ask for seconds!

Tip

Try using 6 miniature pie shells for individual-size treats and decrease the baking time to 25 to 35 minutes or until set.

- **Preheat oven to 325°F (160°C)**
- **Medium rice cooker; fuzzy logic (preferred) or on/off**

¼ cup	coarse stone-ground grits (see tips, page 295)	60 mL
Pinch	salt	Pinch
¾ cup	water	175 mL
¾ cup	granulated sugar	175 mL
2 tbsp	all-purpose flour	30 mL
3	large eggs, lightly beaten	3
½ cup	butter	125 mL
⅓ cup	buttermilk	75 mL
1 tsp	vanilla extract	5 mL
1	9-inch (23 cm) frozen pie shell, thawed	1
1 cup	sliced strawberries	250 mL
	Whipped cream	

1. In the rice cooker bowl, combine grits, salt and water, stirring thoroughly with a wooden spoon or plastic paddle. Set the rice cooker for the Porridge or Regular cycle. Stir thoroughly two or three times while the grits are cooking.
2. When the machine switches to the Keep Warm cycle, transfer grits to a bowl and let cool completely.
3. Meanwhile, in a small bowl, combine sugar, flour, eggs, butter, buttermilk and vanilla. Gradually stir into the cooled grits. Pour into pie shell.
4. Bake in preheated oven for 35 to 40 minutes or until set. Let cool slightly in pan on a wire rack and serve warm, or let cool to room temperature and refrigerate until chilled. Arrange strawberries on top and add a dollop of whipped cream before serving.

Sticky Rice with Mango

Makes 4 servings

Every time I make this sublime Southeast Asian dessert, the combination of refreshing mango, zesty mint and sticky rice transports me right back to the beaches of Phuket.

Tips

You can use white sesame seeds if black aren't available.

For information about rice cooker sizes, see page 13.

● **Medium rice cooker; fuzzy logic (preferred) or on/off**

1 cup	Thai white or black sticky rice, soaked overnight, rinsed and drained	250 mL
¼ tsp	salt	1 mL
2 cups	water	500 mL
½	vanilla bean	½
½ cup	packed brown sugar	125 mL
⅛ tsp	salt	0.5 mL
1	can (14 oz/400 mL) coconut milk	1
4	small ripe mangos, sliced	4
	Fresh mint leaves	
	Toasted black sesame seeds	

1. In the rice cooker bowl, combine rice, salt and water. Set the rice cooker for the Sweet/Sticky or Regular cycle.
2. When the machine switches to the Keep Warm cycle, let stand for 10 minutes, then transfer rice to a bowl.
3. Meanwhile, scrape seeds from vanilla bean and place in a saucepan; stir in brown sugar, salt and coconut milk. Heat over medium-low heat, stirring to dissolve sugar, until steaming. Remove from heat. Discard vanilla pod.
4. Pour 1 cup (250 mL) of the coconut milk mixture over rice and stir to combine. Let stand for 30 minutes to blend the flavors.
5. Place a scoop of sticky rice on a small plate and arrange mango slices alongside it. Garnish with mint leaves and sprinkle with sesame seeds. Serve the remaining coconut milk mixture in a small serving bowl for diners to spoon over top.

Traditional Rice Pudding

Makes 6 to 8 servings

Have a hankering for a traditional homemade rice pudding? Use this as a base or enjoy it alone for a delectable bowl of comfort.

Tips

For a lower-fat version of this recipe, replace the whole milk with 2% milk.

This recipe can be prepared up to 2 days ahead. Store in an airtight container in the refrigerator.

● **Medium to large rice cooker; fuzzy logic only**

⅔ cup	Arborio rice	150 mL
4½ cups	whole milk	1.125 L
½ cup	packed dark brown sugar	125 mL
2	large eggs	2
½ tsp	ground cinnamon	2 mL
2 tsp	vanilla extract	10 mL

1. In the rice cooker bowl, combine rice and milk. Set the rice cooker for the Porridge cycle.
2. When the machine switches to the Keep Warm cycle, whisk together brown sugar and eggs until well combined. Add ½ cup (125 mL) of the hot rice mixture, 1 tbsp (15 mL) at a time, vigorously stirring with a wooden spoon to incorporate.
3. Add egg mixture to the rice cooker bowl, stirring to combine. Close the lid and let stand for 10 to 15 minutes, stirring two or three times, until thickened. Stir in cinnamon and vanilla. Transfer to a bowl and serve warm, or cover with plastic wrap, let cool to room temperature and refrigerate until chilled.

Easy Rice Pudding with Caramel Apples

Makes 4 servings

Arborio rice turns into a creamy pudding. Adding fragrant caramel apples to this already decadent dish makes it a perfect autumn dessert.

Tips

It's fun to double the caramel sauce for this recipe and put out extra apple slices for guests so they can dip them in caramel as they enjoy their rice pudding.

For information about rice cooker sizes, see page 13.

- • **Medium rice cooker; fuzzy logic only**
- • **Candy thermometer**

¾ cup	Arborio rice	175 mL
⅓ cup	granulated sugar	75 mL
⅛ tsp	salt	0.5 mL
1	2-inch (5 cm) cinnamon stick	1
1	large egg	1
1½ cups	whole milk	375 mL
1 cup	heavy or whipping (35%) cream	250 mL
1 tsp	vanilla extract	5 mL

Caramel Apples

⅓ cup	firmly packed light brown sugar	75 mL
Pinch	salt	Pinch
3 tbsp	light (white or golden) corn syrup	45 mL
3 tbsp	heavy or whipping (35%) cream	45 mL
2 tbsp	butter	30 mL
1	Granny Smith or other tart cooking apple, cut into ⅛-inch (3 mm) wedges	1
	Finely chopped toasted almonds (see tip, opposite)	

1. In the rice cooker bowl, combine rice, sugar, salt, cinnamon stick, egg, milk, cream and vanilla. Set the rice cooker for the Porridge cycle.
2. When the machine switches to the Keep Warm cycle, let stand while you prepare the caramel apples.
3. *Caramel Apples:* In a medium saucepan, combine brown sugar, salt, corn syrup, cream and butter. Heat over low heat, stirring constantly, for about 4 minutes or until sugar is dissolved. Increase heat to medium-high and bring to a boil. Boil, without stirring, for about 11 minutes or until mixture registers 238°F (114°C) on candy thermometer. Let cool slightly.

Tip

To toast whole almonds, spread them in a single layer on a baking sheet. Bake in a 325°F (160°C) oven, stirring often, for 5 to 10 minutes or until light brown and fragrant. Immediately transfer to a bowl and let cool completely before chopping.

4. Spread caramel sauce onto apple wedges and sprinkle almonds on top.
5. Spoon rice pudding into martini glasses or other serving bowls. Arrange caramel apple wedges on top. Serve immediately.

Variation

Easy Rice Pudding with Candied Apples: Instead of making the caramel sauce, combine 1 cup (250 mL) granulated sugar, $\frac{1}{2}$ cup (125 mL) water, $\frac{1}{4}$ cup (60 mL) light (white or golden) corn syrup and $\frac{1}{4}$ tsp (1 mL) red food coloring in a medium saucepan. Bring a boil over high heat, then reduce heat to medium-high. Boil for about 20 minutes or until mixture registers 300°F to 305°F (149°C to 152°C) on candy thermometer. Remove from heat and let bubbles subside. Dip apple slices in candy mixture, place on a baking sheet lined with parchment paper and let cool before arranging on top of rice. Omit the almonds.

Pumpkin Rice Pudding

Makes 4 servings

Fresh pumpkin creates a distinct flavor loved by many. Serve this dessert for a perfect end to an autumn holiday dinner party.

Tips

This recipe can be prepared up to 2 days ahead. Store in an airtight container in the refrigerator.

You can make the pumpkin purée up to 24 hours before preparing the rest of the recipe. Let cool to room temperature and store in an airtight container in the refrigerator. Bring back to room temperature before adding in step 3.

Store any remaining purée in an airtight container in the freezer for up to 3 months.

- **Preheat oven to 450°F (230°C)**
- **Shallow baking pan**
- **Food processor**
- **Medium rice cooker; fuzzy logic only**

1	pie (cooking) pumpkin (1½ to 2 lbs/ 750 g to 1 kg), halved and seeded	1
1 tbsp	butter	15 mL
2 tsp	granulated sugar	10 mL
⅔ cup	Arborio rice	150 mL
4½ cups	whole milk	1.125 L
½ cup	packed dark brown sugar	125 mL
2	large eggs	2
⅓ cup	crystallized ginger, finely chopped	75 mL
½ tsp	ground cinnamon	2 mL
2 tsp	vanilla extract	10 mL

1. Arrange each pumpkin half cut side up on a sheet of foil. Top each with half the butter and half the granulated sugar. Wrap separately in foil and place cut side up in baking pan. Bake in preheated oven for about 1 hour or until tender. Open foil and let cool slightly, then scoop flesh into food processor and purée until smooth. Measure out 1¼ cups (300 mL) pumpkin purée and set aside.

2. In the rice cooker bowl, combine rice and milk. Set the rice cooker for the Porridge cycle.

3. When the machine switches to the Keep Warm cycle, whisk together pumpkin purée, brown sugar and eggs until well combined. Add ½ cup (125 mL) of the hot rice mixture, 1 tbsp (15 mL) at a time, vigorously stirring with a wooden spoon to incorporate.

4. Add egg mixture to the rice cooker bowl, stirring to combine. Close the lid and let stand for 10 to 15 minutes, stirring two or three times, until thickened. Stir in crystallized ginger, cinnamon and vanilla. Transfer to a bowl and serve warm, or cover with plastic wrap, let cool to room temperature and refrigerate until chilled.

Indian-Spiced Rice Pudding

Makes 4 servings

Cardamom pods and rose water make a lovely and unique flavor combination in this simple, aromatic pudding.

Tips

Rose water is water infused with Damask rose petals. It is used in a variety of Middle Eastern cuisines. You can find it at Middle Eastern and Indian markets. Substitute orange extract or orange flower water if rose water isn't available.

Edible rose petals contain notes ranging from sweet to spicy. They can be found at some farmers' markets and grocery stores.

For information about rice cooker sizes, see page 13.

• Medium rice cooker; fuzzy logic only

¾ cup	white basmati rice, rinsed and drained	175 mL
3 tbsp	granulated sugar	45 mL
¼ tsp	ground nutmeg	1 mL
1	cardamom pod	1
2 cups	whole milk	500 mL
1 cup	heavy or whipping (35%) cream	250 mL
½ cup	sweetened condensed milk	125 mL
1 tsp	vanilla extract	5 mL
¼ cup	slivered almonds	60 mL
¼ cup	golden raisins	60 mL
1 tsp	rose water (see tip, at left)	5 mL
	Additional slivered almonds	
	Edible rose petals (optional)	

1. In the rice cooker bowl, combine rice, sugar, nutmeg, cardamom pod, milk, cream, condensed milk and vanilla. Set the rice cooker for the Porridge cycle.
2. When the machine switches to the Keep Warm cycle, discard cardamom pod and stir in almonds, raisins and rose water.
3. Spoon pudding into small bowls, sprinkle with almonds and garnish with rose petals, if desired. Serve warm or chilled.

Creamy Brown Rice Coconut Pudding

Makes 4 servings

Enjoy delicious, creamy pudding while reaping the benefits of healthy brown rice. The proof is in the pudding!

Tips

You may substitute ½ tsp (2 mL) ground cinnamon for the cinnamon stick.

For information about rice cooker sizes, see page 13.

• **Medium rice cooker; fuzzy logic or on/off**

1 cup	long-grain brown rice, rinsed and drained	250 mL
½ tsp	salt	2 mL
2 cups	water	500 mL
1 cup	granulated sugar	250 mL
1	2-inch (5 cm) cinnamon stick	1
1	can (14 oz/400 mL) coconut milk	1
2 cups	whole milk	500 mL
½ tsp	almond extract	2 mL

1. In the rice cooker bowl, combine brown rice, salt and water. Set the rice cooker for the Regular or Brown Rice cycle.
2. Meanwhile, in a medium saucepan, combine sugar, cinnamon stick, coconut milk, milk and almond extract. Bring to a boil over medium-high heat; boil, stirring, until sugar is dissolved. Reduce heat to low and keep warm.
3. When the machine switches to the Keep Warm cycle, stir in coconut milk mixture. Close the lid and let stand for 10 minutes, stirring two or three times. Discard cinnamon stick. Serve immediately or hold on the Keep Warm cycle for up to 1 hour. Serve warm or let cool slightly.

Coconut Red Rice Pudding

Makes 4 servings

Tropical flavors in the coconut bring a sweet twist to this traditional rice pudding favorite and make an ultra-festive dessert suitable for any dinner party.

Tip

Cardamom is a fragrant spice that lends flavor to curries, chai and rice pudding. It also stimulates metabolism and aids digestion.

• Medium rice cooker; fuzzy logic or on/off

½ cup	red cargo rice, rinsed and drained	125 mL
½ cup	Thai jasmine rice, rinsed and drained	125 mL
¼ tsp	salt	1 mL
2 cups	water	500 mL
½ cup	packed brown sugar	125 mL
¼ tsp	ground cardamom	1 mL
1	can (14 oz/400 mL) coconut milk	1
½ cup	half-and-half (10%) cream	125 mL
2 tsp	almond extract	10 mL
¼ cup	golden raisins	60 mL
2 tbsp	coarsely chopped pistachios	30 mL
1 tbsp	finely grated lemon zest	15 mL

1. In the rice cooker bowl, combine red cargo rice, Thai jasmine rice, salt and water. Set the rice cooker for the Regular or Brown Rice cycle.

2. Meanwhile, in a medium saucepan, combine brown sugar, cardamom, coconut milk, cream and almond extract. Bring to a boil over medium-high heat; boil, stirring, until sugar is dissolved. Reduce heat to low and keep warm.

3. When the machine switches to the Keep Warm cycle, stir in coconut milk mixture and raisins. Close the lid and let stand for 10 minutes, stirring two or three times. Serve immediately or hold on the Keep Warm cycle for up to 1 hour. Serve garnished with pistachios and lemon zest.

Thai Black Sticky Rice Pudding

Makes 4 servings

The combination of black rice and a coconut garnish creates a sophisticated black and white dessert for an elegant dinner party.

Tips

To toast sesame seeds, spread seeds in a single layer on a baking sheet. Bake in a 325°F (160°C) oven, stirring often, for 10 to 15 minutes or until light brown and fragrant. Immediately transfer to a bowl and let cool.

For information about rice cooker sizes, see page 13.

• Medium rice cooker; fuzzy logic (preferred) or on/off

¾ cup	Thai black sticky rice, soaked overnight, rinsed and drained	175 mL
1½ cups	water	375 mL
½ cup	packed brown sugar	125 mL
½ tsp	salt	2 mL
1	can (14 oz/400 mL) coconut milk	1
	Sweetened shredded coconut	
	Toasted sesame seeds (see tip, at left)	

1. In the rice cooker bowl, combine rice and water. Set the rice cooker for the Sweet/Sticky or Regular cycle.
2. Meanwhile, in a small saucepan, combine sugar, salt and coconut milk. Bring to a boil over medium-high heat; boil, stirring, until sugar is dissolved. Reduce heat to low and keep warm.
3. When the machine switches to the Keep Warm cycle, stir in coconut milk mixture. Close the lid and let stand for 10 minutes, stirring two or three times. Serve immediately or hold on the Keep Warm cycle for up to 1 hour. Serve warm or at room temperature, garnished with coconut and sesame seeds.

Amaranth Raisin Pudding

Makes 4 servings

In Greek myths, amaranth represents immortality. The vitamins and protein in amaranth make for a healthy pudding that is so delicious you'll want to live forever. Serve warm, with more milk, if desired.

Tips

For plumper raisins, add them halfway through the cooking cycle.

To toast whole almonds, spread them in a single layer on a baking sheet. Bake in a 325°F (160°C) oven, stirring often, for 5 to 10 minutes or until light brown and fragrant. Immediately transfer to a bowl and let cool completely before chopping.

- **Medium rice cooker; fuzzy logic only**

1 cup	amaranth	250 mL
3 cups	whole milk	750 mL
¼ cup	raisins	60 mL
¼ cup	almonds, toasted and finely chopped (see tip, at left)	60 mL
1 tsp	finely grated tangerine zest	5 mL
¼ tsp	ground cinnamon	1 mL
¼ cup	unsweetened apple juice	60 mL
1 tsp	vanilla extract	5 mL

1. In the rice cooker bowl, combine amaranth and milk. Set the rice cooker for the Porridge cycle.
2. When the machine switches to the Keep Warm cycle, stir in raisins, almonds, tangerine zest, cinnamon, apple juice and vanilla. Close the lid and let stand for 10 minutes. Serve immediately or hold on the Keep Warm cycle for up to 1 hour.

Bulgur Pudding with Candied Ginger and Figs

Makes 4 servings

The combination of a Middle Eastern grain, sweet figs and spicy ginger creates a pudding with a subtle bite. Serve with more milk, if desired.

Tip

For a lighter touch, use fat-free evaporated milk in place of the half-and-half.

Crystallized Ginger

Crystallized ginger can be found at well-stocked grocery stores, but it's easy to make it from scratch. Peel and thinly slice 1 lb (500 g) gingerroot. In a large saucepan, combine 6 cups (1.5 L) granulated sugar and 6 cups (1.5 L) water. Bring to a boil over high heat; boil, stirring, until sugar is dissolved. Add ginger, reduce heat and boil for 45 minutes. Drain and place on a rack to dry for 30 minutes, then toss with enough granulated sugar to coat. Let dry on waxed paper. Store in an airtight container at room temperature for up to 6 weeks.

- **Medium rice cooker; fuzzy logic only**

¾ cup	coarse bulgur	175 mL
2 tbsp	packed brown sugar	30 mL
1½ cups	water	375 mL
1 cup	whole milk	250 mL
1 cup	dried figs, chopped	250 mL
½ cup	toasted sliced almonds (see tip, page 252)	125 mL
¼ cup	crystallized ginger, chopped	60 mL
¼ tsp	ground nutmeg	1 mL
½ cup	half-and-half (10%) cream	125 mL
	Additional toasted sliced almonds	

1. In the rice cooker bowl, combine bulgur, brown sugar, water and milk. Set the rice cooker for the Porridge cycle.
2. When the machine switches to the Keep Warm cycle, stir in figs, almonds, ginger, nutmeg and cream. Close the lid and let stand for 10 minutes. Serve immediately or hold on the Keep Warm cycle for up to 1 hour. Serve warm, garnished with almonds.

Variation

Substitute 1 cup (250 mL) rinsed quinoa for the bulgur. Omit the water and increase the milk to 3 cups (750 mL).

Polenta Pudding with Raspberry Topping

Makes 3 to 4 servings

This creamy, satisfying dessert is like taking a bite of summer.

Tips

Use any combination of frozen berries.

For information about rice cooker sizes, see page 13.

● **Medium rice cooker; fuzzy logic only**

¾ cup	granulated sugar, divided	175 mL
½ cup	coarse-grain yellow polenta	125 mL
Pinch	salt	Pinch
2 cups	whole milk	500 mL
10 oz	thawed frozen raspberries	300 g
½ tsp	finely grated lemon zest	2 mL
1 tsp	vanilla extract	5 mL

1. In the rice cooker bowl, combine ½ cup (125 mL) of the sugar, polenta, salt and milk, stirring for 15 seconds with a wooden spoon or plastic paddle. Set the rice cooker for the Porridge cycle. Stir thoroughly two or three times while the polenta is cooking.
2. Meanwhile, in a small saucepan, combine raspberries and the remaining sugar. Heat over medium-low heat, stirring until sugar is dissolved. Remove from heat.
3. When the machine switches to the Keep Warm cycle, stir in lemon zest and vanilla. Close the lid and let stand for 10 minutes. Serve immediately or hold on the Keep Warm cycle for up to 1 hour. Serve warm, topped with raspberry mixture.

Variation

Substitute stone-ground grits for the polenta and decrease the milk to 1½ cups (375 mL).

Matthew's Chocolate Peanut Butter Polenta Pudding

Makes 6 to 8 servings

Polenta is a healthy base for this dessert, inspired by my husband's love for peanut butter and my obsession with chocolate. What a perfect pair!

Tips

If you'd prefer a crunchier texture, use crunchy peanut butter.

For information about rice cooker sizes, see page 13.

● **Medium rice cooker; fuzzy logic only**

1 cup	coarse-grain yellow polenta	250 mL
½ cup	packed dark brown sugar	125 mL
Pinch	salt	Pinch
4 cups	whole milk	1 L
½ cup	semisweet chocolate chips	125 mL
¼ cup	smooth peanut butter	60 mL
¼ cup	butter, cut into pieces	60 mL
1 tsp	vanilla extract	5 mL

1. In the rice cooker bowl, combine polenta, brown sugar, salt and milk, stirring for 15 seconds with a wooden spoon or plastic paddle. Set the rice cooker for the Porridge cycle. Stir thoroughly two or three times while the polenta is cooking.
2. When the machine switches to the Keep Warm cycle, stir in chocolate chips, peanut butter, butter and vanilla. Close the lid and let stand for 10 minutes. Serve immediately or hold on the Keep Warm cycle for up to 1 hour. Stir thoroughly before serving. Serve warm.

Variation

Add 1 mashed banana with the peanut butter.

Rocky Road Polenta Pudding

Makes 6 to 8 servings

Here's a rockin' variation on an American favorite. Fluffy marshmallows, crunchy almonds, decadent chocolate and creamy polenta pudding combine to satisfy any sweet tooth.

Tip

To toast whole almonds, spread them in a single layer on a baking sheet. Bake in a 325°F (160°C) oven, stirring often, for 5 to 10 minutes or until light brown and fragrant. Immediately transfer to a bowl and let cool completely before chopping.

• Medium rice cooker; fuzzy logic only

1 cup	coarse-grain yellow polenta	250 mL
½ cup	packed dark brown sugar	125 mL
Pinch	salt	Pinch
4 cups	whole milk	1 L
½ cup	semisweet chocolate chips	125 mL
¼ cup	miniature marshmallows	60 mL
¼ cup	almonds, toasted and chopped (see tip, at left)	60 mL
¼ cup	butter, cut into pieces	60 mL
1 tsp	vanilla extract	5 mL

1. In the rice cooker bowl, combine polenta, brown sugar, salt and milk, stirring for 15 seconds with a wooden spoon or plastic paddle. Set the rice cooker for the Porridge cycle. Stir thoroughly two or three times while the polenta is cooking.

2. When the machine switches to the Keep Warm cycle, stir in chocolate chips, marshmallows, almonds, butter and vanilla. Close the lid and let stand for 10 minutes. Serve immediately or hold on the Keep Warm cycle for up to 1 hour. Stir thoroughly before serving. Serve warm.

Quinoa Banana Pudding with Dried Mango

Makes 4 servings

Mild, nutty quinoa is an intriguing ingredient in this sumptuous dessert, while the dried mangos bring a tropical fruit finish.

Tips

For more intense banana flavor, add ½ tsp (2 mL) banana extract with the vanilla.

For information about rice cooker sizes, see page 13.

- **Medium rice cooker; fuzzy logic or on/off**
- **Blender or food processor**

¾ cup	quinoa, rinsed and drained	175 mL
1½ cups	water	375 mL
2	ripe bananas	2
2 tbsp	packed light brown sugar	30 mL
¼ tsp	salt	1 mL
1½ cups	whole milk	375 mL
½ tsp	vanilla extract	2 mL
¼ cup	dried mangos, chopped	60 mL

1. In the rice cooker bowl, combine quinoa and water. Set the rice cooker for the Regular or Brown Rice cycle.
2. Meanwhile, in blender, purée bananas, brown sugar, salt, milk and vanilla until smooth. Transfer to a saucepan and bring to a simmer over medium-high heat. Reduce heat to low and keep warm.
3. When the machine switches to the Keep Warm cycle, stir in banana purée. Close the lid and let stand for 10 minutes, stirring two or three times. Serve immediately or hold on the Keep Warm cycle for up to 1 hour. Serve garnished with mangos.

Tapioca Pudding

Makes 6 to 8 servings

This American classic is a beloved favorite and works perfectly as a warm dish now or a cold dish later.

Tips

This recipe contains raw egg whites. If the food safety of raw eggs is a concern for you, substitute $1/4$ cup (60 mL) pasteurized liquid egg whites (or separate 2 pasteurized whole eggs, if available).

Experiment with medium pearl tapioca for a bigger bite.

Make sure you're not using instant or quick-cooking tapioca for this recipe.

• Medium rice cooker; fuzzy logic only

$1/2$ cup	small pearl tapioca (not instant)	125 mL
$1/2$ cup	granulated sugar	125 mL
$1/2$ tsp	salt	2 mL
2	large eggs, separated	2
3 cups	whole milk	750 mL
1 tsp	vanilla extract	5 mL

1. Place tapioca in the rice cooker bowl. In a 4-cup (1 L) measuring cup or a bowl, whisk together sugar, salt, egg yolks and milk. Pour over tapioca and stir to combine. Set the rice cooker for the Porridge cycle.
2. When the machine switches to the Keep Warm cycle, transfer pudding to a large bowl and stir in vanilla.
3. In a small bowl, beat egg whites until soft peaks form. Fold into pudding. Serve warm or chilled.

Variation

Bombay Tapioca Pudding: Substitute coconut milk for half the milk. Add 2 cardamom pods with the milk and discard them before serving.

Double Berry Tapioca Pudding

Makes 6 to 8 servings

The berries add vibrant color for a cheerful dessert, perfect for the holiday season!

Tip
This recipe contains raw egg whites. If the food safety of raw eggs is a concern for you, substitute ¼ cup (60 mL) pasteurized liquid egg whites (or separate 2 pasteurized whole eggs, if available).

Fennel

Fennel hails from the Mediterranean region and is an extremely versatile plant. Fennel seeds can be ground into a spice, the bulb makes a wonderful vegetable and the leaves are used as herbs. Similar to anise and licorice in flavor, fennel seeds are used in India to freshen breath and aid in digestion, so they are commonly chewed after meals.

- **Medium rice cooker; fuzzy logic only**
- **Blender or food processor**

½ cup	small pearl tapioca (not instant)	125 mL
½ cup	granulated sugar	125 mL
½ tsp	salt	2 mL
2	large eggs, separated	2
3 cups	whole milk	750 mL
1 cup	strawberries	250 mL
1 cup	blueberries	250 mL
1 tbsp	granulated sugar	15 mL
½ tsp	fennel seeds, toasted and ground (see tip, page 196)	2 mL
Pinch	ground cardamom	Pinch
1 tsp	vanilla extract	5 mL
	Additional strawberries and blueberries	

1. Place tapioca in the rice cooker bowl. In a 4-cup (1 L) measuring cup or a bowl, whisk together ½ cup (125 mL) sugar, salt, egg yolks and milk. Pour over tapioca and stir to combine. Set the rice cooker for the Porridge cycle.
2. Meanwhile, in blender, purée strawberries, blueberries, 1 tbsp (15 mL) sugar, fennel seeds and cardamom until smooth. Measure out 1 cup (250 mL) of the berry purée.
3. When the machine switches to the Keep Warm cycle, transfer pudding to a large bowl and stir in berry purée and vanilla.
4. In a small bowl, beat egg whites until soft peaks form. Fold into pudding. Serve warm or chilled, garnished with berries.

Variation

Tropical Tapioca Pudding: Substitute chopped pineapple and papaya for the strawberries and blueberries. Garnish with toasted sweetened shredded coconut.

Index

Library and Archives Canada Cataloguing in Publication

Chin, Katie
    300 best rice cooker recipes : also including legumes and whole grains / Katie Chin.

Includes index.
ISBN 978-0-7788-0280-8

1. Cooking (Rice). 2. Electric rice cookers. 3. Cookbooks.
I. Title. II. Title: Three hundred best rice cooker recipes

TX809.R5C45 2011   641.6'318   C2011-903180-9